CHANGING CLOTHES IN CHINA

To John

Antonia Finnane

Changing Clothes in China
Fashion, History, Nation

Columbia University Press
New York

Columbia University Press
Publishers Since 1893
New York, Chichester, West Sussex

Library of Congress Cataloging-in-Publication Data

Finnane, Antonia.
  Changing clothes in China : fashion, modernity, nation / by Antonia Finnane.
    p. cm.
  ISBN 978-0-231-14350-9 (cloth : alk. paper) — ISBN 978-0-231-51273-2 (ebook)
  1. Clothing and dress—China—History. 2. Fashion—China—History. 3. China—Social
life and customs. I. Title.

  GT1555.F56 2007
  391.00951—dc22

2007007239

∞
Columbia University Press books are printed on permanent and durable acid-free paper.
This book is printed on paper with recycled content.
Printed in India

c 10 9 8 7 6 5 4 3 2 1

CONTENTS

The author and publishers wish to thank The University of Melbourne, and the Faculty of Arts and School of Historical Studies in The University of Melbourne, for their contributions to the cost of producing this book.

ACKNOWLEDGEMENTS

This project was supported by an Australian Research Council Discovery Grant; by publication, travel, and conference grants from The University of Melbourne, the Faculty of Arts, and the Department of History; and by a three month fellowship at the Center for Chinese Studies, National Central Library, Taipei.

Research was conducted in a number of different libraries and archives. I am grateful to the staff of the institutions involved, especially Bick-har Yeung of the Baillieu Library at the University of Melbourne, and Lo-pei Kneale of the same library; Zhou Deming, Shanghai Municipal Library; Xing Jianrong, Shanghai Municipal Archives; Bruce Williams, East Asian Library, University of California–Berkeley; and Keng Li-chun, Vera Ma and the staff of the Center for Chinese Studies at the National Central Library. Li Meng and Cheng Li-jung provided research assistance in Shanghai and Taipei respectively. Chandra Jayasuriya created the map, Lee McRae assisted with the graphics, and Clare Chandler and Emily Dunn corrected the proofs. I hope the present book does credit to their combined efforts on my behalf. A number of people, some completely unknown to me personally, kindly gave me permission to use images they own at no cost. I thank Luna Zhang, Arthur Hacker, Glenn Roberts, Ferry Bertholet, Lily Lee and Sue Wiles on this account.

Colleagues around the world have encouraged and facilitated the research for this book through conferences, workshops, academic and other hospitality, collaboration, and conversations at different stages of the project. I thank in particular Hsiung Ping-chen, You Chien Ming, Yeh Wen-hsin, Paola Zamperini, Tina Mai Chen, Gail Hershatter, Lise Skov, Karl Gerth, Lai Chi-kong, Robert Bickers, Craig Clunas, Sucheta Mazumdar, Elisabeth Croll, Valerie Steele, Wu Jen-shu, Julia Strauss, Helen Dunstan, Anne McLaren, Vera Mackie, Li Jinyu and, as ever, Xu Minhua. My colleagues in the Department of History have provided a supportive and collegial research environment over the course of this project. I am particularly grateful to Richard Pennell for introducing me to Hurst.

Special thanks are due to Dorothy Ko, who read the entire manuscript in draft, and commented on it in detail; and also to my daughter, Therese Fitzgerald, who did the same for an earlier draft. Siobhan Fitzgerald helped with editing the graphics, Genevieve and Bernard kept me company on a memorable research trip, and my husband John contributed a variety of research materials including many photographs, some of which appear in the pages that follow. I am glad finally to have the opportunity to express appreciation to them all.

May, 2007   A.F.

LIST OF ILLUSTRATIONS

Fig. 1.1 Well-to-do men around the turn of the twentieth century. They are clad in long gowns (*changpao*), the standard garment for non-labouring men. The man on the far left wears a "horse [riding] jacket" (*magua*), while his companion on the right wears a sleeveless vest (*majia*), also standard items in the gentleman's wardrobe. The style of hat was peculiar to the Qing dynasty, as was the queue—the single long braid of hair that is just visible on the two figures to the left. Spectacles had been in use for around three centuries.

Fig. 1.2 The trousers (*ku*) and shirts (*shan*) worn by these men are large, loose and comfortable, allowing maximum coolness in the summer months. The man on the far right wears expensive, embroidered shoes, similar to those worn by his counterpart in Fig. 1.1. The men are too well dressed to be labourers, but the fact that they are not wearing gowns shows that they are not from the educated stratum either. They may be shopkeepers, or retainers in a wealthy household.

1
INTRODUCTION
FASHION, HISTORY, NATION

A century ago, people in China dressed in clothes very different to those worn today. The man about town was usually clad in a jacket and long robe (Fig. 1.1). The well-born woman, rarely to be seen in public, wore a long jacket over a pleated skirt, her hair commonly constrained by a wide embroidered or bejewelled band. Labouring people, men and women alike, wore jacket and trousers. Trousers, cut wide or narrow, were standard wear for Han (Chinese) people, whether or not concealed by an outer garment (Fig. 1.2).

The country was then ruled by Manchus, and had been for more than two and a half centuries. Manchu and Han men dressed alike in the Manchu robe, but Manchu women were readily distinguished from Han women by their distinctive hairstyles, platform shoes, and long robes (Fig. 1.3). The distinctions were sometimes blurred. In the imperial capital, Beijing, Han courtesans might dress in Manchu style, and Manchu fashions showed the influence of Han dress. On the edges of the empire flourished other styles of dress, some similar to and others radically different from either Han or Manchu clothing. The wearers were aboriginal peoples of lands that had been brought into the empire at a relatively late date.

The foreigner's dominant impression of clothing in China was of a simple, monotone culture. Alicia Little (d. 1926), British traveller and social activist, characterised China at the turn of the century as "the land of the blue gown."[1] She also commented, however, on the beauty of the coloured and embroidered silks and satins worn by Chinese women of a certain class.[2] Men, too, often dressed brilliantly. If this was not obvious to the casual observer, it was because men who could afford silks and satins did not throng the streets like their cotton-clad compatriots but were carried around in curtained sedan-chairs, much as their descendants travel in cars with darkened windows to conceal them from the public eye.

---

1 Alicia Little, *Land of the Blue Gown* (New York: Brentano's, 1902).

2 Alicia Little, *Intimate China: The Chinese as I Have Seen Them* (London: Hutchinson & Co., 1901), 124.

Fig. 1.4 The main elements of Qing dress were preserved by men in China till the middle of the twentieth century, although with modifications. Most obviously, jackets (*magua*) and gowns were both closer-fitting in the twentieth century than they had been in the nineteenth. Although the gown was still widely worn in the 1930s, these three men from Gansu may well have looked provincial and old-fashioned in Nanjing, where they arrived as envoys to the Nanjing government in early 1937.

Fig. 1.3 (*Right*) Well-dressed women in the late nineteenth century, photographed by John Thomson. The Manchu woman (right) has dressed her hair in the *ruyi* (sceptre) style, and is wearing a long gown (*changpao*). The girl on the left is wearing Han Chinese dress. Her hair is in the "Suzhou bent" (*Suzhou jue*) style. Her extravagantly wide-sleeved jacket (*ao*) is typical of nineteenth-century Chinese women's dress and influenced a similar trend in Manchu dress, as can be seen from the albeit more modest sleeves on the Manchu woman's gown. The skirt (*qun*) was often pleated, although not in this case.

Simple or elaborate, clothing worn in China at this time was often admired by foreigners, but it was changing even as they beheld it. Men in blue gowns were beginning to wear felt caps and leather shoes. These items were the harbingers of a far-reaching vestimentary revolution that over the next half century was to transform the clothing culture in urban China and in much of rural China as well. Hemlines rose, along with collars. Homespun gave way to machine-woven cloth, often made in foreign lands. Styles came and went as quickly as governments.

Some individual garments survived this revolution, to be brought out of trunks for ceremonial occasions or as party costumes long after they had ceased to be customary wear.[3] Others, most notably the man's long gown, were highly resilient, maintaining their status as daily wear through the vicissitudes of the

---

3 See Zhang Ailing, *Duizhao ji: kan lao zhaoxiangbu* (Juxtapositions: Looking at an old photo album) (Hong Kong: Huangguan chubanshe, 1994), where Zhang is photographed in an oversized man's jacket from the Qing period, given to her by an uncle.

Republican era (1911–1949) (Fig. 1.4) and into the early years of the People's Republic. Generational change, helped along by the political climate, finally achieved the eradication of the last vestiges of the distinctive, variegated clothing culture that had flourished under the Manchu monarchs.

The historical significance of this revolution was recognised while it was in process. Clothing that had commonly been worn by the well-to-do at the beginning of the century was being displayed in Chinese museums by the 1930s (Fig. 1.5). But close documentation of the process was lacking, whether in Chinese or English. Even Japanese accounts, among the best for the Republican era, focused more on a remnant tradition than on contemporary shifts in clothing styles.[4] In 1958, A.C. Scott, formerly employed by the British Council for Cultural Relations in Nanjing, published a small book that traced changes in twentieth-century Chinese dress.[5] Full of astute observations and charmingly illustrated with pen and ink drawings, it probably had few readers at the time. Western interest in Chinese clothing tended to take the form either of comments on the so-called "Mao suit," or of antiquarian fascination with imperial or "dragon" robes, such as the one Scott himself smuggled out of China when he left in 1949.[6]

In China, the political climate in the Maoist era was unfavourable to research into fashion and costume history. A dress reform campaign launched in 1955 featured a few discussions of historical clothing, but these were soon drowned out by the hubbub of the Hundred Flowers movement and the subsequent anti-rightist campaign.[7] In 1964 the eminent Shen Congwen embarked on an archival research project on clothing of the imperial era, but the project ground to a halt in the Cultural Revolution. Shen was sent down to the countryside to raise pigs and many of his research notes were destroyed.[8]

Towards the end of the century, the historicisation of twentieth-century dress did begin in earnest. In China, it was stimulated by the rapid growth of the cloth-

---

4 See Nagao Ryūzō, *Shina minzokushi* (Folk customs of China), (Tokyo: Shina minzokushi kankōkai: 1940-1942), Vol. 6; Aoki Masaru, *Pekin fūzoku zufu* (Beijing customs, illustrated), in Uchida Michio, ed., (Tokyo: Heibonsha, 1964).

5 A.C. Scott, *Chinese Costume in Transition* (Singapore: Donald Moore, 1958).

6 A.C. Scott, *Actors are Madmen: Notebook of a Theatregoer in China* (Madison: The University of Wisconsin Press, 1982), 220. On dragon robes, see Schuyler V.R. Cammann, *China's Dragon Robes* (New York: Ronald Press Co., 1952). Cammann taught at Yale-in-China from 1935. He later became Professor of East Asian Art at the University of Pennsylvania.

7 See Antonia Finnane, "Yu Feng and the 1950s Dress Reform Campaign: Global Hegemony and Local Agency In the Art of Fashion," in Yu Chien Ming (You Jiaming), ed., *Wu sheng zhi sheng (II): jindai Zhongguo funü yu wenhua, 1600-1950* (Voices Amid Silence II: Women and Culture in Modern China, 1600-1950) (Taipei: Academia Sinica, 2003), 235-68.

8 Wang Yarong and Wang Xu, "Shen Congwen and His Book on Ancient Costumes," *China Reconstructs* XXIX, 11 (November 1980): 28-33.

ing export sector and accompanying research and development activities in institutes of textiles, fashion and design. Old clothes were transformed from discards into antiques (Fig. 1.6). In the West, Chinese costume history was fostered by a rise of popular interest in Chinese exotica, as a vast marketplace of Chinese collectibles was opened up for international consumption. Museums were quick to exploit this market, and from the 1990s onward Chinese historical clothing culture was celebrated in one international exhibition after another. Lavishly illustrated catalogues were vehicles for the publication of new research in textile and garment history.[9]

Fig. 1.5 A quarter of a century after the abdication of the last emperor, Qing clothing had become museum pieces, as shown in this display in the Shanghai Municipal Museum, ca 1936.

The present book is one of many manifestations of the recent resurgence of interest in Chinese fashion history. Inspiration for the book was sparked by an essay by Zhu Runsheng, the son of famed Republican-era writer Zhu Ziqing (1898–1948). In 1932, the widowed Zhu Ziqing remarried and brought his new wife down from Beijing (then Beiping) to see his parents and children in Yangzhou. Runsheng later recalled their astonishment at first beholding their stepmother, who was wearing a *qipao*, high heels, and glasses. "At that time," he wrote, "very few women in Yangzhou wore high heels, and in the beginning I harboured feelings only of strangeness and alarm towards this new mother."[10]

---

9 "Evolution and Revolution: Chinese Dress, 1700s-1990s," Powerhouse Museum, Sydney, 25 June 1997-July 1998; see Claire Roberts, ed., *Evolution and Revolution: Chinese Dress, 1700s-1990s* (Sydney: Powerhouse Museum, 1997). "China Chic: East Meets West," Fashion Institute of Technology Museum, New York, February-April 1999; see Valerie Steele and John Major, *China Chic: East Meets West* (New Haven, Yale University Press, 1999). "Fashioning Mao," Victoria and Albert Museum, London, 13 October 1999-23 April 2000. "Every Step a Lotus: 19th Century Chinese Shoes for Bound Feet," Bata Shoe Museum, Toronto, 24 January 2001-31 December 2001; see Dorothy Ko, *Every Step a Lotus: Shoes for Bound Feet* (Berkeley: University of California Press, 2001). "Powerdressing: Textiles for Rulers and Priests" from the Chris Hall Collection, Asian Civilizations Museum, Singapore, 12 December 2005-9 April 2006; see Wong Hwei Lian and Szan Tan, eds, *Powerdressing: Textiles for Rulers and Priests from the Chris Hall Collection* (Singapore: Asian Civilizations Museum, 2006).

10 Zhu Runsheng, "Runer de mianhuai–yi fuqin Zhu Ziqing" (Runny's fond recollections: remembering my father Zhu Ziqing), *Yangzhou wenxue* 18 and 19 (1990), 17.

Fig. 1.6 A pedlar of old clothes spreads her wares on the pavement in an early morning market at Chenghuang Temple, Shanghai. Among the items in her bundle were a 1930s *qipao* and a hand-sewn pair of Chinese-style black silk trousers, lined with fine quality pin-stripe wool. Both these items were purchased by a local fashion historian for a planned clothing museum.

Only six or seven when his father remarried, Zhu Runsheng recalled this momentous occasion in family life mainly in terms of his stepmother's modern clothes. What his grandparents thought of this new daughter-in-law is not recorded, but perhaps they too were startled. Yangzhou, clearly, was a very provincial town compared to places where women wore high heels. On this point, Runsheng's memoir is confirmed by the caustic comments of a visitor to Yangzhou. In 1934, the Jiangsu province Commissioner of Education Yi Junzuo, found it "difficult to find many modern women in Yangzhou."[11] In the 1930s, clearly, China was a place where women could be categorised as modern or not modern, and clothing was a major signifier of the position a woman occupied on the spectrum of modernity. The unmodern women Yi Junzuo saw in Yangzhou fell into three categories: old women smoking pipes, middle-aged women wearing old-fashioned trousers bound at the ankles, and young women wearing flowers in their hair.[12] Modern women such as Zhu Runsheng's stepmother wore high heels with a *qipao*, the high-collared one-piece garment that in 1932 was rapidly gaining ascendancy as standard wear for urban women.[13] Often satirised by cartoonists (Fig. 1.7), the *qipao* acquired weighty political, social and moral meanings, and provoked fierce debates that centred finally on a single ques-

11 Yi Junzuo, *Xianhua Yangzhou* (Chatting at leisure about Yangzhou) (Shanghai: Zhonghua shuju, 1934), 16.

12 Ibid.

13 The *qipao* has been the subject of numerous studies over the past decade. See inter al., Bao Mingxin and Ma Li, eds, *Zhongguo qipao* (China's *qipao*) (Shanghai: Shanghai wenhua chubanshe, 1998); Hazel Clark, *The Cheongsam* (Hong Kong: Oxford University Press, 2000); Beverley Jackson, *Shanghai Girls Get All Dressed Up* (Berkeley and Toronto: Ten Speed Press, 2005); Bai Yun, *Zhongguo lao qipao—lao zhaopian lao guanggao jianzheng qipao de yanbian* (The traditional *qipao* of China: evidence of its [stylistic] changes in old photographs and old advertisements) (Beijing: Guangming ribao chubanshe, 2006).

tion: "what should Chinese women wear?"[14] This book is in large part a history of this problem.

It is also, self-evidently, a history of Chinese fashion. In 1913 a feature article in the *New York Times* introduced the topic of new dress styles in Shanghai with a rhetorical question and answer: "The fashions in China? It never occurred to you, perhaps, that there were any!"[15] To the extent that people in the West thought about Chinese clothing at all, they would certainly have been in agreement with the writer. Fashion could not then be spoken of in non-Western contexts in the same casual way as it was mentioned in Europe. Even now, fashion studies are powerfully informed by the privileged association of fashion with Western modernity. In a history of Chinese fashion, then, what fashion means in the Chinese context needs to be clarified.

Fig. 1.7 "Modern miss in high heels," depicted in a 1935 cartoon by Zhang E (1910–1995). The girl's voluptuous figure is revealed by the tight-fitting *qipao*, and she takes care not to walk on the earth that her poor peasant compatriots are hoeing.

Fashion, history and early modernity

In a pioneering historical study first published around forty years ago, Fernand Braudel described fashion as peculiarly a feature of Western history. He identified it as apparent in some form in Europe from the fourteenth century onward, and used it as a point of demarcation between the West and the rest. His counter examples to Europe in this respect were "India, China, and Islam," civilisations characterised by "unruffled times and ancient institutions."[16] In these civilisations, people wore dress that was customary rather than fashionable. Of the

---

14 See Antonia Finnane, "What Should Chinese Women Wear? A National Problem," *Modern China* 22, 2 (April 1996): 99-131.

15 *New York Times* 3 August 1913.

16 Fernand Braudel, *Capitalism and Material Life, 1400-1800*, trans. Miriam Kochan (New York: Harper Colophon Books, 1967), 231.

mandarin's robes, Braudel wrote that they "scarcely changed in the course of centuries, but then Chinese society itself scarcely moved at all."[17]

Such an understanding of the Chinese past was deeply grounded in Western views of Asia. In the early nineteenth century Hegel described China and India as lying outside the domain of history, waiting to be initiated into the process of development and change on which Europe had long since embarked. Braudel's equation of the stasis of dress with the stasis of society in China was entirely consistent with Hegel's historiography, and for a long time was the only possible view of China's vestimentary past. In the twentieth century's most famous literary treatment of fashion in China, "A Chronicle of Changing Clothes," Zhang Ailing anticipated Braudel's conclusion. "We cannot really imagine the world of the past," she wrote, "so dilatory, so quiet, and so orderly that over the course of three hundred years of Manchu rule, women lacked anything that might be referred to as fashion."[18]

In recent years, however, Hegelian constructions of the world have been challenged by significant historical research focused on the centuries just prior to Hegel's own lifetime. Arguably, "l'empire immobile"[19] was after all not entirely motionless. The monetisation of the economy, the extension of urbanisation, new forms of urban institution, the expansion of printing, new literary forms and new styles of art were among the signs of change in Chinese society between the sixteenth and eighteenth centuries. A scrutiny of clothing practices in these centuries might then yield conclusions rather different from those drawn by Braudel, or indeed by Zhang Ailing.

Most theorists and historians of fashion agree with Braudel in defining fashion as peculiarly a feature of Western society. In a useful survey of fashion theories, Joanne Entwhistle takes exception to two different critiques of "the nature of fashion as an aspect of western modernity," partly on grounds of the failure of the authors to define fashion in a way that might validate their critiques.[20] Change, she points out, is not the same as fashion. But the authors in question—Jennifer Craik, and Ruth Barnes and Joanne B. Eicher—were correct to sense a certain ethnocentricity in fashion studies. If they failed to substantiate their arguments

---

17 Ibid., 227.

18 Eileen Chang (Zhang Ailing), "A Chronicle of Changing Clothes," trans. Andrew F. Jones, *positions: east asia cultures critique* 11, 2 (Fall 2003): 429.

19 The term is taken from the title of a not very old published book, Alain Peyrefitte, *L'empire immobile, ou, Le choc des mondes: récit historique* (Paris: Fayard, 1989).

20 Joanne Entwhistle, *The Fashioned Body: Fashion, Dress, and Modern Social Theory* (Cambridge: Polity Press, 2000), 46-7. See Jennifer Craik *The Face of Fashion: Cultural Studies in Fashion* (London: Routledge, 1994), and Ruth Barnes and Joanne B. Eicher, eds, *Dress and Gender: Making and Meaning in Cultural Contexts* (New York: Berg, 1992).

fully, it was in no small part because they were writing before a substantial body of empirical research on clothing cultures in non-Western societies was available.

A decade later, the fact remains that little is known in the English-speaking world about changes in material culture in non-Western societies. Criticising the assumptions of writers on consumption in the "early modern world," Craig Clunas pointedly asked in 1999 what these writers meant by "the world," and whether any of them knew anything about practices of consumption anywhere outside of Europe and North America. [21] His own research on material and visual culture in the late Ming provided one of the cornerstones for the construction of an "early modern" period in Chinese history, with all that such a periodisation implies in terms of social change over time.[22]

A profound ignorance of Chinese historical clothing culture is evident in some influential works on fashion. The oft-cited Quentin Bell, like Braudel, associated fashion with the West's dynamic forward movement, its engagement with the future. Again, like Braudel, he used the Chinese case as a counterfactual, writing: "no doubt there were variations in Chinese dress from dynasty to dynasty of a kind that Western eyes would hardly notice ... but [change there] occurs at the speed of a rather hesitant glacier ..." But he did not know too much about Chinese clothing in times past. "The Chinese family of the last [i.e. nineteenth] century," he asserted, "looked very much like a Chinese family of the classical age."[23] A comparison of paintings from different periods of Chinese history might have alerted him to substantial changes in dress over this long period at least.

Bell should not be judged too harshly on this account. When he was writing, the great spate of publications of Chinese artworks that would help familiarise non-specialists with the visual culture of imperial China was decades away in the future. He took advantage of such materials on Chinese dress as were then available to him, and at the micro-level of sartorial detail not much more has been published since. Contemporary historians of China, with access to works in Chinese and Japanese, face much the same problem as both Bell and Braudel did: a specialist literature on clothing culture in Chinese history that has only recently begun to expand, and is generally too broad in its coverage of space and time to provide any sense of local, short-term sartorial trends and practices.

Whether more knowledge would have produced a different historical treatment by either Bell or Braudel is a moot point, but it is worth considering how someone in nineteenth-century China might have summarised changes in Western dress on the basis of perusing a book of European costume through the ages.

---

21 Craig Clunas, "Modernity Global and Local: Consumption and the Rise of the West," *American Historical Review* 104 (December 1999): 1497-511.

22 See Craig Clunas, *Superfluous Things: Material Culture and Social Status in Early Modern China* (Cambridge: Polity Press, 1991).

23 Quentin Bell, *On Human Finery* (London: Allison and Busby, 1947), 59.

Men's dress, certainly, began to change radically from around the beginning of the fourteenth century: long robes were abandoned in favour of styles—hose and doublet, then trousers, and finally the suit—that delineated the body. But women, as Anne Hollander writes, for centuries continued to wear "variations of the dress," with long sleeves and skirts, paired always with some covering for the head.[24] Necklines eventually dropped, especially for evening wear, and the bodice became very tight-fitting. Yet from the fourteenth century onward, women's clothing consisted mainly of a dress with fitted bodice, narrow sleeves, and a full skirt. Our notional Chinese reader may well have thought this costume very different from that worn by women in China, but probably only an informed eye would have detected the differences in detail that in the West defined fashion. The neo-classical experiment of the early nineteenth century, yielding empire-line dresses, provided a departure from the norm, but it was notably short-lived.

Recent work on Chinese dress in the sixteenth to nineteenth centuries, revisionist in intent, shows evidence of short-term changes in urban fashions, and a high degree of consciousness of their significance.[25] Whether this amounts to "fashion" depends on how fashion is defined. Given the analytical purposes and uses of the term, Entwhistle is right to distinguish between "change" and "fashion." She failed to recognise, however, that when fashion is defined very narrowly on the basis of particular empirical detail about "a particular sort of society,"[26] the possibility of any other clothing culture being described as "fashion" is by definition excluded. At the very least, this creates terminological problems in how to describe or analyse the phenomenon of short-term shifts in taste and consumption evident in non-Western urban societies that featured social mobility, late imperial (early modern) China being a case in point.

From a survey of ways in which Chinese clothing was described by Europeans in the sixteenth to nineteenth centuries, and even afterwards, it would appear that their accounts were shaped less by the garments than by how they saw them, or more precisely by the repository of ways they had of describing what they saw. The contents of the repository changed over time. As Chapter Two of the present book shows, the early cohorts of Western writers on China, composed mainly of missionaries, did not treat clothing culture as a mark of differentia-

---

24 Anne Hollander, *Sex and Suits: The Evolution of Modern Dress* (New York: Kodansha International, 1994), 45.

25 E.g. Wu Renshu, "Mingdai pingmin fushi de liuxing fengshang yu shidafu de fanying" (Popular styles of clothing among the common people of Ming times, and the reaction of the gentry), *Xinshixue* 10, 3 (September 1999): 55-109; Lin Liyue, "Yishang yu fengjiao—wan Ming de fushi fengshang yu 'fuyao' yilun," (Costumes and customs: late Ming clothing trends and the discourse of "outrageousness") *Xinshixue* 10, 3 (September 1999): 111-57. See further, Chapter Three.

26 Entwhistle, *The Fashioned Body*, 48.

tion between East and West. That was an innovation of their successors in the nineteenth century, when European imperialism was at high tide.

Imperialism was accompanied, as Edward Said has shown, by orientalism, the study of "the East."[27] This branch of learning had certain deficiencies as a body of scientific knowledge about Asia but provided Europeans with some useful ways of describing themselves (e.g., Europeans were *not* superstitious, backward, unhygienic, effeminate, or slavish). In this period, not surprisingly, China was described—in binary opposition to Europe—as lacking in fashion among many other things. This perceived lack threw fashion in Europe, and Europe's self-appointed place in the vanguard of history, into sharp relief. Yet at this very time something that looks very like fashion—rapid change and heady consumption—was a topic of growing interest to Chinese writers commenting on their own society.[28]

Efrat Tseëlon's periodisation of European fashion is useful for thinking about the Chinese context. Tseëlon identifies three historical eras of fashion: the classical, the modern, and the postmodern. In this schema, the classical era falls between the fourteenth and eighteenth centuries, when the expansion of trade and the rise of urban elites were posing a challenge to the feudal order. Since the word "classical" is intimately associated with antiquity in European history, this first era might be better termed the "early modern". In any case, at this time fashion did not possess the volatility and whimsicality by which it was to become known in later centuries, and the distinction between courtly and common dress continued to be evident.[29]

China in this same period did not have a feudal order, but it did have a bureaucratic order dominated by an educated landowning class that during these same centuries, and particularly from the sixteenth century onward, was being challenged by the expansion of trade and the rise of urban elites. It could certainly be said to have lacked fashion if fashion is defined as a uniquely Western phenomenon. On the other hand, as Chapter Three shows, some people's clothing in seventeenth-century China could be described in terms of *shiyang* (contemporary styles) and *xinshi* (new or recent times), and the wearers of such clothing were criticised by conservative commentators in ways similar to their counterparts in Europe.

The question of fashion in China is less controversial for the post-imperial era, when the industrialisation of textile production was proceeding apace, and a self-consequential middle class was emerging to view. Early signs of a sharp rupture with conventional styles of the Qing became apparent in the late nineteenth

---

27 Edward Said, *Orientalism* (London: Routledge & Kegan Paul, 1978).

28 See Chapter Three.

29 Efrat Tseëlson, "Fashion and the Signification of Social Order," *Semiotica* 91 (1992): 1-14, cited in Entwhistle, *The Fashioned Body*, 44.

婦＝女＝裝＝束＝之＝進＝化＝馬甲的改良～

Fig. 1.8 "Progress in women's fashions: the reform of the vest." The vest (*majia*) was a sleeveless top, although the term is also used for an undergarment, much like its English equivalent. Published in 1931, the twentieth anniversary year of the 1911 revolution, this cartoon by Hu Yaguang (b. 1901) depicts progress and improvement in women's fashions since the beginning of the twentieth century.

century and multiplied around the turn of the twentieth. In the early twentieth century the Qing empire gave way to a Chinese nation that in various and some-times ill-defined ways showed itself bent on improvement and progress. Clothes, and indeed the very bodies of people in China, were implicated (Fig. 1.8).

The pattern of change was by no means uniquely Chinese. Yedida Kalfon Stillman has described the transformation of Arab dress, beginning earlier in the nineteenth century, as involving "the progressive abandoning of traditional, loose-flowing garments ... in favour of Western tailored clothes." The new styles were evident first among the "westernised Christian and Jewish protegés of the foreign powers," and then among members of the ruling elite and the military forces. Finally, "a new élite of European-educated Arab students ... was also in the forefront of adopting Western-style dress."[30]

This account could readily be adapted to describe the Chinese case. Chinese Christians, compradors, and Western-educated students were among the pioneers of tailored clothing for men, and while the Manchu ruling elite hung on desper-ately to the vestimentary order that defined its ascendancy, it did countenance the reform of military uniforms in the last decade of Qing rule. A general rise in

---

30 Yedida Kalfon Stillman, *Arab Dress From the Dawn of Islam to Modern Times: A Short History* (Leiden: Brill, 2000), 161-5.

Fig. 1.9 Bound feet and Chinese dress. The bride is wearing a floral *qipao* with long tulle veil, a typical wedding ensemble for modern young women in the 1940s. She is wearing high heels but her feet are badly deformed from binding in childhood. The groom is in a Sun Yatsen suit, which was typically worn by government officials.

militarism in Chinese society at this time affected fashion trends generally, as discussed in Chapter Four, and also helped to bring down the dynasty. The new ruling elite, like the khedives in Egypt at an earlier date, adopted Western suits.

After this, even Westerners could hardly fail to note the transformation of aspects of Chinese dress. The 1913 *New York Times* feature article mentioned above commented on changes in the cut of skirts, the popularity of various styles of shoes, and the rise in consumption of hosiery. Nanjing Road and Fuzhou Road were identified as the places to observe the Shanghai smart set.[31] At the same time, ways of talking about Chinese dress continued to be characterised by a vocabulary that defined it in opposition to Western dress. Although such terminological differentiation can serve to tell the reader what was distinctive about each clothing culture, in practice it has often meant describing Chinese dress in terms of *what it is not*, most notably that it is not fashionable or modern. Thus despite the lively sartorial spectacle in Shanghai, the fact that most Chinese people wore Chinese clothes has frequently obscured the facts that some of these clothes were highly fashionable, were featured in fashion spreads in the mass media, and were worn because they were popular that year.

This point is well illustrated in Pang-mei Natasha Chang's widely-read book *Bound Feet and Western Dress*. In the title of her book Chang nicely encapsulated the sartorial paradoxes entailed in being a Chinese woman in the early twentieth century. The book is an autobiography, in which the story of Chang's aunt, Zhang Youyi, as related to her niece, is intertwined with a self-reflexive commentary on Chang's own American life and her struggle

---

31 *New York Times* 3 August 1913.

with the issue of a Chinese-American identity. Zhang Youyi was unhappily married to the poet Xu Zhimo (1896–1931), a celebrated writer of the May Fourth period. The episode in the marriage that gave rise to the title concerned Youyi's commenting to her husband that the Western-style dress worn by a certain woman did not go well with her bound feet. He took advantage of this comment to say that was precisely why he wanted a divorce—implying that Youyi was culturally foot-bound, despite her natural feet.[32]

The awkward fit between old-style feet and modern fashions is shown in a wedding photo (Fig. 1.9) in which the bound feet of the bride show to apparent disadvantage at the end of legs inadvertently exposed by a high hem-line. The bride is not wearing Western dress, but her dress is modern all the same—a garment quite different from that which her mother would have worn as a bride. The quality of the material and the professional cut of the garment, together with the bride's veil, make-up and bearing, suggest that this young woman's bound feet had carried her confidently, or at the very least determinedly, into a new vestimentary regime. In places where foot-binding was slow to disappear, the distinctive look of the small-footed woman with a modern hemline was probably quite common.

Considering the phrase "bound feet and Western dress" in light of this photograph prompts the question of why its variant, "bound feet and Chinese dress," would not be equally jarring. The answer must lie in how Western and Chinese clothing are respectively imagined, especially in a context suggested by "bound feet." The meaning of "Western dress" is clear. Zhang Youyi would not be referring here to the customary dress still worn in parts of rural Europe but to clothes like the smart dress and hat that Xu Zhimo bought for her immediately on her arrival in France.[33] "Chinese dress," by contrast, might suggest to the reader something like the costumes depicted in nineteenth-century ethnographic or historical accounts. In Zhang's own mind, it might have signified clothes such as those worn by her foot-bound mother.

As Zhang herself shows, clothing in China was rapidly changing in the years she spent in Europe—the early 1920s. On her return in 1925 she was astonished to see in the Shanghai streets "men with hair slicked back and pointed leather shoes, girls with waved and bobbed hair, in white gauze shirts with tight brassieres clearly visible underneath, knee-length skirts and high-heeled shoes worn over flesh-coloured stockings."[34] Her memory of brassieres for this period is probably faulty, since they were not introduced

---

32 Pang-Mei Natasha Chang, *Bound Feet and Western Dress* (New York: Doubleday, 1966), 122.

33 Ibid., 103-4.

34 Ibid., 168.

into China till 1927, but her general impression of street fashion is consistent with the intensification of the fashion system in Shanghai in the 1920s. What she does not recall here is the fashionable dress in which she herself must have been dressed when she left Shanghai five years earlier—the skirt and blouse typical of the May Fourth era—which Xu Zhimo found to be the dress of a "country bumpkin."

A photo of Youyi and her sisters published in *Bound Feet and Western Dress* illustrates the different fashions of 1920s Europe and China. One sister is wearing calf-length pants, leather shoes and the abbreviated Chinese-style blouse that was paired either with pants or a skirt in the 1920s. The brush-across fringe of her hairstyle proclaims her attention to a fashionable look. Another is wearing a very stylish *qipao* of classical cut, which became modish in the 1920s. Chang's caption for the photo shows how difficult it has been even for the empathetic observer to see Chinese clothing as modern, for it includes the comment: "Notice [Zhang Youyi's] decidedly Western dress and striped hat in contrast to her traditional sisters."[35] Here "Western" serves as an antonym for "traditional." The logical correlative is that "modern" must serve as an antonym to "Chinese." In fact the sisters' clothes are decidedly modern. To describe them as "traditional" is in effect to suggest that Chinese culture lacked the impulse for or experience of fashion.

Among Western observers in early twentieth-century China, Ida Pruitt was unusually well-attuned to the nuances of Chinese dress. When she first met old Madam Yin, the subject of one of her two famous books, she saw that:

Her clothes were cut with great style and distinction. The coat was wide and came to her knees. The long sleeves were straight and wide. The trousers were bound in at the ankle above the little triangle of starched white cotton stockings and the tiny cotton black shoes. The narrow straight standing collar buttoned around a firm neck. Her grey hair was combed back into the conventional chignon on the nape of her neck—"modern" yet Chinese, uninfluenced by Western ways.[36]

Pruitt demonstrated in this passage her ability to see Chinese fashion. To assert that Madam Yin was "uninfluenced by Western ways" overstates the case. Western ways were part of the context for Chinese life in the Republican era. Yet Pruitt was right to indicate the specific character of Chinese modernity. Madam Yin had not adopted Western dress, but she did not look old-fashioned either. She dressed elegantly, in a manner consistent with her age, but also in a way attuned to the times. She was a fashionable dresser.

---

35 Chang, *Bound Feet and Western Dress*, following 92.

36 Ida Pruitt, *Old Madam Yin: A Memoir of Peking Life, 1926-1938* (Stanford: Stanford University Press, 1979*)*, 4.

Fashion and national politics

This book begins with an enquiry into ways of thinking about Chinese historical clothing culture, with a focus on Western representations in Chapter Two,
and on a Chinese counterfactual in Chapter Three. Together these chapters
provide a reflection on the concept of fashion in relationship to late imperial
China, as anticipated in the short discussion above. Before too quickly accept-
ing or rejecting the applicability of the word "fashion" to clothing in imperial
China, it seems important to identify the various registers in which the word
"fashion" is used. Clearly, to describe long skirts as the reigning fashion in
Europe for centuries is to use the word lightly. But, as Chapter Three shows,
"fashion" can be used more pointedly than this to describe short-term shifts
in taste in urban China in the late imperial period. If the dynamics of clothing
production and consumption were very different then from the situation in
the 1920s, so too was that the case in Europe. Europe and China may well
have had different historical trajectories in this respect, but Europe's historical
experience of fashion should not be allowed to negate China's.

As Chapter Four makes clear, the fall of the Qing dynasty marked a vestimentary as well as a political rupture in China: the President of the Republic
of China in 1912 was dressed very differently from a Manchu emperor. The
political upheaval of the 1911 Revolution occurred during a period of economic change that was facilitating the emergence of a modern fashion industry
in China. By the 1920s, capitalism, industrial production, advertising, fashion
magazines and department stores were all present in major urban centres.
Chapter Five traces these developments in Shanghai, which in the early decades of the twentieth century established its place as the fashion capital of
China. The pace of change in urban clothing was quickening even before the
fall of the dynasty and accelerated afterwards, resulting in a sequence of major
stylistic shifts over the course of the century. Shanghai maintained its place as
trendsetter through most of this period. Even in the sartorially conservative
years of the Cultural Revolution, it continued to provide the benchmark for
what to wear.

The volatility of fashions in the twentieth century matched vicissitudes in
national politics, to a point where a series of political regimes through the
century was matched by a parallel series of vestimentary regimes. A comparison of photo montages with the headlines in Shanghai's popular press would
immediately suggest a political chronology of Chinese women's fashions in the
twentieth century. The *xinhai* (1911) revolutionary period was characterised
by the close-fitting jacket with high collar, and the May Fourth era by skirt
and jacket-blouse. With the Nationalist Revolution of 1926-8 and growing
Japanese pressures on Chinese sovereignty, clothing was increasingly invested
with nationalist meanings, summed up in the women's *qipao* and the men's
changpao, discussed in Chapters Six and Seven. The Communist Revolution

was represented by the cadre suit (*ganbu zhifu*), discussed in Chapter Eight, while the Cultural Revolution was characterised by the popularity of military uniforms, as shown in Chapter Nine. Finally, the reform era gave rise to a variegated, globalised wardrobe with Chinese characteristics, the subject of Chapter Ten.

Quentin Bell took strong exception to the idea of certain formal directions in fashion being a response to political circumstances. He cited by way of example the popularity of Parisian fashions in England when Britain and France were at war during the Napoleonic era.[37] The appropriation of French styles for English consumption in this period, however, was hardly conceivable outside the context of the complex relationship between the two countries. A comparable case in China involves the rise of the *qipao*, a garment with multiple origins but associated in its very name with the Manchus (the *qi* people), the target of China's first nationalist revolution in 1911. Similarly, Chinese fashions were popular in Japan in the late twenties and early thirties, a period encompassing sharp conflict between the two countries.[38] In England again, the kashmir shawl and other items of oriental clothing became popular during a period of conquest of India.

The relationship between national politics and fashion is not simple, predictable, or steady. Practices of appropriation and emulation are matched by practices of opposition and subversion, and instances of governmental regulation. In China, the Qing state had strong expectations of what people should wear, and after the fall of the dynasty a succession of central and provincial governments made sporadic efforts to regulate clothing styles, particularly for women. More broadly, the domestic political climate over the past century has affected the tenor of local interaction with fashion currents in the wider world; it has had an impact on gender relations, with implications for gender differentiation in dress codes; and it has profoundly influenced the domestic economy, with effects on production and consumption, and especially on discretionary spending, which is a pre-requisite for a fashion regime.

The primacy of politics in China should not be allowed to distract attention from other significant mediators in the process of vestimentary change. New forms of technology, industry, commerce, and communications were central to this process, and cannot be explained simply as outcomes of political events. Likewise, identity formation, so important to sartorial decisions, is by no means entirely reducible to the effects of the political climate. But for much of the twentieth century, China was mired in a constantly transmutating strug-

---

37 Bell, *On Human Finery* (London: Anisson and Bushy, 1947), 97.

38 Ikeda Shinobu, "The Allure of Women in Chinese Dress," paper presented at a conference on New Gender Constructs in Literature, the Visual and the Performing Arts of Modern China and Japan (University of Heidelberg, 28-31 October, 2004).

Fig. 1.10 Wearing the flag. This cartoon from the 1911 Revolution era shows women's garments fabricated from a print featuring over-all pattern of the five-stripe flag of the Republic. The text reads: "If it's weird and wonderful, Shanghai is sure to have it: jacket and trousers adorned with the national flag."

gle for its survival, its sovereignty, and its international standing. Its citizens might blithely disregard sumptuary and sartorial rules and regulations, but like their counterparts the world over, they generally heeded the call of the nation. In complex, sometimes unobvious or contradictory ways, they wore the nation on their backs (Fig. 1.10).

2

WAYS OF SEEING

Between the late sixteenth century, when Matteo Ricci (1552–1610) first donned a Chinese robe, and the late nineteenth, when Sun Yatsen (1866–1925) cut off his queue and put on a suit, a diffuse body of knowledge about Chinese clothing gradually took shape in European societies. Visitors to China in these centuries liked to write about what they saw there, and their contemporaries liked to read about it. What people in China wore was not often prominent among the topics discussed in the various letters home and learned tomes produced in these centuries. Nonetheless, it is the rare general work on China that fails to mention what Chinese people looked like and how they dressed, and many early published works anyway included illustrations. These works gave Europeans an idea of what people wore on the other side of the Eurasian land mass. They also provided the foundations for the fanciful apprehension of far Cathay that was expressed in eighteenth-century chinoiserie.

For a number of reasons, the eighteenth century was an important period of transition in Western views of China. This century has been referred to as a "blank space" in Sino-Western relations, with reference especially to the decades after 1728, when the Yongzheng emperor banned missionaries from activities in the provinces.[1] "Watershed" might be a better metaphor, since what was said after the eighteenth century was quite different from what said before. Writings by missionaries in China in the sixteenth and seventeenth centuries show that men of those times tended to find Chinese habits comparable to their own. The nineteenth-century literature shows a contrary instinct: Chinese had come to be seen as the opposite to whatever Europeans were. Differences that had been perceived as mere variables when viewed across sixteenth-century space became sharp contrasts when viewed from the perspective of nineteenth-century time.[2] This shift was fun-

---

1 Zhu Weisheng, *Coming Out of the Middle Ages: Comparative Reflections on China and the West*, trans. and ed. Ruth Hayhoe (Armonk: M.E. Sharpe, 1990), 113.

2 See Donald M. Lowe, *History of Bourgeois Perception* (Chicago: University of Chicago Press, 1982).

damental to the terms in which people in China would respond to the challenge to their vestimentary heritage.

Early modern commentaries

In the mediaeval world, dress styles in Europe and China were fundamentally similar. East and West, the clothing for the genteel classes was a modified drapery. The clothes were shaped by cutting and sewing, but on loose and flowing lines. Men and women alike wore long robes. In the second half of the fourteenth century, the robes of European men began to shrink, so that hemlines finally reached not much below the crotch. From this time distinctions between men's and women's dress in Europe were marked, not in terms of fabric and ornamentation but in their relationship to the body. Men's clothes delineated the shape of the body, while women's, as Anne Hollander writes, continued till the twentieth century to be "variations of the dress," a garment with long sleeves and long skirts that might be thinned out or thickened up according to the dictates of fashion but was essentially "of great antiquity and great sobriety."[3] This sobriety was countered by a development that Hollander also notes: the armour-like bodice that defined the woman's upper body in a fashion unique to Europe from the fourteenth century to the early twentieth.

Despite these contrasts, Europeans in China in the sixteenth and seventeenth centuries were on the whole inclined to describe Chinese clothes in terms of how they resembled their own. The Portuguese Dominican Gaspar da Cruz (1520–1570), who arrived at Guangzhou in 1556, recorded that Chinese women "wear long petticoats like the Portugal women, which have the waist in the same manner that they have. They make curtseys, as our women do, but they make three together and very hastily."[4] Similarly, the Italian Ricci, resident in China between 1582 and 1610, commented of the tunics worn by both women and men that they had "loose long sleeves, Venetian style ..." while the Spanish Juan Gonzales de Mendoza (1545–1618) wrote that "their women do apparell themselves very curiouslie, much after the fashion of Spaine," and moreover dress their hair "with great care and diligences, as do the women of Genouay ..."[5]

This practice of analogy was extended to the whole domain of the body: its deportment, its tools and accessories, its natural characteristics. Ricci found commonality with the Chinese in "their methods of eating and sitting and sleeping," i.e., they used tables, chairs and beds; and also in their use of the fan, which

---

3 Hollander, *Sex and Suits*, 46.

4 Gaspar da Cruz, "Treatise in Which the Things of China are Related at Great Length," in C.R. Boxer, ed., *South China in the Sixteenth Century* (Lichtenstein: Nendeln, Kraus Reprint, 1967), 149.

5 Juan Gonzalez de Mendoza, *The History of the Great and Mighty Kingdom of China* [1588], trans. R. Parkes, Sir George T. Staunton, ed., (London: Hakluyt Society, 1853), 31.

was deployed very much as Europeans used gloves in that "both alike seem to be employed much more frequently as a matter of display or as a small gift token of friendship."[6] Mendoza knew nothing of a "yellow" race unless it were that in "Tartary." His China, like his Europe, was inhabited by a variegated people: "Those of the prouince[7] of Canton (which is a whot country) be browne of colour like to the Moores: but those that be farther within the country be like unto Almaines [Germans], Italians and Spanyardes, white and redde, and somewhat swart." Elsewhere it strikes him that some are "more yealow," and these he likens again "unto the Almans, yelow and red colour."[8]

The tendency to find likeness everywhere, evident also in the graphic arts (see Fig. 2.1), was broadly consistent with the proclivity of the men of these times to admire Chinese society and culture and consider it in some respects equal and in others complementary to European civilisation. Gottfried Leibniz considered it "a singular plan of the fates that human cultivation and refinement should today be concentrated, as it were, in the two extremes of our continent," by which he meant Europe in the west, and China in the east.[9] At this time, humanity was regarded as one, composed of the children of Adam and Eve, or

Bourgeoise de la Chine

Si l'air faisoit la dignité
On diroit que cette Chinoise
Bien loin d'estre simple Bourgeoise
Seroit dame de qualité

Fig. 2.1 A well-to-do woman of seventeenth-century China—not too different from her French counterpart? The couplet reads "If manner makes for dignity, one would say that this Chinese, far from being a simple *bourgeoise*, must be a lady of quality." After engraving by Nicholas Bonnart (?1636–1718), "Bourgeoise de la Chine."

---

6 Matteo Ricci, *China in the Sixteenth Century: The Journals of Matthew Ricci: 1583-1610* [1615], trans. Louis Gallagher, S.J. (New York: Random House, 1953), 25.

7 The spelling in the original is duplicated here.

8 Mendoza, *The History of the Great and Mighty Kingdom of China*, 11, 30. Variations in spelling as in the original. It is to be noted that John Francis Davis made a similar statement at a much later date, but he did so in protest against what he felt to be misrepresentations by his contemporaries, and had moreover probably read Mendoza. John Francis Davis, *The Chinese: A General Description of the Empire of China and its Inhabitants* (New York: Harper and Brothers, 1836), 254, cited in Patricia Ebrey, "Gender and Sinology: Shifting Western Interpretations of Footbinding, 1300-1890," *Late Imperial China* 20, 2 (December 1999): 6.

9 Donald Lach, *The Preface to Leibniz' Novissima Sinica: Commentary, Translation, Text* (Honolulu: University of Hawaii Press, 1957), 68.

more precisely of the descendants of Noah. Considerable effort was expended on trying to reconcile the chronologies of the Bible and the Chinese classics, so sure were some early missionaries that only a few errors separated them.

By the nineteenth century, science had led to doubts about the essential sameness of human beings of different colours, physiognomies and genders. In the 1840s, Père Brouillon, S.J., drew attention to the disparity between the China described in the letters of earlier missionaries and that portrayed by his contemporaries:

Some might find that, even with all due allowances, it is difficult to reconcile our observations with those of our predecessors, and that the Chinese of the Edifying Letters could not be the same people as those of whom we speak, except if their portrait had been embellished by the fathers of former times or disfigured by us.

His solution for this paradox was that China had declined sadly since the days of the Kangxi Emperor (r. 1661–1722), and was now scarcely recognisable as the same place.[10] In this same work he showed that whatever the actual changes in Chinese society over this time, there had certainly been a shift in the style of analysis of that society. "What most strikes the missionary on his arrival in China," he observed, "is the contrast offered by the customs of his new country when compared to those of European nations." [11] In sharp contrast to Ricci, who could find similarities even between Chinese fans and European gloves, Brouillon could find no similarities between the two cultures at all.

The passage of centuries between Ricci and Brouillon had witnessed the rise of the British Isles as a centre for the dissemination of knowledge of China, first via translations of books from the French and Italian and subsequently through first-hand reports. Indeed, in some respects the shift in the tenor of European sinology was a shift in the site of production from the continent to Britain, which early promised to deliver its audience a different sort of China. In 1748 Baron George Anson (1697–1762) delivered a broadside at China in response to his unfriendly reception in Canton in 1744. This was the year that Montesquieu published a critique of the despotic system of government in China, a system he held to be based on fear. Anson's account suggested, by contrast, that there was nothing to fear: his ship alone was probably a match "for all the force the Chinese could collect."[12]

---

10 Père Nicolas Brouillon, *Mémoire sur l'état Actuel de la Mission du Kiang-nan 1842-1855* (Paris: Julien, Lanier et Cie, Editeurs, 1855), 178-9.

11 Ibid., 239-40.

12 Richard Walter, *Lord Anson's Voyage Around the World, 1740-1744* [1748] (London: G.S.L. Clowes, 1928), cited in Paul Rule, "The Tarnishing of the Image: From Sinophilia to Sinophobia," in Michel Cartier, ed., *La Chine entre amour et haine: Actes du viiie colloque de sinologie de Chantilly* (Paris: Desclée de Brouwer, 1998), 101. Rule documents the familiarity of major French philosophers with Anson's writings.

Even before Anson's account was published, scepticism about this distant paradise was being voiced in England, informed apparently by a determination to be suspicious of anything that came out of Popish Europe. In his "Preface to the Translation of Father Lobo's Voyage to Abyssinia," Samuel Johnson paid credit to the descriptive powers and credibility of Lobo's account, which he held to be praiseworthy especially in light of the "partial Regard paid by the *Portuguese* to their Countrymen, by the *Jesuits* to their Society, and by the *Papists* to their Church ..."[13] In the same article he expressed impatience with the transcendental, utopian quality of treatises on China among other places, for: "The Reader will find [in Lobo's account] ... no Chinese perfectly Polite, and compleatly skill'd in all Sciences."[14]

During the eighteenth century, the English were busy defining themselves in opposition to Catholic Europe, manoeuvring for their destined place in history. Late starters in the race for overseas trade, they were improving their odds at the very time that the Jesuits' fortunes were on the wane. With them, there arose a new sinology. Its first practitioner was George Thomas Staunton (1781–1859), who learnt Chinese as a boy when he accompanied his father, George Leonard Staunton (1737–1801), on the Macartney embassy's historic voyage to China in 1793. In his maturity, George Thomas would produce a new edition of Mendoza's history, a work of interest to him because it was the first detailed account of China to be read widely in England. But before the sinological works came the travellers' tales, beginning with Anson's *Voyage*, continuing half a century later with Staunton senior's "Authentic Account" of the Macartney embassy,[15] and then proliferating in extraordinary number through the nineteenth century.

William Alexander (1767–1816), draughtsman with the Macartney embassy, provided a folio of illustrations to accompany Staunton's account. These were subsequently published separately, with commentary, under the title *The Costume of China*.[16] The title was not entirely appropriate to the contents, for the illustrations included as many landscapes as portraits, but it probably added to the book's market value. Its publication followed closely on the appearance of another book by the same name, produced by the same publisher. Compiled by

---

13 Samuel Johnson, "Preface to the Translation of Father Lobo's Voyage to Abyssinia," in *Johnson: Prose and Poetry* [1735] (London: Rupert Hart-Davis, 1969), 16.

14 Ibid., 15.

15 Sir George Staunton, *An Authentic Account of An Embassy From the King of Great Britain to the Emperor of China* (London: W. Bulmer and Co., 1797).

16 William Alexander, *The Costume of China Illustrated in Forty-Eight Coloured Engravings* (London: William Miller, 1805). The version consulted for the writing of the present book, from The University of Melbourne Baillieu Library Rare Books Collection, is the French edition, which is more accurately entitled than the English original: *Costumes et vues de la Chine* (Paris: Chez Nepveu, 1815). On Alexander's paintings of China, see Susan Legouix, *Image of China: William Alexander* (London: Jupiter Books, 1980).

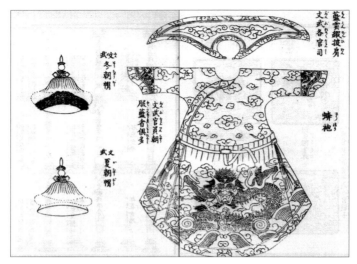

Fig. 2.2 Elements of Qing dress as depicted by Nakamura Tadahide for his encyclopaedic work on Qing customs. The garment depicted here is Qing dynasty court dress (*chaofu*), and is distinguished from other official and common gowns by the skirt style of the lower part of the garment, a phenomenon discussed in the following chapter. The shoulder collar (*pijian*) may also have been in use before the Qing (see Wilson, *Chinese Dress*, 29). Note the horse shoe cuffs on the robe, and the style of the official hats (winter above, summer below).

Fig. 2.3 Nineteenth-century Qing dynasty courtrobe, acquired by George ("Chinese") Morrison presumably after the end of the dynasty in 1912. The cut of the bodice and the decorative design differ from the sketch by Nakagawa, but the horse shoe cuffs and gathered skirt are as he depicted.

24

George Mason (fl. ca 1800), who had been resident for some years in Canton, this earlier work consisted of sixty engravings of scenes of Chinese life based on watercolours by a Chinese artisan whose name appears on the engravings as Pu Qua. With a text in both English and French, it was clearly aimed at a cosmopolitan readership.[17] The publisher's production in the space of five years of these two large, expensive volumes, both with illustrations in full colour, both called *The Costume of China*, is testament to European interest in what Chinese actually looked like.

Qing costume

The vestimentary regime to which Earl Macartney (1737–1806) and his gallant band were exposed had been in place for one and a half centuries.[18] When the Manchus assumed rule over China in the middle of the seventeenth century, they maintained the social and political distinctions between their Chinese subjects and the ruling group and its allies. The latter included the Mongols, and also Chinese who had fallen to Manchu servitude prior to the Manchu invasion of China. The success of Manchu rule was predicated upon ensuring the collaboration of Chinese, particularly men of the scholar class who could provide them with the bureaucratic expertise necessary for governing China.

The identification of servants of the state with the state itself was partly established by a dress code. Chinese men were forced to shave the front of the head and wear the remainder in a long queue, in conformity with Manchu custom. Officials now wore conical straw or bamboo hats adorned with red silk cords in the summer, and fur-trimmed hats of blue satin in the winter, both of which gave quite a different impression from the black gauze, square, or Confucian hats of the Ming.[19] A single long robe continued to be the main garment for men of education or social standing, but the great wide sleeves of the Ming dynasty robe were replaced by close-fitting sleeves with distinctive horse-shoe shaped cuffs (Figs 2.2, 2.3). The

---

17 George Henry Mason, *The Costume of China. Illustrated by Sixty Engravings with Explanations in English and French* (London: W. Miller, 1800). On Mason and his book, see Craig Clunas, *Chinese Export Watercolours* (London: Victoria and Albert Museum, Far Eastern Series, 1984), 33-42. A selection of prints with commentary from Alexander's and Mason's works have been reprinted in a single edited volume, William Alexander and George Henry Mason, *Views of 18th Century China: Costumes, History, Customs* (London: Studio Editions, 1988).

18 Good, scholarly (i.e. documented) accounts of dress under the Manchus include John Vollmer, *Ruling from the Dragon Throne: Costume of the Qing Dynasty (1644–1911)* (Berkeley: Ten Speed Press, 2002); Zhou Xun and Gao Chunming, *Zhongguo gudai fushi fengsu* (Ancient Chinese costume) (Taibei: Wenjin chubanshe, 1989), 205-34; Zhou Xibao, *Zhongguo gudai fushi shi* (History of ancient Chinese costume) (Taibei: Nantian shuju, 1989), 472-502.

19 Verity Wilson, *Chinese Dress* (London: Victoria and Albert Museum, 2001), 27. See further, Chapter Three.

Fig. 2.4 Auguste Racinet used Chinese export paintings to illustrate Chinese costume. From left to right: a gentleman in everyday blue gown, wearing an official's summer hat and carrying a fan; an official in full dress, wearing a *bufu* (coat with rank badge) or *waitao* (overcoat over his split gown), and with horse-shoe shaped cuffs in the Manchu style; Manchu woman wearing a surcoat over her long gown, the gown having horse-shoe cuffs; Han woman wearing a *pifeng* over her pleated skirt, with a sash and fan, in a posture very like that of a woman depicted by Pu Qua.

dress of the defeated Ming dynasty could only be assumed at death. Women were exempt from these pressures. Thus it was said: "Men must submit, not women; the young must submit, not the old; the living must submit, not the dead."[20]

The regulations governing the dress of nobles and officials during the Qing dynasty are notable for being directed more towards differentiation of rank than of gender. A Chinese diplomat in France in the later nineteenth century noted with surprise and disapproval the absence of a system of signs of rank on the dress of European women.[21] In China, the wife of an official wore a plaque on her outer garment that matched that of her husband, plainly declaring to all who saw her that she partook of his rank (Fig. 2.4). Gender differentiation in dress was obvious, without being exaggerated. The "dragon robes of noblewomen," observed Cammann, "were distinguished by extra bands of ornament below the water pattern on the upper sleeves, while women's robes in general were slit only at the sides,

---

20 Eileen Chang, "Chinese Life and Fashions," *Lianhe Wenxue* (Unitas) 3, 5 (1987): 66. This is the English-language original of Zhang Ailing's "Gengyi ji," quoted elsewhere in this book via the translation by Andrew Jones. For an explication of the various versions of the essay, see notes by Jones in Chang, "A Chronicle of Changing Clothes,"427-8.

21 Tcheng-Ki-Tong, *Les Chinois Peints par Eux-mêmes* (Paris: Calmann Lévy, 1884), 228-9.

and not at the front and rear as the men's were."[22] The front and rear slits were to allow horse riding. The differentiation was gradually lost to common knowledge so that tailors, when reproducing these robes for sale to foreign collectors, confused the methods for sewing them up.[23] The slit robe was a sign of social status, and in the imperial family male robes were slit at both front and sides.[24]

Regional and status variations in Chinese dress were observed, described and graphically depicted in the picture books by Mason and Alexander, and also in export watercolour and gouache paintings by Cantonese artisans, of whom Pu Qua—Mason's illustrator—was just one example.[25] They passed into general currency via copies for illustrations in later works about China, or about costume and customs around the world (Fig. 2.4).

Fig. 2.5 "Chinese Soldier," portrayed in a not very flattering light by François Boucher (1703–1720).

Reproductions were occasionally distorted and fanciful, but, in general, depictions of Chinese garments in the nineteenth century (a "long" nineteenth century if we take 1793 as a starting point) are more closely observed than those produced in earlier European works. In the Mason and Alexander collections, the graphic representations are detailed and are glossed by descriptive and explanatory commentaries: the "Tartar lady" in "her habit of ceremony;" a peasant family, with "the Mother ... in the dress of the northern provinces;" the tradesman, wearing a sleeveless jacket of silk with "a collar made of the same," and so on.[26]

---

22 Cammann, *China's Dragon Robes*, 66.

23 Cammann cites the example from the Metropolitan Collection in New York which has "both the noblewoman's sleevebands and the slits proper to a man's robe." Ibid., 66-7.

24 Zhou Xun and Gao Chunming, *Zhongguo gudai fushi fengsu*, 212.

25 Clunas, *Chinese Export Watercolours*. Huang Shijian and Shao Jin, eds, *Shijiu shiji Zhongguo shijing fengqing: sanbai liushi hang* (Street scenes in nineteenth-century China: the 360 professions) (Shanghai: Shanghai guji chubanshe, 1999), 1-30.

26 Alexander and Mason, *Views of 18th Century China*, 176, 196, 222.

Fig. 2.6 William Alexander's portrait of a "family from the northern provinces." Note the very full trouser legs, caught in at the woman's ankles in the typical northern way. The tunic does not look quite right. It should have a side fastening. The long-stemmed pipe, depicted also by Racinet, was a familiar sight in China. According to Lord Macartney, even small children could be seen smoking.

Mason and Alexander agreed on the general good sense of Chinese dress, which they found well adapted to the climate. An exception to this rule was to be found in the dress of the military, which Alexander described as "clumsy, inconvenient, and inimical to the performance of military exercise," and elsewhere again "cumbrous, and for the southern provinces almost suffocating, being lined and quilted."[27] He had a more serious charge to make, alleging that the "army of China cannot be considered formidable, their troops being naturally effeminate, and without the courage of European soldiers."[28] The grounds on which he based this conclusion are not clear, since he was witness to no battles, but the comment bears on one aspect of Chinese society on which European commentaries are consistent over time: its inferiority to Europe in military matters (Fig. 2.5).

The second thing to attract adverse comment was the practice of footbinding, concerning which Mason observed:

It may be considered as no small alleviation to the anguish of poverty, that peasants in all countries are blest with more perfect use of their limbs than the generality of their superiors—enfeebled by voluptuous indolence. This is more particularly the situation of a poor Chinese female, whose meanness of condition is stamped by the appearance of her full-formed feet, a mark of vulgarity which even a tradesman's daughter would feel miserable to display.[29]

Mason was writing of the south, where natural feet were common among farming and labouring women. Alexander, executing a family portrait in the north (Fig. 2.6), commented in astonishment on the "extraordinary custom" of footbinding, practised even by peasant women who "pique themselves on the smallness of their feet, and take great care to adorn them with embroidered silk shoes, and bands for the ankles, while the rest of the habiliments display the most abject poverty."[30]

27 Ibid., 68, 164.

28 Ibid., 132.

29 Ibid., 206.

30 Ibid., 196.

The engagement with the issue of footbinding, which was to excite Europeans to a vicarious indignation for another century, may properly be said to be a mark of the nineteenth-century literature on China and certainly dominates discussions of women's dress. It was intimately connected with an emerging trope in European society: the status of women as a criterion for the status of a civilisation.

Footbinding and the status of Chinese civilisation

From the sixteenth century onwards, it is the rare account of Chinese society that does not mention footbinding.[31] The early missionaries almost startle the modern reader with their matter-of-fact presentation of the practice. "From their childhood," noted Cruz, "[women] squeeze their feet in cloths, so that they may remain small, and they do it because the Chinas do hold them for finer gentlewomen that have small noses and feet."[32] Ricci shrugged it off with a speculation: "Probably one of their sages hit upon this idea to keep them in the house."[33]

Very different were the descriptions in the nineteenth-century literature.[34] It was a practice "unnatural and inhuman," presenting "to the Western eye a very uncouth appearance," leading to "a stunted frame, a sallow complexion, and an irritable temper," producing "real deformity, and a miserable tottering gait." It was "an absurd practice" and "an evil custom."[35] George 'Chinese' Morrison (1863–1945) was rare in his defence of the practice, citing the Chinese as saying "it is very important that their feet should be bound short so that they can walk beautifully with mincing steps, swaying gracefully and thus showing to all that they are persons of respectability."[36]

---

31 See Dorothy Ko, "Bondage in Time: Footbinding and Fashion Theory," *Fashion Theory* 1, 1 (1997): 3-28; Ebrey, "Gender and Sinology."

32 Cruz, "Treatise," 149.

33 Ricci, *China in the Sixteenth Century*, 77.

34 Ebrey, on the basis of a much broader survey than has been conducted in the present book, identifies a "rough chronology" of ways of talking about footbinding, and concludes that "progress in understanding the practice was slow" ("Gender and Sinology," 25). To imagine the possibility of progress on this issue is to suppose a degree of epistemological continuity over this whole period, which is clearly at variance with the argument being developed here.

35 John Barrow, *Travels in China* (London: T. Cadell and W. Davies, 1806), 73; Rev. Justus Doolittle, *Social Life of the Chinese* [1865] (Taipei: Ch'eng-wen Publishing Company, 1966), Vol. II, 198; Edwin Joshua Dukes, *Everyday Life in China; or Scenes Along River and Road in Fuh-kien* (London: The Religious Tract Society, n.d.), 37; Edmund Plauchut, *China and the Chinese*, trans. Mrs Arthur Bell (London: Hurst and Blackett, 1899), 243; J. Dyer Ball, *The Chinese at Home, or The Man of Tong and His Land* (London: The Religious Tract Society, 1911), 42; Henri Borel, *The New China*, trans. C. Thieme (London: T. Fisher, 1912), 124.

36 G.E. Morrison, *An Australian in China* [1895] (Hong Kong: Oxford University Press, 1985), 14.

Along with the commentary came pictures: bound feet shod and bound feet bare, as much isolated from their owners as the limb that was removed from the drowned woman in the Pearl River and sent back to England for scientific analysis.[37] It is not unusual to see Chinese women graphically represented by portrayal of this limb alone, a practice probably starting with George Leonard Staunton (Fig. 2.7). John Francis Davis (1795–

Fig. 2.7 Bound feet, naked and shod, depicted by William Alexander to illustrate the "unnatural custom" described by George Staunton.

1890), a precocious sinologist and author of one of the more detailed critiques of footbinding in the early nineteenth century, used the Staunton illustration (rendered by William Alexander) in his own book, *The Chinese*, first published in 1836.[38]

The commentary on footbinding was informed by an idea novel to eighteenth-century Europe: that the status of women in a society was a primary index to the standard of civilisation in that society. John Barrow (1764–1848), secretary to the Macartney embassy, commenced his "Sketch of the State of Society in China" with a clear statement of the principle: "It may, perhaps, be laid down as an invariable maxim, that the condition of the female part of society in any nation will furnish a tolerable just criterion of the degree of civilisation." He went on to note that, in his "own happy island," the proper appreciation of women commenced only with the reign of Elizabeth, men's manners before that time being somewhat "too rough." Here he echoed Voltaire, who regarded the regency of Anne of Austria in the 1640s "as the beginning of France's reign as the most civilised and sociable country on earth."[39] In Barrow's view, the women of antiquity had suffered a degradation "as impolitic as it is extraordinary," but the Chinese excelled even the ancients in the humiliations and restraints they imposed upon women. They deprived them of the use of their limbs and confined them indoors, or alternatively used and abused them in the fields as they might their oxen and asses.

The strength of Barrow's response to the "condition of women" in China was bound up with debates in Europe itself, past and present. In seventeenth-

---

37 See Ebrey, "Gender and Sinology," 18.

38 Ibid., 7–8.

39 Dena Goodman, *The Republic of Letters: A Cultural History of the French Enlightenment* (Ithaca: Cornell University Press, 1994), 10.

century France, some had been strongly of the opinion that women should be "invisible in their homes," that veils should be revived, that wives should "have no conversation themselves, look at and contemplate only their husbands ..."[40] In debates on the women and the family, as also on the organisation of the polity, China served as a reference point. Jacques Chaussée, an ardent proponent of marriage as a cure for the ills of French society, particularly those arising from salon culture, used Chinese society as an example of an ideal where occupation and social status were fixed by birth.[41] He was not aware, of course, of the rise of courtesan culture in China at that very time, or of the increased social mobility which had been characteristic of Chinese society in key regions since the second half of the sixteenth century, prompting very much the same debates in China as in France.[42]

There was more to the development of this discourse than simply a relocation of issues from one society to another. Barrow's historical treatment of the issue of women shows a shift from representation in space to a representation in time. Chinese society, he elsewhere suggested, had not changed since the mid-sixteenth century, while Europe over the past century and a half had enjoyed "progressive improvements."[43] Likewise Macartney knew for a fact that before the days of Marco Polo "the Chinese had reached their highest pitch of civilisation" but that in recent times they had regressed rather than advancing, so that "they are actually become a semi-barbarous people in comparison with the present nations of Europe."[44] This shift was paradoxically accompanied by another marked feature of nineteenth-century writings: the employment of a perspective of cultural relativism.

Cultural relativism and vestimentary practices

Cultural relativism in Europe had its formal beginnings with imagined Asiatics commenting on European societies. Montesquieu, working from earlier examples, turned this into a definitive genre with *The Persian Letters*, first pub-

---

40 Carolyn C. Lougee, *Le Paradis des Femmes: Women, Salons, and Social Stratification in Seventeenth-Century France* (Princeton University Press, 1976), 85.

41 Ibid., 92.

42 See Susan Mann, "Learned Women in the Eighteenth Century," in Christina K. Gilmartin et al., eds, *Engendering China: Women, Culture and the State* (Cambridge, Mass.: Harvard University Press, 1994), 27-46. Mann, *Precious Records: Women in China's Long Eighteenth Century* (Stanford: Stanford University Press, 1997), and Dorothy Ko, *Teachers of the Inner Chambers: Women and Culture in Seventeenth-Century China* (Stanford: Stanford University Press, 1994).

43 Barrow, *Travels*, 28.

44 J.L. Cranmer-Byng, *An Embassy to China: Being the Journal Kept by Lord Macartney During his Embassy to the Emperor Ch'ien-lung, 1793-1794* (London: Longmans, 1962), 222.

lished in 1721. A long list of "letters" follows—not immediately but over time.[45] The potential of this genre to mirror for Europeans their own prejudices is well demonstrated by the fictional Hwuy-Ung, supposedly a political exile living in Melbourne at the end of the nineteenth century, who had this to say of Western dress practices:

These remarkable people, contrary to us, like clothes that imprison them. Their thick coats fit tightly around their arms and body, narrow trousers restrict the movement of their knees, tough leather pinches their feet, and hats unyielding in shape grip their heads ... They have a great number of slits in their clothes leading into small bags, a curious device for retaining objects such as coins, a cloth for the nose, a watch, papers, tobacco, pipe, matches, and many other things.[46]

The unknown author of this account was prefigured by members of the Macartney embassy. Lord Macartney himself asked why footbinding should elicit expressions of disgust when no such response was inspired by circumcision, or even castration, to which "the Italian opera has long reconciled us ..." Moreover, he noted, in England in recent years, "thread-paper waists, steel stays and tight lacing were in high fashion, and the ladies' shapes were so tapered down from the bosom to the hips that there was some danger of breaking off in the middle of exertion."[47]

At a somewhat later date, the Reverend Justus Doolittle (1824–1880) echoed Macartney when he concluded a lengthy and dispassionate description of footbinding with the observation that:

While foreign ladies wonder why Chinese ladies should compress the feet of their female children so unnaturally, and perhaps pity them for being the devotees of such a cruel and useless fashion, the latter wonder why the former should wear their dresses in the present expanded style, and are able to solve the problem of the means used to attain such a result only by suggesting that they wear chicken-coops beneath their dresses, from the fancied resemblance of crinoline skirts, of which they sometimes get a glimpse, to a common instrument for imprisoning fowls.[48]

---

45 Charles De Secondat, baron de Montesquieu (1689–1755), *The Persian Letters* [1721], trans. C.J. Betts (Harmondsworth: Penguin Books, 1993); Oliver Goldsmith, *Citizen of the World, or Letters from a Chinese Philosopher Residing in London* (London: G. Cooke, 1762); Goldsworthy Lowes Dickinson, *Letters From a Chinese Official, Being An Eastern View of Western Civilisation* (London: R.B. Johnson, 1901); J.A. Makepeace, *A Chinaman's Opinion of Us and of His Own Country* (London: Chatto and Windus, 1927); André Malraux, *The Temptation of the West* [1926], trans. Robert Hollander (Chicago: University of Chicago Press, 1992).

46 Roger Pelissier, *The Awakening of China 1793-1949*, trans. Martin Kiefer (New York: Capricorn Books, 1962), 45.

47 Cranmer-Byng, *An Embassy to China*, 226-7.

48 Doolittle, *Social Life of the Chinese*, 203.

These two examples are from people who, whether from their experience in China or by virtue of their general world view, felt some sort of empathy for Chinese society and were capable of ridiculing their own. Yet the rhetoric of cultural relativism was by no means confined to sinophiles. John Barrow, when commenting on the appearance of Chinese women, showed the sourness which characterised his general attitude towards China:

Never were poor women fitted out in a style so disadvantageous for setting off their charms as those who made their appearance on the banks of the Peiho … Bunches of large artificial flowers, generally resembling asters, whose colours were red, blue or yellow, were stuck in their jet-black hair, which, without any pretensions to taste or freedom, was screwed up close behind, and folded into a ridge or knot across the back of the head, not very unlike (except in the want of taste) to the present mode in which the young ladies of England braid their locks.[49]

Later, in Suzhou, Barrow observed women "dressed in petticoats, and not in trowsers;" but the novelty of "the superior style of dress and the appearance of the women in public at this place" excited him only to a diatribe against the practices of concubinage and prostitution.

John Barrow was a man hard to please. He did not, however, forget himself so far as to neglect the principles of his liberal education, for he piously concluded his discussion of footbinding with the comment that "we had certainly no great reason to despise and ridicule the Chinese, or indeed any other nation, merely because they differ from us in the little points of dress and manners, feeling how very nearly we can match them with similar follies and absurdities of our own."[50] Here he literally repeated Macartney's concluding paragraph on the same subject, for the earl had drawn attention to "how little right we have to despise and ridicule other nations on the mere account of their differing from us in little points of manners and dress, as we can very nearly match them with similar follies and absurdities of our own."[51] The men on the embassy must all have talked about this matter at length, for Staunton, too, says, "they who recollect the fashion of slender waists in England, and what pains were taken, and sufferings endured, to excel in that particular, will be somewhat less surprised at extraordinary efforts made in other instances." All the same, Staunton was not much convinced by this reflection, for he quite failed to see the point of a practice injurious to health and elegance alike, "for *grace* is not *in her steps*, or animation in her countenance."[52]

Cultural relativism emerges in the nineteenth-century literature as a trope, a figure of discourse, that in fact bore little relationship to the dynamics of the

49 Barrow, *Travels*, 72.

50 Barrow, *Travels*, 74.

51 Cranmer-Byng, *Embassy to China*, 230.

52 Staunton, *An Authentic Account*, 425.

interaction between individual Europeans and Chinese. It was used by sinophiles and sinophobes alike. Arthur Smith's years of residence in China in the later nineteenth century failed to persuade him of the cultural logic of Chinese dress, which he found "clumsy, pendulous, and restrictive of 'personal liberty.'" He deplored its general irrationality. The lack of woollen textiles in the nation was extraordinary, the padded cotton worn in the place of wool was at best inconvenient, the mittens which stood in for gloves were clumsy, the absence of pockets was annoying, the dearth of underclothing and night-clothing was injurious to the health and undoubtedly responsible for high levels of neo-natal mortality. Nor did the aesthetics of Chinese dress compensate for its manifold impracticalities.

Yet Smith recognised the equal and opposite position of the Chinese observer, noting that "the foreign sack-coat, the double-breasted frock-coat (not a single button of which may be in use), and especially the hideous and amorphous abortion called a 'dress-coat,' are all equally incomprehensible to the Chinese ..." Furthermore, "if the dress of the male foreigner appears to the average Chinese to be essentially irrational and ridiculous, that of the foreign ladies is far more so. It violates Chinese ideas of propriety, not to say of decency, in a great variety of ways."[53]

It is worth comparing Smith, writing in the late nineteenth century, with John Barrow and George Mason, active around a century earlier. Smith voiced opinions very like Barrow's: both men were essentially antipathetic to Chinese culture, in its vestimentary aspect at least. Barrow's comment on women's lack of "pretensions to taste and freedom" in dressing their hair was echoed by Smith, who commented that "Chinese women, so far as we have observed, have no other kind of head-dress than that which, however great its failure viewed from the unsympathetic Western stand-point, is intended to be ornamental."[54] Mason, by contrast, recorded appreciatively that women in China comb up their hair "very nicely, and braid and coil it on the head with much neatness; sometimes it is fastened with a gold bodkin or two." This description was not far removed from one provided by da Cruz more than two centuries earlier.[55] But Mason was like Barrow and Smith rather than like da Cruz when he commented of footbinding: "the Chinese ladies are ridiculed by the European nations on account of this deformity, which is the result of fashion only, whilst they do not consider, that, unsightly as it may be, it is perfectly consistent with those peculiar principles of modesty and decorum which the Chinese profess."[56] This sort of remark, so often to be found in nineteenth-century commentaries, would hardly have occurred to da Cruz.

---

53 Arthur Smith, *Chinese Characteristics* (Shanghai: North China Herald, 1899), 160-1.
54 Ibid.
55 Alexander and Mason, *Views of 18th Century China*, 18 (cf. Cruz, "Treatise," 149).
56 Ibid.

Gender differentiation in cultural relativism

Although the practice of cultural relativism in analyses of Chinese society was not linked to like or dislike of China, it was linked fairly consistently to something else: in brief, it came to the fore most frequently in connection with observations of women. Montesquieu and Goldsmith perhaps set the tone for this. Montesquieu's Persian, writing home from Paris, expressed horror at "the artful composition of [the women's] complexion, the ornaments with which they deck themselves, the care that they have of their bodies, the desire to please which occupies them continually, [which] are so many stains on their virtue, and affronts to their husbands."[57] Likewise, Goldsmith's fictitious "citizen of the world," the Chinese philosopher Lien Chi Altangi, found the ladies in London "horribly ugly; I can hardly endure the sight of them; they no way resemble the beauties of China ... They like to have the face of various colours, as among the Tartars of Coreki, frequently sticking on, with spittle, little black patches on every part of it, except the nose."[58]

Since Goldsmith had his Chinese correspondent regarding black teeth, broad faces, small feet and thin lips as the hallmarks of beauty, he was not failing to laugh at the Chinese as well as at the English. Nonetheless, it would be difficult with such an explicit example before him for any well-read Englishman to articulate the prejudices of his time without remembering Lien Chi Altangi's Lockean reflections:

When I had just quitted my native country, and crossed the Chinese wall, I fancied every deviation from the customs and manners of China was a departing from nature; I smiled at the blue lips and red foreheads of the Tonguese ... but I soon perceived that the ridicule lay not in them but in me; that I falsely condemned others of absurdity, because they happened to differ from a standard originally founded in prejudice or partiality.[59]

While it is true that both the Persian letters and the Chinese letters satirised many aspects of European society, the examples involving female beauty and habits are particularly pointed. While the deployment of these examples was directed at satirising society as a whole rather than merely women, the synecdoche was not particularly effectual because women were not seen as having universal or general significance. In dress as in other respects, a society was more commonly represented by reference to its male members. John Barrow early made it plain that when he spoke of the dress of "the common people," he was speaking of the dress of men. Women were appended. More than a century later, J. Dyer

---

57 Montesquieu, *Persian Letters*, 49.

58 Goldsmith, *Citizen of the World*, Vol. I, 14.

59 Ibid., 12.

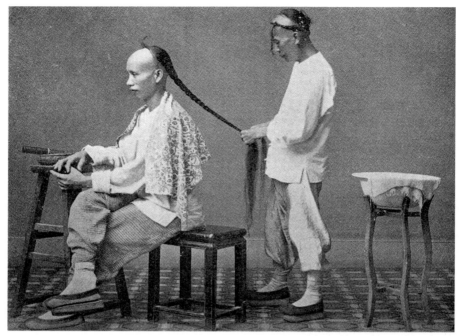

Fig. 2.8 "Braiding the queue," from the collection of the Religious Tract Society. The front of the head was shaven clean, while the hair at the back was cultivated to its maximum length. As shown by the figure on the right, workers would wind the queue around the head to keep it out of the way. Judging by the tesselated tile floor, the photo is of two servants in a Western-style household. Similar scenes were to be seen on the street, where barbers normally plied their trade.

Ball (1847–1919) was to qualify the name of his book *The Chinese At Home* with the subtitle "The Man of Tong and his Land."[60]

What the man of Tong wore was much less likely than the woman to excite the observer to invocations of cultural relativism. Justus Doolittle, who hedged his observations about footbinding with references to the extraordinary fashions of foreign women, had no such qualifications to make about the queue (Fig. 2.8): "The tonsure and the caudle-like appendage proclaim, *'I am not my own master. I cannot even dress my hair according to my pleasure. I do not conceal my political condition and character. My head shows that I am a slave to the Tartar emperor.'"*[61] Using the principle of cultural relativism, Doolittle could have argued that the queue had become simply a matter of custom in China, and that

---

60 J. Dyer Ball, *The Chinese at Home, or The Man of Tong and His Land* (London: The Religious Tract Society, 1911).

61 Doolittle, *Social Life of the Chinese*, 243.

the Manchus were at least as Chinese as the Normans were English. But the man of China, unlike the woman, was judged on universal principles.

The split between approaches to male and female China in English commentaries tended to deepen with the passage of time. Modernisation in the Chinese treaty ports allowed some expressions of optimism about women, alternating with the utterances of sympathy for their plight, but in the depiction of the men, mockery makes an appearance. Arthur Smith (1845–1932) came close to this in *Chinese Characteristics,* with his description of Chinese modes of dress as irrational. J. Dyer Ball took it a step further in a chapter on "How John Chinaman Dresses," which commences: "Imagine a people going about in pyjamas (and badju) the whole day long, and one will get some idea of the common costume of the male section of the nation."[62] In the course of this heavily humorous account, John Chinaman's virility was impugned. "In England," Ball wrote, "men have given up the contest with women as to who shall deck themselves more profusely in the colours of the rainbow, and retired in favour of the fairer sex, content that they should have the monopoly of adornment. In the Far East man still retains supremacy, though woman runs him close in this respect."[63] It may well have been such mockery that in the end drove some Chinese men from their comfortable robes into the stiff, progressive suits of Savile Row, a transformation already underway when Ball's book was published.

In contrast, what Chinese women wore presented Europeans with a problem that confounded their sense of progressive time. Progress placed much store on clothing, which separated the savages from the civilised, but the essential decorum of Chinese women's dress challenged Western observers, whose own clothing culture fostered a deep tension between tendencies to conceal and to reveal the body in its sexual aspect. The contradiction was set forth clearly by Leo Tolstoy, who in "The Kreutzer Sonata" railed against "those detestable jerseys, bustles, and naked shoulders, arms, almost breasts," which were part of a new economy of sexuality that commoditised women's bodies in a way appallingly opposed to the natural way of arranged marriage observed among "the Chinese, Hindus, Mohammedans, and among our own working classes."[64]

Tolstoy's opinion was virtually echoed by the Chinese diplomat Zhang Deyi (1847–1919), sometime minister to Great Britain, who was urbanely well-disposed to the human species in all its variety but took as much exception to the beauty aids of the fashionable European woman as his Brit-

---

62 Dyer Ball, *The Chinese at Home,* 225.

63 Ibid., 230.

64 Leo Tolstoy, "The Kreutzer Sonata," in *Great Short Works of Leo Tolstoy,* trans. Louise and Aylmer Maude (New York: Harper and Rowe, 1967), 370, 372.

Fig. 2.9 Comfort, economy and modesty: the ascribed hallmarks of Chinese women's dress. "Chinese Lady Simply Dressed," photographed by Mr R. Beauchamp.

ish counterpart might have to bound feet. Corsets and bustles he regarded as "the product of a very vicious mind."[65] Alicia Little found that this was not the sum of Chinese disapprobation. "To the Chinese," she wrote, "a foreign woman's tight-fitting dress showing her figure is very indecent ... I avoid wearing anything that shows the figure, in China, as far as I can."[66]

On the important criterion of propriety, Chinese women's dress met with strong approval from Europeans. William Alexander found "an engaging modesty in the Chinese habit,"[67] and so too did James, Bishop Bashford (1849–1919), who in a later century described Chinese women's dress as much more "comfortable, economical, modest and becoming" than that of their European counterparts.[68] Even J. Dyer Ball was forced to admit that "in the case of the girls quite enough is put on to satisfy even the Occidental in his idea of what is right and fit"[69] (Fig. 2.9).

Comfort, as the bishop noted, was another criterion on which women's dress was approved. Isabella Bird (1831–1904) found the ideal travelling ensemble to be "a Chinese woman's dress with a Japanese *kurumaya*'s hat, the one perfect travelling hat, and English gloves and shoes"[70] (Fig. 2.10). Like most

65 Zhang Deyi, *Diary of a Chinese Diplomat* [1872] (Bejing: Foreign Languages Press, 1992), 265.

66 Little, *Land of the Blue Gown*, 61.

67 Alexander and Mason, *Views of 18th Century China*, 18.

68 James Bashford, *China: An Interpretation* [1916] (New York: Abingdon Press, 1922), 141.

69 Ball, *The Chinese at Home*, 226.

70 Mrs J.F. Bishop [Isabella L. Bird], *The Yangtze Valley and Beyond* (London: John Murray, 1899), 206.

Fig. 2.10 Left: Isabella Bird in Manchu (or hybrid) dress: a sleeveless robe (*bijia*) worn over a wide-sleeved robe or, possibly, a jacket (*ao*). The original caption declares this to be Manchu dress, but the sleeves are more typical of a Han jacket. For this studio photo, Bird has donned a Chinese cap or head-band (*leizi*) (the image is not quite clear), rather than the wide-brimmed Japanese hat she favoured for travelling. The latter appears in the sketch on the right, in her own depiction of Japanese wet-weather garb.

foreigners, Bird looked askance at the bound feet of Chinese women, but she also noted "the extreme comfort of a Chinese woman's dress in all classes, no corset or waist-bands or constraints of any kind," and became so accustomed to it that after her China travels were over, she could not again "take kindly to European dress."[71] Alicia Little could not have agreed more. "After spending any length of time amongst the Orientals," she wrote, "I think every one must

---

71 Bishop, *The Yangtze Valley and Beyond*, 242. By "Chinese dress", Bird may have meant Manchu or mixed Manchu-Han dress. Concerning the *kurumaya*'s hat, Lafcadio Hearn (*Glimpses of an Unfamiliar Japan* (London: Osgood, McIlvaine and Co., 1894)) writes: "My kurumaya calls himself 'Cha.' He has a white hat which looks like the top of an enormous mushroom," which seems a fair description of the hat depicted in Fig. 2.10 (right). Bird herself described her travelling dress in Japan as including "a Japanese hat, shaped like a large inverted bowl, of light bamboo plait, with a white cotton cover, and a very light frame inside, which fits round the brow and leaves a space of 1½ inches between the hat and the head for the free circulation of air. It only weighs 2½ ounces, and... light as it is, it protects the head so thoroughly, that, though the sun has been unclouded all day and the mercury is at 86°, no other protection has been necessary." Bishop, *Unbeaten Tracks in Japan* (London: John Murray, 1905), 33. This then would seem to be the "one perfect travelling hat" mentioned above, though it must have looked very odd wedded to Chinese women's clothes.

feel that our European dress is lacking in grace and elegance."[72] She remarked wonderingly on the persistence with which European women continued to martyr themselves on the altar of fashion in the heat of a Chinese summer: "Their dresses are tight-fitting, their shoes are thin, their heels are high, and in this hothouse air surcharged with moisture the least movement must produce consequences disastrous to their new gloves. Thus cheeks are pale and expressions sad, as they are carried to and fro in sedan chairs ..."[73]

It is tempting to conclude from these observations that in beholding Chinese women, Europeans retreated from their new linear perspective, one that placed societies at different points of development in history, to an older understanding of difference across space rather than through time. The generic woman could not be as deeply historicised as the man. Although an advanced society was held to treat women better than did a backward society, the women themselves—closer to nature, less capable of rational thought, more childlike—were not clearly positioned in relationship to each other on the evolutionary ladder. Chinese women dressed differently from European women, but in some ways better than them. Their clothes were not obviously backward or ludicrous in the way that the clothes of Chinese men were. They could be ridiculed only to the same degree that women's clothes everywhere invited ridicule. Footbinding, it is true, was regarded as barbaric, but in this respect, the agency of Chinese women was hardly admitted. Their feet were the fault of their culture.

Conclusion

The engagement with footbinding and the employment of a perspective of cultural relativism are two features that distinguish nineteenth-century, mainly Anglophone commentaries on China, from those of the sixteenth to eighteenth centuries, mostly written by Catholic missionaries from the continent. The features are in essence mutually opposed, since footbinding was both a practice peculiar to Chinese culture and also was used by nineteenth-century Europeans to denigrate that culture. What allowed them to be simultaneously present was the placement of cultures in a hierarchy of progressive time. The difference between the two periods was not so much one of like and dislike, admiration and contempt, as that people of the earlier time saw the Chinese as being rather like themselves while people of the later found them to be utterly different.

The historical production of a certain way of talking about Chinese clothing underpinned the trajectory of vestimentary change evident in the early

---

72 Little, *Intimate China*, 61.

73 Little, *Land of the Blue Gown*, 21.

twentieth century. The radical transformation of dress in twentieth-century China was not due to what Europeans had to say specifically on the subject. Rather, clothing, and more generally the physical appearance of people in China, came under pressure along with other aspects of Chinese culture as European hegemony was extended through the nineteenth-century world. Nineteenth-century perceptions of Chinese clothing culture as lacking in dynamism and innocent of fashion were a well-developed aspect of the civilisational discourse which helped to effect this hegemony.

For people in China, this eventually posed the problem of how to reduce the difference between Chinese and Europeans in their allotted positions in the hierarchy of cultures and races, and to overcome the associated evolutionary and historical time-lag, while at the same time insisting on a cultural difference necessary to nationalist identity. The transformation of their clothing culture was a response to the former imperative; the pattern of transformation showed a sensitivity to the requirements of the latter. But along the way to a new clothing culture, Chinese fashion setters forgot that their forbears had been alert to the demands of the market and the nuances of contemporary choices in what to wear. They became complicit in the conclusion that China simply lacked fashion.

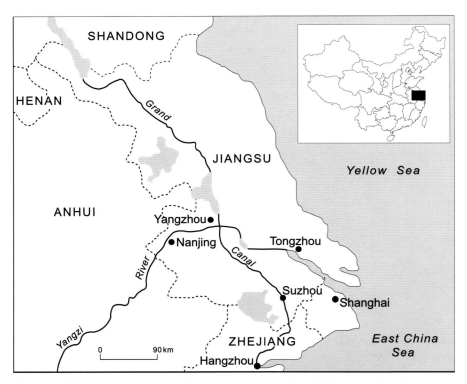

The lower Yangzi valley showing places mentioned in the text. In the Ming dynasty, the provinces of Jiangsu and Anhui made up the single province of Nan Zhili (the Southern Metropolitan province), centred on Nanjing. Tongzhou, then part of Yangzhou prefecture, is now known as Nantong.

3
FASHIONS IN LATE IMPERIAL CHINA

What does it mean to speak of fashion in a Chinese historical context? Fashion, surely, can be identified in many periods of history, and in many places. It is related to taste, consumption and urbanisation. It entails short-term vicissitudes in vestimentary choices, and indicates the presence in particular societies of dynamic relationships between producers and consumers. In other words, fashion is distinguishable from a fashion industry, which is a modern phenomenon grounded in the industrial revolution. China did not have a fashion industry before the twentieth century, but it did have a lively trade in textiles—interregional and international—that was accompanied by an attention in Chinese cities to what was à la mode. Greater exposure to Chinese domestic life and closer familiarity with non-canonical Chinese texts would have alerted Western observers to this fact.

Fashion in China is historically associated most closely with Shanghai, which became the major centre of foreign investment and residence in the late nineteenth century. In the first half of the twentieth century, Shanghai was a voracious centre of consumption of everything from opium to clothes,[1] but before the Opium War in the nineteenth century, and the creation of the Treaty Port system which allowed foreign settlement in Shanghai among other places, it was a relatively modest place. Suzhou, Hangzhou, Yangzhou and the Ming dynasty's "Southern Capital," Nanjing, well exceeded it in economic and cultural productivity, and also in historical importance as sites of social and cultural change (see p.42).[2]

---

1 See Leo Ou-fan Lee, *Shanghai Modern: The Flowering of a New Urban Culture in China, 1930–1945* (Cambridge, Mass.: Harvard University Press, 1999); Sherman Cochran, ed., *Inventing Nanjing Road: Commercial Culture in Shanghai, 1900-1945* (Ithaca: East Asia Program, Cornell University, 1999).

2 The idea of "Shanghai as fishing village" before the Opium War has been challenged by Linda Cooke Johnson in *Shanghai: From Market Town to Treaty Port 1074-1858* (Stanford: Stanford University Press, 1995), but Michael Marmé has shown that miscalculations of the city's engagement in trade led her to overestimate its historical significance by a wide margin. See Marmé, *Suzhou: Where the Goods of All the Provinces Converge* (Stanford: Stanford University Press, 2005), 245, 323-4, n. 70.

Clothing is among the indices to the dynamism of these centres of southern culture. In the early seventeenth century, Gu Qiyuan (1565–1628) wrote of women's fashions in Nanjing that "thirty years before, they changed only once in ten years," while now "not three or four years" passed before some new style was apparent.[3] Suzhou at this time was performing something of the role played in Europe by Paris, setting the tone for new and extravagant styles of clothing.[4] In Hangzhou, one Xu Dunqiu recalled around 1614 that half a century earlier his school friends all "wore hats of [black] gauze and clothes of white cotton. Among them, only one or two well-born youths wore coloured clothing. Now everyone wears coloured clothing and white cloth is nowhere to be seen."[5]

As for Yangzhou:

The women [here] have nothing to do but sit around making up their faces, competing with each other in artful adornment. Their hair ornaments are of worked gold and jade, with pearls and kingfisher feathers added here and there. Their bedding is finely embroidered, their underclothing bright and gay. They are extravagant to the last degree.[6]

Extravagance and fashions are not the same thing. It is the commentary on change as expressed through consumption, not on expenditure per se, that permits us to talk about fashions in this period. This commentary is quite explicit. The clothing made and worn in Tongzhou (in Yangzhou prefecture) included "long skirts, generous collars, wide belts, [and] fine linings." These garments were all subject to "rapid changes, known as "contemporary styles" (*shiyang*). This is what is called outrageous dress (*fuyao*)."[7] In the late Ming, there was much talk of "outrageous dress." The chatter accompanied a proliferation of disturbing new fashions in the prosperous cities of the lower Yangzi valley.[8]

Signs and symptoms of Ming fashions

When Zhu Yuanzhang (1328–1398) established the Ming dynasty in the late fourteenth century, he was determined to rid the empire of the barbarian ways of the Yuan era, including barbarian clothes. This meant abandoning the close-fitting tunics favoured by the Mongols and a return, ideally, to the styles of

---

3 Wu Renshu, "Mingdai pingmin fushi de liuxing fengshang yu shidafu de fanying," 74.

4 Craig Clunas, "The Art of Social Climbing in Sixteenth-Century China," *The Burlington Magazine* 133, 1059 (June 1991): 370; Timothy Brook, *The Confusions of Pleasure: Commerce and Culture in Ming China* (Berkeley: University of California Press, 1998), 220-2.

5 Lin Liyue, "Yishang yu fengjiao—wan Ming de fushi fengshang yu 'fuyao' yilun," 124.

6 *Jiangdu xianzhi* (Gazetteer of Jiangdu county), Wanli edition (1597), 7.28b-29a.

7 Lin Liyue, "Yishang yu fengjiao—wan Ming de fushi fengshang yu 'fuyao' yilun," 125.

8 Ibid. See also Wu Renshu, "Mingdai pingmin fushi de liuxing fengshang yu shidafu de fanying," 96-100.

the Tang dynasty.[9] Garments retrieved from tombs show that this restoration project was at least partially realised, but also provide evidence of the sustained influence of the far north on Chinese clothing.[10] To eradicate all traces of Yuan culture was of course impossible, especially given the continued residence in China of descendants of the original Mongol invaders and to this heritage were added new currents of influence arising from trade and other movements between China and neighbouring lands.

Wu Jen-shu points to three different manifestations of fashion in the Ming. One was fascination with the exotic: horse-hair skirts (*maweiqun*) from Korea, and a military-style tunic (*kuzhe*) apparently inspired by nomad warriors from the north. Both these (male) fashions developed first in the capital, perhaps due to the tribute trade missions that regularly made their way to Beijing, paying obeisance to the Son of Heaven before making their way to the markets. Weaving horse-hair was a rare skill in China when the Korean horse-hair garments first appeared, but by the late fifteenth century local weavers had mastered the art and were stealing the tails of horses owned by metropolitan officials to supply themselves with the materials necessary for the manufacture of the cloth.[11]

As for the military-style tunic, this evolved into the very commonly worn *yesa*, a garment with gathered or pleated skirt that became popular among well-to-do men in the sixteenth century. Wang Shizhen (1526–1590) interestingly documents the *yesa*'s rise in social status. In the course of the sixteenth century it gradually displaced two other styles of tunic to the point that "when grandees are attending a banquet, they must needs wear the *yesa*." In his view, this was a case of military dress triumphing over refined clothing, and probably of barbarian triumphing over Chinese.[12] The *yesa* appears to have shared some formal features with the Qing dynasty court robe referred to in the preceding chapter (see Figs 2.2, 2.3). This suggests that the flared or gathered skirt—whether or not integrated with an upper garment—was a common look in male clothing across the far north, and had different points of entry into China.[13]

---

9 Zhou Shaoquan, "Mingdai fushi tanlun" (An essay on Ming costume), *Shixue yuekan* 6 (1990): 34.

10 Shelagh Vainker, *Chinese Silk: A Cultural History* (London: The British Museum Press, and New Brunswick: Rutgers University Press, 2004), 156.

11 Wu Renshu, "Mingdai pingmin fushi de liuxing fengshang yu shidafu de fanying," 66-7.

12 Wang Shizhen describes three different garments evolving from the *kuzhe*: one was the *yesa*; another was the "tangerine robe" (*chengzi yi*), worn with a cord around the waist; and the third was the "Daoist gown" (*Daopao*), worn without the cord. Ibid., 67. See also entry on *yesa* in Zhou Xun and Gao Chunming, eds, *Zhongguo yiguan fushi da cidian*. (Dictionary of Chinese Costume) (Shanghai: Shanghai cishu chubanshe, 1996), 205. On Wang Shizhen, see Barbara Yoshida-Krafft, "Wang Shih-chen," in *DMB*, Vol. II, 1399-405.

13 On the disputed origins of the court robe, see Wilson, *Chinese Dress*, 35; Vollmer, *Ruling from the Dragon Throne*, 63-9.

Fig. 3.1 Two common hat styles of the Ming dynasty. Left, Xu Guangqi (1562–1633) in an anonymous portrait wearing the *wusha* (black gauze) hat that in historical dramas is often used to represent a Ming figure; right, Gu Mengyou (1599–1660) portrayed by Zeng Jing (1568–1650) (detail), wearing a *piaopiao* (fluttering) hat, with flaps before and behind, of the sort frequently portrayed in Ming illustrations.

In a wide-ranging study of social life in Ming China, Chen Baoliang has documented further evidence of "barbarian" influence on clothing, especially with reference to the persistence of Yuan terminology and styles. In the north, men wore a Mongol style of hat that they called "barbarian hat" (*humao*), while a sort of hooded cloak worn by women was also of Mongol origin. The *bijia*, or long vest, was of Mongol origin, and so was the *zhisun*, a single colour garment which in the Ming was worn as regular dress by military officials. The words, no doubt like the garments, were Chinese approximations of the Mongol terms. Chen notes the lasting use of some Mongol words for clothing in places even as far from the north as Hainan Island.[14]

A second manifestation of Ming fashion lay in a return to the styles of antiquity—a retro trend quite separate from the sanctioned restorationism of the late fourteenth century. In the words of Gu Qiyuan, "costume in the Southern Capital before the Jiajing and Wanli reigns [i.e. before 1522] was rather simple. Officials wore the biretta, scholars the square hat, and that was all. In recent years everyday there is a difference, every month something new. So what gentlemen wear now goes by all sorts of names: the Han cap, the Jin cap, the Tang

---

14 Chen Baoliang, *Mingdai shehui shenghuo shi* (A history of social life in the Ming dynasty) (Beijing: Zhongguo shehui kexue chubanshe, 2004), 206-7.

cap …" and so on.[15] This observation incidentally points to the importance of the hat in the male wardrobe in China (Fig. 3.1): it was an important signifier of social status, as well as, apparently, a convenient site of fashion experiment. But not only hats were involved in this retro movement: Tang-style satins and Song-style brocades were all the rage, accompanying a revival in the popularity of the fourth-century calligrapher Wang Xizhi (ca 302–ca 368) and the Yuan dynasty painter Zhao Mengfu (1254–1322): "at present, a partiality for antiquity prevails throughout the empire."[16]

The third manifestation lay in obvious novelty. Wu Jen-shu explains this in terms of retro fatigue: the resource to antiquity ran its course and invention replaced renaissance. An example he offers is the Chunyang hat (named after a Daoist immortal): this combined Han and Tang styles but was also a departure from both. The Chunyang hat was emblematic of the "new and strange" (*xinqi*) clothing that so frequently receives mention in late Ming texts. In the second quarter of the seventeenth century it was said to be extremely popular among youth, all of whom looked with contempt upon the ancient styles.[17]

These "new and strange" styles flourished in a period otherwise known for the phenomenon of social climbing.[18] The tendency to social emulation, famously identified by both Thorstein Veblen and Georg Simmel as a driving force behind fashion,[19] was a significant factor in the vestimentary environment of the late Ming. Sumptuary regulations restricting the use of certain fabrics and types of adornment to people of certain status were flouted with impunity by commoner or merchant families that had profited from the commercialisation of the economy in the sixteenth and seventeenth centuries.[20] Nor were these solid citizens alone in breaching former dress codes. "Nowadays," complained one writer, "the very servant girls dress in silk gauze, and the singsong girls look down on brocaded silks and embroidered gowns."[21]

It is difficult to squeeze all fashions into the social emulation category without qualification. When Chinese were taking their fashions from "barbarians," clearly more than social status was at issue. The same can be said of respectable women

---

15 Wu Renshu, "Mingdai pingmin fushi de liuxing fengshang yu shidafu de fanying," 68.

16 Ibid., 70.

17 Ibid., 70-1.

18 Clunas, "The Art of Social Climbing."

19 Thorstein Veblen, *The Theory of the Leisure Class: An Economic Study of Institutions* (New York: B.W. Huebsch, 1912); George Simmel, "The Philosophy of Fashion" [1904], *American Journal of Sociology* 62, 6 (1957): 541-58.

20 Clunas, "The Art of Social Climbing," 370-1. See also Sarah Dauncey, "Illusions of Grandeur: Perceptions of Status and Wealth in Late-Ming Female Clothing and Ornamentation," *East Asian History* 25-26 (December 2003): 61-2.

21 Clunas, "The Art of Social Climbing," 370.

looking to the demi-monde for inspiration. According to Yu Huai (1616–1696): "The clothes and adornment associated with southern entertainment were taken as the model everywhere … The length of gowns and the size of sleeves changed with the times. Witnesses referred to this as à la mode (*shishizhuang*)."[22] To put Yu Huai's statement simply, the courtesans of the south established (women's) fashions for the empire. This may even have been through street fashion, for in the early seventeenth century prostitutes were on the streets in increasing numbers. "In the big cities they run to the tens of thousands," wrote Xie Zhaozhe (1567–1624); "but they can be found in every poor district and remote place as well, leaning by doorways all day long, bestowing their smiles, selling sex for a living …"[23]

Considered in tandem, "barbarian" styles and courtesan styles seem to indicate marked gender differentiation in sources of influence on Ming fashions. They broadly accord with the established dichotomies of north/south and outside/inside (*wai, nei*), and their influence was manifested, generally speaking, along gender lines. But they probably owed much of their appeal to the same factor: a certain ambiguity associated with the appropriation of exotic, exogenous, or in general "outside" practices that gave the ensuing fashions a provocative charm. This ambiguity is well illustrated in an episode in the sixteenth-century erotic novel *Jin Ping Mei* (Plum in a Golden Vase) when Ximen Qing comments admiringly of his fetchingly dressed third and fifth consorts that they look like a pair of sing-song girls.[24] He gets snapped at for his pains, but that is not because his concubines do not want to look like courtesans. On the contrary, they closely scrutinise the clothes and adornment of the sing-song girls who visit their household, and with whom they must compete for the favours of their lord and master.[25]

Changing styles of women's dress

Prostitutes, whether high-class courtesans or common street girls, very probably served as the models for the painters whose depictions of women have left us with a visual impression of various sorts of clothing worn by women in the Ming and Qing dynasties. These paintings, in combination with book illustrations, artefacts from tombs, and textual references, point to a number of major stylistic variations in late Ming women's dress: the classic short jacket (*ru*) worn with skirt and short overskirt (*yaoqun*); the skirt worn with long jacket (*ao*); the open-sided gown or long vest (*bijia*); the long over-jacket (*pifeng*), and the "paddy-

---

22 Lin Liyue, "Yishang yu fengjiao," 128.

23 Xie Zhaozhe, *Wuzazu* (Five miscellanies) (Taibei: Weiwen, 1977), 196. On Xie, see Leon Zolbrod and L. Carrington Goodrich, "Hsieh Chao-che," *DMB*, Vol. I, 546-50.

24 Hsiao-hsiao-sheng, *The Golden Lotus: A Translation from the Original of Chin P'ing Mei*, trans. Clement Egerton, (New York: Paragon Books, 1959),Vol. I, 145.

25 See further, Dauncey, "Illusions of Grandeur," 58-9.

Fig. 3.2 The short-waisted style common in Ming paintings of women is here portrayed by Ren Xiong (1798–1856), in a work not too different to one painted by Chen Hongshou (1598–1652) two centuries earlier. This charmingly stylized depiction shows a skirt (*changqun*), and overskirt (*yaoqun* or *weishang*) with sash, and a cape or shawl (*pijian*) worn over short upper garment with long, close-fitting sleeves (*duanru* or *yaoru*). Ren Xiong *Yaogong qiushan tu* (Jade palace, autumn fan), nineteenth century.

field" or patchwork gown (*shuitianyi*).[26] Of these, the paddy-field gown is overtly the most eccentric and would appear to fit into the category of "outrageous dress" excoriated by commentators. Constructed of small, varicoloured squares of cloth, it may have been inspired by Buddhist robes, since Buddhist monks liked to make use of small off-cuts of fabric, discarded or donated, in accordance with the Buddha's own preference.[27] As a fashionable garment, a paddy-field gown would surely have been regarded as irreverent.

Historically, the most interesting development in Ming women's dress is the increasing prevalence of long upper garments at the expense of the high-waisted style of the *ru* or short jacket worn with skirt. This amounted to a major change in the architecture of Chinese women's dress, and presaged the long reign of the *ao* or long jacket during the Qing. The short jacket and skirt (*ruqun*) is the most commonly depicted women's fashion in figure paintings of the Ming and continued to be portrayed by artists right up until the nineteenth century, although late depictions are almost certainly based on earlier paintings or drawings rather than on life (Fig. 3.2).[28] The ensemble

---

26 Zhou Xun and Gao Chunming, *Zhongguo lidai fushi* (Chinese costume through history) (Shanghai: Xuclin chubanshe, 1994), 244-54.

27 Wong Hwei Lian and Szan Tan, eds, *Powerdressing: Textiles for Rulers and Priests from the Chris Hall Collection*, Ex. Cat., (Singapore: Asian Civilisations Museum, 2006), 395. There seems to be no extant example of a paddy-field gown, but the Chris Hall collection does include several fine examples of patchwork.

28 Ren Xiong's depiction of a woman with fan (see Fig. 3.2) echoes a painting by Chen Hongshou, *Dui jing shi nü* (Lady looking in a mirror), which shows a woman in identical dress and comparable pose. See Liu Rendao, ed., *Zhongguo chuanshi renwu minghua quanji* (Col-

has a passing resemblance to the *hanbok* or *kimono*, in sharp contrast to the *ao-qun* (long jacket and skirt), which is the most familiar women's ensemble from the Qing.[29]

A prominent feature of women's dress in the late Ming was the over-gown (*pifeng*, *pi'ao*), which had virtually disappeared from China by the nineteenth century but appears to have been widely worn as everyday dress in the sixteenth and seventeenth centuries.[30] Chen Bao-liang traces the *pifeng* back to the late Tang, but as her own illustrations make clear, the generic garment underwent major shifts in style. An early depiction of the garment in its most frequently represented style is to be found in a painting by Tang Yin (1470–1524).[31] A native of Suzhou, and commercially one of the most successful artists of his time, Tang Yin executed numerous paintings

Fig. 3.3 The long coat depicted here is probably a garment referred to in Ming texts as the *pifeng*, also known as the *beizi*, which in the late Ming appears with great frequency in graphic representations of women. The outer garment in each case is of plain cloth, the skirt of printed. The women's faces are powdered to accent the brow, the nose, and the chin. Tang Yin (1470-1524), *Meng Shu gongji tu* (Palace Ladies of Meng of Shu).

lected figure paintings of the Chinese heritage) (Beijing: Zhongguo xiju chubanshe, 2001), Vol. 2, 322.

29 The terminology for Ming dress, both in the original texts and in the secondary literature, is relatively unstable. Different regional terms were used for the same item of clothing, and different items of clothing were worn in different places, so that there is some variation between north and south, and also over time. The term *ru* can serve as a synonym for *shan* or *ao*, themselves interchangeable terms, and while it generally refers to a short garment, the term "*changru*" (long *ru*), also exists. Zhou and Gao describe this as the precursor to the *ao*. Zhou Xun and Gao Chunming, *Zhongguo yiguan fushi da cidian*, 221. The term *ru* is used in *ruqun* in Hua Mei, *Zhongguo fuzhuang shi* (History of Chinese dress) (Tianjin: Renmin meishu chubanshe, 1989), 73, but is not employed in Zhou Xibao, *Zhongguo gudai fushi shi*, 413-14.

30 Meng Hui, "Pifeng xiaoshi" (A little knowledge about the *pifeng*), in Meng Hui, *Pan Jinlian de faxing* (Pan Jinlian's hairdo) (Nanjing: Jiangsu renmin chubanshe, 2005), 81-103. Meng Hui provides an example of a short *pi'ao*, but the majority of her references and illustrations are to long garments. It is possible that the term *pi'ao* does refer to the shorter version.

31 Li Chu-tsing, "T'ang Yin," in *DMB*, Vol. I, 1256-9.

Fig. 3.4 A ball game in the grounds of a sixteenth-century bawdy house, as illustrated in an early edition of the novel *Jin Ping Mei* (Plum in a Golden Vase). The men are members of a ball club, entertaining themselves and the onlookers by playing kickball with one of the ladies of the house, Cassia. She is described in the text as wearing a crimson skirt under a white silk front-fastening jacket (*ao*) coat, with her hair done in "the Hangzhou style." The illustration shows her wearing a full-length front-fastening overgarment with overlong sleeves, the latter a common feature in illustrations and paintings of women's dress in this period.

that portrayed beautiful Suzhou women dressed in fashionable clothing.[32] The Palace Ladies of Meng of Shu, perhaps his most famous work, purports to be of courtesans in the court of the Meng Chang (919-65), in Sichuan, during the interdynastic wars of the tenth century (Fig. 3.3). In the colophon, the painter refers to the "Daoist garb" allegedly worn by the women at Meng's behest. This might explain why they are portrayed wearing over-gowns rather than the short jacket and skirt common in other paintings of "beauties" in the Ming, including by Tang Yin.

It was no doubt changes in the dimensions of the *pifeng* that occasioned some of the carping about women's clothing in the late Ming. Hems were descending and sleeves growing larger in the sixteenth century. With sleeves trailing well below the finger tips and descending hems threatening to cover skirts completely, the *pifeng* came perilously close to looking like a man's tunic (Fig. 3.4). Hence the anxieties expressed by the distinguished official Huo Tao, who as Minister of Rites in Nanjing attempted in 1537 to reverse the trend:

Men's and women's styles differ in length. A woman's upper garment is level with her waist, her lower garment meets with the top: earth supports heaven. A man's upper garment covers his lower garments: heaven embraces earth. When a woman's [upper] garment covers her lower garments, there is confusion between male and female.[33]

---

32 Ibid. On Suzhou in the Ming, see Marmé, *Suzhou*.

33 Huo Tao, *Wei'ai wenji* (Wei'ai's collected prose), quoted in Lin Liyue, "Yishang yu fengjiao," 137. On Huo Tao's dress reform efforts, see Fang Chaoying, "Huo T'ao," in *DMB*, Vol. I, 681.

Fig. 3.5 Both the *ruqun* (short jacket and long skirt) and *pifeng* (overgarment or coat) make an appearance in this early Qing painting. The artist was an astronomer and court painter in the Kangxi era (1661–1722). Jiao Bingzhen, *Shinü tu* (Pictures of ladies), album leaf.

Portraits and other representational works of the early Qing suggest that the *pifeng* and *ruqun* were styles that lasted into the early eighteenth century (Fig. 3.5),[34] while the photographic record shows that they were not evident in the nineteenth. This prompts questions about the common supposition that under the Manchus, Han Chinese women clung to the fashions of their predecessors. Clearly, the long, figure-concealing *pifeng* had much in common not only with the man's gown but also with the Manchu women's gown. Perhaps this helped dislodge the short jacket in favour of a longer one—the *ao*—which finally rendered the *pifeng* redundant. In any event, a garment which is rarely discussed and of which there are few surviving examples apparently had a critical role to play in the costume drama of Ming and Qing China. Its disappearance from the Han wardrobe and effective replacement by the *ao* contributed to the emergence of a distinctively Qing look in Han women's dress.

Qing fashions: the example of Yangzhou

The Qing dynasty is imagined as a much less exciting, less inventive period than the late Ming, except perhaps in terms of empire-building, and overall less is known about its material culture even though so many more material remains from that time are preserved in museums around the world. Not surprisingly, it is viewed also as a regime under which fashion experienced a decline.[35]

Before too quickly dismissing this era as uninteresting for fashion history, it is worth looking at what might actually have been written on the subject by those familiar with what people wore in those times. Evidence from Yangzhou, for example, suggests a steady consumption of fashion from the late sixteenth to the

---

34 See Shen Yizheng, comp., *Lidai meiren huaxuan* (Selected paintings of beauties through the ages) (Taibei: Yishu tushu gongsi, 1999), 102-39.

35 Kenneth Pomeranz, *The Great Divergence: China, Europe, and the Making of the Modern World Economy* (Princeton: Princeton University Press, 2000), 155.

nineteenth centuries and beyond. The materials are not abundant, but what they have to say permits a more nuanced vestimentary history than one written simply in terms of the dragon robes which dominate museum holdings. Local fashion trends here hint at the richer history that might result from a more broadly based study of textiles and clothing production in the Qing.

Situated north of the Yangzi River well upstream from Shanghai, Yangzhou lay far from the coast and was out of immediate reach of foreign trade, which made it something of a backwater in the early twentieth century. In earlier centuries, however, it had been a large and prosperous city with a lively leisure economy.[36] The salt merchants who dominated local society were among the wealthiest men in China, renowned for their gardens and patronage of theatre and painting, as well as for more vulgar sorts of consumption.[37] In some respects a peculiar place, Yangzhou was also a participant in broader movements of social change involving commerce, social mobility, and changing gender configurations in urban China in the sixteenth to nineteenth centuries.[38]

In the late Ming, Yangzhou began to challenge Suzhou's position as the premier centre of wealth and consumption in the lower Yangzi valley. Suzhou was much the larger city, with a much sturdier economy,[39] but the expansion of the salt merchant presence in Yangzhou during the sixteenth century resulted in an extraordinary concentration of liquid capital there, and a growth in luxury consumption that was favourable to fashion. "Suzhou style" and "Yangzhou style" (*Su shi, Yang shi*) emerged as parallel, notionally contrasting but probably mutually influential modes of dress.[40] The city was sacked and its residents massacred in 1645, but in the early decades of the Qing it regained and even improved on

---

36 The classic, oft-cited essay on this city is Ping-ti Ho, "The Salt Merchants of Yang-chou: A Study of Commercial Capitalism in Eighteenth-Century China," *Harvard Journal of Asiatic Studies* 17 (1954): 130-64. Specialist studies of the city include Tobie Meyer-Fong, *Building Culture in Early Qing Yangzhou* (Stanford: Stanford University Press, 2003) and Antonia Finnane, *Speaking of Yangzhou: A Chinese City, 1550-1850* (Cambridge, Mass.: Harvard University Asia Center, 2004).

37 See Ho, "The Salt Merchants of Yang-chou." On opera in Yangzhou, see Colin P. Mackerras, *The Rise of Peking Opera: Social Aspects of the Theatre in Manchu China* (Oxford: Clarendon Press, 1972), Chapter 3. On gardens, see Zhu Jiang, *Yangzhou yuanlin pinshang lu* (An appreciation of the gardens of Yangzhou) (Shanghai: Shanghai wenwu chubanshe, 1984); on art patronage, see Ginger Cheng-chi Hsü, *A Bushel of Pearls: Painting for Sale in Eighteenth-Century Yangchow* (Stanford: Stanford University Press, 2001).

38 For a review of this historiographical shift, see Harriet Zurndorfer, "From Local History to Cultural History: Reflections on Some Recent Publications," *T'oung Pao* LXXXIII (1997): 387-96.

39 See Marmé, *Suzhou.*

40 Wei Minghua, *Yangzhou shouma* (Thin horses of Yangzhou) (Fuzhou: Fujian renmin chubanshe, 1998), 153 ff.

Fig. 3.6 Young girl depicted by Wu Youru (d. 1893) in a *pipa*-cut jacket and pleated skirt in the fish-scale style. Her hair is cut with a fringe in the "number one" style, so-named for forming a straight line across the forehead, like the character for *yi* (one). The little boy's hair is in the "potty lid" (*mazi*) cut, one of a number of styles for small boys that involved shaving part of the head. Right, a much shorter version of the *pipa*-cut jacket is worn by this well-dressed military mandarin, photographed by John Thomson in the nineteenth century.

its name for the good life. The poet and dramatist Kong Shangren (1648–1718), resident in Yangzhou in the 1680s, complained about the "accountants, clerks, slaves and servants" of wealthy households in the city, because they were inclined to "dress up in flashy clothes, putting on airs in order to snub others."[41] His contemporary Li Gan complained: "In all the empire, it is only in the prefectural city and suburbs of Yangzhou that clothes have to follow the times."[42] Li Dou,

41 Richard Strassberg, *The World of K'ung Shang-jen: A Man of Letters in Early Ch'ing China* (New York: Columbia University Press, 1983), 144.

42 Jonathan S. Hay, *Shitao: Painting and Modernity in Early Qing China* (New York: Cambridge University Press, 2001), 12. Translation adapted.

the great chronicler of eighteenth-century Yangzhou, had much the same to say: "Clothes worn in Yangzhou are always in the newest style (*xin yang*)."[43]

From a morphological point of view, stylistic changes over this century and a half might seem slight compared to those in contemporary Europe, but much is probably hidden from the eye. That Manchu women were influenced by Han fashions is well known. In 1839, during the imperial marriage draft, the emperor ordered punishments to be meted out to the fathers of girls who were wearing wide sleeves in emulation of Han fashion.[44] The impact of Manchu styles on Chinese dress is less well documented, but clearly extended beyond the expectation that literati wear the Manchu long gown. A good example of its influence is the popularisation of the so-called *pipa* cut for the front of a jacket or vest. The *pipa* vest is familiar in Chinese costume history as a common item of dress among Manchu women in the late Qing. Numerous photos and surviving garments attest to its popularity.[45] The origins of the style appear to lie in the Manchu informal riding coat, which for ease of mounting the horse was cut short on the front left side.[46] In eighteenth-century Yangzhou, this style was affected by the likely lads who hawked food around the time of the Qing Ming (Grave-sweeping) festival in spring. According to Li Dou, they vied with each other to make an impression in their *pipa* jackets of indigo or lilac.[47] Han women rarely wore the *pipa* vest, but they could deploy the *pipa* cut on their jackets, a style depicted in the late nineteenth century by Wu Youru (Fig. 3.6).

To look only at the shape of a garment and not at the material from which it was constructed is to overlook an important aspect of clothing culture in China, and indeed more broadly in the early modern world. The sites of Chinese fashion in the late imperial era were not quite the same as in modern Europe: cut and fit were less significant than the quality and colour of the fabric. Li Dou itemised the different sorts of cloth that went in and out of fashion in Yangzhou: silks and satins in different colours rapidly succeeded each other in popularity.[48] Hairstyles were also subject to fashionable changes—much like hats for men. This meant a thriving market in false hairpieces and hair adornments. According to Li Dou, Yangzhou women dressed their hair differently from women in other places—the apricot style, the double swallow style, and so on, but the fashion here seems to

---

43 Wei Minghua, *Yangzhou shouma*, 143.

44 See e.g. Evelyn S. Rawski, *The Last Emperors: A Social Hierarchy of Qing Imperial Institutions* (Berkeley: University of California Press, 1998), 41.

45 Photographs taken by Stephane Passet in Beijing and Mukden for Albert Kahn in the period 1909-1912, preserved in the musée Albert Kahn at Boulogne-Billancourt, include a number of Manchu women wearing this style of vest.

46 See Vollmer, *Ruling from the Dragon Throne*, 60, Fig. 3.2.

47 Zhou Xun and Gao Chunming, *Zhongguo yiguan fushi da cidian*, 243.

48 Wei Minghua, *Yangzhou shouma*, 143.

have spread to other places.[49] Both textiles and hairstyles continued to be a focus of fashion interest in the early twentieth century.

Fashion, the times, and the world

While Li Dou was writing, European fashion was gathering pace, and within a few decades of the publication of his famous guidebook, it had acquired the velocity by which fashion is often identified, moving from yearly and seasonal change to changes of "every week, every day, almost every hour."[50] In this era, as we have seen, Europeans began to describe Chinese dress mainly with an eye to how it varied from their own. Thus Père Eugène Estève in 1843 found that Chinese costume was based on principles fundamentally opposed to that of European dress: while European men doffed their hats to show respect, the Chinese kept theirs on; Europeans wore black for mourning, Chinese white; Europeans used pockets, Chinese a purse; Europeans cultivated a full head of hair, Chinese shaved their heads, and so on.[51]

A feature that distinguished European clothing in the early nineteenth century from that in the seventeenth was the industrialisation first of textile production and then of tailoring in Britain, France and elsewhere. This made way for the fashion houses of the second half of the century, and the appearance, as Giles Lipovetsky notes, of "fashion as we understand it today."[52] Consequently, fashion is commonly described as a product of industrial capitalism, even if most historians and theorists of fashion find it difficult to clearly differentiate between the fashion of, for example, early modernity, and that of recent times.[53] This nexus leads to a simple conclusion, as indicated in Chapter One of the present book: fashion can be found only in the context of the mass market of industrialised societies, which voraciously consumes all that is offered and then demands more.

Theories of consumption have, however, been changing, with effects on theories of fashion. In Germany, argues Daniel Purdy, fashion was produced by print culture, not by industrialisation.[54] In challenging the direct link between industrialisation, mass consumption, and fashion, Purdy opens the way for thinking about fashion mentality and practices in a context distinct from the fast world of the thoroughly modern city. Communications, both in the form of travellers and

---

49 Ibid., 153.

50 Giles Lipovetsky, *The Empire of Fashion: Dressing Modern Democracy*, trans. Catherine Porter (Princeton: Princeton University Press, 1994), 21.

51 Brouillon, *Mémoire sur l'état actuel de la Mission du Kiangnan*, 239-40.

52 Lipovetsky, *The Empire of Fashion*, 55-7.

53 Elizabeth Wilson, *Adorned in Dreams: Fashion and Modernity* (London: Virago, 1985), 16.

54 Daniel L. Purdy, *The Tyranny of Elegance: Consumer Cosmopolitanism in the Era of Goethe* (Baltimore: Johns Hopkins University Press, 1998).

tourists on the continent and in the form of magazines, leaflets and postcards, could produce new visions of how one should look.

The first fashion journal hit the streets in Germany when the beginnings of a popular press were yet a century away in China. But between China and Europe there were clearly other forms of communication in operation. In the realm of art and of *objets d'art* more generally, the effects of East-West contact are apparent in the palaces of both places during the eighteenth century.[55] Tea-drinking in England and tobacco smoking in China were both effects of East-West trade. Well-born Europeans dressed in silks and satins woven in distant Suzhou, among other places. And in 1755, someone in China purchased the following cargo from the good ship *Drake*: "Imbossed Carpets, 359 pces;" "Hairbines, 100 pces;" "Hair Camblets, 32 pces;" and "Long Ells, 4,899 pces."[56]

It has been common to make light of the significance of Western goods in China, a position frequently justified by reference to the famous letter in which the Qianlong emperor informed George III of England: "The productions of our Empire are manifold, and in great Abundance; nor do we stand in the least Need of the Produce of other Countries."[57] But the cargoes of the *Drake* and its long line of successors were of course absorbed into Chinese life. The carpets must have ended up on the floors of particular houses, and the "Long Ells" transformed into no doubt expensive clothing. More and more people must have been dressed in such clothing as time went on, because there was a growth in exports of English woollens to China in the late eighteenth century. The amounts were small in comparison to the size of the Chinese population, yet in urban markets, supplying around 5 per cent of the population, there were effects.

In Yangzhou, clocks and watches were one obvious sign that goods of Western origin were enriching local commodity culture, and incidentally affecting fashions. Clocks and watches receive short shrift in discussions of the China trade, perhaps because so many of them were purchased simply for presentation to the emperor.[58] But according to Lin Sumen, a younger contemporary of Li Dou, watches and clocks were significant consumer items in Yangzhou at least by 1808.[59] They were also significant fashion accessories. A watch was hung from

---

55 Jessica Rawson and Jane Portal, "Luxuries for Trade," in *The British Museum Book of Chinese Art*, Jessica Rawson, ed., (London: British Museum Press, 1992), 281-2; Pamela Crossley, *A Translucent Mirror: History and Identity in Qing Imperial Ideology* (Cambridge, Mass.: Blackwell, 1997), 281.

56 Hosea Ballou Morse, *The Chronicles of the East India Company, Trading to China, 1635-1834* (Oxford: Clarendon Press, 1926), Vol. V, 32.

57 Ibid., Vol. II, 248.

58 Ibid., Vol. III, 62.

59 Lin Sumen, *Hanjiang sanbai yin* (Three hundred sonnets from the Han River [Grand Canal]) (Yangzhou, 1808), 7.5b-6a.

the girdle of the wearer, and girdle hooks, used in place of the Western pocket to carry items of daily use, were themselves becoming more elaborate. They were made of white jade or aged bronze, and "in recent custom, large ones were more admired." In Yangzhou, a Western watch cost "several tens of taels" with the price varying according to the accuracy of the mechanism.[60] Since the price for a Western watch is given, it can be presumed that Chinese-made watches were also available—the products, perhaps, of workshops in other Lower Yangzi cities such as Nanjing, Hangzhou, and Suzhou.[61] The first Chinese clock-making manual was published in 1809,[62] but Chinese clocks were being crafted well before this date.[63]

It has often been asserted that Chinese interest in foreign manufactures before the late nineteenth century was one of disinterested curiosity at best, and the well-known Chinese fascination with watches and clocks has been viewed as comparable to an interest in mechanical toys.[64] This view is not sustainable in face of evidence that clocks and watches were actually used to tell the time. Zhao Yi (1727–1814), head of the prestigious Anding Academy in Yangzhou in the 1780s, was derisive of their efficacy in this respect. His experience of clock owners while he was serving the Grand Council in Beijing was that "those who own these things forget meetings."[65] This negative assessment paradoxically points to a direct relationship between the mechanical clock and times of meetings. Correspondingly, Lin Sumen records that chime clocks were used in Yangzhou by "people in a hurry," i.e. not just by people who wanted to keep up with the Chengs.[66]

If how to tell the time was changing, that was quite in keeping with the changing of the times. Around the turn of the nineteenth century, the relation-

---

60 Ibid., 7.5b-6a.

61 Catherine Jami, "Western Devices for Measuring Time and Space: Clocks and Euclidian Geometry in Late Ming and Ch'ing China," in Chunchieh Huang and Eric Zürcher, eds, *Time and Space in Chinese Culture*, (Leiden: E. J. Brill, 1995), 191-2. See further, Benjamin A. Elman, *On Their Own Terms: Science in China, 1550-1900* (Cambridge, Mass.: Harvard University Press, 2005), 206-8.

62 Ibid., 192-3.

63 Guo Fuxiang, "Guanyu Qingdai de Suzhong" (On the Suzhou clocks of the Qing dynasty), *Palace Museum Journal* 1 (2004): 65-76.

64 Carlo Maria Cipolla, *Clocks and Culture, 1300-1700* (London: Collins, 1967), 87-8; David Landes, *Revolution in Time: Clocks and the Making of the Modern World* (Cambridge, Mass.: Harvard University Press, 1983), 43-5.

65 Catherine Pagani, "Europe in Asia: The Impact of Western Art and Technology in China," in Anna Jackson and Amin Jaffer, eds, *Encounters: The Meeting of Asia and Europe, 1500-1800* (London: V & A Publications, 2004), 309.

66 Lin Sumen, *Hanjiang sanbai yin*, 7.5b-6a.

ship between world trade and material culture in Yangzhou was firming. To judge by Lin Sumen's catalogue of goods, consumers in early nineteenth-century Yangzhou could buy a range of products that in their youth were hardly known. Wind screens had become popular in Yangzhou "in the last ten or so years." A type of large table napkin (*wodan*), in former days used only by "very refined dinner guests", had recently become commonplace. Gauze lanterns such as those used in yamens were "in recent days" also used for lighting in the Yangzhou markets. Rain protectors were increasingly employed for the comfort of passengers in open sedan chairs.[67] The use of tobacco by both men and women had become prevalent, and jade receptacles were widely used as tobacco containers.[68] Household pets became more and more exotic: they included Cantonese chickens and "Western" rats, the latter housed in finely wrought cages.[69]

In the context of this flourishing city of goods, Lin Sumen's commentary on dress in Yangzhou assumes significance as a reflection on consumer choice and product innovation. He presents his inventory in a chapter called "new and curious clothing," which is less suggestive of fashion than the term "*shiyang*" (contemporary styles) mentioned above, but nonetheless evokes the shock of the new as well as echoing late Ming discourse on "outrageous dress." A number of examples concern highly informal dress. These include the "Arhat wrapper" (*Luohan ta*), a short-sleeved jacket of Chinese linen or grasscloth worn by fat men on hot days; the yellow grasscloth jacket (*huang caobu gua*), likewise good for summer wear because it absorbed sweat; and the cicada jacket (*mengzuo gua*), a short-sleeved garment worn by women at their toilet.[70] Others relate to the social pretensions of servants. The "happy bird gown" (*xiquepao*) was made in imitation of the long gown with vest, but was economically constructed from cloth remnants as a one piece garment, the gown with sleeves and skirts being of one colour, the trunk of another. This was much affected by bondservants, a class theoretically enfranchised early in the eighteenth century but apparently continuing in the form of household retainers at least into the early nineteenth century. "Frivolous servants" otherwise set great store by trousers of double-threaded black silk (*hei jiansi ku*).[71]

These several items provide some insights into domestic clothing. Although servants might be seen abroad in their trousers of double-threaded black silk, it is doubtful that even the fattest of their masters would be seen out of doors in an Arhat wrapper. From the perspective of "fashion" such garments perhaps hardly count apart from some indication of social emulation in happy bird gowns. Other

---

67 Ibid., 3.9b, 3.11a, 5.14a, 3.12a, 3.14a.

68 Ibid., 9.6b-7a.

69 Ibid., 7.3b, 7.4b, 5b-6a; 6.7a, 8.7a-8a.

70 Ibid., 6.1a-b.

71 Ibid., 6.1a.

Fig. 3.7 Well-dressed women with servant, all in Han clothing, in the late nineteenth century. The sleeves of the silk jackets are moderately wide; more exaggerated versions are evident in other photographs. Decorative borders were very popular in the late Qing. The points of bound-foot shoes are just visible beneath the hems of the richly embroidered skirts. Despite the concealing front panel, it is clear that the woman on the left is wearing a pleated skirt.

items, however, show developments in street wear plausibly worn by fashion-setters: "watermelon" hats (*xiguading*) sported by men, and "lotus leaf collars," that were basted to the shoulders of the outer garment and easy to remove.

Three further items are suggestive of distinctively fashionable developments. The first two are specific to women's dress. One is the "five-terrace sleeves" (*wutaixiu*) of women's jackets, described by Lin Sumen as recently reaching a width of around one foot and six inches (Chinese measure), as compared to the one foot of earlier times.[72] The sleeves were embroidered in five layers, hence the name, and the thick embroidery rendered them stiff as armour, so that rather than falling, the arms were held akimbo, like someone pushing a cart. This latter description resonates with images from photographs in the late Qing, in which women's arms do seem to be held akimbo. The breadth or narrowness of sleeves, like the width of skirts in Europe, was a mark of fashion in nineteenth-century China.[73]

Another example of fashion in early nineteenth-century Yangzhou was the "hundred pleats skirt" (*baizhequn*) (Fig. 3.7). Preserved examples of Qing dynasty skirts show variation between the straight and pleated. The latter were clearly more expensive, requiring more material and more work. In Beijing in the 1860s, the "fashionable skirt" (*shiyang qun*) was the so-called "fish-scale hundred pleats skirt," each pleat featuring an overlay of silk ribboning in a wave pattern, so that the overlapping pleats gave an impression of fish scales.[74] Pleated skirts had a hoary ancestry in China, so it must be supposed either that these were newly popular in Yangzhou in particular or that their "newness and curiousness" lay in

---

72 Ibid., 6.4b.

73 *Xianshi gongsi 25 zhounian jinian ce* (Sincere Company 25th anniversary commemorative volume) (Shanghai Municipal Archives, Q227-84, 1925), 302.

74 Zhou Xun and Gao Chunming, *Zhongguo yiguan fushi da cidian*, 284.

Fig. 3.8 Suburbs of a Chinese City, probably based in part on Yangzhou, as depicted by William Alexander, 1793.

the material of which they were made. According to Lin Sumen, "pleated skirts made of crepe have the advantage of falling very softly; this is a new style."[75]

The third item brings us finally to the international context of Yangzhou dress in the early nineteenth century. The denomination is "butterfly shoes" (*hudielü*), and the description provided by Lin Sumen is of shoes with a large butterfly sculpted on toe and heel from velvet or satin, with small butterflies featured on either side. These shoes were lined with English wool, camlets, down, or Ningbo silk.[76] Here can be found the beginnings of an answer to what happened to the imports of English cloth in China before the opening of the Treaty Ports and the rampant growth of Sino-Western trade in the second half of the nineteenth century. Since Ningbo silk was an alternative to English cloth as lining for these shoes, we can safely say that British imports were easily naturalised within an established Chinese context of commerce and manufacture, and also that Yangzhou fashions in the early nineteenth century had a context in world trade.

Lin's inventory draws attention to how little has yet been written about clothing in Qing China. Costume histories ranging from Shen Congwen's monumental survey to more interpretative studies focus in the main on standard clothing items and their more obvious features, such as dragon robes, riding jackets, horse-shoe cuffs, and embroidered shoes for bound feet. The variety of fabrics, the range of garments, and stylistic shifts involving other than the "glacial" changes mentioned by Quentin Bell, all demand attention. Macartney embassy member George Staunton, who actually saw Chinese clothing first hand, commented like Bell that the changes in fashion were many less than in Europe at

75 Lin Sumen, *Hanjiang sanbai yin*, 6.5a.

76 Ibid., 6.2a.

the same time.[77] This may have been so, but Staunton was looking on China from much the same perspective as Hegel would adopt, one that blocked the view of such changes as were underway. The Macartney embassy passed by Yangzhou on the return from Beijing in 1793. They glimpsed its walls, "ancient and covered with moss," but they could not see within (Fig. 3.8).[78]

Judging by watches and clocks in Yangzhou in 1808, either things had changed very rapidly indeed in China since 1793, or what the emperor said in his letter to George III failed to reflect consumer "needs" within Chinese society. Perhaps there is an element of truth in each of these statements, and the turn of the century was, as Joanna Waley-Cohen remarks, also the turn of an era.[79] If so, nothing could better symbolise the new era than that the man in a hurry should

Fig. 3.9 A merchant in his fur coat, photographed by John Thomson ca 1870. A jacket in the National Gallery of Victoria, similar to the one portrayed here, is made of red fox fur, but furs were sourced from a variety of local and exotic animals. They were used for trimming and lining and for the manufacture of hats as well as for coats, long and short. This was one item that American traders had no trouble in selling to Chinese purchasers.

be measuring out his time with chime clocks. Wearing his watermelon skin cap, and a belt adorned with jade hooks for carrying his watch and tobacco pouch, with a grasscloth jacket to change into if the day turned warm, and a rain protector to place over his sedan chair in case of wet weather; his wife in a pleated crepe skirt with five-terrace sleeve jacket—the man about town in early nineteenth-century Yangzhou presents a figure rather specific to his own time.

Fashions in the 1840s

Lin Sumen's poems can usefully be read in conjunction with a work on Yangzhou penned half a century later. Zhou Sheng's *Dream of Yangzhou* is a memoir of the

---

77 Pomeranz, *The Great Divergence*, 152.

78 Barrow, *Travels in China*, 516.

79 Joanna Waley-Cohen, *The Sextants of Beijing: Global Currents in Chinese History* (New York: Norton, 1999), 132.

city, and particularly of its courtesan quarters. The author was a native of nearby Zhenjiang, across the Yangzi from Yangzhou. He arrived in the city in 1842, apparently for an extended visit. The memoir contains a number of diverting comments on fads, fashions, and trends in Yangzhou life, including servants dressing up like their masters, respectable women dressing their hair like prostitutes, the cheapness of watches and the different sorts of fur (including Japanese leopard fur) available for winter coats (Fig. 3.9). Most pertinently to the topic of fashion, he comments on the fickleness of women's taste in clothes: a garment made one year, he complained, would be abandoned in the wardrobe the next.[80] Like Lin Sumen, Zhou Sheng documents changes in clothing practices. Silk gauze had become popular for summer wear, apparently replacing the grasscloth noted by Lin and used even for trousers. Variegated silk, made from wefting multi-coloured silk threads against a warp of blue, was being used for women's garments, although not yet for men's.[81] He also comments on foreign imports, including watches, down, and woollen cloth for winter garments.[82]

Zhou conveys better than Lin Sumen a sense of a clothing culture that featured consumer choice. For a self-proclaimed simple man, he had a great deal to say about what he himself liked to wear: Hangzhou silk gauze, Su-Hu crepe, Hangzhou silk, and wool. He liked Grand Council jackets, which were casual and comfortable, and easy to wear under an outer garment;[83] he liked jade or blue coloured lining for his garments, and a particular style of footwear called "spread-soled Chancellor shoes" (*putian tianguan lü*). He was sensitive to public opinion, and especially ridicule, writing that on one occasion, "when the weather suddenly cleared, I was walking along the street still in my stilt shoes [used in wet weather]. Some people scoffed at me saying, 'What heavy rain!' Only wet-and-dry shoes have oiled soles without stilts, suitable for both sunny and rainy days. Most people wear these on overcast days."[84]

A community of taste, a diversified and volatile clothing culture, and a broader context of commodity innovation and circulation are all suggested in Zhou's memoir. He was choosy about his own dress, and particularly fond of wool for winter wear. What is the significance of the fact that Chinese consumers could dress in wool? A suggestion of how the wearing of wool was experienced is to be found in his analysis of fabrics. "Undergarments," he wrote, "should be soft, as they cling to the body; outer garments should be hard, as they define the shape of

---

80 Jiaodong Zhou Sheng, *Yangzhou meng* (Dream of Yangzhou) (Taipei: Shijie shuju, 1978), 44-6.

81 Ibid., 45.

82 Ibid., 45.

83 *Junjigua* or *junjipo* were short-sleeved jackets which had their origin as writing jackets, with only the right sleeve cut short for ease in brushwork.

84 Jiaodong Zhou Sheng, *Yangzhou meng*, 45.

the body." Among hard fabrics he identified court satin, but he himself favoured "the hard feel of woollen cloth."[85]

Herein lies an intimation that foreign cloth was facilitating the construction of the self, and that it informed Zhou Sheng's understanding and presentation of himself. Certainly his observations of clothing in Yangzhou were intimately related to his own sartorial experience in a way that starkly differentiated them from Lin Sumen's, not to mention Li Dou's. This might be attributed to the different literary genre within which he was writing, but comparing his first-person narrative with contemporary novels suggests that his observations about clothing in Yangzhou were framed by a new sort of consciousness about dress, the body, and identity: one crystallising in precisely the years he was in Yangzhou.

Fashion, fiction and modernity

The 1840s were years of profound significance in Chinese history. The Opium War of 1840–1842 had far-reaching implications for Chinese society and in China is regarded as marking the beginning of "modern history". From the end of this decade a new and definably modern fiction began to emerge in China, and along with the new fiction came new fashions.[86] These were represented both graphically—most famously by the illustrator Wu Youru (1867–1910)—and textually. Popular novels such as the homoerotic *A Precious Mirror for Ranking Flowers* and the courtesan tale *Shanghai Flowers* displayed a preoccupation with identity that was expressed in part by references to a changing material culture, including what people wore.[87]

An early example of this new fiction was a Yangzhou novel called *Dreams of Wind and Moon*, which bears a preface dated 1848 and was presumably composed recently to that year.[88] Judging by the story, the pseudonymous author was a minor literatus familiar with the city's brothels, not unlike Zhou Sheng. The story centres on the relationships of a number of courtesans with a corresponding number of male characters and is remarkable for the attention paid to the physical layout of the city.[89] Its attention to dress is equally pronounced, which is less remarkable. As Paola Zamperini has noted, "scholars of Chinese fiction are familiar with the long, seemingly endless descriptions of clothes of almost every

---

85 Ibid.

86 David Der-wei Wang, *Fin-de-Siècle Splendor: Repressed Modernities of Late Qing Fiction, 1849–1911* (Stanford: Stanford University Press, 1997).

87 Paola Zamperini, "Clothes that Matter: Fashioning Modernity in Late Qing Novels," *Fashion Theory* 5, 2 (2001): 214.

88 Hanshang mengren, *Fengyue meng* (Dreams of wind and moon) [1848] (Beijing: Beijing daxue chubanshe, 1988). The phrase "wind and moon" is a metaphor for seduction.

89 Patrick Hanan, "*Fengyue Meng* and the Courtesan Novel," *Harvard Journal of Asiatic Studies* 58, 2 (December 1998): 345-72.

new character introduced to the readers."[90] The details of the clothes worn by the characters, however, deserve attention.

In the early chapters of this novel the reader is introduced to Yangzhou via the perambulations of its various characters as they move around the city streets, in and out of teahouses, visiting the brothels in the Nine Lanes of the Old City, shopping, listening to story recitals and opera, looking at Western paintings and peep-shows in the Parade Ground, taking a boat out to Lower Buy-and-Sell Street on the north moat and thence out to the lake, where they behold the ruined gardens built by salt merchants in the preceding century. They do all this dressed up in fashionable clothing (*xinshishi*, lit. "new time style") fabricated from Western cloth (*yangbu*), sporting watches, carrying tobacco pouches, the girls elaborately made up.[91] This is how Lu Shu dresses the morning after his arrival in Yangzhou, as he prepares to make some social calls:

He changed into a fashionable, high, bridge-shaped hat of broadcloth, vermilion in colour with best-quality tassels; clad himself in a lined robe of double-blue corded silk and a silken belt with dragon and tiger hooks of white jade from which were suspended a watch, a fan, an ornamental purse, a small knife and so on. Over this he wore a lined jacket of natural-coloured silk.[92]

Thus garbed, Lu Shu strolled through the streets to visit Yuan You, another of our heroes. But this outfit does not constitute the totality of what he needs for the day. Before or behind him trots his retainer, who is carrying Master Lu's visiting cards, his water-tobacco pouch, a small hat, and a clothes bag. The purpose of this extra baggage shortly becomes clear: "At Yuan You's request, Lu Shu changed his hat for the smaller one. He also took off his jacket, handing it to Small Happiness, and put on a lined riding jacket in its place."[93]

The act of changing clothes is in this way delicately dove-tailed into movements from home to street, inside to outside, and back again. The detail of the clothes is consistent with that of the physical surrounds, so that the portraits of the individual characters resonate with the urban environment. This environment increasingly bore signs of the world economy to which the city was now linked via the Yangzi River and Shanghai. Lu Shu does not only carry a watch; his hat is made of broadcloth, an English import. English cloth is everywhere apparent. When Wei Bi sets off to hire a boat, he does so with a portmanteau of multi-colored English printed cloth lined with jade-coloured silk, and his serviette is also of English printed cloth. What's more, he has to pay the boatman in Western coin (*yangqian*, presumably Spanish silver dollars).[94] The repeated

---

90 Zamperini, "Clothes that Matter," 196.

91 Hanshang mengren, *Fengyue meng*, 10, 14, 28, 30, 37, 54.

92 Ibid., 14.

93 Ibid., 15.

94 Ibid., 21-2. On the circulation of Spanish dollars, see Yen-p'ing Hao, *The Commercial*

references to foreign cloth suggest that the author was carefully constructing a cast of characters who were to be read as products of changing times.

In Chinese literary history, *Dreams of Wind and Moon* has quietly established a premier position at the vanguard of the new fiction of the late Qing. Patrick Hanan regards it as China's first identifiable "city novel."[95] Alexander Des Forges proffers it as the earliest example of the reality novel, a genre characterised by the claims of the fictionalised author to be telling a tale of things he himself observed rather than relying on past texts to legitimate his narrative.[96] On these grounds, it seems reasonable to think about the fashionable society of early nineteenth-century (i.e. pre-1850s) Yangzhou in terms of its location in the modern world, and its engagement with modern times and particularly modern sensibilities.

Two years after *Dreams of Wind and Moon* was penned, the Taiping Rebellion erupted. Occupied three times by the rebels, Yangzhou suffered massive destruction from which it never really recovered. Fittingly, the novel was subsequently rewritten as a Shanghai novel, its streets and alleyways recast as Shanghai places that were in actuality being frequented by the merchants, artists, scholars and fashionably-dressed courtesans who a century earlier might have been treading the streets of Yangzhou.[97] The original version survives as evidence of an urban culture that in its own time was very "up to date," in striking contrast to the situation a century later.[98]

In Shanghai, fashion would come into its own: restless, overblown, excessive. The context for its efflorescence in early twentieth-century China more broadly was the intensifying consumption in modernising cities that were now nodes in international as well as regional trading networks. Yet this recognisable, modern fashion had roots in the fashions of earlier times. Urban markets in late imperial China were sensitive to cultural change, and these markets responded to new values in the vestimentary realm. This was evident not only in the limbo period of the late eighteenth to early nineteenth centuries, when China was increasingly engaged in world trade, but also in the sixteenth and seventeenth centuries, when silver from the New World was facilitating the monetisation of the economy. New fashions were fostered by economic and social change in both periods, and

---

Revolution in Nineteenth-Century China: the Rise of Sino-Western Mercantile Capitalism (Berkeley: University of California Press, 1986), 35-40.

95 Hanan, "*Fengyue Meng* and the Courtesan Novel," 349.

96 Alexander Des Forges, "From Source Texts to 'Reality Observed': The Creation of the Author in Nineteenth-Century Vernacular Fiction," *Chinese Literature: Essays, Articles, Reviews* 22 (2000): 67-84.

97 Hanan, "*Fengyue Meng* and the Courtesan Novel," 349.

98 On Yangzhou in the 1930s, see Antonia Finnane, "A Place in the Nation: Yangzhou and the Idle Talk Controversy of 1934," *Journal of Asian Studies* 53, 4 (November 1994): 1150-74.

were accompanied by an intensification of urban identity made evident in print culture. It is not surprising, then, that such a very lively fashion scene should emerge in Shanghai in the early twentieth century. Granted the particularities of the economic and social environment of the Treaty Port era, such a scene was not at all inconsistent with the past.

Fig. 4.1 Contemporary print of the negotiations at Shimonoseki. Li Hongzhang, identified by his trademark white beard and moustache as well as by the Chinese characters above, is depicted at the front of the Chinese team on the left. Itô Hirobumi is the seated figure in the Japanese team on the right. Note the dress swords, the ceremonial sashes, and the medallions.

4

SOLDIERS AND CITIZENS

In 1895, Chinese high official Li Hongzhang (1823–1901) met with Japanese Prime Minister Itô Hirobumi (1841–1909) to negotiate settlement of the Sino-Japanese war of 1894. The two men had comparable standing in their countries. The Japanese emperor was wont to complain about Itô's ambitions, saying that he thought he was to Japan as Li was to China or Bismarck to Germany.[1] In sartorial terms, however, the two men presented a contrast (Fig. 4.1). Japan had adopted Western clothing for official dress some years earlier. In China, that would not happen until the dynasty fell. Consequently, while Itô wore dress uniform to the meeting, Li wore his official robes. To Western eyes, Itô must have looked like a solider, and Li like a cleric.

1895 can be considered a year of some significance in the history of Chinese dress. The defeat profoundly affected the Chinese literati, the cap-and-gown wearing class on whose compliance the Manchus depended for their survival. After the Treaty of Shimonoseki, the old ways could no longer be maintained. Already in 1892 one official was proclaiming: "if we wish to alter the bureaucracy, establish a parliament and reform the examination system, we must begin by changing to western dress."[2] In Taiwan, which was ceded to Japan at Shimonoseki, the new rulers made it clear that queues were to go, along with opium and bound feet.[3] In Shanghai, reformers founded societies for the prevention of

---

1 Yoshitake Oka, *Five Political Leaders of Modern Japan: Itô Hirobumi, Ôkuma Shigenobu, Hara Takashi, Inukai Tsuyoshi, and Saionji Kimmochi*, trans. Andrew Fraser and Patricia Murray (Tokyo: University of Tokyo Press, 1986), 20.

2 Wang Ermin, "Duanfa, yifu, gaiyuan: bianfalun zhi xiangwei zhiqu" (Cutting hair, changing dress, altering the calendar: symbolic indicators of reform), in *Zhongguo jindaide weixin yundong—bianfa yu lixian taojihui* (Research Conference on the modern Chinese reform movement—reform and the establishment of the constitution) (Taipei: Institute of Modern History, Academia Sinica, 1981), 61.

3 Wu Wenxing, "Riju shiqi Taiwan de fangzu duanfa yundong" (The movement for un-binding feet and cutting hair in Taiwan during the Japanese occupation), in Li Youning and Zhang Yufa, eds, *Zhongguo funüshi lunwenji* (Collected essays on the history of Chinese women) (Taipei: Taiwan shangwu yinshuguan, 1988), 469.

footbinding and the education of girls: bound feet had become a symptom of national weakness.[4] And in Beijing, a radical clique of scholars began a campaign for influence at court that culminated in the failed reform movement of 1898 but led in the longer term to wide-reaching reforms, including reforms in dress.

The leader of the 1898 reformers, Kang Youwei (1858–1927), later articulated a relationship between dress and international relations. "At the present time," he wrote, "the myriad nations are all in communication and are as one moving towards veneration for oneness. It is just in our country that clothes are different, so that sentiments cannot be close and friendly relations between nations cannot be achieved."[5] Such a view was consistent with his ideal of universal civilisation, in which the many nations would be as one. But he saw also that "cutting hair and changing clothes" was necessary for national defence: "In Europe and America, men all cut their hair a hundred and more years ago. Over the last few decades they daily have new machines and refinements in the military arts. So if everyone [in China] cuts his hair, the whole nation will become soldiers."[6]

This last observation nicely encapsulates the link between militarism and dress that was to become evident in the transformation of the Chinese wardrobe in the last years of the Qing dynasty. No sharp rupture in civilian wear occurred, but rather a steady undermining of established vestimentary codes as the once despised figure of the soldier gained in social prestige and political importance. In the opening years of the twentieth century, the ground was laid for an association between military culture and Chinese dress that was to be periodically reaffirmed over the following decades.

New uniforms for a new army

The time of intensifying contact between China and foreign powers—including Japan—was marked by the militarisation of European societies and the rise of nationalism, evident, as Marc Ferro has written, in "the advance of education, the press, sport and mysticism [that] led to a re-creation, in national terms, of duty, of

---

4 Chia-lin Pao Tao, "The Anti-Footbinding Movement in Late Ch'ing China: Indigenous Development and Western Influence," *Jindai Zhongguo funüshi yanjiu* 2 (June 1994): 150-1; 155-7.

5 Wang Ermin, "Duanfa, yifu, gaiyuan: bianfalun zhi xiangwei zhiqu," 62. According to Luke Kwong, Kang Youwei did not actually memorialise the Guangxu emperor on clothes reforms although he liked to claim he did. Luke S.K. Kwong, *A Mosaic of a Hundred Days: Personalities, Politics and Ideas of 1898* (Cambridge: Mass.: Council on East Asian Studies, 1984), 201, 318. Cf. Edward J.M. Rhoads, *Manchus and Han: Ethnic Relations and Political Power in Late Qing and Early Republican China, 1861-1928* (Seattle: University of Washington Press, 2000), 65.

6 Li Zhigang (Lai Chi-kung), "Xianxiang yu yingzao guozu: jindai Zhongguo de faxing wenti" (Imagining and constructing nationhood: hairstyles in Modern China), *Si yu yan* 36, 1 (1998): 110.

obedience, to constituted authority."[7] Patriotic histories—and what other sort were there?—portrayed the patria as under siege and filled the centuries with national heroes who had fought off invaders or died in the attempt. The half-century preceding the First World War was a period when the English, French and Germans were falling in love with war, and so were the Japanese. China followed suit.

Chinese culture is often thought of as favouring literary over martial skills; hence the saying: "good iron is not beaten into nails; good men are not made into soldiers." The Manchus helped foster this self-perception on the part of the Chinese, laying claim to a martial (*wu*) identity in a society that gave primacy to literary (*wen*) ideals.[8] Paradoxically, the Manchus' own military weakness relative to the foreign powers in the nineteenth century excited a militarist response in Chinese society.[9] Liang Qichao (1873–1929), Kang's most famous disciple, saw the proper appreciation of martial qualities as part and parcel of the "renewal of the people," and Liang's own disciple, Cai E (1882-1916), having graduated from the Japanese military academy Shikan Gakkō in 1904, held that "to train a good solider is actually to train a good citizen."[10] In the end, the Qing court was forced to take a comparable view, and almost despite itself set in train a sequence of events that would fill the country with soldiers.

The armed forces were the vanguard of vestimentary change in China. After the crushing defeat by Japan in 1894, the court embarked on a stuttering project of reform of the military forces, only to suffer an even more humiliating defeat in 1900, when the anti-foreign Boxer Rebellion led to the occupation of Beijing by an alliance of foreign powers.[11] In 1901, the first of a series of sweeping institutional

---

7 Marc Ferro, *The Great War, 1914-1918*, trans. Nicole Stone (London: Routledge and Kegan Paul, 1973), 13.

8 Mark Elliot, *The Manchu Way: The Eight Banners and Ethnic Identity in Late Imperial China* (Stanford: Stanford University Press, 2001). On the *wu–wen* dichotomy in Chinese culture, see Kam Louie, *Theorising Chinese Masculinity: Society and Gender in China* (New York: Cambridge University Press, 2002), 1-21.

9 On the militarisation of Chinese society in the late Qing see Philip Kuhn, *Rebellion and its Enemies in Late Imperial China: Militarisation and Social Structure, 1796-1864* (Cambridge, Mass.: Harvard University Press, 1970), and for a critique, Edward McCord, "Militia and Local Militarisation in Late Qing and Early Republican China: The Case of Hunan," *Modern China* 14, 2 (1 April 1988): 184. In what respects militarisation was "causal" in this period is not at issue in the present chapter, which is concerned mainly with demonstrating the development of a militarist ethos.

10 Hans van de Ven, "The Military in the Republic," *The China Quarterly* 157 (June 1997): 357. See also, Douglas R. Reynolds, *China 1898-1912: The Xinzheng Revolution and Japan* (Council on East Asian Studies, Harvard University, 1993), 153.

11 On military modernisation in Canton, see Edward J.M. Rhoads, *China's Republican Revolution: The Case of Kwangtung, 1895-1913* (Cambridge, Mass.: Harvard University Press, 1975), 56-8.

Fig. 4.2 Chinese regular soldiers of the Green Standard, ca 1900, carrying muskets, and wearing the regulation *haoyi* (jacket with insignia). The round badge, which adorned both front and back of the jacket, bore the number of the soldier's regiment and the name of his commander. Neither soldier has shaved the front of his head for a few days, which is a sign either of great lack of discipline or of mourning.

Fig. 4.3 In 1911, even soldiers fighting for the Republic still had their queues, which they sometimes wore tucked up inside their caps. Note the different sorts of hats worn by spectators in the background.

reforms was announced as the court began a last-ditch attempt to restore its empire, and in 1902, with the aid of German and Japanese advisors and instructors, a "New Army" was created. Its infantry was drilled according to German practice and dressed in German-style uniforms, which were already in use in Japan.[12] The loose trousers of infantrymen were replaced by narrow-legged pants, tailored in the Western style. The loose jacket was supplanted by a body-fitting coat. The cone-shaped hats with the red tassels worn by military officials gave way to peaked caps, and cloth boots gave way to leather.[13] In brief, the soldier in China began to look less picturesquely Oriental and more like his counterpart elsewhere in the world (Figs 4.2, 4.3).

Japan's influence on China was pervasive in this period, and intensified after 1905, the year in which Japan defeated Russia in a short war conducted over control of Manchuria and the Korean peninsula, while revolution erupted in Russia itself. In China, Japan's victory illustrated the potential of an Asian power to gain ascendancy over a European one, and the revolution demonstrated the possibility of popular revolt against imperial rule. Both served to heighten the prestige of the martial ideal in China. In 1906, "everyone," according to the military attaché at the French embassy in China, wanted to don military uniform and undertake military drill.[14]

Also, in 1905, the old examination system that had served as the pathway to bureaucratic office was abandoned. The resulting vacuum in the education system was partially filled by new military schools, so popular that they were forced to turn away thousands of disappointed applicants. In Japan, Chinese students enrolled in military academies in growing numbers. New education regulations promulgated by the Qing dynasty in 1909 explicitly promoted an ideal of military citizenship—*junguomin zhuyi*.[15] In this year, Canton's Christian College in China (later Lingnan University) introduced summer uniforms modelled on those worn at the USA's West Point Military Academy. A year later the college started up a Boy Scouts troupe, and all pupils in the primary and lower middle

---

12 On Japanese military instructors and their eventual displacement of German advisers, see Reynolds, *China 1898-1912*, 151-60.

13 Zhongguo dier lishi dang'anguan (Second Historical Archives of China), ed., *Minguo junfu tuzhi* (Illustrated account of military uniform in the Republican era) (Shanghai: Shanghai shudian chubanshe, 2003), 4-16. It is pointed out in this volume (4-5), that reforms of uniform commenced in the 1890s, but were not standardised or universal. An exception was the navy, into which white sailor suits were introduced in 1898.

14 Ralph L. Powell, *The Rise of Chinese Military Power, 1895-1912* (Princeton University Press, 1955), 192.

15 Sally Borthwick, *Education and Social Change in China: The Beginnings of the Modern Era* (Stanford: Hoover Institution Press, 1983), 82.

Fig. 4.4 Left: This studio photo of Lin Xiantang with some companions in Fuzhou, ca 1904, illustrates perfectly the brilliance of the clothing worn by well-born young men in the late Qing, and the comparative sobriety even of formal Western dress. Brought up in Japanese-occupied Taiwan, Lin Xiantang distinguished himself sartorially from his Chinese friends. In Taiwan, where Chinese-style clothing was still the norm, his suit would have marked him as one of the elite.

Fig. 4.5 Below: Well-to-do young men in the early Republic, looking much more soberly dressed than their counterparts of earlier times.

school had to acquire the modified military uniforms worn by Boy Scouts around the world.[16]

In this environment, a man could feel some satisfaction in appearing in military dress. Li Zongren (1890–1969) entered the Military Elementary School in Guangxi in 1908 and later recalled his uniform with some pride:

One of our uniforms was made of very fine quality wool and the others of ordinary wool. Each of us was also provided with a woolen overcoat ... Although dressed in modern uniforms and leather shoes, most of us still wore our long queues, an incongruity that was considered handsome in those days.[17]

Circumstances had changed since the scholar reigned supreme. "The status of the soldier has been transformed," wrote George Morrison. "The relative ranks of civil and military have been reversed ... Good families now send their sons as officers."[18]

The militarisation of civilian dress

Under the Qing, the changes in military and school uniforms were the most visible, the best documented, and also the only changes to be sanctioned by the imperial government. But modifications in civilian wear took place alongside these changes. Sun Fuyuan (1894–1966), born in the year of the war with Japan, remembered clearly the dress of his boyhood years:

The young man of that time was done up in many-coloured splendour: a robe of almond yellow Huzhou crepe, a jacket of sky-blue Nanjing silk; a sash of snow-coloured Hangzhou silk; shoes with whited soles, embossed with flowers and clouds green as sunflowers or red as dates; what with trousers, ankle straps, paper fan, spectacles cord, little melon-skin hat topped with a precious stone—looked at with modern eyes, one wonders what he was on about! Of course I mention these colours and materials haphazardly, but I think they were common, not exceptional. And if a young man dressed like this, even more so was it the case for a young woman.[19]

Such a description accords with the details of garments in the price-list supplied by Fu Chongju (1875–1917) for men's clothing in Chengdu around the time of the 1911 Revolution. A multi-coloured fully embroidered garment cost

---

16 Huang Juyan, ed., *Jindai Guangdong jiaoyu yu Lingnan daxue* (Modern education in Guangdong and Lingnan University) (Hong Kong: Commercial Press, 1995), 163, 172.

17 Tong Te-kong and Li Tsung-jen, *The Memoirs of Li Tsung-ren* (Boulder: Westview Press, 1979), 21.

18 *The Times* 21 October 1911: 6. See also Donald Sutton, *Provincial Militarism and the Chinese Republic: The Yunnan Army, 1905-1925* (Ann Arbor: University of Michigan Press, 1980), 14-20.

19 Sun Fuyuan, "Xinhai geming shidai de qingnian fushi" (Young people's dress in the period of the 1911 Revolution) in *Sun Fuyuan sanwen xuanji* (Collected essays of Sun Fuyuan) (Tianjin: Baihua wenyi chubanshe, 1991), 184-5.

eight or nine taels of silver; a robe of best qual-
ity Hangzhou flowered
silk lined with sheepskin,
twenty six dollars; of best
quality Hangzhou flow-
ered silk, eleven dollars
fifty; and for a patterned
or plain cotton-padded
gown of Huzhou crepe,
eight dollars forty.[20] But to
Sun's memory, this style of
dress began to change from
around from 1900: "the
clothing worn by the young
bit by bit changed from
red and green to black and
white. Starting with the top
of the head, the use of oil

Fig. 4.6 In 1906, a teacher in an old-style classroom is confronted by a student in a new-style uniform.

gradually became less frequent ..." Hairdress became simpler: tassles disappeared from the end of pigtails, until finally the pigtails themselves began to disappear. Dress became more sober (compare Figs 4.4, 4.5). The white-soled embroidered cloth shoes gave way to brown leather shoes, where they could be afforded.[21]

"We may like to think that the military and the civilian are distinct worlds," observes Nicholas Sullivan, "... But in men's fashion the military is there all the time."[22] In Sun Fuyuan's youth, the reformed education system of the late Qing provided a bridge between these "distinct worlds" so that young scholars inevitably began to look more and more like young soldiers. The education re-forms were essentially those that had been suggested by the reformers of 1898 and quashed at the time of the palace coup. In 1901 the chastened court or-dered the establishment throughout the country of Japanese-style schools that would teach a new curriculum, combining modern and classical studies. Primary school boys were to be trained in calisthenics and middle school boys in military calisthenics; every school was to have a military drill ground.[23] Naturally, this physical education would not be undertaken by boys in gowns (see Fig. 4.6).

---

20 Fu Chongju, *Chengdu tonglan* (Looking around Chengdu) (Chengdu: Bashu shushe, 1987), Vol.II, 70.

21 Sun Fuyuan, "Xinhai geming shidai de qingnian fushi," 185.

22 Paul Fussell, *Uniforms: Why We Are What We Wear* (Boston: Houghton Mifflin, 2002), 197.

23 William Ayers, *Chang Chih-tung and Educational Reform in China* (Cambridge, Mass.: Harvard University Presss, 1971), 205-9.

Fig. 4.7 Advertisement for Yi Jing, makers of uniforms for soldiers and students in Guangzhou. The prospective buyer is urged to make his way to Datong Street, outside Taiping Gate. The uniforms depicted are for the troops of the regular army, right to left: top rank, first division dress uniform; top rank second division dress uniform; third rank, third division, regular uniform. The text on the lower left draws the reader's attention particularly to the fact that the company manufactures straw hats, "most suitable for students and army personnel in the summer season."

In place of the long robe, male students began to don trousers and jacket, a form of dress that generically had been associated mostly with the peasantry or the uneducated rank-and-file of the old-style armies.[24] Straw boaters or military peaked caps replaced the traditional round cap. School uniforms were often modelled directly on military uniforms, as was the case in Japan, and commercial suppliers of military uniform touted for custom among students (Fig. 4.7).

Campaigning against the queue

A symbiosis between army and schools was apparent again in the trend away from the queue after 1900. To cut or to keep the queue was foremost among the controversies over dress (broadly defined) in the late Qing, quite overshadowing the issue of footbinding in political significance. In the middle of the seventeenth century, the refusal by Han men in some Chinese cities to wear the queue had resulted in the slaughter of tens of thousands of townspeople. These massacres were recalled by revolutionaries in the late Qing, adding grist to the mill of anti-Manchu feeling.[25] The queue came to be regarded as symbol of national humiliation, a view put with unintended comical effect by Javanese-born Oei Hui-lan when she attempted to explain its origins:

The custom of the queue dates back to the invasion of China by the Manchus. They made the Chinese shave their heads, except for a section at the top they had them braid; then

---

24 See Susan Brownell, *Training the Body for China: Sports in the Moral Order of the People's Republic* (Chicago: University of Chicago Press, 1995), 38.

25 Peter Zarrow, "Historical Trauma: Anti-Manchuism and Memories of Atrocity in Late Qing China," *History & Memory* 16, 2 (2004): 67-107.

Fig. 4.8 Undated photograph of Sun Yatsen in exile, before the 1911 Revolution.

they used the braids as reins when they rode over the Great Wall on the backs of the humiliated Chinese. Curiously, the queue eventually became recognised and so much the fashion that the Manchus themselves, forgetting it was originally an emblem of servility, adopted it ...[26]

As peculiar a distortion of history as this was, it eloquently expressed latter-day understandings of the queue. Hui-lan's father, the sugar mogul Oei Tiong-ham, hated the queue and "concealed it when he went out, winding it around his head under a straw hat." He cut it off around 1907, after the death of his own father.[27]

Chinese overseas led the way in queue cutting. For nineteenth-century emigrants, it was not necessarily a sign of disaffection with the dynasty, merely one of acculturation. In the last decade of the Qing dynasty, however, political haircuts made their appearance. Sun Yatsen cut off his queue in 1895, "a step of great importance," he later recalled. He was in hiding from the Qing authorities in Japan at the time, and had a haircut by way of a disguise (Fig. 4.8).[28] A long line of queue cutters followed. Chung Wing-kwong (1866–1942), from the same county as Sun, was a provincial graduate of 1894, the year of China's defeat in the Sino-Japanese War. He joined Sun's Revive China Society in 1896, converted to Christianity in 1899 (like Sun before him), cut his hair, and adopted Western clothing.[29] The fiery Zhang Binglin (1868–1936) cut off his queue in 1900, declaring it a thing of shame, laughed at by the Japanese and regarded with contempt by Europeans. Like Chung he adopted Western clothing.[30]

---

26 Madame Wellington Koo (Oei Hui-lan) with Isabella Taves, *No Feast Lasts Forever* (New York: Quadrangle, 1975), 27-8.

27 Ibid., 27.

28 Lyon Sharman, *Sun Yat-sen, His Life and Its Meaning: A Critical Biography* (Stanford: Stanford University Press, 1934), 40.

29 Huang Juyan, ed., *Jindai Guangdong jiaoyu yu Lingnan daxue*, 28, 49, Fig. 51; 171, Fig. 264.

30 Lung-kee Sun, "The Politics of Hair and the Issue of the Bob in Modern China," *Fashion Theory* 1, 4 (1997): 354.

Such acts, for all their symbolic power, were undertaken for the most part by figures then on the periphery of Chinese society: revolutionaries, Christians, exiles and expatriates. The army and the schools, by contrast, were mass institutions embedded in Chinese society, institutions that the late Qing court was bound to foster as its chosen sites of reform and progress. For this reason, the hairstyles of soldiers and schoolboys possessed great social significance. Although the court defended the queue almost to the bitter end, it contributed to the scale of the controversy centred on it by regulating modifications of its length among soldiers and policemen. This caused angst in some quarters (notably among policemen in Beijing) while in others it served only to encourage calls for getting rid of the queue altogether.[31]

If Beijing policemen were fond of their queues, schoolboys found them irksome. Despite what Li Zongren had to say about the queue and modern military uniform, slouch caps or boaters worn as part of school uniform showed up the quaintness of the queue and was felt by school pupils to be an incongruous appendage.[32] Practical management of the queue was also burdensome. Chen Jinbiao (b. 1898), from the conservative town of Xinzhu in Taiwan, was accepted into the Kokugo Gakkō around 1923. At that time, one in ten of his fellow-students still had a queue, which they had been able to maintain because their mothers or elder sisters had helped them do their hair. Away at school, they cut them off.[33] Although Chinese students in Japan were the forerunners of the student revolution in hairstyles,[34] in China itself, the military schools that were training new-style soldiers became hotbeds of dissent over hair-cuts. In 1906–7 a wave of queue-cutting occurred in schools, most notably in the military schools of Hangzhou.[35]

In the limbo period between the 1911 Revolution and the abdication of the last emperor in early 1912, the Qing government finally permitted its subjects-cum-citizens freedom as to how they should cut their hair.[36] No such freedom was allowed by the new regime, which handed down an interdict against the queue before government had even been stabilised. The army and police were recruited to the task of cutting off queues, and violent struggles ensued between queue-cutters and queue-keepers (Fig. 4.9). The Trotskyist Chen Bilan

---

31 Rhoads, *Manchus and Han*, 113. Michael Godley, "The End of the Queue: Hair as Symbol in Chinese History," *East Asian History* 8 (December 1994): 65-6.

32 Rhoads, *Manchus and Han*, 113.

33 Pan Guozheng, *Zhuqian sixiangqi: lao zhaopian shuo gushi* (Thinking about Zhuqian: tales from old photos) (Xinzhu: Zhushi wenhua chubanshe, 1995), Vol. 2, 42-3.

34 Wang Xing, *Bainian fushi chaoliu yu shibian* (One hundred years of fashion trends and global change) (Hong Kong: Shangwu yinshuguan, 1992), 29-30.

35 Rhoads, *Manchus and Han*, 113-14; Godley, "The End of the Queue," 67.

36 Ibid., 209.

(1902–1987) amusingly recalls her en-
counter with this campaign. Chen was
raised in a district—Taohua village in
Hubei—where only the daughters of
the big landlord and overseas students
were raised with natural feet. Her father belonged to the latter category and
from Japan wrote stern letters home,
forbidding the women of the family
to bind his daughter's feet. One day,
sometime after the 1911 Revolution,
she was out in the fields with her aunt,
playing bare-footed, when a regiment
passed by. Seeing this large-footed
child with a long plait, some soldiers
in the regiment assumed she was a boy
and were about to cut off the "queue"
when her aunt came to the rescue and
assured them she was indeed a girl-
child, despite her large feet. Hilarity
ensued on all sides.[37]

Fig. 4.9 This man, suffering the ignominy
of having his hair removed by force, had
already stopped shaving the front of his
head. He was probably retaining his queue
till a haircut was quite safe.

The queue long outlived the campaign against it, surviving for a quarter
of a century or more in conservative pockets of urban society or remote rural
areas. For many men, despite its origins, the queue had come to be identified
with Chinese culture, the more so because of reactive sentiments associated with
response to the Western powers. Its passing left a vacuum that was partially
occupied by a variety of eccentric haircuts adopted by men who were unsure of
whether the dynasty had gone for good, and who also did not know exactly how a
Chinese head should look if not shaven at the front with a rope of hair behind.[38]
Nationally, the most famous person to retain the queue was the warlord Zhang
Xun (1854–1923), who demanded the same of his army. In 1917 the "Queue
Army" briefly put the last emperor back on the throne.[39]

By-and-large, the transformation of men's dress in the early twentieth century
followed a world-wide trend to greater simplicity and sobriety, and a trimmer fit.
A greater technological sophistication of materials and design was evident, especially in the popularisation of leather footwear. The Western suit was a rare sight,
except on foreigners, but Western hats proliferated: boaters, felt caps, Hombergs

37 Chen Bilan, *Wode huiyi* (My memoirs) (Hong Kong: Shiyue shuwu, 1994), 12.
38 See further Lung-kee Sun, "The Politics of Hair," 354-5.
39 *BDRC*, Vol. I, 68-72.

Fig. 4.10 Yi Jing advertisements for hats (detail). The customers are all wearing caps, but one shelf is piled high with boaters, which are also displayed on the counter, along with a pair of leather shoes.

(Fig. 4.10). As in the late Ming, headwear was obviously an important site of male fashion. Around 1911, Fu Chongju commented amusedly on hats in his hometown in the western province of Sichuan:

Hat styles in Chengdu change yearly. Large hats are mostly in Beijing style, small in Suzhou or Hangzhou style. Among small hats, there has recently emerged an inelegant type, like a melon skin with an unadorned border, resembling the headband of a young female impersonator [from the Beijing opera]. When four or five borders are added, it looks as if a number of small hats are being worn at once. Last year, there was something known as the "pacification hat." Now, except for among the Tibetans who have adopted it as a uniform, no one in the province wears one.[40]

From photos—and indeed from Fu Chongju's price list, which lists varieties of hats from different places—it is evident that a comparable variety of hats was common in many places around the time of the 1911 Revolution. In Beijing, self-made man Liu Xisan made a fortune patenting a straw hat, and sold "fashionable hats for different seasons" from three different shop fronts. A rival business relied on sales of "little melon caps" to compensate for the drop-off in sales of court wear.[41] Hat and haircut together served to signify a certain zeitgeist, as shown in the memoir of French-educated agriculturalist Sheng Cheng (b.1899):

Civilized China is a man with short hair, wearing a grey cap or a black felt hat, going to meetings, singing the song of revolution and crying: "Long live the Republic!" Barbaric China is a man in a pigtail wearing satin slippers, shutting himself up in his Ivory Tower, passing his time in reading the canons of old and kneeling before the shadows of the past.[42]

Although the "civilized" man was a civilian rather than a soldier, he was a civilian who participated in the revolution and supported the Republic. The grey

---

40 Fu Chongju, *Chengdu tonglan*, Vol. II, 66.

41 Madeleine Yue Dong, *Republican Beijing: The City and Its Histories* (Berkeley: University of California Press, 2003), 158.

42 Sheng Cheng, *Son of China*, trans., Marvin McCord Lowes (London: George Allen and Unwin, 1930), 206.

Fig. 4.11 Liang Qichao and his daughter in 1911. Liang had been living in exile in Japan since 1898; hence his elegant Western suit and short hair. Sishun was eighteen at the time of this photo, and in another era would almost certainly have been married off by this time, her hair done up, and wearing a skirt. Her feet were probably never bound. She is dressed in the simple top and narrow trousers that were popular at the time. This photo provides a good idea of how the Chinese jacket could resemble a Manchu gown—a few more inches to the length of the garment and it would have looked to all intents and purposes like a Manchu woman's dress.

cap or black felt hat were civilian alternatives to the military cap that Sheng Cheng himself donned when he joined the student militia in support of the *xinhai* (1911) Revolution and helped usher China into a new era.

The fashionable effects of natural feet and education

Among women, undoubtedly the most dramatic vestimentary change concerned footwear, and was related to the abandonment of footbinding. The woman with natural feet was the natural counterpart to the man without a queue. The *yin* side of Sheng Cheng's "civilised China" was "a woman with her feet unbound, passing freely in and out of the house." Correspondingly, the *yin* side of "barbaric China" was "the woman who keeps to her woman's apartment, nursing her beauty and shaping her feet until they are like lilies of gold."[43] "Lilies of gold" is a translation of the term *"jinlian"*—alternatively rendered in English as "golden lotus." The expression is used, both in Chinese and English, as a euphemism for bound feet.

A detailed history of the anti-footbinding movement has yet to be written, but its close association with movements of national renovation, reform, and revolution is obvious from all accounts.[44] Kang Youwei was an early activist,

---

43 Ibid.

44 For a succinct overview of the movement, see Chia-lin Pao Tao, "The Anti-footbinding Movement in late Ch'ing China," 141-78. Dorothy Ko presents a revisionist account, with a focus principally on the state-sponsored movement under Yan Xishan (1883–1960) in Shanxi

founding an anti-footbinding society in 1885 and forbidding footbinding in his own family. Women from both the Kang and Liang families were present at an international forum of women against footbinding held in Shanghai in 1895.[45] Anti-footbinding societies proliferated over the turn of the century, dedicated not only to the abolition of footbinding but to the provision of women's education and vocational training.[46] Education and natural feet proved to be mutually influential fashions, and students dominated the ranks of a new generation of large-footed girls. Activists in Zhejiang at the time of the establishment of the Foot Unbinding Society in Hangzhou in 1903 looked enviously at the example of Canton where "girls' schools are springing up, and eight or nine out of every ten have unbound their feet."[47]

Dorothy Ko has correctly drawn attention to "the misogynist attitude expressed [in the anti-footbinding movement] toward women with bound feet."[48] In 1900, the Hanlin Academician Cai Yuanpei (1868–1940), destined to become China's foremost revolutionary educationalist, made it known that he wished to marry a woman who was literate and had natural feet.[49] These laudable ideals were not so laudable from the perspective of women whose feet had already been bound. What had been beautiful and desirable became ugly and unwanted. Revolutionaries in their droves abandoned small-footed wives for large-footed, educated women.[50] In the longer term, the marriage market no doubt helped put footbinding in disfavour even among conservatives.

A confusion of dress codes was among the consequences of the movement against footbinding. Alicia Little was surprised to be introduced to a woman in a Manchu robe who turned out to be a daughter of Kang Youwei. "She wore Manchu dress," recorded Little, "which puzzled us, as she is Cantonese. Her father

---

province in the early Republican era; see Ko, *Cinderella's Sisters: A Revisionist History of Footbinding* (Berkeley: University of California Press, 2005), 38-68. On the Nanjing regime's efforts, see Yang Xingmei, "Nanjing guomin zhengfu jinzhi funü chanzu de nuli yu chengxiao" (The Nanjing government's prohibition of footbinding: efforts and effectiveness), *Lishi yanjiu* 3 (1998): 113-29.

45 Little, *Intimate China*, 383.

46 Xia Shaohong, *Wan Qing wenren funü guan* (Literati views of women in the late Qing) (Beijing: Zuojia chubanshe, 1995), 3-14.

47 *Zhejiang chao* 2 (1903), 2-4.

48 Ko, *Cinderella's Sisters*, 68.

49 *Bainian shishang: ershi shiji Zhongguo shehui fengqing huajuan* (One hundred years of contemporary trends: an illustrated volume on the social ambience in twentieth-century China), *Zhongguo qingnian banyuekan* 23 (1999): 6.

50 Well-known examples are Sun Yatsen, Lu Xun, Guo Moruo, Chen Duxiu, and Chiang Kaishek. Recognising the difficult social position of their arranged-marriage wives, some abandoning husbands—including Lu Xun and Guo Moruo—refrained from actually divorcing their wives.

Fig. 4.12 Chinese comprador Ma Yue and family, late Qing. The women of this family are dressed in Han clothing, but with the exception of the servant on the far right, are all wearing Manchu platform shoes. From photo album dated 25 February 1903.

Fig. 4.13 An elderly woman, dressed in the clothing of the north-western provinces, shows off her bound feet with tiny embroidered shoes and neat ankle wrappings.

had never allowed her feet to be bound, ... thus she, like several other Chinese ladies, considered the dress of the Manchus, who never bind feet, the most convenient" (Fig. 4.12).[51] From this, it appears probable that natural feet looked exceedingly odd with the Chinese pleated skirt, as though the wearer were a man dressed up as a woman.

Embroidered shoes for bound feet were a great source of sartorial pride among Han women, and even the poor and humble paid close attention to this aspect of their wardrobe (Fig. 4.13). In well-to-do families small fortunes could be spent on materials and hours in embroidering the intricate patterns, good-luck symbols, or fashionable motifs that would make clear both the skills of the sewer—particularly important in a future daughter-in-law—and the status of the family.[52]

51 Little, *Intimate China*, 383.

52 Dorothy Ko, *Every Step a Lotus: Shoes for Bound Feet* (Berkeley: University of California Press, 2001), 81-92.

With the abandonment of footbinding, women did of course have the choice to embroider large shoes, but large shoes were such a comical matter when connected with women that psychologically it may well have been easier to opt for a different style of footwear altogether.

Clearly, the Manchu platform shoe was among the choices in footwear available to non-Manchu women with large feet. The other sort of shoe available to natural-footed women was the European-style leather shoe. This was probably the footwear of choice for Chinese girl students in progressive Japan.[53] In Shanghai, narrow pants and jacket were provocatively worn with bound feet clearly in evidence;[54] but as natural feet became more common, Western-style leather shoes became more popular, eventually achieving unrivalled status as the most fashionable items of footwear. They are to be seen on the feet of a number of well-to-do young women pictured in these pages, including Liang Qichao's daughter and the daughters of Sun Yatsen. No doubt the daughters of Kang Youwei eventually donned them as well.

Schools were powerful agents of vestimentary change among girls, and not always in predictable ways. Regulations for school dress issued by the Board of Education in 1907 were consistent with Confucian conservatism but also made plain the tensions between old and new expectations of the place of girls in society. The standard recommended school dress consisted of simple cotton garments. This meant a break away from the silks and satins commonly worn by girls of the social class from which the students were largely drawn. The long jacket or modified robe (*changshan*) and trousers were set by the Board as school uniform, but the over-garment proved far too amenable to fashionable variety for everyone's comfort. The more concealing skirt was preferred in some quarters.[55]

To a surprising degree, the militarised education provided to boys in the Qing decades—especially in the last years—was matched by the curriculum in girls' schools.[56] The winds of change in China had produced a climate conducive to

---

53 See the case of Wang Lian, discussed in Joan Judge, "Talent, Virtue, and the Nation: Chinese Nationalism and Female Subjectivities in the Early Twentieth Century," *The American Historical Review* 106, 2 (June 2001): 789.

54 Luo Suwen, "Lun Qingmo Shanghai dushi nüzhuang de yanbian, (1880-1910)" (On changes in urban women's clothing in late Qing Shanghai, 1880-1910), in Yu Chien Ming, ed., *Wu sheng zhi sheng(II): jindai Zhongguo funü yu wenhua, 1600-1950* (Voices Amid Silence (II): Women and Culture in Modern China, 1600-1950) (Taipei: Academia Sinica, 2003), 135-6.

55 Paul J. Bailey, "'Unharnessed Fillies': Discourse of the 'Modern' Female Student in Early Twentieth Century China," in Lo Jiu-jung and Lu Miaw-fen, eds, *Wu sheng zhi sheng(III): jindai Zhongguo funü yu wenhua, 1600-1950* (Voices Amid Silence (III): Women and Culture in Modern China, 1600-1950) (Taipei: Academia Sinica, 2003), 334.

56 Fan Hong, *Footbinding, Feminism and Freedom: The Liberation of Women's Bodies in Modern China* (London: Frank Cass, 1997), 81-7.

Fig. 4.14 Schoolgirls at the Beiyang Girls' Public School bid their teacher farewell. The girls are dressed in a uniform of highly fashionable design: a close-fitting, knee-length tunic with high collar and straight pants.

Fig. 4.15 In West Fan Lane, scandal is caused by "a girl student with cropped hair and large feet, wearing a long robe, looking like a boy, hand in hand with a boyfriend …" She is taken along to the police station for questioning.

changed expectations of daughters. Wood-block prints, bought by every family to paste up on doorways and within the house to celebrate the New Year, showed girl students practising calisthenics or in bizarre military uniform, practising military drill.[57] The Chinese Women's Gymnastic School, established in Shanghai in 1907, embraced a motto that encapsulated the relationship between girls' physical education and the national interest: "Build up the Chinese People's Health and Throw Away the Humiliation of the Title of 'Sick Man of Asia.'"[58] From schools with names like Patriotic Girls'

57 See Tanya McIntyre, "Images of Women in Popular Prints of the Early Modern Period," in Antonia Finnane and Anne McLaren, eds, *Dress, Sex and Text in Chinese Culture* (Melbourne: Monash Asia Institute, 1998), 58-80.
58 Fan Hong, *Footbinding, Feminism and Freedom*, 87

School or Help Strengthen (the Nation) School, students emerged to take part in nationalist agitations.[59]

The top-and-trousers—*shanku, aoku*—ensemble worn by girl students must have directly influenced general fashion trends in this period. That girl students could, with relative impunity, appear in public enabled young women of this class to set trends in a way once reserved for common women—the women of the "mean" classes. The *shanku* was donned by students, by prostitutes, and eventually by respectable married women. To wear a skirt over the trousers was a conventional, modest and conservative alternative: thus a teacher might wear a skirt to distinguish herself from her students. But visual representations from the opening years of the Republic suggest that the *shanku* was quite widespread in fashion-conscious China, and worn without too much discrimination of age and status (see Fig. 4.14).

The appearance of girl students in public also had an impact on hairstyles. Female students usually wore their hair in a single long braid, but paid great attention to how they dressed the hair at the temples. Different styles of fringe became popular: the "word for one" (*yizi*) style, cut straight across in a horizontal line like the Chinese character for one; the swallow-tail (*yanwei*) style, featuring a wing of hair at either side of the temples (see Fig.4.14); the hanging silk (*chuisi*) style, which involved a lock of hair descending down the centre of the forehead; and the "rolled-up blind" (*juanlian*) style.[60] Rarely, a girl might cut her fringe off altogether (see Fig. 4.15). Cutting the hair and otherwise dressing it modishly were prohibited by the Board of Education, apparently with little effect.[61]

The permeability of gender boundaries

Although girls did not shave their heads at the front, as their brothers had to, sardonic comments about their braids in this period show that the girl student's "queue" was capable of arousing anxiety about its gender significance.[62] In other respects, too, schooling facilitated a blurring of conventional gender roles and of ascribed gender identity, with little girls being sent off to school dressed like little boys. Wang Zheng's collection of oral histories of women contains a number of examples. Lu Lihua (b. 1900), later the founder of a gymnastic school for girls in Shanghai, was the second daughter in a family without sons, and her father

---

59 On the Patriotic Girls' School, see Mary Backus Rankin, *Early Chinese Revolutionaries: Radical Intellectuals in Shanghai and Chekiang, 1902-1911* (Cambridge, Mass.: Harvard East Asian Series, 1971), 68, 96-7. For girls' schools involved in the anti-imperialist activities in Canton, see Rhoads, *China's Republican Revolution*, 131, 137.

60 Zhou Xun and Gao Chunming, *Zhongguo yiguan fushi da cidian*, 350.

61 Bailey, "Unharnessed Fillies," 333-4.

62 Paola Zamperini, "On Their Dress They Wore a Body: Fashion and Identity in Late Qing Shanghai," *positions: east asia cultures critique* 11, 2 (2003): 311.

decided to raise her as a boy, sending her off to school in boy's clothing—gown and jacket. Likewise Wang Yiwei (b. 1905) recalled, "both my parents brought me up as if I were a boy," while Chen Yongsheng (b. 1900) remembered that her father, a returned student from Japan, "endorsed equality between men and women. He sent all his sons and daughters to school … I do not know why, but in Beijing my father dressed my brothers, my sisters, and me in boys' clothes."[63]

These few examples suggest quite a widespread readiness among Chinese people of a certain class to re-imagine their daughters as sons, or boy-equivalents.[64] Li Hongzhang's daughter, married off against her wishes to a man much older than herself, brought up her own daughter as a son. In adulthood, this daughter was called "uncle" by her nieces and nephews. An early photo shows mother and children clad in the conventional richly embroidered clothes of the late Qing gentry, except that the little girl was dressed like her brother. Her feet were never bound, she received a good education, and married only late in life.[65] She was an inspiration to her niece, the talented Zhang Ailing.

The most famous cross-dresser of this era was Qiu Jin (1877?–1907), who became a myth and an inspiration in her own time. The daughter of a well-to-do family, Qiu Jin in 1904 abandoned her husband and children to join the off-shore revolution in Japan. The years 1904–1905 were a time of intensifying political activity among Chinese overseas students and exiles in Japan. Qiu Jin joined in turn the Restoration Society, led by Zhang Binglin, and the Revolutionary Alliance, founded by Sun Yatsen. She studied physical education in Tokyo, and trained in fencing and archery at the Martial Arts Society. Surviving photos of her show the restless vestimentary search for a new identity: the subdued Chinese woman of the turn of the century, wearing a conventional jacket, hair neatly constrained by the gentlewoman's headband; the Japanised woman with dramatically bouffant hair-style, a small but highly emblematic sword in hand; and different examples of men's dress—the long robe and sleeveless vest of the Chinese man at leisure, complete with the umbrella; the Western suit, cap and cane of the progressive man of the world (Fig. 4.16). She was an outspoken propagandist against footbinding.[66]

---

63 Wang Zheng, *Women in the Chinese Enlightenment: Oral and Textual Histories* (Berkeley: University of California Press, 1999), 148, 225, 261.

64 On this subject, see Elisabeth Croll, *Changing Identities of Chinese Women: Rhetoric, Experience, and Self-Perception in Twentieth-century China* (Hong Kong: Hong Kong University Press; London, Atlantic Highlands: Zed Books, 1995), 38-40.

65 Zhang Ailing, *Duizhao ji*, 50.

66 Qiu Jin (Ch'iu Chin), "An Address to Two Hundred Million Fellow Countrywomen," in Patricia Buckley Ebrey, ed., *Chinese Civilisation and Society: A Sourcebook* (New York: Free Press, 1981), 248-9. On Qiu Jin, see Mary Backus Rankin, "The Emergence of Women at the End of the Ch'ing: the Case of Ch'iu Chin," in Margery Wolf and Roxane Witke, eds, *Women in Chinese Society* (Stanford: Stanford University Press, 1975), 39-66; and more

Qiu Jin's cultural heroes were women warriors, most notably the legendary Hua Mulan.[67] Hua Mulan, somewhat controversially represented in a Disney animation in recent years, was historically celebrated in China primarily on account of her filiality. When the dynasty (variously given as the Liang (502–557) or the Northern Wei (386–534) was under threat, she took her ailing father's place in the army, serving as a soldier for twelve years in the guise of a man.[68] Qiu Jin took the example of Hua Mulan almost literally, perhaps imagining herself taking the place of her father in the coming revolution. As principal of Datong Normal College (in Hangzhou) in 1907 she drilled her girl students in military gymnastics, almost to the exclusion of other pursuits, and caused scandal by riding around town dressed in men's clothing. "My aim is to dress like a man!" she proclaimed. "If I first take on the appearance of a man, then I believe my mind too will eventually become like that of a man!"[69]

A contemporary of Qiu Jin, one "Woman of Hunan," astutely took exception to women having to become men to achieve historical prominence, sorrowfully referring to the case of Hua Mulan.[70] Yet as Elisabeth Croll has shown, gender in Chinese society at this time shows evidence of being very highly performative, embedded in social roles that could be played by people of whatever sex.[71] Much as men on the stage played women's roles, so in actual life daughters could in certain situations serve as sons, sisters as brothers, and aunts as uncles. Dressed in men's clothes, they could save the nation, or alternatively receive an education—which in a context where education was linked intimately to nation self-

---

recently, Fan Hong and J.A. Mangan, "A Martyr for Modernity: Qiu Jin, Feminist, Warrior and Revolutionary," *International Journal of the History of Sport*, 18 (2001): 27-54; Robyn Hamilton, "Historical Contexts for a Life of Qiu Jin," PhD dissertation, Department of History, The University of Melbourne, 2003.

67 Among other heroines were the women of the Yang family, said to have commanded armies in defence of the Northern Song dynasty, and Qin Liangyu (d. 1648), who did the same in defence of the Ming. For a discussion of these and other women warriors, see Louise Edwards, "Women Warriors and Amazons of the Mid Qing Texts *Jinghua yuan* and *Honglou meng*," *Modern Asian Studies* 29, 2 (1995): 225-55; and Sufen Sophia Lai, "From Cross-Dressing Daughter to Lady Knight-Errant: the Origin and Evolution of Chinese Women Warriors," in Sherry J. Mou, ed., *Presence and Presentation: Women in the Chinese Literati Tradition* (New York: St. Martin's Press, 1999), 77-107.

68 Lai, "From Cross-Dressing Daughter to Lady Knight-Errant," 81-8.

69 Fan Hong and J. A. Mangan, "A Martyr for Modernity," 38. See also Hu Ying, *Tales of Translation: Composing the New Woman in China, 1899-1918* (Stanford: Stanford University Press, 2000), 141-4.

70 Wang Zheng, *Women in the Chinese Enlightenment*, 41-2. The writer, identified only as *Chunan nüzi* (Woman of Human), set forth her ideas in a women's paper published in Japan in 1903, before Qiu Jin's rise to national prominence.

71 Croll, *Changing Identities*, 38-40.

Fig. 4.16 Qiu Jin in various guises: the proper Chinese wife (top left), the Japanese woman warrior (top right), in Manchu dress (bottom left), and Western men's dress, complete with felt cap and walking stick.

strengthening, might mean very much the same thing. Ling Shuhua (b. 1904), born into a large and powerful family, was sent to Japan with three of her siblings at the early age of seven. She recalled in her English-language autobiography that before this time she had been inspired by tales of women who disguised themselves as men to participate in the civil service exams.[72]

The social roles being played by these various "cross-dressers" obviously varied from one individual to the next. In Qiu Jin's case, the adoption of men's dress was intimately bound up with the development of a military persona, a persona that she propelled into action on the national stage. With her cousin Xu Xilin (1873–1907), she planned an uprising that was meant finally to topple the dynasty. She set out a structure for the Restoration Army, which was going to carry out this historic mission, and designed uniforms for its troops. Her vision of soldiers in white turbans, wearing short black jackets emblazoned with the character *guang* (glorious) shows romantic, heroic, folk-historical origins, but generals and senior officers were to wear a sash across the chest, like the ceremonial sashes sported by Western officers. She pictured the troops going into battle behind a white flag adorned with the single character *Han* (Chinese), and carrying three-cornered flags of yellow cloth with the words *fu Han* (restore the Han) written in black thereon.[73]

The plot was sprung before the army could be formed and Qiu Jin was executed in July 1907. In death as in life she inspired a martial ideal among women. Little girls heard of her exploits, which in their minds probably merged with those of Hua Mulan.[74] Her students, the Yin sisters, carried on Restoration Society activities in Shanghai after her death[75] and were at the forefront of military activities in 1911 (Fig. 4.17). For a few months from October 1911, girls in uniform became a common sight in key Chinese cities as enthusiastic young women joined special army units set up to provide communication and medical services.

Naturally, military uniform did not become common dress for women any more than it did for men. While photographs attest to the actual practice of young women donning military dress in 1911–12, the idealised girl of a progressive, civilised China was better summed up by the cover illustrations of a new journal, *Women's Times*. Simply clad in jacket and trousers, such a girl might

---

72 See discussion in Shu-mei Shih, *The Lure of the Modern: Writing Modernism in Semicolonial China* (Berkeley: University of California Press, 2001), 219-20.

73 Qiu Jin, "Guangfujun junzhi gao" (Draft military organisation of the Restoration Army), in *Qiu Jin xianlie wenji* (Collected writings of the martyr Qiu Jin) (Taipei: Zhongguo Guomindang zhongyang weiyuanhui dangshi weiyuanhui, 1982), 156-7.

74 Wang Zheng, *Women in the Chinese Enlightenment*, 179, 225, 291, 295.

75 Qiu Zhengang, "Guangfuhui you yi nüjie Yin Weijun" (Yin Weijun: another heroine of the Restoration Society), in *Zhejiang xinhai geming huiyilu xuji* (Memoirs of the 1911 Revolution in Zhejiang: continued) (Hangzhou: Zhejiang renmin chubanshe, 1984), 64-72.

be imagined as playing tennis (Fig. 4.18), or more typically as on her way to school, umbrella in one hand, book in the other. Nonetheless, for a girl of good family (*liangjia*) to wear a military uniform illustrates better than any other sartorial event at this time both the permeability of gender boundaries in China, and the degree to which established dress codes had become destabilised over a period of ten to fifteen years. In these respects, the history of the late Qing foreshadowed later cycles of vestimentary change in China.

Fig. 4.17 The Yin sisters of Zhejiang, students of Qiu Jin, flanking an unidentified woman.

Towards "xinhai" fashion

Xinhai, the Chinese designation for the year 1911, seems an appropriate term for a fashion that was developing just before the Revolution and that flourished in the early years of the Republic. Ida Pruitt described this fashion from a photograph of Old Madam Yin: "It showed her as a young matron, dressed in the tight sleeves and flaring high collar, the tight coat with the flair at the knees, and the long tight trousers that had been so fashionable in the early years of the Republic."[76]

The trend towards this very neat, streamlined style can be observed in various representations of women's dress in the last decade of Qing rule. The cut of clothes shifted from wide to narrow, colours changed from brilliant to delicate or dark, gaily embroidered lotus slippers gave way to leather shoes, skirts were abandoned in some cases altogether. Of course, these developments are to be observed mainly among certain sorts of women, such as those from educated families who themselves were now expected to gain an education, or alternatively courtesans, who wore the new fashions in highly exaggerated forms; but they showed the way in which the national wardrobe was changing, to the extent that a wardrobe could be afforded.

The narrow cut of clothes familiar from photos of the revolutionary period was evident in some quarters as early as 1903, as is clear from the comments made by Jin Tianhe in the revolutionary publication, *Warning Bell for Women*. Jin attributed the new cut to Western influence, of which he did not approve,[77]

---

76 Pruitt, *Old Madam Yin*, 79.

77 Aiguo ziyouzhe Jin Yi (Jin Tianhe), *Nüjie zhong* (Warning bell for women) (Shanghai, 1903), 15.

but unlike in Europe, where close-fitting fashions involved "compressing the waist and protruding the bosom" (a style that appalled Jin),[78] the new style in China favoured straight lines. The breasts were undoubtedly flattened by a breast cloth, and continued to be so until the anti-breast binding movement, the introduction of the brassiere and the rise of the *qipao* during the Nanjing decade. Especially where skirts were not worn, the female figure thus presented was rather boyish, or at least a good counterpart to the male figure in military dress (Fig. 4.19).

The "flaring high collar" to which Pruitt refers in her description of (young) Madam Yin's clothes was known in Chinese as *yuanbaoling*, or "ingot collar", apparently due to its shape (high at the jaw, low at the back of the neck).[79] It emerged as a feature of both men's and women's dress

Fig. 4.18 The civilized girl of the Republic —dressed in close-fitting, high-collared *ao*, trousers of narrow cut, and large-footed shoes. On the front cover of an early women's magazine, she is depicted running around a tennis court.

that encapsulated the relationship between civil and military dress. The genealogy of the collar in Chinese clothing is obscure. It made an appearance in the late Ming,[80] and appears in a number of portraits from the seventeenth and eighteenth centuries, including portraits of the Yongzheng emperor's consort,[81] but it was not a common feature of costume before the twentieth century. The robes and jackets of the Ming and Qing periods were round-necked, occasionally sporting a well-defined neck-band. Collars, made and sold separately, were donned for decorative

---

78 Ibid.

79 Luo Suwen, "Lun Qingmo Shanghai dushi nüzhuang de yanbian," 136.

80 Meng Hui, "Pifeng xiaoshi," 99.

81 See Liu Rendao, ed., *Zhongguo chuanshi renwu minghua quanji*, Vol. 2, 314-17. The portraits, on silk, are part of the Palace Museum Collection in Beijing.

Fig. 4.19 *Xinhai* fashions. Sun Yatsen's daughters, son and daughter-in-law photographed for a French newspaper in 1912. Left to right: Kam Yuen (Jinyuan), Kam Yeem (Jinyan), Fo (Ke), and Chen Shuying. Sun's daughters are wearing what was the height of fashion at the time: close-fitting jacket (or sleeveless jacket in the case of the elder), with the extremely high collar which is the true mark of the fashions of this era. The younger daughter is wearing trousers without a skirt. The elder daughter's feet look quite small, and were possibly bound. The daughter-in-law, apparently pregnant, wears a pocket-watch pinned to her breast. The Western clothes worn by Sun Fo are also typical fashion of the era.

effect, warmth, and formal (official) wear.[82] Made from satin or fur, if the wearer was rich, they were fastened around the throat over the jacket neckline.

A late Qing reference to "the so-called 'stand-up collars' worn on everyday clothing" in Chengdu points to the popularisation of this item, and an intermediate stage in its development from an occasional to a regular feature of dress.[83] Around this time, the collar was being integrated into standard garments of both the Chinese and Manchu wardrobes—the jacket and robe. For Han women, it was the defining feature of the long jacket that they wore over either skirt or trousers, and it remained so through the first few years of the Republic. Graphic representations suggest that the rise and rise of the collar can be dated to the years following 1905, or in other words to the years in which the military schools were gaining increased popularity and men in uniform were becoming *comme il faut*. After 1913, it would never again reach the dramatic heights it achieved at the height of *xinhai* fashion, but then again, it never entirely disappeared. The stand-up collar somehow became the defining sign, the *sine qua non*, of Chinese dress.

The new look developed at a time of national crisis that was favourable to the figure of woman acquiring a high degree of political significance. The consequences of the national crisis for the representation and self-representation of women were not entirely predictable. Since the discourse of national reform and

---

82 Zhou Xun and Gao Chunming, *Zhongguo gudai fushi fengsu*, 216.

83 Fu Chongju, *Chengdu tonglan*, Vol. 2, 69.

renovation featured woman as the bearer of cultural tradition,[84] it could have encouraged an atavistic move back to historical forms of dress and an aggressively Neo-Confucian approach to wives and daughters such as that manifested by conservative reformers in the mid-nineteenth century. As it happened, the pull of tradition was overwhelmed by the call of the future. Girls were caught up in the slip-stream of institutional reforms affecting their fathers and brothers. In the early years of the twentieth century, new images of Chinese women in all sorts of new social roles gained wide currency. In magazines written by and for women, the state of the nation was discussed side by side with how to cut out garments and wash out stains.[85] In fiction written by women, assertive and often novel roles were imagined for Chinese women, present and future: they become teachers, journalists, doctors, and political activists. They equipped themselves with first-aid kits and hand-guns in preparation for the revolution.[86] Not surprisingly, women in actual life began to wear clothes that were quite different from what had been worn even ten years earlier.

Citizens of the Republic

On 1 January 1912, a khaki-clad Sun Yatsen arrived in Nanjing to a triumphant welcome from supporters of the new, provisional Republic of China. When official ceremonies began that evening, Sheng Cheng later recalled, "there was not a pigtail to be seen. Frock coats and top hats were everywhere. For the mandarin robe, the satin slipper, the fringed hat, the red button, the long hair of old, it was a night of weeping."[87] Few statements could better encapsulate the semiotics of dress in the highly political society that was China.

New regulations for formal wear handed down by the Beijing government in 1912 confirmed this trend, ordaining frock coats and top hats as the proper dress for male representatives of Chinese society. In the detailed booklet setting out expectations for how people in the Republic should look, men's wear was divided into high formal and regular formal wear, those categories were in turn divided into morning and evening wear. The top hat was designated for high formal wear,

---

84 Theodore Huters, *Bringing the World Home: Appropriating the West in Late Qing and Early Republican China* (Honolulu: University of Hawai'i Press, 2005), 289, n. 22.

85 Of the early women's magazines, *Nüzi shijie* (Women's world), published between 1904 and 1907, had a particularly strong focus on domestic tasks, such as cutting out clothes, washing, and cooking. It may have provided a model for later, more sophisticated magazines, which despite their more varied content commonly included patterns of clothes.

86 Ellen Widmer, "*Honglou meng ying* and Three Novels by Women of the Late Qing," Paper presented at International Symposium on Women, Nation and Society in Modern China (1600-1950), Taipei: Research Institute of Modern History, Academia Sinica (23-25 August, 2001), 13.

87 Sheng Cheng, *Son of China*, 198.

Fig. 4.20 Under the Republican regime, the long gown and jacket worn with bowler hat was an acceptable alternative to the Western morning (or evening) suit as semi-formal dress. High formal wear, again with morning and evening styles, was worn with the top hat. After *Zhonghua minzu fuzhi*.

being replaced by the bowler or Homberg for day wear. Bow-ties and neckties appear to have been acceptable alternatives for all but high formal evening wear. Chinese dress worn with a bowler hat was acceptable as regular formal wear, but it is worth noting that no Chinese alternative is presented for high formal wear (Fig. 4.20). This means that ceremonial wear was definitively European, although perhaps understood as conforming to international standards.

For women, who from this time were more often to be seen at public formal occasions, there was only one form of formal wear and it was Chinese in style: the typical close-cut, high-collared jacket of the Republican era worn over a pleated skirt, as shown in the cartoon above (Fig. 4.21). The failure of authorities to stipulate for women a European style that might have corresponded with the man's suit shows that the idea of women as bearers of the cultural tradition had after all taken root. Colours were designated for the clothing of both sexes—shades of grey and blue for men's daily wear, and black for formal wear; light and dark equally acceptable for women. The booklet was printed by the National Products Support Society, and the regulations included some strong advice on which fabrics should be used: Chinese silk, cotton or hemp. For men's clothes, the origins of cloth were problematic from the point of supporting national products. China did not yet have a developed fine wool industry, and silk and cotton were not suitable for most of the stipulated male dress styles.[88]

As commentators then and later have noted, the change of regime signalled by the 1911 Revolution was not complete, far-reaching, or thorough. Old wine was everywhere being poured into new bottles, old cloth being cut in new styles. Nonetheless, a sudden flurry of interest in Western fashions after the collapse of the Qing attests to a sense of rupture with the past and orientation to a future in which China was definitively part of the modern, "civilised" world community. To Bao Tianxiao, it appeared that the loss of the dynasty meant the defeat of Chinese by Western fashions. "European and American merchants won the women over," he wrote. "High heels came in, sheer silk stockings appeared. One marvel succeeded the next. Battle was joined over beauty and finery. Who would have believed it?"[89]

The change of political regime had almost instantaneous effects in the retail industry. Within ten days of the October 10 uprising the *Shenbao* daily paper in Shanghai was carrying advertisements for Western clothes (*yangzhuang*) and "civilised" hair-cutting and styling implements (see Fig. 4.22).[90] Recently to this time, advertisements for Western or Western-style products were limited to commodities such as electric lights, gramophones, and sock-knitting machines. Outlets such as Whitelaw's Department Store, developed in the first instance to supply the needs of the tens of thousands of Westerners in the city, were soon advertising for Chinese custom. A sale in the summer of 1913 shows the range of ready-made goods that Chinese customers might buy: white shirts, leather belts, spencers, lace-up canvas shoes, umbrellas, socks, sock suspenders.[91]

Footwear was prominent among such goods, as reported in the *New York Times* that same summer. The reporter described a shoe-shop in Shanghai's Fuzhou Road: one display window was devoted to cloth shoes, for both bound

---

88 Dazongtong gongbu, *Zhonghua minzu fuzhitu* (Nanjing: Guohuo weichihui, 1912). (The work lacks pagination.) These points are discussed in detail in Henrietta Harrison, *The Making of the Republican Citizen: Political Ceremonies and Symbols in China 1911-1929* (Oxford: Oxford University Press, 2000), 58-9.

89 Bao Tianxiao, *Yi shi zhu xing de bainian bianqian* (One hundred years of change in food, clothing, accommodation and travel) (Hong Kong: Dahua chubanshe, 1973), 39.

90 *Shenbao* 20 October 1911; 27 October 1911.

91 *Shenbao* 8 June 1913; 22 June 1913.

Fig. 4.21 A cartoon in the pictorial press made fun of the new clothing regulations, parodying the instructions above and adding a jingle below: "Short and long, high and low, old and new—a very funny mix."

Fig. 4.22 In this advertisement a Republican soldier is depicted holding two flags: the one on the right carries the characters for Republic of China, while the one on the left states "welcome, compatriots." The "compatriots" are being welcomed to 115 South Sichuan Road, in the International Settlement, where they can change to Western clothes and cut their hair.

and natural feet; the other was devoted to leather shoes, of which some were fashioned like their cloth counterparts while others were high-heeled, looking very like those worn by the fashionable milady in the West. The stocking, according to the same writer, was beginning to make inroads, to a point where even bound-footed women desired them, and hosiers "were busy with new models designed to meet the exigencies of feet cramped to the size of a doll's."[92]

The body's other extreme—the head—was of course the part most commonly associated with the change of regime, due to the sudden disappearance of millions of queues, many by force. But Luo Dunwei (b. 1898), a native of Hunan, recalled the hairstyles of the revolutionary period primarily in terms of women's hairstyles (Fig. 5.23). "With the coming of the revolution," he wrote, "what most attracted people's attention was that women's hairdos changed in a big

---

92 *New York Times* 3 August 1913.

way. Every woman with the slightest claim to being new-style began to wear a hair-roll that was popularly known as 'the butterfly do.'" [93] Little boys, probably including himself, would prance behind such women chanting rhymes such as "Butterfly head, butterfly head,/ Talks freedom, likes freedom," which appeared not to bother these new-style young women at all. Like the single plait, the "butterfly do" was open to antipathetic readings. As Luo went on to say, "freedom" had particular meanings when made in reference to a woman, and the equation of the butterfly hairdo with freedom meant that this hairstyle could readily be interpreted as signalling sexual availability.[94]

An anxiety about the confusion of culture, gender and status being produced by ways of dressing was widely evident in the early years of the Republic. A journalist for *Shenbao* reported bemusedly in 1912 that "Chinese are wearing foreign clothes, while foreigners wear Chinese clothes; men are adorned like women and women like men; prostitutes imitate girl students, and girl students look like prostitutes."[95] Cao Fangyun of the YWCA expressed concerns about women wearing provocative clothing and "novel and outlandish" forms of dress, such as Western men's hats and coats. In such clothes, she opined, Chinese women were risking the loss both of their "natural character" and their dignity, for such clothes were making them a laughing-stock. "With China at the present turning point," she wrote, "I dearly hope that everyone will think twice before converting the quality costume (*zhuangshu*) of our women into styles neither Chinese nor Western, male nor female."[96]

In the vestimentary realm, the transition from the late Qing to the early Republic—*Qingmo Minchu*—was marked by uncertainty and a quality of liminality. Photographs of Qiu Jin as man or woman, Japanese, Chinese or Western, soldier or citizen, together with images of Sheng Cheng dressed either in military uniform or in Western suit, graphically encapsulate the dynamic possibilities of how to dress in this transitional period. People in China were literally crossing a threshold from subjecthood to citizenship, however imperfectly citizenship was to be realised. In later decades there were to be even more dramatic shifts and a much more widespread transformation in clothing styles, affecting many more people; but at no other time was vestimentary change so confused, its orientation

93 Luo Dunwei, *Wushi nian huiyi lu* (Memoir of fifty years) (Xinzhu, Zhongguo wenhua gongyingshe, 1952), 14.

94 Ibid.

95 Quoted in Tao Ye, "Minchu funü de xinzhuang" (New fashions among women in the early Republic), in Shandong huabao chubanshe "Lao zhaopian" bianjibu (Shandong pictorial publishing, "Old photos" editorial section), ed., *Lao zhaopian* (Old photos), no. 1 (Jining: Shandong huabao chubanshe, 1996), 105.

96 Cao Fangyun, "Yifu lüeshuo" (A few words about clothing), *Nüduobao* 2, 4 (cumulative number 16) (July 1913): 11-14.

Fig. 4.23 A popular hairstyle around the time of the 1911 Revolution. The text reads: "If it's weird and wonderful, Shanghai is sure to have it (no. 3): the newest style of hair roll for women." Signed by "You" (i.e., a surname, not the second personal pronoun). The sketch, the third in a series, matches the description of a "butterfly do"—hair wound around two ends of a stick to form a butterfly shape.

so uncertain, its possibilities so many. Who and what to be in the absence of an emperor—soldier or citizen, Chinese or Western-cum-international, male or female—was nowhere more clearly expressed than in the variety of ways in which people dressed.

5
THE FASHION INDUSTRY IN SHANGHAI

In the 1920s, a fashion industry took shape in China. It was characterised by mechanised textile production, advertising through billboards and newspapers, the proliferation of pictorial magazines, the emergence of the graphic artist as fashion designer, promotion of retail outlets, competition between local and foreign products, and fashion parades. It is possible to speak of "fashions" in China before this time, and to conceptualise especially urban dress in terms of fashion regimes; but in China as in Europe, the fashion industry by definition exists by virtue of capitalism and industrialisation. In 1920s China, activities surrounding the production and consumption of clothing become systemically linked to the point where a fashion industry can be said to exist. Its development was most obvious in Shanghai, which in this decade became the undisputed fashion capital of China.

Shanghai emerged as China's major port city during the nineteenth century and had since served as the country's main site of cultural experiment, economic development, and social change. It was to retain this role for the greater part of the twentieth century, becoming a point of reference nationwide in standards of what to be and how to do. In nationalist iconography it was rivalled only by Beijing, the national capital before 1928 and after 1949, and by the poor, remote, and distinctly unfashionable town of Yanan, where the ideological framework of Maoism was refined in the 1940s. The fashion industry was one sign of Shanghai's economic, social, and cultural dynamism.

In the eyes of both Chinese and foreigners, Shanghai seemed a foreign city. To the Chinese it was "the ten-mile Western quarter," (*shili Yangchang*), a city of "blue-eyed missionaries" and of foreign ways. Its tall buildings, electric lights and mechanised transport astonished visitors from the inland, and the bold young women in their fashionable, body-revealing clothes were an affront to conservative Chinese sensibilities. In Mao Dun's fictional representation, Shanghai impressed itself on Old Mr Wu in the first instance as a place where

101

Fig. 5.1 Republican-era Shanghai, showing the greater part of the International Settlement and the French Concession, and the Chinese City. The Bund is visible on the far right, flanking the Huangpu River. Nanjing Road, Shanghai's major shopping precinct, runs east to west from the Bund, passing north of Shanghai Race Course (now the Shanghai Museum of Modern Art) before turning into the great residential street of the Settlement, Bubbling Well Road (Now Nanjing Road West). Yates Road (now Shimen Road), crowded with well-patronised tailoring businesses, ran south from Bubbling Well Road, changing names to Rue Soeurs at the border of the International and French jurisdictions. Three blocks further south it met Avenue Joffre (Huaihai Road), where Russian residences and businesses were concentrated. Suzhou Creek, shown at the top of the frame, demarcated the Hongkou (Hongkew) district, part of the International Settlement, where the Japanese population was concentrated.

Fig. 5.2 Shanghai's famous "Bund," showing the architecture which has continued to be the city's most distinctive feature. The Hong Kong Shanghai Bank (red roof), customs building (clock tower) and Cathay Hotel (green pinnacle) are all in sight.

young women wore "light silk dresses [that] barely concealed their curves, their full, pink-tipped breasts and the shadow under their arms."[1]

In his 1920 guide to Shanghai, the missionary Charles Darwent was at pains to emphasise the city's Chineseness,[2] but for Westerners, the signs of Europe evident in gunboats, banks and well-paved roads often overwhelmed impressions of the Chinese environment (Fig. 5.2). "Part of the French Concession," wrote journalist George Digby, "very closely resembled a French colonial town," while the International Settlement "despite its cosmopolitan character ... was predominantly British." Resident in Carter Road, off the more famous Bubbling Well Road, and employed by the China Press, the Shanghai Times and the Shanghai Mercury in turn, Digby was "gratified by the essentially English surroundings in which [he] spent a large part of every day."[3] Harold Isaacs, long resident in the city, regarded its Chinese residents as "in effect a colonial population."[4]

---

1 Mao Dun [Shen Yanping], *Midnight*, trans. Hsu Meng-hsiung (Beijing: Foreign Languages Press, 1979), 13-14.

2 See Lee, *Shanghai Modern*, 15-16.

3 George Digby, *Down Wind* (New York: E.P. Dutton & Co., Inc., 1939), 11-12.

4 Lee, *Shanghai Modern*, 307.

Fig. 5.3 Guo Jianying's cartoon, "A wife's unhappiness." The sketch illustrated a bitter little joke: "Modern wife out with her husband looks at his face and gives a sigh. "Will you look at that!" she says. "My silk stockings, leather shoes, gloves, handbag, the new hat I bought today, everything I have goes with my new outfit. The only thing that doesn't match is your "unmodern" yellow face. Oh, what can be done about it!"

Was Shanghai a colonial city?[5] Leo Ou-fan Lee, clearly irritated at the inferences flowing from the category "colonial", argues that China has to be distinguished from the colonies. In his view, "China was victimised but never fully occupied by a Western power," and Chinese intellectuals had a cosmopolitan rather than a colonial mentality. They were not like Indian or African writers, who were "forced by their colonial education to write in the language of their colonial masters" and emerged—in Homi Bhabha's famous formulation—"mimic men" who were "almost the same but not white."[6] The modernity of Chinese literature, he insists, was forged with local materials.

Much the same argument could be mounted on the basis of what Chinese people wore. The fashion industry was forged by Chinese entrepreneurs, and the modernity of Chinese dress in Shanghai, particularly in the 1930s, was obviously indigenous as well as cosmopolitan. World fashion was imprinted on Chinese styles. Nonetheless, in its clothing as in other aspects of cultural production—including literature—Shanghai society manifested some deep anxieties that do not seem qualitatively different from those evident in Bombay or Calcutta in the same period. In both China and India, as indeed in the Gold Coast (Ghana), nationalists talked about clothing and cloth in reference to culture, politics, and the economy.[7] "Almost the same but not white" is

---

5 See Bryna Goodman, "Improvisations on a Semicolonial Theme, or How to Read a Celebration of Transnational Urban Community," *The Journal of Asian Studies* 59, 4 (November 2000), 889-926; see esp. 915-23 for a critical discussion of colonialism as a way of understanding Shanghai in the 1890s.

6 Lee, *Shanghai Modern*, 309-10. Lee engages here with Homi K. Bhabha's essay, "Of Mimicry and Man: The Ambivalence of Colonial Discourse," in Homi K. Bhabha, ed., *Location of Culture* (London: Routledge, 1994), 86-90.

7 On Ghana (formerly Gold Coast), see Jean Allman, "'Let Your Fashion be in Line with our

exactly the phenomenon on which Guo Jianying (1907–1979) commented in a cartoon in the 1930s about how a modern (Chinese) man should look (Fig. 5.3).

These anxieties were creative, and contributed to the production of Shanghai fashion. They were fertilised by a growing circulation of commodities and innovations in technology. From spinning factories to humble knitting needles, from the Singer sewing machine to the Toyoda loom, new tools for the production of cloth and clothing facilitated the diversification of the Shanghai wardrobe. When Arno Pearse, General Secretary

Fig. 5.4 Woman spinning, ca 1871. Note the headdress, which John Thomson describes as typical in the Shanghai area. Photograph by John Thomson.

of the International Federation of Master Cotton Spinners' and Manufacturers' Associations, visited the Oriental Engineering Company in Shanghai in 1929 he found that its seven hundred workers were "principally engaged on textile machinery." They were making looms on a Japanese model (Toyoda), importing from England "only the crank-shafts of the looms."[8] This combination of Chinese capital and skilled labour, Japanese design, and British parts nicely summarises the global flows of technology and culture that produced the Shanghai industrial complex, and in tandem, a fashion industry.[9] The origins of this industry lie in the later nineteenth century, when the "imperialism of free trade" was at high tide. Fashion was inevitably embroiled in the ensuing political struggles.

Ghanaian Costume': Nation, Gender, and the Politics of Cloth-ing in Nkrumah's Ghana," in Jean Allman, ed., *Fashioning Africa: Power and the Politics of Dress* (Bloomington: Indiana University Press, 2004), 144-65.

8 Arno S. Pearse, *The Cotton Industry of Japan and China: Being the Report of the Journey to Japan and China* (Manchester: International Federation of Master Cotton Spinners' and Manufacturers' Associations, 1929), 162.

9 On the global context of Republican-era Shanghai, see further Wen-hsin Yeh, "Shanghai Modernity: Commerce and Culture in a Republican City," *The China Quarterly* 150 (June 1997): 381-2.

A textile industry
for Shanghai

In her famous essay, "A Chronicle of Changing Clothes," the self-confessed "clothes-mad"
Zhang Ailing nostalgically imagined "all the
clothing handed down for generations" being hung out to air in June. Suspended in an
orderly row from bamboo poles, they would
form a corridor along which she could walk,
"flanked by walls of silk and satin," occasionally pausing to press her forehead on a piece
of gold brocade that someone had embroidered long ago.[10] She was twenty-two years
old when she penned the essay, and living in
wartime Shanghai. A century after the foreign
settlement on the banks of the Huangpu River
had begun to take shape, half a century after
the Jubilee celebrations organised by the Brit-
ish-dominated Shanghai Municipal Council,
the city was in Japanese hands. Her nostalgia
was no doubt related to the occupation.[11]

Fig. 5.5 Li Hongzhang in informal
dress. The great statesman of the
day, he was by chance connected to
the history both of spinning mills
and sewing machines in China.
Photograph by John Thomson.

The clothing culture to which Zhang
referred consisted of hand-made garments, produced in an earlier, simpler
time when cloth, too, was made by hand, and so too the yarn from which the
cloth was woven. In the West, household production of yarn and cloth was in
steep decline in the early decades of the nineteenth century, and in Britain was
hardly known after 1815. In nineteenth-century China, by contrast, spinning
and weaving were well-established small-scale household industries (Fig. 5.4).
Even in wealthy households they were sometimes practised by the womenfolk,
for these were the staples of "women's work" (nügong) and proper pastimes
for wives and daughters in good Confucian homes. Commercial production of
yarn and cloth was heavily concentrated in the Lower Yangzi Delta prefecture
of Songjiang, which included the county of Shanghai. Well before Treaty Port
days, Shanghai itself was the premier producer and major entrepôt in the interregional cotton trade.[12]

---

10 Eileen Chang, "A Chronicle of Changing Clothes," 428.

11 On Zhang Ailing in relationship to occupied Shanghai, see Nicole Huang, *Women, War,
and Domesticity: Shanghai Literature and Popular Culture of the 1940s* (Leiden: Brill, 2005),
passim; and with reference to this essay in particular, ibid., 151-8.

12 Hanchao Lu, "Arrested Development: Cotton and Cotton Markets in Shanghai, 1350-
1843," *Modern China* 18, 4 (October 1992): 491-522.

Mechanised textile production in Shanghai began in the 1870s with the establishment of silk filatures, using machinery imported from France and Italy. Cotton spinning followed. In 1890, Zhang Ailing's great-grandfather, Li Hongzhang (Fig. 5.5), established China's first cotton textile mill. After years in the making, it was dramatically engulfed by fire in 1893 but in the meantime it had proved profitable. By 1895, five other mills had been established in China, all but one in Shanghai. In this year, the signing of the Treaty of Shimonoseki cleared the way for foreign powers to establish factories on Chinese territory, resulting in an immediate expansion in the number of mills. By the end of the dynasty, Shanghai was home to eight foreign, four Chinese, and three Sino-foreign mills, out of a total of twenty-eight in China as a whole.[13] These were important features in the city's socio-economic landscape. They served to consolidate Shanghai's position in the urban hierarchy and underpinned the continued growth and diversification of its population.

During and just after the Great War, cotton spinning in China expanded enormously, filling the hiatus created when the workers of Europe left their factories for the front. Around 1921, the year that the Chinese Communist Party was founded in Shanghai, "the profit [from investment in spinning] often exceeded 100 per cent of the capital."[14] A crisis in 1923–1924 disrupted growth, but not terminally. In the 1920s, imports of raw cotton to supply the industry grew steadily, accompanied by exports of Chinese yarn and cloth to Southeast Asia and beyond.[15] Wuxi, Nantong, Qingdao and Tianjin among other cities now all had mills, but Shanghai had the most. At the end of 1928, it accounted for just over half of the country's mechanised spinning and weaving capacity.[16]

The price advantage of factory-produced over home-spun yarn quickly served to make household spinning redundant. This was partly because yarn was highly commercialised in the pre-industrial era, being bought up from cotton-producing regions by cotton-dearth regions for the production of local cloth. Mechanised weaving was slower to make an impact because the greater proportion of

---

13 Albert Feuerwerker, "Handicraft and Manufactured Cotton Textiles in China, 1871-1910," *The Journal of Economic History* 30, 2 (June 1970): 345.

14 M. T. Chou, "Report on Industrial and Social Survey," in Heintzleman to Secretary of State, July 23 1923. File no. 893.40, General Records of the Department of State [USA], RG59 (National Archives), 3.

15 Wang Yuru, "Economic Development in China Between the Two World Wars (1920-1936)," in Tim Wright, ed., *The Chinese Economy in the Early Twentieth Century: Recent Chinese Studies* (New York: St Martin's Press, 1992), 69. On the crisis, see Marie-Claire Bergère, *The Golden Age of the Chinese Bourgeoisie, 1911-1937*, trans. Janet Lloyd (Cambridge: Cambridge University Press, 1989). Wang departs from Bergère in pointing out further growth in the later twenties.

16 Evan B. Alderfer, "The Textile Industry of China," *Annals of the American Academy of Political and Social Science* 152, *China* (November 1930): 185.

Fig. 5.6 Shanghai industrialists: cotton king Rong Zongjing, silks manufacturer Cai Shengbai, and Philip Gockchin (Guo Quan), founder of Wing On enterprises.

woven cloth, used to clothe the vast rural population, was the product of surplus peasant labour and made by them for their own use.[17] Moreover, in the early years of the Republic improved handlooms were efficiently producing superior cloth that was highly competitive with the best machine-made cloth. Nonetheless, machine-woven cloth, whether of foreign or domestic origin, made gradual inroads into the textile market. On the eve of the anti-Japanese war, domestic machine-made cloth accounted for an impressive 45 per cent of total cloth consumption, or more than half of all locally produced cloth.[18] By the late thirties, then, a large number of people outside the big cities, living in little towns far from the coast, were probably buying machine-made cloth to make their clothes. Much of this cloth was produced in Shanghai, or arrived from abroad via Shanghai.

Evan Alderfer observed in 1930 that "considerable credit for the development of the Chinese cotton manufacturing industry is due to the activities of foreign entrepreneurs." In evidence, he tabulated ownership of mills by nationality. In 1928, there were only three British-owned mills to seventy-four Chinese, but there were forty-three Japanese mills, and the number of Japanese looms (13,981) actually exceeded Chinese (13,907).[19] The machinery used for these mills was still mostly imported from Britain. Under these circumstances, it would not be hard to argue that the industrialised textile industry in China was imperialist in character, as political activists of the time proclaimed. Indeed, in 1925, a lock-out at a Japanese mill in Shanghai precipitated the May Thirtieth Movement, involving nation-wide demonstrations and strikes that fuelled in turn the Northern Expedition and the Nationalist Revolution of 1928.

At the same time, foreign investment and enterprise stimulated local competition, giving rise to a stratum of Chinese capitalists who were the recognised princes of industry in Shanghai (Fig. 5.6). Rong Zongjing

---

17 Xu Xinwu, "The Struggle of the Handicraft Cotton Industry Against Machine Textiles in China," *Modern China* 14, 1 (January 1988): 41.

18 Ibid., Table 3.

19 Alderfer, "The Textile Industry of China," 187.

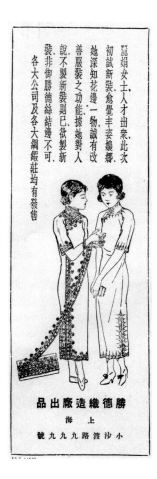

品出廠織德勝
海 上
號九九九路渡沙小

Fig. 5.7 Advertisement for Shengde Weaving Factory lace trim, "sold in every large business and silk store." The girl on the left is portrayed as the one in the know about beauty and elegance. She understands how a decorative border can beautify a garment. She tells her companion: "You can't just make a new dress and that's it; if you want to make a new dress, you have to use Shengde silk trimming."

(1873–1938), the "cotton king" of China, founded the Shenxin Cotton Spinning Corporation with a single mill in 1916; by 1935 it accounted for a quarter of the total number of spindles in the country.[20] Cai Shengbai (1894–1977), a graduate of the Massachusetts Institute of Technology, took over management of the Meiya Silk Weaving Company in 1919, when it was a business of fourteen mechanised looms in a single factory. By 1934, it was a multi-site company with over a thousand looms and more than three thousand employees.[21] In the same period, the Kwok brothers built up the Wing On Textile Manufacturing Company to a three-mill enterprise with two thousand looms, 240,000 spindles, and a workforce of more than fourteen thousand. Philip Gockchin (Guo Quan, 1879–1966) was inspired to extend the family business in this direction by the strength of anti-Japanese feeling in Shanghai, which he sensed—correctly—was favourable to Chinese industry.[22]

The rapid development of mechanised production in Shanghai was evident in a range of industries between the wars. Migrants flocked to the city to find work in flour mills (another Rong brothers' enterprise), rice mills, canning factories, cigarette factories, and factories for the production of candles and soap. A power plant—"one of the largest in the world"—supplied the city with electricity, and a new gas plant "declared by engineers to be the most modern in the world," began operations

---

20 Leonard T.K. Wu, "The Crisis in the Chinese Cotton Industry," *Far Eastern Survey* 4, 1 (16 January 1935): 1-4.

21 *SDHB*, 5, 6 (16 January, 1934). Cai remained profitably engaged in his business through the war years, but far-sightedly turned his attention to real estate in Hong Kong after the war. In the 1950s, he settled in Australia. *MGRW*, 1369.

22 Yen Ching-hwang, "Wing On and the Kwok Brothers: A Case Study of Pre-War Overseas Chinese Entrepreneurs," in Kerrie L. MacPherson, ed., *Asian Department Stores* (Richmond: Curzon Press, 1998), 63.

in 1934.[23] But cotton mills were the main sign of Shanghai's industrialisation in the early twentieth century. In the 1930s, Shanghai was one of the world's great cotton manufacturing centres.

In the textile and apparel industries, the important plants apart from cotton mills were devoted to silk (reeling, weaving, lace-making) and knitwear.[24] Lace-making was an important adjunct to fabric production. Widely used for decorative trim on fashionable Chinese clothes, lace was introduced to China by Catholic nuns in the convent at Xujiawei, the old Catholic settlement west of the city. By 1925, it was a well-established handicraft that had a major commercial outlet in the Cathay Lace Company, at 19 Nanjing Road, and another in The Hip Seng Company, at 21 Nanjing Road.[25] Industrial lace-making thus flourished in the face of considerable competition from the competitively-priced hand-made item. Around 1935, there were thirty-nine silk lace factories of various dimensions in Shanghai, and their products were used creatively to trim and adorn garments that were often quite simple in cut and plain in fabric (Fig. 5.7).

The changing structure of urban society in China was among the significant consequences of the mechanisation of cotton spinning and associated industries. In 1920s Shanghai, a substantial working class supplied factory labour as well as providing a seed-bed for trade unionism and the Communist Party. The need for technical and managerial staff for China's new industries was in part supplied by overseas-trained personnel, but some leading industrialists took important initiatives to develop local expertise. The Rong brothers were exemplary in this regard. They established training institutes to ensure a steady supply of personnel with expertise in textile technology, engineering, and management.[26] The demand for managerial, technical, clerical, accounting and other services to support the industrial machine contributed to the growth of a middle class that provided discriminating consumers for textiles among many other goods.

Tailoring and technology

In the midst of all these changes, the familiar figure of the tailor remained important in Chinese society. In Shanghai, the city where everyone "paid attention

---

23 *All About Shanghai: A Standard Guidebook* [1934-5], (Hong Kong: Oxford University Press, 1983), 30.

24 Ibid., 29.

25 Allister Macmillan, comp. and ed., *Seaports of the Far East: Historical and Descriptive Commercial and Industrial Facts, Figures, & Resources* (London: W.H.& L. Collinridge, 1925), 107-8.

26 Zhang Zhongli, "The Development of Chinese National Capital in the 1920s," in Tim Wright, ed., *The Chinese Economy in the Early Twentieth Century: Recent Chinese Studies* (New York: St Martin's Press, 1992), 53.

to clothes rather than people" (*zhi zhong yishan, bu zhong ren*), tens of thousands of tailors served the vestimentary needs of a portion of the three million or more people living in 1930s Shanghai.[27] Tailors sat behind some of the best-known shopfronts: the Hongxiang fashion store, established in 1917 and featuring a sign-board with calligraphy by Cai Yuanpei; Rongchangxiang tailors in Nanjing Road, the most famous place for men's Western suits; and the Yunshang Fashion Company, near Jing'an Temple Road, discussed further below.[28] In Tianjin, the Shanghai of the north, one of the best known names in high society in the 1920s was Sun Xiaobian (Little Queue Sun), tailor. Sun was a weather-beaten, rustic-looking fellow who dressed in a plain gown and still sported a queue. Despite his unpromising appearance he could evidently cut like an angel, and his services were in high demand.[29]

Local historians date the origins of new-style "fashion" tailoring in Shanghai to the middle of the nineteenth century, when one Zhao Chunlan, a native of Chuansha—not far from Shanghai—was taken under the wing of an American missionary. In 1851, he travelled to the USA, returning after a year to open a tailor's shop specialising in Western clothes.[30] The clientele for such a business can only have been expatriates. Although Western clothing was occasionally worn by Chinese people in the second half of the twentieth century, in Shanghai the practice probably did not extend much beyond the entertainment quarter.

The tailor shops that sprang up in emulation of Zhao's co-existed with the "tote-a-bag tailors" (*lingbao caifeng*), who carried their trade from door to door. In 1886, a trade association to service these tailors was established. Its quarters were behind the Temple of the City God in the Chinese city, south of the international concession, but the tailors must have served a population beyond the walls of the old city because large numbers of Chinese were now living in the foreign concessions. A.S. Roe, who visited China three years before the 1911 Revolution, recorded the visit of a "tote-a-bag tailor" to a house in a town in the interior, where she was staying:

---

27 Lu Hanchao gives an estimate of 40,000 tailors in Su Guang tailor shops in 1946. To these must be added tailors in Western-style tailor shops and the big department stores. Lu Hanchao, *Beyond the Neon Lights: Everyday Shanghai in the Early Twentieth Century* (Berkeley: University of California Press, 1999), 256.

28 Tang Zhenchang, *Jindai Shanghai fanhua lu* (The flowering of modern Shanghai) (Hong Kong: Shangwu yinshuguan, 1993), 104; Lu, *Beyond the Neon Lights*, 257.

29 *BYHB* 11 January 1928.

30 Shanghaishi difangzhi bangongshi (Shanghai municipal local gazetteer office),, Zhuanyezhi: Shanghai riyong gongyepin shangyezhi: Diwupian, fuzhuang xie mao shangye: diyijie, yange (Gazetteer of professions: the Shanghai trade in industrial goods for everyday use: chapter five, the clothes, shoes and hats trade: section 1, historical development). www.shtong.gov.cn/node2/node2245/node66046/node66055/node66156/node66167/userobject1ai61750.html. Accessed 9 August 2006.

Fig. 5.8 Tailors in the workroom of Sincere Department Store.

He arrived with his paste-pot, his iron, his needle and thread, and his 'grey mouse'—in other words, a tiny bag the size of a mouse filled with chalk, through which a little cord to draw, in order to mark out seams to be cut. In true contrariwise fashion, Chinese tailors chalk the table and not the material, and place the latter in the chalked-out divisions. Their accurate calculations, resulting in great economy of cloth, would be a lesson to many a cutter-out in Western lands. Finally, after about three days' work, behold a dainty garment complete in every detail—the buttons, cords, braided trimming, etc. etc., have all been evolved from the one length of silk plus the paste-pot and the iron and Chinese ingenuity.[31]

In Republican-era Shanghai, as women became more mobile, tailors became less so. They set up store themselves, or were employed by large fabric and tailoring entreprises (see Fig. 5.8). The small-time, "corner store" tailors were known as Su-Guang tailors, apparently in reference to the prestige of Suzhou and Guangzhou dress styles in the old regime.[32] Western tailoring came to be dominated by men from Ningbo, the ancestral town of much of Shanghai's population. Before 1949, Shanghai had around 420 Ningbo tailor shops that specialised in the manufacture of Western suits, accounting for more than half the total number of such shops.[33]

---

31 A.S. Roe, *China as I Saw It: A Woman's Letters from the Celestial Empire* (London: Hutchison & Co., 1910), 319.

32 Lu Hanchao, *Beyond the Neon Lights*, 255.

33 Ibid. See also, Jiang Weimin, exec. ed., *Shimao waipo: zhuixun lao Shanghai de shishang shenghuo* (given English title: Vogue grandma: in searching of the fashionable life of the old Shanghai) (Shanghai: Sanlian shudian, 2003), 44.

Aspiring fashion designer Zhang Qianying, who spent some years studying fashion in the USA, complained about both the Su-Guang tailors, whom she felt lacked a vision of modern clothing, and also about new clothing companies, whose proprietors had progressive ideas but lacked the technical skills needed to realise them. Her stated mission, on her return to Shanghai in 1936, was to improve the quality of fashionable clothing.[34] But foreigners tended to think highly of Shanghai tailors. Mary Ninde Gamewell, an American missionary, wrote in 1916 that tailors specialising in European women's clothes were highly skilled copyists: "Show him a picture in a fashion book ... and he will evolve something, which if not an exact reproduction, comes incredibly near it."[35] Carl Crow, first journalist and then advertiser extraordinaire in Shanghai, must have been of the same opinion, for he presented his old London-made suits to his tailor for reproductions to be made in lieu of going to London. The tailor obliged to the point of transferring the labels from the originals to the new garment.[36]

In late 1937, after the beginning of the Sino-Japanese war, a great influx of refugees from Germany—joined by Austrians in 1938—introduced a new figure into the Shanghai fashion scene: the Jewish tailor. A number of refugees made a living in Shanghai through the rag trade, some on the basis of professional expertise developed in Europe. Until the end of 1941, they had quite a large European clientele because the international concessions remained unoccupied by Japan until the beginning of the Pacific war.[37] The degree to which they interacted with or influenced the local fashion scene is unclear, but Bao Mingxin, from Donghua University's Fashion Institute, attributes a degree of influence to one Erwin Leschziner. Leschziner operated a business called "Modelle" at the Cathay Hotel in the late thirties, and then—in conjunction with a Chinese partner, K.P. Lee—set up a business called "Bond Street" at 61 Nanjing Road, the now address of a multi-tenant complex that accommodates fashion boutiques among other businesses.[38] This is listed in a 1944 directory as specialis-

34 Zhang Qianyu, "*Shizhuang xinjiang*" (New comments on fashion), *Kuaile jiating* 1 (1936): 28-9.

35 Mary Ninde Gamewell, *The Gateway to China: Pictures of Shanghai* (New York and Chicago: Fleming H. Revell Company, 1916), 57.

36 Carl Crow, *400 Million Customers: The Experiences—Some Happy, Some Sad of An American in China and What They Taught Him* [1937], (Norwalk: Eastbridge, D'Asia Vue Reprint Library, 2003), 239.

37 Antonia Finnane, *Far From Where? Jewish Journeys from Shanghai to Australia* (Melbourne: Melbourne University Press, 1999), 114-15. A few of the former Shanghai residents interviewed for this book made a living by making apparel or fashion accessories. See ibid., 86-7.

38 See Bao Mingxin, "Shanghai Fashion in the 1930s," in Jo-Anne Birnie Danzker, Ken Lum and Shengtian Zheng, eds, *Shanghai Modern, 1919-1945* (Ostfildern-Ruit: Hatje Cantz, 2004). Bond Street is incorrectly rendered "Bong Street" in this article, and the name of the tailor is not supplied. I am indebted to Tess Johnston, Old China Hand Research Services,

ing in "Houte [sic] Couture, Ladies Dress Maker, Furs." Since Jewish refugees from Nazi-controlled Europe (though not from Russia) had by that time long since been confined to a restricted residential zone in Hongkou, north of Suzhou Creek, it seems probable that he was dependent on K.P. Lee for his continued employment and especially for the daily pass that enabled him to cross the creek to the former International Settlement.

Women as professional tailors or dressmakers were latecomers to the Chinese economic landscape, but the millions of women at home made the greater bulk of clothing produced in China. "Every family then knew how to make clothes," recalled Ma Wenying, master tailor, of his childhood years. Ma was born into a wealthy family in Linxia, Gansu, part of a powerful clan that dominated political affairs in Qinghai in the Nationalist era.[39] His family could afford any number of tailors to produce its wardrobe. Nonetheless, "my mother enjoyed cutting out clothes for relatives, or for the children, using the *kang* [as a work table] ... This was purely for her own enjoyment."[40] For good clothes, the family brought in hired labour. When the year for his sister's wedding drew nigh, "we asked tailors to come to our house. From morning to night they were engaged in making clothes, for a period of two years ... My sister could not have worn that many clothes in a lifetime."

In the far-western province of Gansu, where Ma Wenying grew up, customary methods of clothing production could be expected to have long continued. Even in Shanghai, however, it is observable that mass-produced ready-to-wear

Fig. 5.9 How to buy a new dress: first, buy the material. This cartoon for Daxin Silk Store (corner of Nanking and Stone Roads) reads, right to left: i) the husband doesn't like her; ii) the reason is, her clothes aren't up-to-date; iii) off to Daxin Silk Store to have a new outfit made; iv) on her return, her husband looks at her with other eyes.

---

for tracking down the details, which she found in the 1939 *Emigranten Addressbuch* and the January edition of the 1944 Dollar Directory.

39 His father, Ma Ji, was Chief of Staff in the North-West Command under the able governor, Ma Bufang (1903-1975). *BDRC*, Vol. II, 474-5.

40 Interview with Ma Wenying, Taipei, 10 January 2001.

apparel was not a standard feature of Chinese life. A retrospective survey conducted in 1989–90 showed that among Chinese residents of pre-Liberation Shanghai, more than half had their clothes made at home while under a quarter used tailors. Only 80 of 503 respondents, around 18 per cent, bought ready-to-wear garments.[41] The results both for the use of tailors and for the patronage of ready-to-wear outlets are skewed by the fact that many bourgeois families fled Shanghai in 1949, as indeed did many tailors. The figures could probably be revised upward to show that around one in four used a tailor while one in five bought ready-to-wear. The combined 45 per cent would represent the modestly prosperous to very rich upper stratum of Shanghai, but the survey was not nuanced enough to account for a mix of methods of obtaining clothing. In a bourgeois Chinese household, the man's suit may have been bought off the rack (at less than half the price of a tailor-made),[42] but the woman's fitted *qipao* would almost certainly have been made by a skilled tailor, while the children's clothes may have been made at home. Nonetheless, ready-to-wear outlets in Shanghai appear to have been few.

One reason for the predominance of home-made and tailor-made clothing over ready-to-wear imported clothing, even among those who could afford it, was the problem of fit. This continues to be a major obstacle in the marketing of international fashions. The standard proportions of bodies differ not only from East to West, but also across regions within broad geographical areas so that clothing stock appropriate for people living in Guangdong Province in the south cannot easily be marketed in Shandong, in the north.[43] Ready-to-wear items appearing in advertisements in the Republican era include raincoats, fur coats, shoes, hats, underwear, hosiery, and children's wear—in brief everything but the central item of the wardrobe, which if imported from the West would in almost every case have needed adjustments before the buyer could wear it in comfort. Many a scrawny young man in 1930s Shanghai took himself off to the gym so as to fit better into his store-bought suit, or else had to ask his tailor to add lining or padding to the suit coat.[44]

In this context, bolts of cloth occupied a central place in the Chinese fashion imaginary. A 1928 advertisement for the Yunshang Fashion Company—"China's only Women's Clothes Company"—showed not a wide range of modern

---

41 Lu Hanchao, *Beyond the Neon Lights*, 328.

42 Jiang Weimin, ed., *Shimao waipo*, 44.

43 Jocelyn H-C Chen, "Investigating Garment Fit Requirements for Fashion Brands in Taiwan: A Case Study Based on Oasis and French Connection." Paper presented at Making an Appearance: Fashion, Dress and Consumption, University of Queensland, St Lucia Campus, Brisbane, 10-13 July, 2003.

44 Jiang Weimin, ed., *Shimao waipo*, 50.

Fig. 5.10. Studio photo of a Singer Sewing Machine teacher, toting her wares to show prospective clients what they, too, might produce if only they had a Singer!

dress styles but rather a wide range of modern patterned textiles.[45] These were to be bought by the yard and taken either to a tailor or back home to be made up according to the design and skills of the housewife. Conspicuous consumption of clothing meant conspicuous consumption of cloth. For a man, a suit of distinction meant a suit made of *taotouliao*—a single length of fine imported cloth that was available as a one-off purchase to him alone, the discriminating, well-heeled customer.[46] For a woman to imagine a new *qipao* meant imagining in the first place the material she would buy, and her shopping expedition involved a visit to the draper's, not to a dress shop (Fig. 5.9). The draper, of course, was often a tailor as well, or at least the employer of a tailor.

Sewing machines

A technological innovation that had the potential to transform the production of clothing was the sewing machine, which achieved a modest presence in Chinese society in the Republican era. The world's earliest sewing machines emerged in the USA in the 1850s.[47] Of the many firms engaged in the race to perfect the machine and capture the market, the most famous was the Singer Company, which ensured its pre-eminence partly by canny salesmanship at home and partly by rapid expansion overseas. In 1896, Li Hongzhang visited its multi-million dollar plant in Scotland, and was presented with two machines as a gift—one for himself and one for the Empress Dowager.[48] Like the Society of Jesus at an earlier date, the Singer Company imagined that if it could make inroads at the pinnacle

---

45 See Ellen Johnston Laing, "Visual Evidence for the Evolution of "Politically Correct" Dress for Women in Early Twentieth Century Shanghai," *Nan Nü* 5, 1 (2003): 104, Fig. 21.

46 Jiang Weimin, *Shimao waipo*, 46-7.

47 Ruth Brandon, *Singer and the Sewing Machine: A Capitalist Romance* (London: Barrie and Jenkins, 1977), 101.

48 *Manchester Guardian* 19 August 1896.

of Chinese society, success was assured at lower levels.[49] Its advertisements were among the earliest in Shanghai's newspapers, and it sought ways to integrate itself into Chinese society, much as it had done in the USA (Fig. 5.10).

The vicissitudes of Singer sales in China have been traced by Robert Bruce Davies, who notes what patience was required on the part of the company to penetrate the market. Singer commenced its China campaign in 1883, with an office at 11 Fuzhou Road, Shanghai, that closed five years later after dismal sales. Machines were subsequently sold through commission by a trading company, but sales were few and due mostly to the demand for European clothes among the foreign population. Hong Kong, with a much smaller population than Shanghai but a greater demand for European clothing, had larger sewing machine sales.[50] When a Chinese delegation of high officials visited the Singer show rooms in New York in 1906, their interest was greatest in machines specially designed for the sewing of military uniforms.[51]

One factor militating against the appeal of the sewing machine in China was the style of Chinese garments and the sort of stitching used to hold them together. There were some fundamental differences in clothing and tailoring technology between East and West generally.[52] In China, although trousers, skirts, and jackets together constituted a wardrobe with some generic similarities to European clothing, modes of cutting and basting differed. European garments used the lock stitch, designed for permanence. A stitch of this strength was indeed needed for European clothes, which were often close fitting and would have burst asunder if a looser stitch were used. Chinese seams, on the other hand, were constructed with chain stitch. European garments also required more sewing overall. Darts were used to shape the clothes to bust, waist and hips. Sleeves were cut separately and fitted onto the body of the garment through a complex process of gathering and easing. Cuffs were separately added, and button-holes cut and bound.

In all these respects, Chinese practice was much more economical. Clothes were loose fitting with a minimum number of separate parts; sleeves were continuous with the body of the garment; seam lines were generally straight, requiring no shaping. Fastenings were sewn onto the garment. A Chinese garment might show evidence of intensive labour: the embroidery might be rich and fantastic, the lotus-shaped collar exquisitely cut, the fastenings elaborate in the highest degree. The underlying structure of the garment, however, was simple

---

49 Robert Bruce Davies, *Peacefully Working to Conquer the World: Singer Sewing Machines in Foreign Markets, 1864-1920* (New York: Arno Press, 1976), 196.

50 Ibid., 203.

51 Ibid., 190-7.

52 Ibid., 174.

Fig. 5.11 1913 advertisement for "Dr William's Pink Pills for Pale People," showing Madam Liu, née Pan, in ruffled splendor in her portrait to the left, and instructing a student at the sewing machine, right. The scroll hanging on the wall to the far right contains the main text of the advertisement: Dr William's Pink Pills can restore weak women to strength.

compared to its European counterpart, and the usefulness of a sewing machine correspondingly diminished.

To overcome market resistance, Singer developed a machine that could sew chain stitch, and began, as in the USA, to offer sewing classes. The company benefited from the new vocational schools founded in the early years of the twentieth century, which used sewing machines for the instruction of their female students in the practical arts. After 1911, Western clothing enjoyed a surge in popularity with corresponding effect on sewing machine sales. A 1913 advertisement for Dr Williams' Pink Pills for Pale People must have been drawing on a familiar figure when it featured the case of Madam Liu Pan, said to be an instructor in the use of sewing machines in Shanghai. Her clothes, with their ruffles, fitted sleeves and shaped jacket, suggest how much a well-dressed woman of the 1910s might have appreciated a sewing machine (Fig. 5.11).

Around this time, Singer was offered competition from Germany. The vast Gritzner factory in Durlach began producing sewing machines in 1872, diversifying later into bicycles and motorcycles. This appears to have been the company responsible for the Likang Brand sewing machine that was advertised in China soon after the 1911 Revolution. The name "Sander, Wieler and Co.," a German trading company based in Hong Kong, appears on advertisements for the machine and must have been responsible for importing it into China. The brand did well enough for either the manufacturer or an agent to establish an office at 116 Sichuan Road, Shanghai, where it opened a sewing school for boys. Shortly before the beginning of the Great War, around one hundred boys were being instructed by six different teachers.[53] The school must have closed during the war, but its popularity among boys before that time hints at the role the sewing

---

53 Tan Jintu, "Fengrenji zai Zhongguo de zaoqi zhuanbo" (The early spread of the sewing machine in China), in Shandong huabao chubanshe "Lao zhaopian" bianjibu (Shandong Pictorial Publishing, "Old Photos" editorial section), ed., *Lao Zhaopian* (Old Photos), No. 37 (Jinan: Shandong huabao chubanshe, 2004), 150-3.

machine may have been assuming in the mass production of certain items of clothing, not least military uniforms.

Sewing machines did eventually become a fixture in Chinese life but the company had to content itself with modest profits for sales never reached the dizzy heights imaginable by reference to the size of the population. Quite apart from the issue of the appropriateness of the machine for the vestimentary environment in China, the average Chinese household was far too poor to invest in such an expensive machine. As Carl Crow memorably recorded, even sewing needles were not easy for foreign companies to sell in Shanghai. Packets of twelve needles of assorted sizes, such as offered to the market by one of his foreign clients, were not marketable to the average Chinese customer, who wanted just one, or at the most three or four, of the one size. A whole packet of different-sized needles was superfluous to the ordinary family's needs.[54]

Similarly, the sewing machine was used economically within Chinese communities. Interviewed in 2001, eighty-year-old Lucia Ko [Gao Huiying], a longtime employee of Singer in post-war Hong Kong, recalled that in the 1920s "My mother had a sewing machine, probably from the time she was first married, and she would make clothes for all our relatives. We had a big family, and my mother would often make clothes for this one or that one." The garments would arrive already cut out, and her mother ran them up on the sewing machine.[55] The Taiwanese tailor Zhang Qi (b. 1922) scraped her resources together to take sewing classes and buy a sewing machine in the late 1930s. She was unable to do this alone, however, and shared the sewing machine in shifts with other trainees until she had enough income to own one outright.[56]

Hand-sewing long continued to be the staple of Chinese tailoring, in both domestic and commercial contexts. As Ma Wenying observed, in his childhood "everyone made clothes by hand; there were no machines."[57] Ma fled from China with his family in 1949 and was apprenticed in Hong Kong to a Shanghai tailor who trained him in the art of making a *qipao*. To this day, all the *qipao*s made in Ma's shop are hand-sewn. In one tailor shop in Shanghai, master tailor Lu uses a sewing machine to make *qipao*s and Chinese jackets (*tangzhuang*) for tourists and local brides-to-be. He learnt his craft from his father, a *qipao* tailor in old Shanghai who stayed on after 1949 to make "people's clothing" (*renminzhuang*). But Lu senior stitched everything by hand until his work unit introduced sewing

---

54 Crow, *Four Hundred Million Customers*, 21.

55 Interview with Lucia Ko, Canberra, 6 July 2001. I am grateful to Cheng Hsiu-cheng for facilitating this interview, and to Anita Chan for introducing me to her mother.

56 Ying Dawei, *Taiwan nüren* (Women of Taiwan) (Taipei: Tianye yingxiang chubanshe, 1996), 322.

57 Interview with Ma Wenying, Taipei, 10 January 2001.

Fig. 5.12 Making socks the old way, as depicted by the eighteenth-century illustrator, Pu Qua. According to George Mason's accompanying text: "the men's stockings are made of stuff, stitched and lined with cotton, with a line of gold thread sewed along the top. These stockings are somewhat misshapen but very warm."

machines in the 1960s.[58] In consequence, any collection of old Chinese clothes is bound to show a predominance of hand-sewn garments, the stitches so tiny and neat that close inspection of seams is needed to ascertain exactly how the garment was put together.

Knitting and knitting machines

The relationship of the sewing machine to actual changes in Chinese fashions remains obscure, since it could be used to baste together clothes of the old cut as well as of the new. But another machine introduced into China early in the twentieth century showed the potential of new manufacturing technologies actually to alter the nature of garments that people in China wore. This was the circular knitting machine used for the manufacture of socks and stockings, which was regularly advertised in the Shanghai press in the opening years of the Republic. The circular knitting machine is now rarely if ever to be seen in private households anywhere, but it was a very popular item in the early twentieth century, especially during the Great War. Like the sewing machine, it was the product of many minds—German, British and American inventors active around the middle of the nineteenth century all contributed to the technology.[59]

---

58 Personal communication, Shanghai, 23 July 2004.

59 Charlotte J. Erickson, *British Industrialists: Steel and Hosiery 1850–1950*, (Cambridge University Press, 1959), 178-80.

It had two great advantages over earlier forms of hosiery production: it removed the need for a seam and it actually shaped the sock.

Before the advent of knitted socks, Chinese socks were made of silk or cotton, cut broadly to the shape of the foot (Fig. 5.12). Knitwear, both socks and underwear, were popularised via imports in the late nineteenth century and prompted the founding of Chinese knitting factories. The *New York Times* report from Shanghai in 1913 quoted in the preceding chapter noted the absence of interest in lingerie in China but the popularisation of stockings. China's first hosiery factory was established in Hangzhou around 1902, its second in Shanghai in 1909. By 1912 power-driven knitting machines were being imported.[60]

Fig. 5.13 1912 advertisement for a (Griswold?) sock-knitting machine (detail). The message written on the "G" can be translated: "Only this machine is capable of increasing your income!" The knitter is wearing the high-collared jacket characteristic of fashions in the very early years of the Republic.

In the West, knitting machines (like sewing machines) were often advertised as money-making investments from which the entreprising housewife could turn a tidy profit after very little instruction and at very little trouble to herself. In a 1912 advertisement made for British supplier (Fig. 5.13)[61] the same pitch is made to Shanghai readers. "The only machine capable of increasing your income!" it proclaims, and: "You can also earn three dollars a day by instructing others!" As in the Pink Pills advertisement, personal testimony in the form of letters was used to sell the product. During the war, as European imports dried up, small factories and cottage industries mushroomed and demand for the hand knitting machine soared. It could be rented as well as purchased outright, and for "a dollar or two" monthly rental, a number of families might invest in one jointly.[62]

Hand knitting of garments, widespread in the early PRC years, was in its infant stages at this time. Commenting on an old photo of a little girl, a contributor to the

---

60 D.K. Lieu, *The Growth and Industrialisation of Shanghai* (Shanghai: China Institute of Economic and Statistical Research, 1936), 40. Lieu provides the following names of early hosiery factories: Ching Luen Knitting Factory (*Jinglun zhenzhi chang*), Shanghai, 1902; Su Luen Knitting Factory (*Sulun zhenzhi chang*), Hangzhou, ca 1920; Tung Hsing Hosiery Factory (*Dongxin wachang*), Tangshan Rd., Shanghai, 1909; Ching Pu Hosiery Factory (*Jinbu wachang*), Paoyuan Rd., Chapei, Shanghai, 1912 (power-driven machines); Ching Hsing Knitting Factory (*Jingxing zhenzhi chang*), 1912+, Shanghai.

61 *Yingshang jie zu zhiwa gongsi* (British Merchants Quick Knit Sock Company), located in 2/19, Canton Rd., Shanghai.

62 Lieu, *The Growth and Industrialisation of Shanghai*, 40.

Fig. 5.14 1924 designs for woollen handknits.

Fig. 5.15 Knitting in 1930s Shanghai. Left, a "very lively young mute girl" learns how to "knit socks, scarves and other items". Right, businesswoman Zhong Yanrong wears a lacy cardigan to advertise her knitting business.

"old photographs" project launched by Shandong Pictorial Publishing Company in the 1990s, guessed that it dated from just after World War II on the basis of the knitted cardigan the child was wearing.[63] It is possible that European handicrafts had an impact in Shanghai during the war through the agency of thousands of Jewish refugees, who unlike the average expatriate lived among poor Chinese and had to make a living in humble ways. Knitting was among the cottage industries that flourished at this time.[64]

But if knitting was popular after World War II, it certainly had a much longer history, one that the difficulties of obtaining wool during the war possibly disrupted. According to a 1924 fashion feature: "Since the rise of education for girls, knitted woollen garments have become very popular. At first it was just children's socks and hats along with women's scarves, but in the past two or three years, in late autumn to early winter, women are more and more knitting woollen tops or vests as outer wear, to guard against the cold" (Fig. 5.14).[65] By the 1930s, hand-knitted garments were being produced, no doubt commercially, at schools for the deaf and dumb;

---

63 Yingzi, "Gege niandai de tongzhuang" (Children's clothing through the ages), in Lao Zhao-pian bianjibu, ed., *Fengwu liubian jian cangcang* (Witnessing the tides of change) (Jinan: Shandong huabao chubanshe, 2001), 102.

64 Finnane, *Far from Where*, 87.

65 *Guowen zhoubao* 2, 13 (26 October 1924).

knitted garments were widely used for children's clothes; and Carl Crow was able to report that women "standing in an alley and enjoying an afternoon chat," or "sitting in rattan armchairs" listening to a Suzhou storyteller, would be knitting as they did so.[66] In 1933, a National Products Year, *Modern Miscellany* introduced readers to Zhong Yanrong, a business woman from Southeast Asia who had returned to China to set up the East Asia Wool Weaving Company (Fig. 5.15). Zhong took advantage of the wave of publicity surrounding national products to hold an exhibition designed to introduce knitting to Shanghai consumers.[67]

Worn under an imported woollen overcoat, the knitted jumper or cardigan helped displace the padded jacket, which was once an indispensable item in the winter wardrobe. Women of the burgeoning middle class were exposed to woollen garments as fashion items in the pages of magazines such as *Happy Family*, *Women's Pictorial*, and *Arts and Life*, which advertised the advantages of knitting and occasionally even provided patterns with detailed stitch sequences and photographic illustrations of different combinations of stitches.[68] The same magazines depicted fashionable young women equipped with wool and needles, as though knitting belonged to the same spectrum of activities as listening to the gramophone, playing golf, or going for a drive.

Advertising

The dissemination of knowledge about new methods of production, new sorts of fabric, and above all new styles, was facilitated by the development of an advertising industry. Advertising was not unknown in China before the Treaty Port period, but it was a rather incidental aspect of the marketing of goods.[69] With the emergence of a mass media, the carefully planned advertisement of commodities at sites separate from both the point of sale and from the commodity itself became a feature of Chinese commercial life. Sewing and knitting machines were among the earliest commodities to be advertised.

The Shanghai daily, *Shenbao*, launched in 1872, played a pioneering role in establishing an advertising culture in China.[70] Founded by a British merchant, Ernest Major, this newspaper at first featured mainly advertisements for foreign firms, but the balance shifted quite quickly. In 1875, Chinese merchants or companies accounted for a quarter of its advertisements. They were unaccustomed to

---

66 Lu Hanchao, *Beyond the Neon Lights*, 258-9.

67 *SDHB* 5, 4 (16 December 1933): n.p.n.

68 *Kuaile jiating* 1 (1936): 30-1.

69 See the discussion in Ellen Laing, *Selling Happiness: Calendar Posters and Visual Culture in Early-Twentieth-Century Shanghai* (Honolulu: University of Hawai'i Press, 2004) 11-20.

70 Barbara Mittler, *A Newspaper for China? Power, Identity, and Change in Shanghai's News Media, 1872-1912* (Cambridge, Mass.: Harvard University Asia Center, 2004), 314-22.

Fig. 5.16 Viewing changing fashions via the calendar poster. Left, advertisement for Shandong Yuxing fabric dyes, showing the jacket-blouse paired with calf-length trousers or skirt, a fashion flourishing in the May Fourth era (late 1910s to early 1920s). Right, complimentary poster for the Great Five Continents' Drugstores, showing two young women in the long *qipao* with very high collar and trim that was fashionable in the thirties. An inset shows the company headquarters, built in 1937. Unlike in the earlier picture, the two figures are depicted as tall and well-formed, in accordance with an emphasis on healthy or "robust" (*jiankang*) beauty at this time.

the practice, had no means of calculating its advantage to them, and the paper's circulation was anyway small (the first issue had a run of only 600).[71] Ten years later more than half the advertisements were placed by Chinese businesses, and by the 1920s, when the daily print run was around 30,000, the proportion had increased to reach around 75 per cent.[72]

A survey of advertisements shows that proportionally few were devoted to clothing and textiles, which is the impression to be gained also from browsing through the paper. The vast majority of all advertisements up to 1925 were for medicines.[73] It is possible that the advertisers were aiming mainly at a male audience, although some ads—dried milk to nourish the wetnurse; Sun-Maid

---

71 Feng Yuemin, "Cong 1875-1925 nian 'Shenbao' guanggao kan Zhongwai 'shangzhan'" (Looking at the Sino-foreign 'commercial war' from advertisements in 'Shenbao', 1875-1925), *Dang'an yu shixue* 2 (2004), 25.

72 Ibid., 28.

73 Ibid.

Seedless Raisins to feed the children; Ponds Vanishing Cream to beautify the self[74]—were obviously directed at women consumers. From 1925 onward, figures of women were more frequently depicted in the paper and advertisements became bolder: the "Sidley" girdle and Maid Marion lingerie are depicted on comely Western damsels; their barely-clad Chinese counterparts emerge from baths to advertise eau de cologne or, less predictably, a National Product thermos;[75] seasonal fashions become a regular feature and advertisements for fabrics proliferate: "NAMRIT—the Indelible Voile," "Tobralco—THE COTTON WASH DRESS FABRIC IN WORLD-WIDE USE."[76]

Since ready-to-wear outlets for clothing were few, advertisements for garments per se are rare, but changing styles were both documented and disseminated through advertisements for other commodities, particularly cigarettes. The big tobacco companies ran highly aggressive advertising campaigns: competition raged between British-American Tobacco and the patriotic Nanyang company ("buy national products!").[77] Their campaigns were conducted through black-and-white advertisements in the daily papers and brilliantly coloured "calendar posters." Calendar posters, so named because the early versions incorporated a calendar on the margins of the advertising poster, were a prominent and distinctive feature of advertising in Republican-era China.[78] Used to advertise cosmetics, pharmaceuticals, and fabric as well as cigarettes, they provide a gorgeous visual record of changing dress styles in the early twentieth century (Fig. 5.16).[79]

Cinema, a significant Shanghai industry, dovetailed neatly with calendar poster advertising. The advertiser was happy to take advantage of the familiarity and popularity of a given actress to sell the product, and the poster painter had an excellent model if she would sit for him, or even if he used a photograph. Movies, according to one fashion designer, were a far more influential source of fashion than fashion magazines,[80] but their impact was heightened by the print media. In the 1930s, a pantheon of Chinese screen goddesses competed successfully for fame with the Hollywood stars, their photos constantly in newspapers and magazines (Fig. 5.17). Via the calendar poster painter, actresses were also drawn inexorably into the world of advertising: Butterfly Wu endorsed Indan-

---

74 *Shenbao* 13 January 1920; 21 August 1920; 28 January 1923.

75 *Shenbao* 7 September 1928; 12 September 1928; 19 September 1928.

76 *Shenbao* 19 September 1928.

77 See Sherman Cochran, *Big Business in China: Sino-Foreign Rivalry in the Cigarette Industry, 1890-1930* (Cambridge, Mass.: Harvard University Press, 1980).

78 See Laing, *Selling Happiness.*

79 See Laing, "Visual Evidence for the Evolution of 'Politically Correct' Dress;" Sherman Cochran, *Chinese Medicine Men: Consumer Culture in China and Southeast Asia* (Cambridge, Mass.: Harvard University Press, 2006), 51-7.

80 *Funü huabao* 31 (August 1935): 31.

Fig. 5.17 Left, Butterfly Wu and Liang Saizhen in a scene from The Star Company's *Madame Mo* (*Mai furen*). The strappy sandals, bare legs, and close-cut *qipao* with trimming were the height of high fashion in the mid-thirties. Above, Butterfly Wu in an advertisement for the Jiuyi Hosiery Factory, located in the French Concession in Shanghai.

threne,[81] and so did Chen Yunshang; Chen appeared also in an advertisement for Toung Foh Kee tailor shop, situated off Carter road, as did the famous Japanese imposter, Li Xianglan (Ri Koran).[82]

The calendar posters were created, for the most part, in Shanghai and Hong Kong, but spread from there to other large cities and small towns, being carried far inland by the agents of tobacco companies. Cigarette cards, sold with or accompanying the packs of cigarettes, presented comparable images in small. The companies were alert to cultural differences between the sophisticated coast and the more conservative hinterland, and they experimented with a range of images that might appeal to different sectors of the market. Zhou Muqiao (1868–1923), a pioneer in the calendar poster art form, was accustomed to depicting women in anachronistic classical clothing of an imagined past, a visual form also quite common in poster advertisements. The latter sort of image—either on posters or on cigarette cards—was

---

81 Indanthrene was a fabric dyed with colour-fast dye of German origin. See Laing, *Selling Happiness*, 210.

82 Deng Ming ed., Gao Yan comp., *Lao yuefenpai nianhua: zui hou yi pie* (The New Year prints of old calendar posters: a last look) (Shanghai: Shanghai huabao chubanshe, 2003), 6-11.

popular in rural areas, a finding that strongly suggests urban-rural differentiation in responses to early twentieth-century fashions.[83]

Pictorials and fashion designers

Another important medium for the dissemination of fashion images was the pictorial magazine, which together with newspapers regularly published fashion designs and photographs of fashionably dressed women. Pictorial papers of the late Qing early demonstrated the appeal of images of young women wearing novel or "civilised" clothes. In the first decade of the twentieth century drawings and even photos of such women were appearing in the Chinese press. Not until the 1920s, however, was a fashionable rhythm of life firmly established, with newspapers and periodicals using new fashion designs to mark the change of seasons. The *National News Weekly* (*Guowen zhoubao*) began to publish seasonal fashion sketches in 1924; the Shanghai daily, *Shenbao,* followed suit in 1925.

Single issue or short run fashion magazines appeared in the mid to late twenties. *Beautiful Dress*, launched in the summer of 1927 by the newly established Society for Research on Beauty in Fashion, aimed to "give expression to true national spirit, promote national goods, and bring into being a style of fashion that is both economical and lovely, so as to provide for the needs of today's society."[84] The founders had in mind the creation of a vestimentary order appropriate to yet another new era in China, when the country would be united "under the party with a flag showing the white sun on a blue sky" (i.e. the Nationalist Party). Black and white drawings of fashionable clothing suitable for a student, a bride, a socialite, and for formal as well as day wear, were combined in the magazine with numerous articles directed at establishing an aesthetic compatible with the aim of robust health for China's womanhood.

Such specialised magazines may have been too costly for the market to sustain in the long term. *Beautiful Dress* should have had an autumn edition, and the editors had to apologise to readers when the second issue appeared only in the winter of that year.[85] A 1926 magazine confusingly named simply *Vogue*, with no Chinese title, appears to have had only one issue, and so too a fashion

---

83 Sherman Cochran, "Transnational Origins of Advertising in Early Twentieth-Century China," in Sherman Cochran, ed., *Inventing Nanjing Road: Commercial Culture in Shanghai, 1900-1945* (Ithaca: East Asia Program, Cornell University, 1999), 54. The two market reports Cochran cites in this regard are from Yancheng and Xuzhou, both in the poor, underdeveloped north part of Jiangsu province. Responses may have varied depending on the character and prosperity of the region.

84 *Mei de zhuangsu* 1, 2 (November 1927), n.p.n.

85 Ibid.

Fig. 5.18 Autumn leaf dress design published in the Sincere Department Store fashion brochure.

Fig. 5.19 Fashion designs by Ye Qianyu, among the most productive designers in the Nanjing decade. Left, short *qipao* over sheer blouse, designed for daywear in late 1929, and published in the founding issue of *Modern Miscellany*; right, Chinese-style trousers and top, designed as casual summer wear, published in *Linglong*.

magazine published by Sincere Department Store in 1930.[86] Both these magazines carried colour illustrations. The Sincere publication was nothing short of sumptuous. The graceful line drawings with watercolour fill and in some instances gold or silver detailing showed imaginative clothing designs that had in common the mandarin collar but were otherwise varied in cut and innovative in decorative effects (Fig. 5.18). Copies of the magazine were very probably available at counters in the store, ready to attract the fashionable shopper's eye. But colour printing was an expensive undertaking in the Chinese publishing world at that time, and these magazines are unusual for the time.

The pictorial papers and magazines (*huabao*) had a wider range of topics, appealed to a male audience (most of them regularly carried photographs of naked European women), and they ran to many issues. The best known of the 1920s pictorials is Shanghai's *Young Companion* (*Liangyou*). Launched in 1926, it was one of the earliest publications of any sort to carry regular fashion features in the form of graphic designs and photographs. Pictorials were soon being published in other

---

86 *Vogue*, (Shanghai) 1926; *Shanghai xianshi gongsi shizhuang tekan* (Shanghai Sincere Company fashion special) (Shanghai, 1930). Both magazines are held in Shanghai Municipal Library.

Fig. 5.20 Fashion show at the Majestic Hotel, 20 October 1930, by the Mei Ya Factory (producer of fine silks). The show was held to mark the company's tenth anniversary.

major cities: Tianjin's *Beiyang Pictorial*, published from 1927, the *Beijing Pictorial*, and the *Feifei Pictorial*—printed in Hong Kong but substantially concerned with Guangzhou. In Shanghai, however, *Young Companion* inspired a proliferation of pictorials not equalled elsewhere: *Modern Miscellany* (*Shidai huabao*), which rivalled *Young Companion* in scale and pictography; *Linglong*, a highly successful pocket-sized magazine, and the *Women's Pictorial*, among others.

The pictorials all manifested an interest in fashion, though the degree of emphasis varied. *Modern Miscellany* was closely associated with the gestating fashion scene. It was underwritten by the poet and essayist Shao Xunmei (1906–1968)—who also invested in the Yunshang Fashion Company—and his artist colleague Cao Hanmei (1902–1975), who included fashion sketches among his activities; and it was designed and edited by some of the most talented graphic artists of the time, including Cao's brothers, Zhang Zhengyu and Guangyu, and Ye Qianyu (1907–1995).[87] The *Beijing Pictorial*, by contrast, never ran fashion design features or published fashion sketches, and the *Feifei Pictorial*, essentially an arts magazine, did so only rarely, although both published photos of fashionable women from high society and the entertainment worlds. The *Beiyang Pictorial*, in contrast, clearly saw fashion news as part of its raison d'être. A single page might carry a fashion design sketch, a report of a fashion parade or clothing exhibition, a photograph of fashionable street wear, and one or more opinion

---

87 Sheng Peiyu, *Sheng shi jiazu: Shao Xunmei yu wo* (The Sheng clan: Shao Xunmei and I) (Beijing: Renmin wenxue chubanshe, 2004), 124; Laing, *Selling Happiness*, 189-90.

pieces or news reports related to fashion.[88] While it focused on the local fashion scene (Tianjin and Beijing), it drew inspiration from Shanghai, publishing photos of Shanghai and sketches by Shanghai designers. The *Beijing Pictorial* also regularly published photos of visitors from Shanghai, especially actresses, singers, and dancers.[89]

The pictorials, and women's magazines generally, provided an outlet for the work of budding fashion designers. Fashion houses as such were unknown in China till the late twentieth century. Designers were graphic artists, who used the popular press as a vehicle for the promotion of new styles.[90] One of the most famous designers of the Nanjing Decade was Ye Qianyu, now better remembered as a cartoonist than a fashion designer but acknowledged by later generations of designers as a pioneer in their trade. Ye was fascinated by the presentation and commoditisation of the female body. His fashion sketches were published in a number of leading pictorials, most notably *Modern Miscellany*—which he helped to produce—and *Linglong, Ladies' Magazine, Women's Pictorial, Young Companion*, and *National News Pictorial* (Fig. 5.19).

According to his autobiography, Ye was responsible for Shanghai's first fashion show, perhaps in 1926, held at Whitelaw's Department Store in Nanjing Road. "A British patterned textiles company sought me out through an advertising company," he recalled, "wanting me to organise a fashion show so as to promote its new products. For this show, I not only designed the fashions and edited the printed patterns but also ran around to the dance halls to sign up some dancing girls as temporary models."[91] Fashion shows were thereafter a familiar feature of Shanghai life (Fig. 5.20), and were mounted in other large cities as well—Guangzhou, Tianjin, and even in staid Beijing, where an exhibition of the "ancient and the modern" was held in January 1928.[92]

Another cartoonist-cum-fashion designer, Guo Jianying, was closely associated with *Women's Pictorial*, which he was appointed to edit in 1934. Guo's professional career was largely in the world of banking and commerce, but between graduating from St John's University in 1931 and taking up a diplomatic position in Japan in 1935, he firmly stamped his mark on cartooning in Shanghai.[93] A

---

88 *BYHB* 11 January 1928.

89 See e.g. *BYHB* 22 February 1930, where a photo of Ruan Lingyu is one of three of Shanghai visitors to "Ping"—i.e. Beiping.

90 Laing, *Selling Happiness*, 189.

91 Ye Qianyu, *Xixu cangsang ji liunian* (Telling of the changing landscape, remembering the passage of the years) (Beijing: Qunyan chubanshe, 1992), 30.

92 *BYHB* 11 January 1928.

93 Chen Zishan, ed., *Modeng Shanghai: sanshi niandai yangchang baijing* (Shanghai modern: a hundred scenes from the Western sector in the 1930s) (Guizhon: Guangxi shifandaxue chubanshe, 2001), preface.

Fig. 5.21 Left, front cover for *Women's Pictorial*, by Guo Jianying, showing a *qipao* design but not looking too different from a 1932 cartoon of "one of Shanghai's famous modern products"— a predatory *qipao*-clad woman with a man on a leash (above).

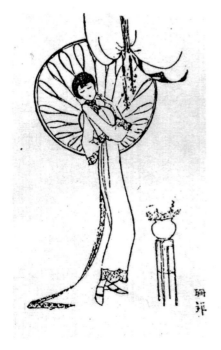

Fig. 5.22 Women in the production of fashion. Left, design for formal wear by Shanghai artist "Miss S.F. Li" (Li Cefei). Right, Tan Xuerong models her own design on the front of *Modern Miscellany*.

Fig. 5.23 "Image of Nanjing Road" by Ye Qianyu. The young lady wears a lace-trimmed *qipao* and fashionable shoes; the rural immigrant behind her has or had half-bound feet, and wears old-fashioned trousers and jacket. They are standing in front of Sincere Department Store; in the window is a mannequin with a European face, wearing a fur-lined coat.

collection of his bitter, misogynist cartoons was published by *Young Companion* in 1935. He employed much the same style in his fashion designs, which dominated the pages of *Women's Pictorial* after his appointment as editor in 1934. The front covers of the magazines during his period of appointment all featured his fashion sketches, which show a strained effort to modify the savagery of his cartoons. (Fig. 5.21).

A number of women were active both as graphic artists—"famous Shanghai artist Li Cefei"—and as clothes designers: "Miss Tan Xuerong wearing her own designs" (Fig. 5.22).[94] Zhang Qianying's *qipao* designs and Zhong Yanrong's knitting business have been mentioned above. Zhang Youyi and Lu Xiaoman, the first and second wives of the poet Xu Zhimo, were both involved in the Yunshang Fashion Company in Shanghai: Zhang had a good head for business, and Lu invested in the venture.[95] But while the names of women do frequently appear in the burgeoning fashion scene, the women themselves on the whole remain obscure. Their works were not published in profusion, and their careers were no doubt cut short by marriage and children, with war and revolution preventing career revivals at a later stage. A youthful Yu Feng (b. 1916) appeared in a fashion feature in *Women's Pictorial* in 1936. A graduate of the Central Academy of Fine Arts in Nanjing, she studied under Pan Yuliang (1895-1977) in the early thirties and became an underground Commmunist Party member during the anti-Japanese war. In the 1940s, she worked as a costume designer in Chongqing, and in the 1950s served as director of a campaign to beautify Chinese dress. She is an unusual example of a woman who, having trained in the Nationalist era, became well

---

94 *SDHB* 1, 4 (16 June 1930): 36; see also ibid. 1, 1 (October 1929): n.p.n., front pages feature.

95 Chang, *Bound Feet and Western Dress*, 180-1; *BYHB* 17 August 1927.

known as an artist and was engaged in fashion design, albeit briefly, in the Maoist era.[96]

The shopping Mecca

The bustling centre of Shanghai's fashion scene during the Nanjing Decade was Nanjing Road, which is still the busiest shopping strip in Shanghai. In a cartoon called "Image of Nanjing Road," Ye Qianyu drew attention to the contrast between wealth and poverty in Shanghai by depicting a fashionable young woman in a lace-trimmed *qipao* alongside an old woman with half-bound feet wearing the simple cotton clothes of the poor. In the background, a European mannequin in a fur coat is posed in a shop window (Fig. 5.23). Almost out of the frame are the characters for the word *xianshi*, which place the scene half-way down Nanjing Road outside the Sincere (*xianshi*) Department Store. The reference to fashion in the figures of the girl and the mannequin is thus reinforced by an allusion to one of the major icons of consumption in Republican-era Shanghai. At the time of its construction in 1917, Sincere was the largest department store in Nanjing, and it long continued to be one of its most successful.

As sites of consumer activity in general, and as significant traders in textiles and apparel, the Nanjing Road department stores had an important part to play in the creation of a fashion environment. The early stores, built in the late Qing, were foreign-owned. Whiteaway, Laidlaw and Co., more commonly known as Whitelaw's, on the corner of Nanking and Szechuen Roads, were specialists in "general apparel", and had a tailoring department "under highly skilled European supervision" (meaning that the tailors were Chinese). Hall and Holtz, at 14 Nanking Road, began as a bakery in 1843 and expanded to become "drapers, outfitters, [and] general furnishers" as well as bakers. In 1925 it owned two furniture factories, baked five thousand loaves of bread a day, and ran a tailoring department—again "under highly skilled European supervision"—that was "operated on lines fulfilling all the most approved ideals of sartorial proficiency ..." Lane, Crawford and Co., at 9a Nanking Road, covered around an acre of ground and had a glass frontage stretching two hundred feet down Nanjing Road. Designed to serve "the classes rather than the masses" (presumably the upper classes), the store included "a tailoring department where under expert European supervision fabrics and workmanship are procurable fulfilling every ideal of quality and sartorial distinction."[97]

Of these stores, it would seem that Lane, Crawford and Co. probably had few Chinese customers, whereas Whitelaws, which advertised in the Chinese press, obviously desired and expected local customers. From 1917, both

96 See Finnane, "Yu Feng and the 1950s Dress Reform Campaign", 235-68.
97 Macmillan, comp. and ed., *Seaports of the Far East*, 76-80.

Fig. 5.24 A 1930s image of Nanjing Road at the corner of Zhejiang Road, showing Wing On and Sincere Department Stores. Sincere (on the right) included a large hotel with accommodation in Chinese and foreign styles.

had to cope with newcomers on the block. The significant stores for Chinese consumers in the twenties and thirties were the big four on Nanjing Road, and especially the two largest: Sincere and Wing On, which opened in short succession in 1917 and 1918. Both these companies had existing branches in Hong Kong and Canton. Sun Sun and Dah Sun followed in 1926 and 1936 respectively.[98] Built by returned overseas Chinese entrepreneurs, and modelled on Sydney's department store Anthony Hordern's (the founders were all from Australia), the stores made available a wide range of imported goods to the Chinese consumer.

To encourage habits of fashion consumption, the department stores took considerable initiatives in promoting new styles. For Wing On, the fashion industry was particularly significant because the company early diversified its investments in Shanghai and entered boldly into textile production.[99] But for all the stores, textiles and apparel were significant retail items. They offered a one-stop service: customers could choose their cloth and adornments in the silk, piece goods and haberdashery departments, then have the garments made

98 Wellington K.K. Chan, "Selling Goods and Promoting a New Commercial Culture: The Four Premier Department Stores on Nanjing Road, 1917-1937," in Cochran, ed., *Inventing Nanjing Road*, 31-2.

99 Shi Lei, "Jindai Shanghai fushi bianqian yu guannian jinbu," 39.

up on site by house tailors. They printed fashion brochures and organised fashion shows, inviting their comely shop assistants to serve as models (see Fig. 6.14). The Shanghai bourgeoisie streamed through the doors.

The arrival of Sincere and Wing On in Shanghai was, writes Wellington Chan, "the critical event that turned Nanjing Road into China's shopping mecca" (Fig. 5.24).[100] Republican-era guidebooks invariably draw attention to this busy road, the "great horse thoroughfare," running westward from the Bund for nearly three quarters of a mile to the racetrack—a hub of Shanghai social life—before mutating into Bubbling Well Road.[101] But it accommodated many outlets for textiles and apparel apart from the big department stores. In 1936 the Shengde Lace Company was supplying its products to eleven different stores on Nanjing Road, including the big four.[102] Among the others were the Chinese Native Products Company at 225 Nanjing Road, established in 1933 by a leading patriotic entrepreneur, Fang Yexian;[103] and the Lao Jiu He Silk and Woollen Goods Emporium (formerly the Silk and *Foreign* Goods Emporium). As Carlton Benson has shown, the Lao Jiu He helped make Nanjing Road a by-word for fashion through publishing a songbook popularised by advertising through songs with lyrics such as "Every one wants new clothes/... In a flash they arrive at Nanjing Road," and: "For real prosperity look at Nanjing Road/... [where] beautiful women come and go in modern fashions."[104]

Guidebooks also make clear the fact that much activity related to fashion happened at other sites. Yates Road, for instance, was a major centre of storefront tailor shops; Avenue Joffre was lined with boutiques run by Russian emigrés producing handbags, selling imported hats and shoes, and making up fur coats;[105] Shanxi Road was "given to women's gear and fancy wares," and Honan Road to silks and embroidered cloth.[106] "Heng Kong My Tailor" was located

---

100 Chan, "Selling Goods and Promoting a New Commercial Culture," 31.

101 See Wm. Fred. Mayers, N.B. Dennys, and Chas. King, *The Treaty Ports of China and Japan* (London: Trübner and Co., 1867), 378.

102 See the large advertisement in *Shenbao* 14 March 1936.

103 Karl Gerth, *China Made: Consumer Culture and the Creation of the Nation* (Cambridge, Mass.: Harvard University Asia Center, 2003), 11. See advertisement in *All About Shanghai*, 108. The store was opened in 1933. On Fang, see *MGRW*, 131-2.

104 Carlton Benson, "Consumers are Also Soldiers: Subversive Songs from Nanjing Road During the New Life Movement," in Sherman Cochran, ed., *Inventing Nanjing Road*, 108.

105 For businesses on Avenue Joffre, see Shanghaishi Huwanqu dang'anju, Shanghaishi Huwanqu difangzhi bangongshi (Shanghai Municipality Human District archives and local gazeteer office), eds, *Huaihailu bainian xiezhen* (One hundred years of photographs of Huaihai Road) (Shanghai: Shanghai shehui kexueyuan chubanshe, 2001).

106 Charles Ewart Darwent, *Shanghai: A Handbook for Travellers and Residents To the Chief Objects of Interest In And Around the Foreign Settlements and Native City* (Shanghai: Kelly and Walsh, 1920), 23.

on Sichuan Road, Fujiwara Shirt Co. on Boone Road, and the Kiang San Shoe Co. on Yuyuan Road.[107] The Toung Foh Kee Tailor Shop was tucked inside Lane 131, at 66 Carter Road. It advertised its obscure location on glamorous posters featuring famous film stars such as Chen Yunshang and Li Xianglan.[108] And beyond the retail outlets were the public places in which the modern city specialised: the theatre, the cinema, and the racecourse; teahouses, cafés, and restaurants; parks, the Bund, and the tree-lined avenues of the French Concession, which together provided an abundance of exhibition spaces where people could see what other people wore. So if Nanjing Road was the shopping street *par excellence* in Shanghai, it was in no small measure because so much fashion, such heady consumption, was observable elsewhere as well.

Conclusion

Industry, investment, location and population were an unbeatable combination in the race for urban pre-eminence in China. They made Shanghai a busy, lively, prosperous city, even if also one where great poverty was apparent. People died on the streets, to be picked up by municipal workers. The poor begged from the rich; rags and silks could be seen side by side. Refugees from floods, drought, and wars supplied the economy with an inexhaustible source of human energy. A vast, inexpensive labour force ensured that Shanghai was above all productive.

As a source of entertainment, newspapers and magazines, books, and images of all sorts, or in other words, as a centre of communications, Shanghai also wielded enormous cultural influence in the rest of the country. In the Jiangxi county of Xunwu, Mao Zedong found that beginning in 1920, people gradually began wearing new-style clothes. These were not made in London or Paris, but in the style of Shanghai or Canton, at that time competing as centres of Chinese modernisation. The Shanghai-style shirt, "cut down the center with rounded buttons and embroidery," was the first to gain currency. In 1926 the Canton-style was on the rise: "seven buttons, four pockets, cut long."[109] This was due to the Nationalist Revolution, based in Guangzhou. With the establishment of the Nationalist Government in Nanjing in 1928, Shanghai's star undoubtedly appeared again on the Xunwu horizon.

It was common for foreigners who visited Shanghai to feel that Shanghai was not quite China. Yet Shanghai was not utterly different from other places. It shared features with Tianjin in the north and Guangzhou in the south, which like it had grown and evolved under the Treaty Port system. Guangzhou—or Guangdong provice more generally—anticipated Shanghai in some respects and

---

107 *All About Shanghai*, 223-4.

108 Deng Ming and Gao Yan, *Lao yuefenpai nianhua*, 9, 11.

109 Mao Zedong, *Report from Xunwu*, trans. Roger R. Thompson (Stanford: Stanford University Press, 1990), 93-4.

contributed to it in others; the large Chinese department stores were evident there first, cinema flourished there, and from there artists, actresses, merchants and politicians made their way north, bringing southern know-how, sophistication and tastes to the Shanghai melting pot.[110] Publications emanating from both Guangzhou and Tianjin had much in common with Shanghai papers and magazines, and were sometimes produced by the same people. The clothes that were worn in Shanghai were worn in these other cities. Indeed, as we have seen in the case of Xunwu, they were worn in places much less notable, much further away from the obvious frontier of modernity in China.

Shanghai's great influence was then not mystifying, peculiar, or untoward; it was a function of its location, half-way between north and south, poised between the oceans and the land, the "gateway to China" as Mary Ninde Gamewell termed it. For Chinese as well as foreigners it was a place of opportunity. Its immense resources made it a magnet for people from all walks of life, and virtually all parts of China. It was associated with flamboyance and decadence, but it was also a hardworking city, with banks and docks and mills that declared its importance as a hub of domestic and international industry and trade. Its capacity for the production and consumption of fashion was a product of linked economic and cultural strengths that it drew from China and from the world in almost equal measures.

---

110 See e.g. Carrie Waara, "Invention, Industry, Art: The Commercialisation of Culture in Republican Art Magazines," in Sherman Cochran, ed., *Inventing Nanjing Road* (Ithaca: Cornell University Press, 1999), 62-3.

6
QIPAO CHINA

In the first two decades of the twentieth century, women's fashions in China consisted of variations of the Chinese jacket or blouse worn with skirt or trousers. All of these garments gradually became shorter, moving in tandem with Europe-

an fashions. By the late 1910s, a new look in Chinese clothes had become obvious: the scoop-hemmed jacket-blouse with wide sleeves and a mandarin collar paired with gathered skirt. This was standard dress among young women around the time of the May Fourth Movement, in the late teens and early twenties. Calf-length pants were fashionable in the same period (Fig. 6.1). Decorous as it might appear from the perspective of the 1930s, the May Fourth style was as controversial as any new fashion when it first loomed on the horizon. Zhou Zhongzheng (1908–1996), daughter of a wealthy and powerful family from Tianjin, clamoured for clothes in this style: "I wanted to wear a skirt instead of trousers; I wanted a short jacket, not a long one." In brief, she wanted to dress up like other girls she saw walking in the park. Her mother refused with the words, "No girl of good family would go about dressed like that."[1]

Fig. 6.1 High fashion in Guangzhou? Skirts and trousers have both become shorter, and the sketch shows an awareness of fashionable attitude. Advertisements, in this case for skin cream, paved the way for fashion sketches that began appearing in papers a few years later. The caption reads: "N.B. top grade national product."

---

1 Chow Chungcheng, *The Lotus-Pool of Memory*, trans. Joyce Emerson (London: Michael Joseph, 1961), 130-1. Chow Chungcheng, i.e., Zhou Zhongzheng, an artist, was the grand-daughter of Qing official Zhou Fu (1837-1921) by his youngest son, Zhou Xuehui.

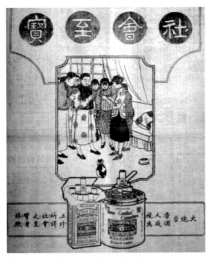

Fig. 6.2 In this sketch for a cigarette advertisement, the girls are wearing typical May Fourth style clothes, and even the hems of the men's gowns are going up.

The modification of women's fashions in the early Republican era is startling on account of the speed and degree of change, especially in light of what men were wearing. A close examination suggests that men's clothing was affected by some of the same trends: the man's riding jacket became very short and close fitting, and even the gown became shorter (Fig. 6.2). But men's clothes were essentially conservative. A 1920s New Year print appropriately depicted a couple of albeit nattily dressed fellows in their long gowns primarily occupied in the act of looking at a transformed, "civilised," street scene, where women in short skirts and jacket-blouses are riding bicycles and driving cars in streets lined with Western-style buildings (Fig. 6.3).

Fig. 6.3 Early Republican-era New Year woodblock print. The busy scene is compositionally similar to some New Year prints of the Qing period, but the details of daily life place it firmly in the twentieth century. The women are wearing the jacket-blouse with skirt and three-quarter pants typical of the May Fourth era. The men wear gaily patterned gowns that had become passé in more progressive sectors of society. One wears a *magua* and trilby, the other a *majia* and slouch cap. The little boys in the picture wear hats, the little girls do not.

Occasional photos and advertisements show that the long skirt and high-collared jacket of *xinhai* fashions survived for a while alongside the May Fourth style, especially among older women, but it is very rare to see the high collar in the 1920s. By the end of the decade the May Fourth style itself was on the way out, to be replaced by the *qipao*, a garment that in the 1930s gained absolute ascendancy. The *qipao* was the main site of fashion in China during the Nationalist period. As such, it became a stage for debates about sex, gender roles, aesthetics, the economy, and the nation.

Both the skirt and jacket-blouse ensemble of the early Republican era and the *qipao* were distinctively Chinese styles of garment, and the abandonment of one for the other is one of the great enigmas of Chinese fashion history in the twentieth century. In many respects, however, Chinese fashions between the wars have much in common with fashions elsewhere in the world. The bob was as controversial in China as in France, androgeny in the twenties excited protests in Shanghai as well as in Paris, and in both places a renewed emphasis on feminine styles characterised the thirties. Throughout Europe and Asia in these decades, a lively critical discourse on women's clothing attested to shared anxieties over family, nation, the past and the future, and a common tendency to express these through reference to the disturbing figure of the modern woman.[2]

The rise of the qipao

The *qipao* (banner gown) is commonly described as a style continuous with the robe worn by Manchu women, a theory buttressed by its name: the Manchus were the *qi* or "banner" people. The connection is rendered more tenuous when the Cantonese term "cheongsam" (*changshan*) is used, a word simply meaning long shirt or robe. *Qishan* (banner garment) was another way of referring to the same item of clothing when it first emerged to light on fashion pages in the middle of the twenties, and in some cases it was simply termed *changpao*, "long gown," the same word used for the man's robe.[3]

Confusion reigns over the origins of the *qipao*, primarily because of its many progenitors. It was manifestly a retro style, appearing around the same time as other re-invented or "reformed" (*gailiang*) Qing garments: the long and short

---

2 Very little comparative research on twentieth-century fashions has been carried out, but the parallels between different national experiences are clear from individual studies. On France, see Mary Louise Roberts, *Civilization Without Sexes: Reconstructing Gender in Postwar France, 1917-1927* (Chicago: University of Chicago Press, 1994), espec. 63-87; on Arab dress, see Stillman, *Arab Dress*, 161-5; on China, Louise Edwards, "Policing the Modern Woman in Republican China," *Modern China* 26, 2 (April 2000): 115-47, espec. 128-35. Edwards, however, distinguishes the Chinese case rather sharply from the Western in ibid., 117.

3 *SDHB* 2, 6 (August 1932): 2.

Fig. 6.4 In the mid-twenties various forms of long garment appeared in the fashion pages of Shanghai publications. Here, two fashion sketches from the same magazine show the early stages of the rise of the *qipao* as a a fashion garment in Shanghai. The garment to the left is referred to as a *qipao*. Note the absence of side splits. The garment to the right is a "qimajia" —a sleeveless tunic worn over a blouse. This garment does have side splits, but is cut low at the neck, unlike the *qipao*.

vests (*majia, chang majia*), and riding jacket (*magua*) (Fig. 6.4).[4] As Shi Lei notes, "the *qipao, majia*, long *majia* and short jacket all fused around 1926."[5] The 1920s *qipao* may well have been quoting Qing dynasty clothing, but it should not be confused with the Qing garment, although the relationship between the two was probably closer in Beijing than in Shanghai.

Zhang Ailing dated the origins of the *qipao* to 1921.[6] She provided no source for this statement, and as she was only one year old in 1921, was obviously not writing from personal observation. Pictorial evidence for such a garment at this time is lacking, apart from her own drawing of a student in an early genera-

---

4 See Laing, "Visual Evidence for the Evolution of 'Politically Correct' Dress," 96.

5 Shi Lei, "Jindai Shanghai fushi bianqian yu guannian jinbu," 38.

6 Chang, "A Chronicle of Changing Clothes," 435. Zhang's date appears to inform assumptions in a number of secondary works that touch on the periodisation of the *qipao*. Shi Lei, in a paragraph that twice cites Zhang, explicitly states that the *qipao* came into prominence at two different dates, first appearing in spring, 1921, and then re-emerging around 1926. No footnote is given for the former date. Shi Lei, "Jindai Shanghai fushi bianqian yu guannian jinbu," 39, 36.

tion *qipao*. Photographs and advertisements attest rather to the ubiquity of some combination of skirt and top among urban Chinese women in the early twenties, the *qipao* achieving dominance only towards the end of the decade. Perhaps Zhang simply hazarded a guess at 1921, on the basis that this new fashion came into being in the course of the twenties.[7]

Helen Foster Snow attributed the change in Chinese fashions in the 1920s directly to the rise of the Guomindang as the premier nationalist party. She did not have a precise idea of the chronology and complex origins of contemporary Chinese dress, but was definite that after "Madame Sun [Song Qingling] adopted Chinese gowns ... one never saw an adult Chinese woman in foreign dress even in the treaty-ports. It was Madame Sun who set the nationalist fashion, presumably as an 'anti-imperialist' new look. Schoolgirls began wearing the blue cotton 'coolie cloth'..."[8]

As the wife of Sun Yatsen, Song Qingling was one of the most photographed women of the Republican era. The visual record shows her sartorial transformation over a period of ten years from the time of her marriage. The wedding photograph, taken in 1915, shows a young woman dressed in the height of European fashion: tailored jacket and skirt; a cameo pendant at her throat, framed by a wide lace collar; a wide-brimmed hat worn at a smart angle; and high-heeled shoes. Sun Yatsen correspondingly wears a suit. They were similarly dressed for the photograph taken for their wedding anniversary in Guangzhou in 1919. In the early 1920s, when Sun was guiding a reformed and revitalised Nationalist Party to power, Song Qingling consistently wore the Chinese skirt and wide-sleeved jacket-blouse typical of the May Fourth era. In Beijing in 1925 she appeared in a simple, A-line *qipao* of dark cloth.[9] The garment had wide sleeves, just like the jacket-blouse, and fell to just above her ankles. The *qipao* was to be her standard form of dress until well after liberation.

---

7 The dates given by Zhang for earlier garments are also inexact. The high-collared narrow jacket and pants that appeared in Shanghai not earlier than 1905 is dated 1890-1910, and the short skirt and jacket-blouse of the May Fourth era appeared only late in the decade 1910-1920 to which she ascribes it. Chang, "A Chronicle of Changing Clothes," 430, 436.

8 Helen Foster Snow, *Women in Modern China* (The Hague: Mouton & Co., 1967), 119. Verity Wilson has suggested that it was not Song Qingling who popularised the *qipao*, but her younger sister, Meiling. Meiling was certainly emulated by fashionable society in the late twenties, but Qingling almost as certainly preceded her in adopting the *qipao*. Wilson suggests, moreover, that Qingling dressed very plainly, without an eye to fashion, but Qingling's photos show the opposite. If her *qipao* was simple, it was also the last word in elegance. Verity Wilson, "Dressing for Leadership in China: Wives and Husbands in an Age of Revolutions (1911-1976)," *Gender and History* 14, 3 (November 2002): 615.

9 As Ellen Johnston Laing points out, I was mistaken in an earlier publication to suggest that Song Qingling adopted the *qipao* after the May Thirtieth Movement. Laing, "Visual Evidence for the Evolution of "Politically Correct" Dress for Women": 99, n. 26.

Fig. 6.5 Song Qingling wearing skirt and jacket-blouse in Guangzhou in 1922, and *qipao* in Hankou, 1927.

Since Song Qingling, the first Chinese woman of any note to have been photographed wearing a *qipao*, wore the garment well before it was widely popularised, and was probably instrumental in establishing its popularity, it is worth dwelling on the sartorial choices she faced in the months of transition between one dress style and another. When she left Guangzhou on 13 November, she was wearing skirt and jacket-blouse. Between then and her arrival at Beijing on 31 December, she and Sun spent four days in Shanghai, nearly a week in Kobe, and more than three weeks in Tianjin. In Shanghai, where they stayed in Sun's house in Rue Molière, she may have been exposed, however briefly, to a much livelier fashion scene than in Guangzhou but that seems unlikely. Sun was fully occupied briefing journalists and meeting political figures in those few days,[10] and she was almost certainly by his side for the duration.

A photo of her by Sun's side on shipboard some days later shows her glamorously dressed in a fur coat and elegant hat. In retrospect, this photo—fittingly taken in the neutral space of international waters—can be seen to represent a

10 Luo Jialun, ed., *Guofu nianpu* (Yearly chronology of the Father of the Nation) (Taibei: Zhongguo guomindang zhongyang weiyuanhui dangshi weiyuanhui, 1985), Vol. II.

liminal moment in her sartorial history. Earlier photos of her in Chinese dress show her invariably wearing skirt and top, whilst in later photos, dating from around the time of Sun's death in Beijing, she is always in a *qipao* (Fig. 6.5). Given that her time in Shanghai was so short, it can surely only have been in Beijing or nearby Tianjin that she had time to have a tailor make up this new style of Chinese women's dress. In Beijing, she and Sun were accommodated in the home of Oei Hui-lan and Wellington Koo, a former Ming palace that Hui-lan's father had purchased when the couple settled in Bejing in 1923. Hui-lan and Wellington were not there at the time, but it is worth pondering whether Qingling had a glimpse of Hui-lan's wardrobe, bound to be in the latest fashion.

Beijing fashions circa 1925

Although Beijing is not commonly imagined as a site of changing fashions in the early twentieth century, Song Qingling's sartorial transformation in early 1925 raises questions about the vestimentary context in which this transformation was possible. A glimpse into daily life in the capital at this time is available through the picturesque record created by the Japanese ethnographer Aoki Masaru (1897–1964), who was studying in Beijing in 1925–6. Highly conscious of the loss of aspects of cultural heritage in Japan in recent times, Aoki was fascinated in Beijing by the spectacle of an old historical culture that he recognised was disappearing before his very eyes. Apparently inspired by Nakagawa Tadahide, who in an earlier era had compiled an illustrated compendium of Qing customs, Aoki set about creating a set of illustrations of Beijing customs at a time of transition. These were finally published in Japan in 1964.[11]

Among the one hundred drawings Aoki created, a number are devoted to displaying a range of individual clothing items that are identified by name on the drawing itself, much like a museum exhibit. A "women's long garment" (*nüchangshan*) is among the items displayed, but this seems simply to be a reference to the Manchu robe, elsewhere in the work frequently depicted on Manchu women.[12] The text makes no reference to the term *qipao*, and the clothing display is otherwise difficult to read in terms of the historical time it was produced. The array of men's hats, for example, includes no example of the felt hats or caps commonly worn in the Republican era.

11 Aoki Masaru, *Pekin fūzoku zufu*. For a Chinese translation of the work, see Aoki Masaru, *Beiping fengsu tu* (Illustrations of Beiping customs), trans. and ed. by Zhang Xunqi (Taipei: Changchunshu shufang, 1978). The work that inspired him, Nakagawa Tadahide, comp. *Shinzoku kibun* [1800] (Recorded accounts of Qing customs) (Tokyo: Heibonsha, 1966), is frequently used by historians of Qing China.

12 Aoki Masaru, *Pekin fūzoku zufu*, Fig. 4.5.

Fig. 6.6 What women in Beijing were wearing, as sketched by Aoki Masaru in the 1920s. The Manchu robe, and May Fourth style skirt and jacket-blouse were both in evidence.

The genre scenes depicted in the same collection tell a different story. Presented with a street scene, Aoki was alive to the infinite variety of dress being worn in Beijing at this time. Felt hats and caps were worn by some men, or straw boaters in the hot summer months, when umbrellas were also much in evidence. So-called "melon-skin" caps with buttons on top abounded in winter, along with fur-lined hats with side-flaps of a style still to be seen in north China in the winter. Haircuts were evident, and even completely shaven heads, but the queue was still worn by many men. Long robes and riding jackets predominated among men's clothing, the poorer wearing simply trousers and jacket.

In depicting women, Aoki consistently drew attention to the difference between Manchu and Han, the former in robes with platform shoes and the handlebar hairdress or hairdo, or in the case of young unmarried women a long braid. Other sources show that Manchu women were abandoning their distinctive dress around this time: "the greater number of banner garments were changed into Han clothing, palace robes were cut down into short jackets and skirts."[13] Such a transformation would be difficult to depict visually, since a Manchu woman dressed in Han clothing looked like a Han woman.

Han dress is shown in greater variety. Seen next to a pair of diminutive Manchu figures, two young Chinese women presented to Aoki's eye above all a typically Han mode of dressing, but it was also a very modern way of dressing: skirts shortened to calf-length, modestly worn with loose pantelettes; an abbreviated jacket-top; large shoes; one girl with bangs, the other with a smart little hat and an abbreviated "clock" mantle (*yikouzhong*) (Fig. 6.6).[14] By contrast, elegantly dressed women

---

13 Li Jiarui, *Beiping fengsu leizheng* (Inventory of Beiping customs) (Shanghai: Shangwu yinshu guan, 1936), Vol. 1, 242.

14 The text does not touch on the fashionableness of any part of these ensembles except for the fringe (bangs). For a photo of the Empress Dowager wearing a clock mantle—pleated at the top into a neckband— see Valery M. Garrett, *Chinese Clothing: An Illustrated Guide* (Hong Kong: Oxford University Press, 1994), 58, Fig. 4.19. A quilted version featuring medallion-style inscriptions of the word *shou* (long life) is published in Chen Juanjuan, "Zhixiu wenwu

depicted wearing formal pleated skirts with long Chinese jackets, out shopping in a New Year print stall, encapsulated the conservatism of the ladies of wealthy, high-born families of Beijing. The latter feature of Beijing society was noted by Oei Hui-lan when she described a diplomatic function in 1923. The American wives, she wrote, were "friendly, very much at ease, and dressed appropriately in light summer frocks." The "reserved Chinese ladies" were clad in a style of formal dress not too different from that stipulated in the regulations of 1912—"a pleated scarlet silk skirt topped by a black jacket embroidered with a series of circles whose number increased according to the husband's rank."[15]

At the other end of the social spectrum, working women and servant girls in Beijing dressed simply in pants and top, older women wearing their trousers bound at the ankle in a practice typical of northern dress. Judging by Aoki's depiction, Beijing prostitutes at this time also wore pants and top, cut short in the leg and sleeve in the fashionable style recognisable from the advertisement above (Fig. 6.1). This ensemble may have been cutting-edge fashion in Beijing, for Aoki elsewhere provided a glimpse of it through a doorway, being worn by an apparently more respectable young girl. Yunying, sister of former emperor Puyi, was photographed in just such clothes around this time.[16] But it was difficult for girls from "good families" to wear such advanced clothes in public, as young Zhou Zhongzheng found in Tianjin.

Although Aoki was able to depict novel elements in Chinese dress in the mid-twenties, the outsider's overwhelming impression of the Beijing crowd was that it was thoroughly Chinese, which to outsiders also meant "traditional." C.P. FitzGerald first visited Beijing in 1924, and having spent time in both Shanghai and Tianjin was struck by just this aspect of clothing in the capital. "At least 99 per cent of the population was dressed in traditional Chinese costume," he wrote. But like Aoki's illustrations, his description of what people wore is as important for the detail as for the generality. While men wore the long gown, "women did not wear this costume at that time: they still wore the wide trousers and rather long jacket. The use of *chang sheng* [sic], the long male gown, adapted with a higher slit above the knee, was just beginning to be the new fashion, a mark of emancipation, among the upper-class Chinese women ..." [17]

---

zhong de shouzi zhuangshi" (The word "longevity" as an adornment on embroidered items), *Gugong bowuyuan kan* (Palace Museum Journal): 16, Fig. 30.

15 Hui-lan Koo [Madame Wellington Koo], *An Autobiography as told to Mary Van Rensselaer Thayer* (New York: Dial Press, 1943), 175.

16 Liu Beisi and Xu Qixian, comps, *Gugong zhencang renwu zhaopian huicui* (Given English title: Exquisite Figure Pictures from the Palace Museum) (Beijing: Zijincheng chubanshe, 1994), 93, Fig. 16.

17 C.P. FitzGerald, *Why China? Recollections of China 1923-1950* (Melbourne: Melbourne University Press, 1985), 30.

Two points in this description deserve particular attention. One is that the *qipao* was already evident among Chinese women of a certain class. The other is that FitzGerald understood the garment in terms not of Manchu origins, but rather of male origins. From these points it can be concluded also that the garment he was describing was distinguishable from the robes worn by Manchu women, which continued to be in evidence on the streets of Beijing at least to the late thirties.[18]

Zhao Jiasheng, an instructor at the Beijing Industrial School, confirmed these points in a guide to best practice in garment cutting, written in April 1924.[19] He based his instructions on the centre-pieces of the Chinese wardrobe so obvious in Aoki's illustrations: the long robe and the short jacket. "The long garment with the large lapel (*dajin changyi*) is the commonly worn men's dress," he wrote, "while the short garment with the large lapel (*dajin xiaoyi*) is the commonly worn women's dress." The "short garment" to which he refers was the *ao* or jacket, worn over trousers and/or skirt. But Zhao went on to note: "recently many women have been wearing the long garment (some people call it a '*qipao*' because Manchu women always dressed up in a long robe (*changpao*)) ... , " and in the very next paragraph he makes reference to the short-sleeved *qipao* (*duanxiu qipao*, i.e. sleeves abbreviated to above the wrist), showing that some modifications of the men's robe for women had already taken place.[20] Like FitzGerald, then, Zhao distinguished between the long garment worn by fashionable or emancipated women, and that worn by conservative Manchus.

In fact, Manchu women had also been experimenting with fashion. Like the Han jacket, the robe had acquired a high collar in the last years of the Qing. The cut had altered, so that the robe no longer hung loosely, and the hemline had ascended. Ornamentation had changed with the times. Photographs of the Manchu nobility in the early Republican era show young women stylishly dressed in modes not dissimilar to the retro *qipao* of a decade later.[21] It can be concluded that the latter took some of its inspiration from the modified dress of Manchu women. Again, a convergence of styles leading to the Nationalist-era fashions must be posited.

Among the cultural circumstances favouring the rise of the *qipao*, the significance of its associations with the imperial past and especially with Beijing,

---

18 Enid Saunders Candlin, *The Breach in the Wall: A Memoir of Old China* (New York: Paragon House Publishers, 1987), 190.

19 Zhao Jiasheng, "Yifu caifa ji cailiao jisuan fa" (Cutting garments and calculating the amount of material), *Funü zazhi* (1 September 1925): 1450-63. The April 1924 date is given at the beginning of the article proper, 1450, after a short introductory paragraph obviously written for the journal itself.

20 Ibid., 1454.

21 Liu Beisi and Xu Qixian, *Gugong zhencang renwu zhaopian huicui*.

Fig. 6.7 Lin Huiyin (1904–1955), budding writer, with Rabindranath Tagore and her fiancé, Liang Sicheng (1901–1972), in Beijing in 1924. A stylish young woman who had lived for some time in London, Huiyin would have been alert to fashionable trends and likely to have been wearing a *qipao* if it had been a well-established garment at that time.

the dysfunctional but magnificent capital, cannot be overlooked. "Peking, glorious Peking," wrote Enid Candlin (though it was only "Beiping" by the time she saw it)—"… so lovely that in spite of centuries of inept government it possessed a superb self-confidence."[22] Oei Hui-lan found it captivating, comparable only to Paris in beauty. In the setting of this ancient city, Song Qingling may have felt that her customary skirt and top were rather provincial, like her southern accent, or suitable mainly for young and unmarried women. Twenty-year-old Lin Huiyin, the future daughter-in-law of Liang Qichao, wore the Chinese-style skirt and top with sleeveless vest when she was photographed in Beijing with Rabindranath Tagore in 1924 (Fig. 6.7), and skirt and top again when she visited the Great Wall later that year. The Soviet political adviser Vishnyakova-Akimova passed through Beijing in 1925, on her way to Canton, and saw "girl students in the traditional short student haircuts and uniform—a black skirt and bright jacket with a high collar—[exchanging] smiles with youths in long robes."[23] Song Qingling, so recently dressed in clothes just like this, seems never to have worn them again.

The fashionable qipao

The *qipao* made an appearance among Shanghai fashion designs in the mid-twenties, when it was included in fashion features in *National News Weekly* in 1924, in *Shenbao* in 1925, in *Young Companion*, launched in 1926, and then in a plethora of other magazines that appeared in the late twenties and thirties. In the mid-twenties it was just one among many possible fashion ensembles and its long-term success was by no means assured. Other fashion items in the summer of 1925 were the scoop-hemmed "wrapper blouse" (*taoshan*), which buttoned up on both sides from underarm to throat and showed off "the beauty of the

---

22 Candlin, *The Breach in the Wall*, 171-2.

23 Vera Vladimirovna Vishnyakova-Akimova, *Two Years in Revolutionary China, 1925-1927*, trans. Steven I. Levine (Harvard: Harvard East Asian Monographs, 1971), 60.

curves of bosom and waist;" a see-through blouse made of transparent gauze with a trim of decorative glass that caught the light; a "cool and breezy blouse" again of transparent summer-weight cloth but this time worn under a vest, and matched with loose pants; a "vest-with-blouse" (*lianbeishan*)—a long sleeveless garment worn over a blouse with floating sleeves, described as "substantially similar to the *qishan*" i.e. to the *qipao*; and a "one hundred pleats skirt" which successfully "blended Chinese and Western fashion"[24] (Fig. 6.8). In the later twenties, the *qipao* gradually came to dominate fashion features, but it coexisted with the skirt and jacket-blouse until around 1930. Like the May Fourth style, it commenced as a fashion for the young, before becoming established as general wear.

◀衫褙聯▶   ◀裝褶百▶

Fig. 6.8 Fashion designs in *National News Weekly* were quite typical of the period. "Vest-with-blouse" (left) and "one hundred pleats skirt" were among the summer fashions of 1925.

Photographs and other visual images, including advertisements, show women in one or the other form of dress, sometimes featuring both styles simultaneously (Fig. 6.9), until the end of the decade.

It seems likely that the *qipao* in its essentially *changpao* or male form proved widely acceptable as winter dress in the first instance, as it could be easily padded—unlike the skirt—and worn to the ankles over long undergarments. Such was certainly the opinion of one Shanghai fashion commentator, who wrote in 1924: "After the Republic [was established], Han women suddenly went in for the *qipao*, to keep their legs warm. [The fashion] began among the sing-song households of the alleyways and gradually spread among high born ladies of the great families. In winter everyone wears the *qipao*."[25] Photographed on a winter's day in 1928, the many members of the Yongjia (Wenzhou) Natural Feet and

---

24 *GWZB* 2, 22 (14 June 1925): 52; 2, 24 (28 June 1925): 37; 2, 25 (5 July 1925): 32, 33; 2, 28 (26 August 1925): 34.

25 *GWZB* 1, 14 (2 November 1924): 32.

庭　家　之　虎　楊

Fig. 6.9 A well turned out family in 1928. The paterfamilias, Yang Hu (b. 1889), was Shanghai military commander in the period immediately following the Nationalist Revolution. His wife is wearing the wide-sleeved jacket-blouse and skirt that dominated fashions in the twenties. Her hat marks her as a member of very modish circles: hats were rarely worn by women in China. Her feet have the bunched-up look which must have been common to women of her age—born in the 1890s, subjected to footbinding in early childhood, then unbinding her feet around 1911, if not before. The two girls are both wearing the wide-sleeved *qipao* of the Nationalist Revolution period. The elder daughter's very short haircut was the height of fashion. Her elegant dress belies its boyishness but would have been regarded as less obviously feminine than her mother's ensemble.

Natural Breasts Society—more likely to be "ladies" than sing-song girls—were all wearing *qipao / changpao* (see below, Fig. 6.22). 1928 is a relatively early year for the *qipao* to have achieved absolute dominance. It is possible that what we are seeing in this photo is a winter "overcoat", and that when spring came, skirts and jacket-blouses were still to be seen.

Although the photographic record makes it clear that the *qipao*'s hegemony was not fully established till the 1930s, contemporary observers were startled by its rapid popularisation. In an article about Shanghai fashion in 1926, Cheng Fangwu (1897–1984) commented that even in Hunan (his native province), "slender young women were sweeping up and down the streets" wearing *qipao*s, a style that had spread "more quickly than any intellectual trend." Nor was the generic garment all that was involved. Over the past year, the "first revolution" in the *qipao* could be observed when a sleeveless style became popular.[26] Cheng must have been referring here to the long vest (*chang majia*), a sleeveless garment worn over a blouse and no doubt easily confused with the *qipao* in the eyes of the

---

26 Cheng Fangwu, "Jiaoyan yudi de weijing" (The beguilingly lovely scarf), *Hongshui* 2, 1 (December 1926), reprinted in Shi Ying, ed., *Minguo shishang* (Fashions of the Republic)? (Beijing: Tuanjie chubanshe, 2004), 88. Cheng Fangwu, responsible for the first translation of the Communist Party Manifesto into Chinese, was a founder of the Creation Society, which produced the periodical *Hongshui* among other publications.

Fig. 6.10 Different styles of *qipao* in Shanghai in the early thirties as modelled by Gong Xiufang (left), a student at Fudan University, and Miss Ji Jingyi, a young "lady" of Shanghai.

uninitiated. But whatever the distinguishing details of the garments he observed, there is no mistaking the impression made on him of a sweeping change in women's fashions at this time.

Beijing style, Shanghai style

In a recent work on the *qipao*, Beijing and Shanghai styles of *qipao* are distinguished from each other, along the well-established lines of division between "capital" and "coastal" cliques (*jingpai*, *haipai*) pertaining in the literary world. In Beijing, according to this analysis, the *qipao* was loose and angular, the garment framing the body; in Shang-

hai, the reverse was the case.[27] Comparing pictorial magazines from Beijing and Shanghai in the early Nationalist period, it is hard to see any steady difference between the styles along regional lines. The square-cut *qipao* was worn in both cities in the late twenties, when it was just beginning to give way to a closer-fitting garment, evident again in both cities.[28] The differentiation applies to time rather than to place, and to some degree also to different social categories and roles (Fig. 6.10).

The relationship between Beijing and Shanghai fashions was confusingly commented on by Oei Hui-lan, who wrote two different autobiographies more than thirty years apart. In her later years she expressed contempt for the fashion scene in Shanghai as she had known it. "The so-called chic Chinese women often wore smartly cut jackets and trousers," she wrote, but she found their tastes vulgar and their pretensions to patriotic wear laughable. Their Chinese-style garments were cut from imported fabrics, and they "wore their hair in the Western fashion,

---

27 Bao Mingxin and Ma Li, eds, *Zhongguo qipao*, 71. I am grateful to Ye Xiaoqing for providing me with a copy of this book.

28 The conclusion is based on a comparison of the 1929-1931 editions of the *Beijing Pictorial*, and Shanghai's *Modern Miscellany* (*SDHB*).

Fig. 6.11 Influencing Chinese fashions? A formal portrait of Oei Hui-lan (Madame Wellington Koo) appears to have influenced the Zhiying Studio advertisement for Scott's Emulsion (cod liver oil). The advertisement duplicates not only the pose of the figure in the photo, but the trim of the *qipao*, the folds of the material at the waist and knee, and the design of the sandals.

going to the French beauty shops."[29] She herself insisted on using local materials, a practice upsetting to "the Shanghai fashion plates, who thought anything foreign desirable and considered imported materials the ultimate chic."[30]

In her 1940s autobiography, however, she recalled being "impressed by the chic of Shanghai's modern young women." They had abandoned "the cumbersome pleated skirt and bulky jacket" in favour of "long, slim gowns, becomingly moulded to the figure," i.e. the *qipao*. To this "revolution" she attributed her own abandonment of European clothes, although she also claimed responsibility for fashionable developments in the *qipao* (Fig. 6.11). "I started a Chinese wardrobe," she states, "and in the process accidentally made several adaptations which, because they were widely copied, set me up as a fashion leader." Among the innovations she claimed were slitting the gown to the knee, wearing lace pantalettes "which were decorative yet concealing," and adding decorative trimming to the side slits and the opening of the gown between collar and underarm.[31]

---

29 Koo, *No Feast Lasts Forever*, 182.

30 Koo, *An Autobiography*, 255-6.

31 Ibid.

代意・人夫張・人夫顧・軍將易考可麥表代美之上會茶
○攝生同平北○　　　　　　　　　爵伯提葛表

Fig. 6.12 Yu Fengzhi (left) and Oei Hui-lan at a diplomatic function in 1932, with representatives from the USA (right) and Italy.

Hui-lan clearly thought that she brought a certain tone to Shanghai from Beijing. She was occasionally joined there by the much-photographed Yu Fengzhi (Madam Zhang Xueliang) (1897–1990), whom she claims to have initiated into the world of fashion (Fig. 6.12), as well as by the daughters of Tang Shaoyi (1859–1938), the sisters of Wellington Koo's deceased wife. She found the Tang women sophisticated and stylish, unlike the rest of the Shanghai smart set. "We used to have fun," she wrote, "setting styles in clothes and watching the Chinese women copy us."[32] Hui-lan's accounts are self-serving, but she was probably correct to intimate that highly-placed women, many resident in Beijing while it was the capital, were influential in establishing fashion trends. In the autumn of 1928 it was reported that sun umbrellas had become a fashionable item because Song Meiling (1897–2003), wife of Chiang Kaishek, always carried one, "whatever the time or place."[33]

Counterparts to the high-born woman from Beijing, and of course Nanjing (capital from 1928), were the social butterfly, the "modern girl," the sing-song girl, and the actress from Shanghai. "Women's fashions in China are mostly created in Shanghai," wrote a Tianjin reporter in 1931, "and women's fashions in general are given reign by singsong girls (i.e. prostitutes, *jinü*) who like to flaunt themselves."[34] The reporter was probably behind the times. Actresses, surely,

---

32 Koo, *No Feast Lasts Forever*, 182.

33 *BYHB* 1 September 1928.

34 *DGB* 22 March 1931, reprinted in Shi Ying, ed., *Minguo shishang*, 77.

Fig. 6.13 The collar as a work of art, here displayed on the throat of actress Huang Naishuang, a leading actress with The Star Company.

had overtaken prostitutes as fashion icons. Starring in stories about contemporary Chinese life, wearing contemporary Shanghai fashions, they wielded much greater cultural influence than any of their contemporaries. They produced the glamour effect that distinguished the name

Fig. 6.14 *Qipao* designs featured at a Wing On department store fashion show, 19–25 May, 1936. The garment on the left has unusual, decorative sleeves, barely covering the shoulder. The bold trim of the garment on the right adds emphasis to the high collar.

"Shanghai" from the names of other cities in China. While Beijing/Beiping could always lay claim to a certain cultural prestige, Shanghai had panache; and although the Shanghai press occasionally manifested an interest in girls from Beijing, it is obvious that these girls were dressed in styles not noticeably different from those flourishing in Shanghai itself.

Between its introduction as a fashion item in Shanghai in 1925 through to its period of clear ascendancy in the 1930s, the *qipao* underwent a series of transformations that saw the hems of both the skirt and the sleeves go up and down while the side seams steadily approached the actual line of the body. It gradually lost what Zhang Ailing criticised as its "angular and puritanical" cut, evolving into a garment cut somewhat closer to the figure than was acceptable to everyone. Decorative trim, as Oei Hui-lan's narrative suggests, was a point of great interest in the design of the *qipao*: lace edging or piping supplied fashion

Fig. 6.15 Fashion sketch of a "qishan" (banner shirt), showing side splits, which were not then a feature of the *qipao*.

on the peripheries of the garment. The collar, gradually ascending up the throat, became a work of art (Fig. 6.13). Spring fashions typically showed new features that added modishness to the garment without disrupting the main form. Frills and ribbons were added for playful effect (Fig. 6.14).

A distinguishing feature in the *qipao*'s evolution, and one that it retained in the essentialised, traditionalised form now evident, was the long side-splits in the skirt of the garment. These varied in length but sometimes extended well up the thigh of the wearer, exciting great controversy. A fashion sketch from May 1925 foreshadows this feature (Fig. 6.15). The garment depicted is described as modelled on the *qipao* but showing new features, most notably the side-splits. The commentary notes: "The *qipao* is not cut to form splits (*bu kai cha*) but in this garment, the splits are very long."[35] As can be seen from the sketch, loose trousers were worn beneath the garment. These were not necessary for the *qipao* in the twenties, which continued to be sewn up at the sides even as it grew rather narrower, as shown in the photo of actress Yang Juqiu (Fig. 6.16). It is plain from the way that Yang is sitting that without splits, the narrow *qipao* was very like a hobble skirt in the difficulties it created for physical movement.

In a curious twist, a short version of the *qipao* became quite popular in the late twenties and early thirties, and legs were fully exposed from the knee down. It was after hems had dropped again and side splits became standard that the exposure of legs became really controversial. In other words, clothes created a perception of exposure much more powerful than was achieved by actual nakedness. Under

Fig. 6.16 Actress Yang Juqiu in a sheath *qipao* without splits, 1929. The garment must have been akin to the hobble skirt in terms of difficulties posed for walking.

---

35 *GWZB* 2, 20 (31 May 1925): 38.

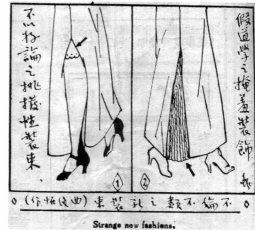

Fig. 6.17 Lu Mei, wife of prominent society figure Xu Ziquan, pictured wearing a *qipao* with pleated insert or underskirt. The same fashion had been mocked in a cartoon on the "muddle of new fashions" earlier in the year.

these circumstances, it was impossible to wear the long *qipao* without having to think carefully about how to manage one's legs (Fig. 6.17).

Breasts and arms were among other points of controversy. When Lu Lihua introduced shorts and tops for physical education in the Liangjiang Physical Education School, she was widely criticised for encouraging display of arms and the bosom as well as legs.[36] At this time, footbinding was still being combated, but feet that were being exposed through fashionable sandal-style shoes were soon to come under censure. Hair—short or long—was also at issue, and permed hair continued to be controversial well into the 1930s. As Lu Xun (1881–1936) drily commented, "A woman has so many parts to her body that life is very hard indeed."[37]

The problem of the bob

The spread of the *qipao* was accompanied by the popularisation of short hair for women (Fig. 6.18). Very short hair appeared sporadically among radical women in the first two decades of the twentieth century before becoming generally established as the hairstyle of choice for young women in the course of the twenties, the same period in which it swept Europe. European fashions, or more precisely American movies, provided one of the contexts for the fashion. The other was

---

36 Wang Zheng, *Women in the Chinese Enlightenment*, 156.

37 Lu Xun, "Anxious Thoughts on 'Natural Breasts'" [1927], in Yang Xianyi and Gladys Yang, trans., *Lu Xun: Selected Works* (Beijing: Foreign Languages Press, 1985), Vol. 2, 355. On feet, see Pei-yen Hsiao, " Body Politics, Modernity, and National Salvation: The Modern Girl and the New Life Movement," *Asian Studies Review* 29 (June 2005): 165-86.

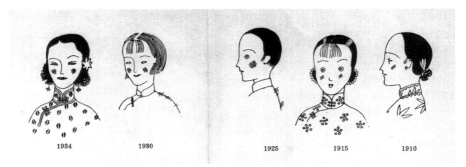

Fig. 6.18 Hairstyle timeline as depicted by Guo Jianying in 1935. The bare forehead of the young woman in the late Qing was replaced by various styles of fringe, the most popular being the "hanging silk" (*chuisi*) style depicted here for the years 1915 and 1930. Long hair worn in a single plait or various sorts of chignon gave way to short hair among very progressive young women in the late twenties, before becoming quite normal in the 1930s. In the 1940s, shoulder-length hair, à la Rita Hayworth, was the fashion.

Fig. 6.19 Studio photo of students with bobbed hair, Chongqing, August 1921.

provided by political struggles and military conflicts in which young women became involved. In 1919, the May Fourth demonstrations against the terms of the Treaty of Versailles brought girl students out onto the streets in force. Ding Ling (1904–1986), destined to join the ranks of famous May Fourth writers, cut her hair at this time, and others followed suit (Fig. 6.19). In Chengdu, girls in one school after another turned up to class with short hair, prompting the warlord regime of Liu Cunhou to issue a blanket prohibition of the practice. The radical *Semi-monthly* responded by denouncing the prohibition, and became the first paper to be shut down during the ferment of the May Fourth era.[38]

The male hairdo—typically a simple short cut or shaved head from the 1911 revolution onwards—was not the only sounding board for women's choices. In a popular novel serialised in the late twenties, author Wang Xiaoyi recorded a hair controversy that preceded arguments over the bob:

"Today the hairdresser is coming," said Madam Hong. "Ask her to try out a hairstyle for you—the S-do, or the abalone-do—and get her to make up the one you like. Don't do your hair in a plait any longer. Fastening the hair high and letting it dangle down looks like you've hung a fly-brush down your back." "I like wearing a plait," said Ding Huiyin, "and I don't like hairdos. Doing your hair up looks awful. If anyone wants to do my hair I'll just cut it all off at the neck. Then see who still wants to give me a hair-do."[39]

As Huiyin's mother indicates, a variety of hairdos were available for women. The two she mentions are among those described by Zeng Nifen (1852–1942), old styles which were revived after 1914: "the butterfly, then the chrysanthemum heart, the coiled queue, the abalone, the S, the horizontal S, and, most recently, the fan style."[40] The simple long plait, by contrast with these, spelt youth, an unmarried state, and probably student status.

War, both at home and abroad, determined that the national struggle of girls' hair would finally be about the bob, not the braid. In Europe, the Great War of 1914–1918 made very short hair the normal hairstyle for men, setting a fashion which quickly became standard worldwide, with very few exceptions. Women in the armed forces in Western countries did not emulate their male colleagues in this respect, and indeed had carefully differentiated uniforms. In China, however, there was little difference between male and female uniforms. After the May Thirtieth Movement in 1925, young women joined the Nationalist Revolution in force, and the woman-as-soldier, a much publicised figure in the 1911 Revolution, again became a common sight. At the age of twenty, Xie Bingying (1906–2000) was one of a number of young women to be accepted at the Central Political and Military School in Wuchang in 1926. Lined up for induction, the new recruits were advised: "All your hair should be cut short. If you can shave it all off, like the men, all the better."[41] One of her friends followed this latter course

---

38 Zhang Xiushu, "Wusi yundong zai Sichuan de huiyi" (A memoir of the May Fourth Movement in Sichuan), quoted in Wang Xing, *Bainan fushi chaolin yu shibian*, 44.

39 Wang Xiaoyi, *Chunshui weibo* (Ripples in spring waters) (Shenyang: Chunfeng wenyi chubanshe, 1997), 9. The story was first serialised in 1926 then published in book format in 1931.

40 Nie Zeng Jifen, *Testimony of a Confucian Woman: The Autobiography of Mrs Nie Zeng Jifen, 1852-1942*, trans. Thomas L. Kennedy (Athens: University of Georgia Press, 1993), 96.

41 Hsieh Ping-Ying, *Autobiography of a Chinese Girl*, trans. Tsui Chi (London: Pandora Press, 1986), 105, 132.

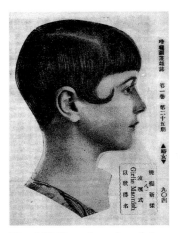

Fig. 6.20 One of a series of short hair styles advertised in *Linglong* magazine. This one is called the "wave" style, after the wave-shaped curl at the side.

and had a crewcut. Dressed in uniforms indistinguishable from that of the men, these women found it easy to slip from feminine to masculine personae. Bingying was consistently called "uncle" by one of her younger army friends.[42]

From around this time, hair-cutting was reported consistently in the press. In Tianjin it was proscribed in girls' schools, except for those in the foreign concession. Girls with short hair circumvented the ban by wearing a hat with two plaits attached, much as in the late Qing men without queues would wear a hat with a false hairpiece hanging down the back.[43] Global fashions converged with domestic political developments to create a favourable climate for the popularisation of short hair (Fig. 6.20). Photos of Colleen Moore and Billie Dove, stars of the silent screen, were used to illustrate foreign models for the fashionable bob in China.[44] Whether because of reaction to foreign influence or simply on account of its androgeny, bobbed hair excited some strong responses, including physical assaults on short-haired women.

In his influential novel *Family*, first published in 1933, Ba Jin narrated a heated conversation between a mother and daughter on the subject of a haircut, which culminated with the daughter in tears, declaring: "I want to be a human being, a human being like a man."[45] The readers of the novel would have had no trouble in recognising the dynamics of this argument, in which the bob becomes a symbol of liberation from the past and from the patriarchy. But in the thirties short hair per se in fact ceased to be a matter of controversy, while very long hair became completely outmoded. In 1935, a journalist for the *Central Daily* was surprised to discover that numbers of women in Shunde county, near Guangzhou, wore their hair in a single plait—a sign, it proved, of their membership of a sisterhood. In north China plaits were now to be seen only on young girls in backward or remote places. If "modern girls" (*modeng de xiaojie*) in the big cities wore plaits, it was sure to be in a novel style designed to proclaim their modishness (Fig. 6.21).[46]

42 Ibid., 136.

43 *BYHB* 13 October 1926.

44 *BYHB* 9 October 1926; 13 November 1926.

45 Pa Chin [Ba Jin], *Family*, trans. Sidney Shapiro (New York: Anchor Books, 1972), 191-203.

46 *Funü xinshenghuo yuekan* (December 1936): 49.

Bound breasts and brassieres

Another subject of furious debate in the early *qipao* era concerned breast-binding. Short hair and "natural breasts" were at this time closely associated with each other. Thus the Yongjia (Wenzhou) campaign for natural breasts, run under the auspices of the Yongjia Women's Association, was simultaneously a movement for short hair (Fig. 6.22). Short hair and natural breasts, together with natural feet, were systemically linked in the minds of activists: they all signified the liberation of women. They met, however, with different receptions in Chinese society. Natural feet were accepted rather quickly, despite some signs of backsliding in the 1920s; and short hair was soon normalised. Breasts were a different matter. They required a new sort of technology, as Western innovations of the early twentieth century showed; and as it proved, the rise of the *qipao* was unfavourable to this particular campaign.

The subject of breast-binding was extensively canvassed in the *Beiyang Pictorial* in 1927, following on a flurry of reports about bobbed hair in late 1926. The stimulus for the paper's interest was provided by developments in Guangdong, where a prohibition against breast-binding was issued in July 1927. Public statements on breast-binding in this context—a topic commonly discussed under the rubric of "the little vest"—were reported in the paper, together with opinion pieces on the importance of natural breasts.[47]

Fig. 6.21 An example of plaits worn in a modish way, 1930, by a girl in an expensive *qipao*.

Movements to cut hair, to prohibit dancing, and a revival in footbinding were being reported in the same months, while military affairs dominated the main news items: Nationalist forces had set off from Guangzhou in July 1926, taken Shanghai in April 1927, slaughtered their communist allies, and were on the way north. Why anyone should have been worried about breast-binding in this context would be a wonder except for the observable link between political instability and cultural preoccupation with the sexual order.

The point to which the *Beiyang Pictorial*'s coverage was heading was advocacy of the brassiere—that marvel of clothing technology invented a few years earlier by a Russian Jewish seamstress in New York. But in a carefully constructed education campaign, the paper commenced with a series of short illustrated articles

---

47 *BYHB* 4 May 1927; 13 July 1927; 20 August 1927.

Fig. 6.22 Members of the Yongjia Short Hair, Natural Breast and Natural Feet Society, Zhejiang, line up for a commemorative photograph, January 1928.

on the "little vest" (*xiaomajia*) or "little shirt" (*xiaoshan*) used by Chinese women as underclothing for the upper part of the body. The series' starting point was the *doudu*, a sort of apron for the upper body, which is frequently depicted on adults in erotic paintings of the late imperial period, and more generally on children (Fig. 6.23). In recent times it has been revived as a fashion garment and can be purchased at many a popular tourist destination in China.

Under the commodious jackets of the nineteenth century, the *doudu* had sufficed as an undergarment. Writing in the early 1940s, a Japanese ethnologist in Taiwan commented that in former times the *doudu* had been worn by everyone, old and young, male and female. The young wore red, the middle-aged wore white or grey-green, the elderly wore black. A little pocket sewn into the top was used by adults to secrete their money and by children their sweets. When a girl got engaged, she would show off her embroidery skills by sending an elaborately worked *doudu* to her fiancé, decorated with bats for good fortune and pomegranates, symbolising many sons. In Taiwan, this bridal offering had been replaced by the early forties: a tie, a fountain pen, or a scarf was given in its place.[48] The value attached to embroidery had no doubt declined, while the *doudu* itself had probably been replaced by a machine-made singlet.

On the mainland, too, the *doudu* had by this time become a thing of the past. Among women it was supplanted by new styles of "little vest," five of which are described in the *Beiyang Pictorial*.[49] All of these differed from the *doudu* in allow-

48 Ikeda Toshio, "Minsu zaji" (Various writings on popular customs), in Lin Chuanfu, ed., *Minsu Taiwan* (Taiwan popular customs) (Taipei: Wuling chuban youxian gongsi, 1994), Vol. 2: 95-108.
49 *BYHB* 8 June 1927; 15 June 1927; 19 June 1927.

Fig. 6.23 The *doudu* or breast-cloth, past and present. It is rare to see a small child clad in a *doudu* now, but woodblock prints of the late imperial period frequently show babies or small children dressed like this little boy. The *doudu* was also often depicted in erotic art, of which the Qing dynasty print (detail) on the right is an example. The print shows a courtesan in a state of semi-undress being pursued by an aroused client. She is wearing no trousers, but retains her *doudu* under her open jacket.

ing tight buttoning across the chest. It is possible that an undergarment of this sort had long co-existed with the *doudu*, for a strapless little vest is depicted on women in book illustrations of the late Ming. Of the styles shown in the *Beiyang Pictorial*, the earliest was still widespread in the north China in the late twenties and was categorised together with the *doudu* as "old style." The most recent was a simple side-buttoned top with shoulder straps, popular in the summer because it was light, and mainly worn by fashionable women. The Western chemise supplied the model for this style (Fig. 6.24).

The little vest was designed to constrain the breasts and streamline the body. Such a garment was necessary to look *comme il faut* around 1908, when (as J. Dyer Ball observed): "fashion decreed that jackets should fit tight, though not yielding to the contours of the figure, except in the slightest degree, as such an exposure of the body would be considered immodest."[50] It became necessary again in the mid-twenties, when the jacket-blouse—a garment cut on rounded lines—began to give way to the *qipao*. At this stage, darts were not used to tailor the bodice or upper part of the *qipao*, nor would they be till the mid-fifties. The most that could be done by way of further fitting the *qipao* to the bosom was to stretch the material at the right places through ironing. Under these circumstances, breast-binding must have made the tailor's task easier.

Curiously, the first form of brassiere in the West, developed by Mary Phelps Jacobs in 1914, served precisely the same function as the little vest in China: it

---

50 Dyer Ball, *The Chinese at Home*, 236.

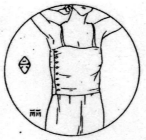

Fig. 6.24 Two of the "little vests" described in the *Beiyang Pictorial*: left, an old style, still widespread in North China in 1927; and the most recent, styled after the Western chemise.

was designed to flatten the breasts, and was marketed under the name "Boyish Form." Ida Rosenthal famously took exception to this denial of a woman's natural physique, and designed a bra with two pockets or cups, that would emphasise rather than reduce the profile of the bust. In 1927, readers of the *Beiyang Pictorial* were exposed to the Rosenthal bra through a series of sketches and photos before being treated to a detailed explanation of how it worked. A technically precise drawing of a bra was supplied (Fig. 6.25), with instructions as to the function of its separate parts: "in the drawing, fingers point to two pouches wherein the breasts are secreted, so that the breasts are supported and constrained without being squashed. In the centre of the garment is a tie that can be used to tighten or loosen [the fit], while at the top, two straps allow suspension over the shoulders. At the back are buttons for fastening."[51]

The bra was one of a number of new items of underwear that not so much transformed the lingerie scene in China as created it. It was "only five years ago," according to a report in 1935, "that distinctive women's undergarments in China were limited to grannies' vests (poor breasts, complaining for who knows how many thousands of years?), undershirts and underpants."[52] Drawers, bloomers, combination petticoats, chemises, slips, and corsets were all available in modern department stores by the early 1930s. But the ways in which these garments were deployed in China were not predictable from the Western experience. The bra rapidly became a sine qua non of the Western woman's wardrobe: the same was not true in China. "Why aren't you wearing a vest?" asks older sister in a 1937 advertisement (Fig. 6.26). Younger sister thinks vests are old-fashioned, and bad for the health, but she is not about to put on a bra. She prefers to wear "a cotton sweatshirt (*hanshan*), the latest product from the Zhenfeng Cotton Knit Factory." Older sister thinks she might buy one the next day, and see how it feels.[53]

---

51 *BYHB* 19 October 1927.

52 Zhang Lilan, "Liuxingjie de beixiju," (Tragedies and comedies in the world of fashion), *Furen huabao* 25 (1935): 9.

53 *Jilian huikan* 168 (1 June 1937): 36.

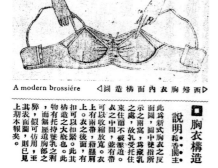

A modern brossiére   ◁ 圖造構面內衣胸婦西▷

□ 胸衣構造

說明 稚香閣主

Fig. 6.25 Meet the bra: an iconic piece of women's underwear makes an appearance in China. The text explains the structure and function of its component parts.

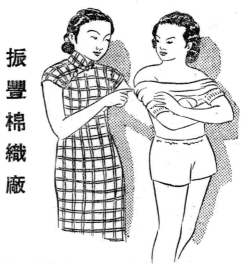

振豐棉織廠

Health was the major issue raised in connection with opposition to breast-binding. In 1926, *Vogue* fashion magazine urged young women who in summer wore Western-style garments not to skimp on their underwear: petticoats, step-ins, chemises, were all appropriate foundation garments. The combination illustrated here (Fig. 6.27) had the advantage of "not binding the breasts," and so being "particularly compatible with [the wearer's] health."[54] The dangers posed to health by breast-binding were set forth eloquently by a medical student who, at a much later date, wrote to the magazine *Life* (*Shenghuo*), lamenting that "the new women of today seek novelty in everything, but maintain old practices when it comes to breastbinding." It is a practice, he averred, that prevents proper development of the breasts, inhibits mammary secretions and was obviously responsible for the breast complaints which brought one in four of the female patients to the clinic operated by the head of his medical school. Lack of scientific knowledge was not limited to women. "Some husbands," he pointed out, "are lacking in common medical knowledge [and] they thoughtlessly rub and mishandle their wives' breasts, causing considerable discomfort and frequently resulting in the formation of lumps which develop into abscesses."[55]

Fig. 6.26 Advertisement for spencer or singlet in place of the Chinese-style "little vest" (*xiao majia*). The breast-flattening "vest" was evidently still worn by many. The *qipao* shown here, with its short, short sleeves, is typical of this period. Cf. the Wing On models above, Fig. 6.14.

The argument that breast-binding was injurious to a woman's children was also advanced, echoing debates over footbinding that related natural feet to maternal health. An admonitory essay in *The Women's Monthly* scolded young women for

---

54 *Vogue* (Shanghai) 1926: 45.

55 *Shenghuo* (1937): 397.

binding their breasts in the interests of fashion and at the expense of their ability to breast-feed their children. The writer gave the unhappy example of her friend whose had bound her breasts so tightly that her nipples had fully inverted: "although she called her husband and slightly older children to help pull them out," she was finally unable to feed her baby, and since the family was too poor to afford a wet-nurse, the child ailed.[56]

These various materials, all from 1930s journals, suggest that ten years or more after the beginning of a campaign against it, breast-binding was still widely practised. In the 1937 Zhenfeng advertisement discussed above, the older sister may be presented as less enlightened than the

Fig. 6.27 Underwear suitable for modern Westernised clothing such as worn in 1926. After *Vogue* (1926): 45.

younger, but she is wearing a modern, close-fitting *qipao*, apparently with a "little vest" flattening her breasts underneath. This is consistent with the photographs of the period. Advertisements of the *qipao* era frequently show women with swelling bosoms, curving hips and exposed legs. In life, the opposite seems to be the case. A comparison of the photo of Oei Hui-lan with an advertisement modelled on the photo is instructive (Fig. 6.11). In the photo, the bust line is only just apparent. In the advertisement, which is otherwise an exact copy of the photo as far as the clothes are concerned, the bodice of the *qipao* has been filled out.

Girl students should logically have had progressive "natural breasts," but they seemed particularly keen to hide the fact that they had any at all (Fig. 6.28). In a society where poor women commonly exposed their breasts in public while breast-feeding,[57] breasts were no doubt considered rather infra-dig by young

---

56 Yan Fu, "Gan sujiechu xiaomajia!" (Hurry up and undo the little vest!"), *Nüzi yuekan* 1,1 (8 March 1933): 36-7.

57 In the 1930s, Hedda Morrison took numerous photos of poor women breast-feeding in the open. See The Hedda Morrison Photographs of China, 1933-1946, Harvard College Library, at hcl.harvard.edu/libraries/harvard-yenching/collections/morrison/. Accessed 21 November 2006.

Fig. 6.28 Miss Jiang Peiying in 1932. She is wearing typical student dress and shows no evidence of the influence of the "natural breast" movement.

women; jokes, looks, and comments about women sporting natural breasts must have been a strong disincentive for them to abandon the concealing little vest.

Modern girls and vestimentary sanctions

To cartoonist Jiang Hancheng, and no doubt to many of his contemporaries, bobbed hair and natural breasts together spelt "flapper" or "modern girl" (Fig. 6.29), a phenomenon who appeared on the Chinese social horizon just as the National Revolution was coming to fruition. The term "modern girl"—a Japanese-cum-English term embedded in a Chinese text—was first used in China in 1927.[58] A counterpart to the Japanese *moga*, the Chinese modern girl was early defined in the English-language press of Shanghai as someone with a bob, make-up, and a short skirt. She was depicted in just such terms by novelists.[59]

The general view of the modern girl was summed up by one writer in a passing reference to the "*modeng gouer*," or "modern doggy." The writer disingenuously glossed the term in parentheses: "N.B., this is just a translation of the sound, and does not mean that they are all dogs."[60] Given the infamous equation between "Chinese and dogs" made in the context of who was not to be admitted to the Public Garden in China, it is extremely unlikely that this transliteration could have been read as other than derogatory. A critic of Western clothing styles frankly admitted the difficulty of using the term "modern" in association with women when she wrote: "The majority of China's fashionable (I do not like to use the term "modern") women desire westernised clothing, high heels and short skirts, imitating Western women in every aspect ..."[61]

---

58 Shu-mei Shih, *The Lure of the Modern: Writing Modernism in Semicolonial China, 1917–1937*, 92.

59 Ibid., 294-5. On the modern girl, see Kendall H. Brown, "Flowers of Taishō: Images of Women in Japanese Society and Art," in Lorna Price and Laetitia O'Connor, eds, *Taishō Chic: Japanese Modernity, Nostalgia and Deco* (Honolulu: Honolulu Academy of Arts, 2001), 19-21.

60 Bing Ying, "Dongluan zhong de Minxi" (Western Fujian in turmoil), *SDHB* 5, 2 (16 November 1933).

61 Hua Sheng, "Cong Deguo de weisheng fuzhuang yundong tan dao Zhongguo shimao funü de yanghua" (Comments on the Westernisation of fashionable women in China from

天乳美
蔣漢澄作

"Chinese flapper"

Fig. 6.29 "The beauty of natural breasts," or "Chinese flapper," showing evidence of a bosom, and sporting a bob.

The modern girl embodied the un-Chinese values that governments, both central and provincial, sought to eradicate from the cultural landscape in the 1930s. Her high heels, hemlines, permed hair, and the very stuff of which her clothes were made, all invited public criticism. The man in the street evidently had much to put up with from her provocative clothing, especially in summer when fabrics were thin and clothes correspondingly revealing (Fig. 6.30). In a letter to a Shanghai magazine, one scandalised fellow appealed to the government to heed the example set by Mussolini and introduce regulations to control what women wore.[62] In Beijing, Shanghai fashions of that summer were reported as "*luohua*" or tending toward nakedness. Women were wearing *qipao*s of thin gauze, without collars or sleeves, shoulders barely covered. The flesh of protruding breasts was shockingly obvious, "the pink nipples" even more so, and "below, a pair of snow white legs, and naked feet mounted on high heeled leather shoes …" When the wind blew, all was revealed. "What difference was there," the columnist queried, "between this semi-naked fashion and complete nakedness?"[63]

But the fully covered woman could attract as much criticism as the barely covered one. Very long *qipao*s, very high heels, brightly or richly patterned materials, all exposed the wearer to reproof.[64] It was not all women who dressed thus, pointed out one critic: "some women dress quite appropriately, and poor women can dress only in rags, with no colour at all." The culprits belonged to another social class: they were women "who had both money and leisure."[65] What was worse, these sorts of women looked modern but were backward in their thinking. Such views were shared by the dress reformers of the Nanjing Decade, who

---

the perspective of the healthy dress movement in Germany), *Linglong* 221 (1936): 167-9.

62 *Shenghuo* 42 (1930): 672.

63 "Shanghai funü luohua zhi xinzhuang" (Nakedness in Shanghai women's new fashions), *Beijing huabao* 4 September 1930.

64 Ke Shi, "Guanyu funü de zhuangsu" (On women's dress), *Dongfang zazhi* 31, 19 (1 October 1934): 205.

65 Ibid.

were bent on de-sexualising the look of the *qipao*-clad woman.

Governmental interventions in women's dress and adornment in the early years of the Nationalist era were broadly consistent with the progressive social agenda of the May Fourth era. In 1928, the year the new government took office in Nanjing, the Internal Affairs Bureau issued a detailed prohibition of footbinding, and set a scale of fines for households that did not comply.[66] In the same year, it decided to ban earrings, "an evil custom in China for several thousand years." It was "inhumane" and "a waste of money."[67] The issue here was overtly ear-piercing, which like footbinding entailed deforming the natural body.

In some respects, the agenda for women during the Nanjing Decade remained true to these early indications. The "fragile beauty" (*bingtai wei mei*) aesthetic of the late imperial period had given way to an explicit preference for a taller, fuller, more robust physique.[68] Models parading national products at a Shanghai fashion show in 1930 fell well short of the standards held by a reporter who complained in print about the unfavourable impression created by "the sight of female compatriots with short stature and weak frames."[69] Strong women were desirable for the nation, as they were in Japan, Germany, and more widely in the 1930s world. Gymnastics, swimming, tennis and other forms of athletic activ-

Fig. 6.30 The clothing on the model used in this 1937 advertisement for *The Arts and Life* pictorial magazine hints at what conservatives were protesting about when they railed against modern women's dress. The cut is so close and the material so thin that the woman's nipples can be seen, while her legs are provocatively revealed by the long splits in the skirt.

---

66 "Jinzhi funü zhanzu tiaoli" (Regulations for prohibition on footbinding), 10 May 1928. Chongqing Municipal Archives, *Jiaoyu* (Education), Vol. 536, Neiwubu yin, 1937.

67 Nagao Tatsuzô Ryûzô, *Shina minzokushi*, 413.

68 Yu Chien Ming, "Jindai Zhongguo nüzi jianmei de lunshu (1920-1940 niandai)" (Modern discourses on the strong beauty of Chinese women, 1920s-1940s), in Yu Chien Ming, ed., *Wu sheng zhi sheng(II): jindai Zhongguo funü yu wenhua, 1600-1950* (Voices Amid Silence (II): Women and Culture in Modern China, 1600-1950) (Taipei: Academia Sinica, 2003), 141-72; Sun Fuxi, "Shenme shi nüxing mei?" (What is beauty in a woman?), *Xin nüxing* 1, 5 (May 1925): 362; Virgil Kit-yiu Ho, "The Limits of Hatred: Popular Attitudes Towards the West in Republican Canton," *East Asian History* 2 (1991): 91-3; Wolfram Eberhard, "What is Beautiful in a Chinese Woman?" in Eberhard, *Moral and Social Values of the Chinese: Selected Essays* (Taipei: Ch'eng-wen Publishing Company 1971), passim.

69 *Shenghuo* 46 (1930): 748-9.

Fig. 6.31 Part of a photo montage featuring Hong Kong swimming sensation Yang Xiuqiong, the star turn in the women's swimming events at China's Sixth National Athletic Meeting, held in Shanghai, 10-20 October, 1935.

ity were promoted in schools and Chinese successes in international sport received an enormous amount of publicity in newspapers and magazines. Female swimmers and gymnasts were not infrequently photographed in their sportswear, to appear in magazine features ostensibly designed to illustrate the unity of beauty and strength (Fig. 6.31). Although the baring of female limbs created some controversy, winning medals for China (an elusive goal) put the scantily clad athlete a long way ahead of the scantily clad society girl in the public arena (Fig. 6.32).

It is also observable, however, that the athletic female body was worryingly close to the revolutionary (i.e. Communist) female body. In Liu Na'ou's short story "Flow," when Jingqiu falls in love with the revolutionary Xiaoying, it is not merely on account of her ideas, as Liu Jianmei writes, but because of "her masculinised body—her healthy dark skin, strong and flexible arms and legs, and short hair."[70] After brutally parting ways with the Communists in 1927, the Nationalists had to break the nexus between women's progress and communism. The New Life Movement, launched in 1934 shortly after the defeat of the Communists in Jiangxi, was one means to this end.

The NLM was predicated on Chiang Kaishek's vision of a militarised (*junshihua*) society in which gender roles were clearly defined in accordance with a reinvented Confucian tradition. In this society, the father would have responsibility for affairs outside the home, the mother for domestic matters; the father had to take care of the present, the mother had to safeguard the future.[71] Women who had learnt in the May Fourth period to defy the "three obediences and the four virtues" were now told that "the New Life Movement has as a principle the

---

70 Liu Jianmei, "Shanghai Variations on 'Revolution Plus Love'," *Modern Chinese Literature and Culture* 4, 1 (Spring 2002): 65.

71 Chen Lifu, 1975 [1934]. "Xinshenghuo yundong yu fumu zhi zeren" (The New Life Movement and the Duties of Parents) [1934], in *Geming wenxian, di liushiba ji, Xinshenghuo yundong shiliao* (Documents on the Revolution, Pt. 68, materials on the New Life Movement) (Taipei: Zhongyang wenwu gongyingshe, 1975), 175.

promotion of traditional morality. The three states of women's dependence and the four female virtues are the traditional morality for women."[72]

Female virtue went together with certain vestimentary expectations. Under the New Life Movement attempts were made to ensure that throats, arms and legs were decently covered. In general, the Movement emphasised neat, plain clothing and a simple diet.[73] Some of the related regulations were applicable to both sexes: clothes had to be neat and clean; hats were to be worn straight (i.e. no rakish angles!); buttons were to be properly fastened; hairnets, eyeshades and slippers were not to be worn outdoors; clothes were to be washed frequently, and no one should be without a handkerchief. Such directives, issued at a time when Japanese pressure on North China was intensifying, prompted wits to mock the Movement as an effort to save the nation by doing up coat buttons.[74]

Other regulations were particularly directed at women. Prohibitions were directed at permed hair, outlandish and provocative clothing, breast-binding, and high heels.[75] In Shandong, governor Han Fuqu (1890–1938) (Fig. 6.33) went in

person to see that all was in order on the streets. When he spotted two women wearing non-standard (*bu he biaozhun*) clothing, he ordered their arrest.[76] The clothing imagined for women in the New Life Movement was to be modern and tasteful, but above all decorous. *Modern Miscellany* provided an example in the early months: a box pleated skirt reaching well below the knees, and a *qipao*-style top with elbow-length sleeves. Respectable pumps encase the model's feet, and she holds a parasol (Fig. 6.34).

Fig. 6.32 Cartoon comparing the strong and decadent forms of modern women in China. The strong woman won medals for China ("China" is written on her shirt); her antithesis wore a *qipao*.

The significance of the parasol—an item popularised by Song Meiling—is revealed in the caption to a newspaper photo of

---

72 Sherman Cochran and Andrew C.K. Hsieh, with Janis Cochran, *One Day in China: May 21, 1936* (New Haven and London: Yale University Press, 1983), 68.

73 Yang Xiaoqing ed., *Xinshenghuo gangyao* (Principles of New Life) (Chongqing: Chongqing gonganju jingcha xunliansuo, 1936), 39. Chongqing Municipal Archives, 774/2.

74 Xu Qingyu, "Xinshenghuo yundong yu wenhua" (The New Life Movement and culture) [1935], in Pamier Shudian bianjibu, ed., *Wenhua jianshe yu xihua wenti taolunji, xiaji* (Collected articles on the establishment of culture and the problem of westernization, part 2) (Taibei: Pamier Shudian, 1980), 155.

75 *Xinshenghuo yundong yaoyi* (Main principles of the New Life Movement) (Wuhan: Hubei Police Bureau Press, 1937), 13-23. Chongqing Municipal Archives 776/2.

76 *Funü shenghuo* 6 (16 June 1936): 1.

Fig. 6.33 Han Fuqu, Chairman of the Shandong Provincial Government, on his way to meet with Chiang Kaishek in early 1937, was met at Pukou Railway Station by General He Yingqin, Minister for War in the Nanjing Government. The party shows a range of forms of male attire: Sun Yatsen suit of dark wool worn by Han himself and another member of his party; gown and jacket worn by two others; a Western suit on the man just behind General He; and military and police uniform.

actress Ding Zhiming. Ding did her bit for China by appearing in public simply clad and carrying a paper parasol, "presenting in pure form the beauty shown in old [Chinese] pictures."[77]

The visual effect of the New Life outfit is in sharp contrast to another ensemble pictured on the same page: a close-fitting lace-trimmed *qipao*-top worn over loose pants by a world-weary model with cigarette in hand.[78] This second photo shows the sort of "non-standard" clothing that was targeted by the Movement: close-fitting, decorative, sexually charged. The woman has obviously bound her breasts, and her hair is permed. She typifies the urban decadence that was held by cultural conservatives, and for that matter by Communists, to be sapping the moral fibre of the Chinese nation.

The New Life Movement was the signature mass movement of the KMT, but a broader historical impulse behind it can be identified. In 1918 Yan Xishan (1883–1960), the military governor of Shanxi, had established a Good People's Movement (*haoren yundong*), which in many respects anticipated the NLM. Yan plundered the classics for cultural norms and held forth on the virtues of the Chi-

---

77 *Shenbao* 25 May 1929.

78 *SDHB* 6, 6 (16 July 1934): 4.

Fig. 6.34 Contrasting styles of dress in the 1930s: left, the demure modern dress with Chinese characteristics designed by the New Life Movement; right, a cigarette-smoking entertainer (this looks like the actress Liang Saizhen) wearing smart, showy leisure-wear.

nese tradition even as he sought to modernise education, improve public health, and liberate women from footbinding.[79] The same cultural conservatism was apparent in Guangdong in the 1930s, where the military governor, Chen Jitang (1890–1954), first launched a movement for the revival of Confucianism,[80] and then began a campaign for general moral improvement involving rectification of relations between the sexes. Women and men were forbidden to swim in the same pool at the same time, dances were prohibited, and couples were not to walk along the street side by side.[81] A Shanghai critic commented sarcastically: "if you know about the affair between [Chen's] wife and the chauffeur, than you'll understand why he has thought up so many [versions of] 'men and women are not allowed'... "[82] (Fig. 6.35).

Vestimentary sanctions were central to Chen Jitang's new moral order. Women employees of the government were ordered to cover up their legs and drop their hemlines.[83] Students were banned from possessing ornate accessories or imported items of clothing. Women in general were prohibited from wearing "outlandish" forms of dress (qi zhuang yi fu). Some quite precise regulations were issued, including that sleeves should extend one (Chinese) inch below the elbow—a stipulation apparently too difficult to enforce because it was subsequently relaxed to "sleeves should reach the elbow."[84] Tailors were prohibited from making "outlandish" garments, and were subjected to police inspections designed to ensure compliance.[85]

---

79 Donald Gillin, *Warlord: Yen Hsi-shan in Shansi Province, 1911-1949* (Princeton: Princeton University Press, 1967), 34-5, 59-78.

80 Xiao Zili, *Chen Jitang* (Guangzhou: Guangdong renmin chubanshe, 2001), 373-7.

81 Ibid., 392.

82 *Manhua shenghuo* (Life in cartoons), *"Funü manhua teji"* (Special edition of cartoons about women), 10 (1935), n.p.n.

83 Xiao Zili, *Chen Jitang*, 389.

84 Ibid., 390.

85 Ibid., 389.

Fig. 6.35 Chen Jitang and his wife, passing through Shanghai on the way to Nanjing, in response to a summons from Chiang Kaishek.

Commenting on these among other sumptuary regulations, *Linglong* magazine remarked in astonishment on the plethora of bans on women's fashions across the country, with particular reference to a ban on permed hair. Recently to the time of writing, the perm had been prohibited in Hangzhou and also among students in Guangdong. In Shanxi, the prohibition was evidently of much longer standing, but in 1935 an extraordinary exception to the rule was made: prostitutes were allowed to wear high heels and have permed hair. "In other words," as the editor noted, "everyone with permed hair and high heels is a prostitute." She went on to query the logic of the exception, since prostitutes, too, were women (*funü*).[86]

In the end, it proved difficult to separate the feminine from the sexual, the progressive from the bold, the independent from the outlandish. Urged on the one hand to have natural breasts and on the other to cover up her elbows, the *qipao*-clad woman was destined to remain on the losing side of a constantly shifting argument. Hu Shi (1891–1962) recognised this conundrum. On a visit to Hong Kong and Guangdong in 1935 he frankly criticised Chen Jitang's campaign, pointing out the inherent paradoxes: "We cannot abuse our power and arbitrarily issue standards [of behaviour] that declare: women's liberation extends to unbinding their feet and cutting their hair, and no further; they are not to perm their hair, wear short sleeves or silk stockings, dance, or wear make-up."[87]

The fact remained that when a national crisis erupted, women were sure to be wearing the wrong clothes. So it happened that when Japan invaded China in 1937, women's dress was immediately at issue. "For the rise and fall of the country," it was proclaimed, "women's adornment bears responsibility." New murmurs against the *qipao* were to be heard, and also against men wearing suits. "National essence" should be preserved. Men should wear the long gown and riding jacket, women should wear the skirt and jacket-blouse. The suggested revival

---

86 *Linglong* 221 (1936): 167. On *Linglong*'s editorial position, see further, Pei-yen Hsiao, "Body Politics, Modernity and National Salvation," passim.

87 Xiao Zili, *Chen Jitang*, 388.

of skirt and jacket-blouse for women points to a residual historical consciousness of Han women's dress under the Manchus, and may have been prompted by a heightened consciousness of Manchukuo, now firmly in the camp of an enemy, under the puppet rule of Puyi, the last of the Qing emperors. In face of this attack, a sturdy defence of the *qipao* as Chinese national dress was mounted. The *qipao* symbolised the "unity of the country" and "complete morality." Implicit was a crude reading of the skirt and jacket, an outfit "divided into two parts," representing a divided nation.[88]

The real problem for advocates of the skirt and jacket, however, was not that it was in two parts, but rather that its time had passed. A year before the Japanese invasion, a contributor to the women's magazine *Happy Family* had commented on the state of Chinese womanhood with a cartoon that divided "female compatriots" into three categories: "one sort is first in knowledge and awareness, another sort is behind in knowledge and awareness, and a third sort lacks knowledge and awareness." The first sort was depicted wearing *qipao* with high heels and "natural breasts", the second in *qipao*, with cloth shoes and bound breasts, and the third barefoot, in Chinese-style jacket and trousers (*shanku*) (Fig. 6.36). The skirt and jacket was nowhere to be seen.

Fig. 6.36 Cartoon by Huang Jiayin in 1936, commenting on "three sorts of female compatriot."

88 Guo Weilin, "Mantan nüren de fushi" (Talking about women's dress and adornment), *Furen huabao* 48 (June-July 1937): 4-6.

7
HER BROTHER'S CLOTHES

The male equivalent of the *qipao* was the *changpao*, or long gown. These two garments were less highly differentiated along gender lines than fashion magazines might suggest. The early *qipao* was cut like a man's robe, as Zhao Jiasheng's 1924 instructions showed, and in 1926, the Jiangnan warlord Sun Chuanfang (1885–1935) proscribed it on this basis.[1] Zhang Ailing frankly declared that women wore the *qipao* because they wanted to look like men. It was a sign, she argued, of the lost illusions of women who had been driven by the failed project of gender equality "to discard everything that smacked of femininity, even to the point of rejecting womanhood altogether."[2] If this seems an overstatement in light of the figure-hugging form that the *qipao* could assume, fundamental similarities between the garments nonetheless did complicate dress choices for men as well as for women who wanted to look like men.

The historical significance of the *changpao* as a Republican-era garment is less than obvious at first glance, because the *changpao* was worn by non-labouring men throughout the Qing dynasty and continued to be the dominant form of male dress for this class in the early years of the Republic. In other words, it offers itself as a vestimentary sign of the essential conservatism of Chinese society. Such an interpretation becomes less appealing when we read in an essay by Lu Xun that in 1934 the preferred garb of the radical male student was the gown and short jacket.[3] And when Ding Ling dresses the heroine of "The Hamlet" in a *changpao* before sending her off to join the revolution, the impression is deepened that the *changpao* was not a timeless garment at all.[4] The *changpao* on a young revolutionary woman clearly had a specific role to play in a nationalist narrative.

---

1 Laing, "Visual Evidence," 101.

2 Chang, "A Chronicle of Changing Clothes," 435.

3 Peter Carroll, "Refashioning Suzhou: Dress, Commodification, and Modernity," *positions: east asia cultures critique* 11, 2 (Fall 2003) 457.

4 Ding Ling, "The Hamlet," in Ding Ling, *Miss Sophie's Diary and Other Stories*, trans. W.F. Jenner (Beijing: Panda Books, 1985), 330.

Fig. 7.1 Yang Xianyi (left) with a colleague, photographed by Cecil Beaton in 1944.

The actual male radicals mentioned by Lu Xun as well as the fictional female radical mentioned by Ding Ling obviously had other garments at their disposal if what they wore was to have any significance in the eye of the reader. The sight of the *changpao* evoked the image of its alternatives. The evocation was immediate and sharp when the wearer was a woman, as demonstrated by contemporary media interest in women dressed in men's clothes—the *changpao*, the Western suit—or in a mixture of garments including those coded variously as Chinese and Western, male and female. The *changpao*-clad man, unlike the woman, could of course pass without comment. He wore what was comfortable, convenient, and common. He was often shadowed, however, by his own alter image in a Western suit, an ensemble he might indeed at times wear, or in which he had appeared in photos taken at an earlier stage of life. Moreover, another form of dress was available to men: the Sun Yatsen suit, of which more will be said shortly, had gained currency in Guangdong during the early twenties, becoming widespread elsewhere after the success of the Nationalist Revolution.

Men in Republican China actually had a greater variety of possible dress ensembles at their disposal than women. Yang Xianyi (b. 1915) summed up the available choices when recalling what he wore in Chongqing during the war: "I never liked to wear a Western suit because it made me feel too colonialist. But I did not wear a Sun Yat-sen type of suit either, because I did not want to look like a bureaucrat. So I was reduced to wearing my shabby long gown" (Fig. 7.1).[5] There could hardly be a clearer statement of the relationship of dress to personal identity. Yang had worn Western suits for years during his study abroad, but back in China he made a conscious choice about what to wear based on how he might "look" or "feel;" in other words, how he would seem in the eyes of others as well as himself.

---

5 Yang Xianyi, *White Tiger* (Beijing, 1999), 116. This book was privately published in a small print run. I am grateful to Li Jinyu for lending me a copy.

The fact that women sometimes appropriated men's dress complicates a reading of men's vestimentary choices as simply variations of male identity preferences. An increasingly complex material culture that was shaped and mediated by China's interactions with the rest of the world provided a range of garments that in practice could be donned by anyone. While the strength of gendered vestimentary codes is evident in the basic adherence of men and women to sexually distinctive forms of dress, the transgression of these codes in life, on the stage and in literature reveals

Fig. 7.2 Men in suits were more often to be seen on the screen than on the street. Here, the pensive heroine of Chen Kengran's 1934 film, "Enemies for Women" (*Nüxing de choudi*) gazes over the ship's rail while her male companions confer. From left to right: Xu Qinfang (the director's wife), Sun Min, Zhao Dan and You Guangzhao.

a more complex set of responses to available social identities than might be suggested by any one of the many images of heterosexual couples that circulated through newspapers, advertisements and on film during the Republican era.

Such images in general conferred great power on the Western suit (Fig. 7.2). The suit had an uneven career in the early twentieth century. Worn by bold young fellows in the late Qing, it was endorsed as official (male) dress by the new Republican administration in 1912. During the 1920s, it was adopted by cosmopolitan, forward-looking young May Fourth intellectuals, who in the 1930s—as discussed below—abandoned it as part of a nationalist reaction against things foreign. But it had by then become the established vestimentary mode in financial circles as well as among employees of Western firms,[6] and during the 1940s it appears to have recovered ground. By the late forties, Shanghai boasted around seven hundred Western clothing shops.[7]

Custom, convenience and cost militated against the general popularisation of the suit at an early date. Suits were expensive and China was poor. One elderly Shanghai resident remembers: "When I was young, it was too expensive to have a Western suit made. I always bought off-the-rack, what used to be called [in English] 'ready made'—that meant an off-the-rack Western suit. Buying a suit

6 Jiang Weimin, *Shimao waipo*, 49.

7 Ibid., 44.

was cheaper than having one made; that way, you could have a few." Another, born around the time of the 1911 Revolution, recalls that in his youth a store-bought suit cost twenty to thirty dollars, and a tailor-made at least twice that price, with the best costing more than a hundred dollars. But among the wearers of suits, the fashion stakes were high. "When everyone got together somewhere, or met for dinner, the first thing you did was look ... look and see what colour your friend's clothes were, whether the material was any good, whether it was made in the USA. American-made clothes were loose, British were tight-fitting."[8]

The ascendancy of the suit, in the view of Lin Yutang (1895–1976), was "simply and purely political;" it was

Fig. 7.3 Women in *qipao*s, men in suits: in this 1936 advertisement, the contrast is deployed in the service of selling the Ford V8 sedan.

associated with the power of "gunboats and Diesel engines."[9] This conclusion pressed towards but failed to capture the full cultural cachet of the suit, which Lin lacked the words to evoke: its concentrated sexuality and intensely (Western) male architectural elegance. In a world of competing male elites, the "simply and purely political" reasons for the appearance of the suit in Chinese society were after all the most significant of all possible reasons. Wearing a suit, the modern man contrasted with his *qipao*-wearing wife in a highly binarised visual image that equated him with worldliness, progress, action, and financial success and her with domesticity, both national because of her dress, and literal because of children at her knee or because of an actual domestic setting. The contrast was used to effect in advertisements for any number of goods for sale in Shanghai and elsewhere during the Republican era (Fig. 7.3).

Even in advertisements, however, the *changpao* was more commonly to be seen than the suit, which was in accordance with majority clothing practice. Not quite interchangeable with the suit, it was nonetheless pre-eminently serviceable for

---

8 Ibid., 44, 49. The Chinese term *xiancheng*, translated here as "off-the rack," literally means "ready made." The less exact synonym has been employed because of the logic of the sentence. The English term "ready made" is used in the original.

9 Lin Yutang, "The Inhumanity of Western Dress," in *The Importance of Living* (London: Heinemann, 1938), 257-62.

Fig. 7.4 Advertisement for Nanyang Great Wall cigarettes. The happy smoker has two sons and a daughter. His wife stands close to the doorway of their home, greeting or farewelling them.

advertising a wide range of products, including pharmaceuticals and cigarettes. From the consistency with which it was deployed in Nanyang "smoke patriotic cigarettes!" advertisements, it can be seen that, as domestic and distinctively Chinese wear (despite its Manchu origins), it challenged the power of women's dress to represent home and the nation. Not too much subtlety is employed in the visual imagery of such advertisements. The man in his *changpao* is the master of his home/country, and the woman in her skirt and jacket-blouse serves him and takes care of her family, thus serving the country (Fig. 7.4).[10]

The appeal of the *changpao* to the patriotic intelligentsia crossed gender boundaries. It was worn by nationalist girl students as well as by their brothers. For her graduation from the Patriotic Girls' School in Shanghai in 1928, Miss Bu Linqing appears to have considered it the most appropriate form of dress in which to receive her certificate (Fig. 7.5), just as Ding Ling found it the appropriate costume for her revolutionary heroine in "The Hamlet." A classical form of dress with deep historical and cultural associations, it was a much more serious garment than the skirt and jacket-blouse, although what it actually said about its wearer, apart from shouting "I am Chinese," was still being sorted out.[11]

Suits and gowns in the Republican era

The problem of what Republican men should wear is evident in the sartorial history of the "Father of the Nation" (*Guofu*), Sun Yatsen, whose photo album shows him wearing a variety of garments in the course of his revolu-

---

10 *Minguo Ribao* 5 February 1925: 8.

11 See Robert E. Harrist, Jr, "Clothes Make the Man: Dress, Modernity, and Masculinity in China, ca 1912-1937," in Wu Hung and Katherine R. Tsiang, eds, *Body and Face in Chinese Visual Culture* (Cambridge, Mass.: Harvard University Asia Center, 2005), 171-96.

愛國女學高級中學畢業生卜霖慶女士之男裝

Fig. 7.5 Miss Bu Linqing wore boy's clothing for the occasion of her high school graduation from the Patriotic Girls' School.

tionary career.[12] Although Sun is one of the few prominent leaders of twentieth-century China to be associated more closely with civil than with military leadership, the significance of the military figure in the early Republic is apparent from his wardrobe. He wore khaki when he arrived in Nanjing to be installed as Provisional President of the Republic, and in 1917, as head of the military government in Canton, he rivalled Yuan Shikai in Prussian splendour (Fig. 7.6). At other times, both before and after the Revolution, he appeared in a Western lounge suit, while late in life he often wore a *changpao*.

According to Israel Epstein, Sun regretted having been photographed in military garb in 1917, preferring to be seen as a civilian leader.[13] This may have been a response to the phenomenon of warlordism, one of the declared enemies of the Nationalist Revolution. As head of a revolutionary party that from 1923 was supported by its own armed forces, Sun could anyway leave the task of wearing military uniform to his subordinates, most notably Chiang Kaishek, head of the newly established Huangpu Academy. Nonetheless, Sun's formal dress as party head was not a Western suit or a robe, but rather an ensemble that looked like a civilian version of military uniform. This was the *Zhongshan zhuang* (Sun Yatsen suit).

The origins of the Sun Yatsen suit are generally attributed to Sun's purchase of a Japanese military uniform from the Rongchangxiang Woollen Fabrics and Western Suits Shop on Nanjing Road—or alternatively to his bringing a uniform back from Japan, and taking it to this shop for alterations. The shop owner, Wang Caiyun (1880–1933), collaborated with Sun in creating a civilian suit out of the uniform. Wang was a native of Fenghua, Chiang Kaishek's home county, and was reportedly acquainted with Sun via this connection.[14] The year was 1920. Sun had recently restructured

12 See Huang Renyuan, exec. ed., *Sun Zhongshan yu guomin geming* (Sun Yatsen and the Republican revolution) (Hong Kong: Shangwu yinshuguan, 1994), passim.

13 Israel Epstein, *Woman in World History: Life and Times of Soong Ching Ling (Mme. Sun Yatsen)* (Beijing: New World Press, 1993), 125.

14 Shi Ying, *Minguo shishang* (Republican fashions) (Beijing: Tuanjie chubanshe, 2005), 150.

Fig. 7.6 Sun Yatsen in khaki, which he adopted as Provisional President of the Republic in 1912. The uniform is quite like the Sun Yatsen suit of later years. Right, Sun in full military dress as head of the military government in Guangdong in 1917.

his political move-
ment in Guangzhou,
creating the Guomin-
dang or Nationalist
Party, which was to
establish a new na-
tional central govern-
ment in Nanjing in 1928. The Sun Yatsen suit was the signature dress of the Nationalist Revolution.

The suit looked much like the military-style school uniform worn in Ja-
pan and—from the turn of the century—increasingly in China as well.[15] In a posthumously published photo of Sun wearing the suit, the *Young Companion* reported "Mr Sun liked wearing students' dress, now called the Sun Yatsen suit (*Zhongshan zhuang*)."[16] The jacket was close-fitting and buttoned down the centre, with square pockets at breast and waist, and was worn over trou-
sers cut in the Western style. In time, its unremarkable stylistic features were invested with deep political significance: the three buttons on each sleeve cuff stood for the Three Principles of the People, the four pockets for the four Nationalist principles and the five front buttons for the five branches of the Nationalist Government.[17] It became popular among young revolutionaries in Canton in the 1920s, and as the Nationalist Revolution gathered pace it spread far inland to become common wear in small provincial towns.[18]

After the Nationalist Revolution, northerners gradually became familiar with the Sun Yatsen suit. The convergence of clothing cultures between south and north at the time of reunification is hinted at in a short article on the Sun Yatsen

---

See also Lu Hanchao, *Beyond the Neon Lights*, 253-4; Harrison, *The Making of the Republican Citizen*, 176-7.

15 John Fitzgerald, *Awakening China* (Stanford: Stanford University Press, 1996), 25.

16 *Liangyou* (November 1926): 16.

17 Shi Ying, *Minguo shishang*, 149.

18 See Mao's reference to Cantonese-style "shirts" in Xunwu, discussed in the previous chapter.

suit published in the *Beiyang Pictorial* around the time that Sun Yatsen's corpse was being removed from Beijing (or Beiping) for burial in Nanjing. An inquiry into its origins by a reporter for the paper yielded the following answer from a long-term fellow of Sun Yatsen's:

One day after the former Premier assumed office as commander-in-chief in Guangdong, he was about to inspect the troops and wanted to put on his commander's uniform, but felt that it was too grandiose and not suitable for the occasion. A Western suit was not what he wanted, either. He was just looking through his travelling chest when he came across a hunting suit he had worn in the past in Great Britain and he felt this was appropriate, so put it on and went out. After that, all the officials had suits made in imitation, and called it the Zhongshan suit. The [suit now known by that name] has undergone some changes, and does not duplicate the original suit worn by the Premier.[19]

This story suggests that the Sun Yatsen suit, like the *qipao*, had a rather complex genealogy. In fact, various other origins have been advanced for the suit, including Western military uniform, Japanese student uniforms, and a style of shirt worn by Chinese in Southeast Asia.[20]

The Sun Yatsen suit had a profound impact in political circles. In 1949, when Mao Zedong emerged as paramount leader of the newly established People's Republic of China, he resisted pressure from his chief of protocol to don a suit and black leather shoes. "We Chinese have our own customs," he said. "Why should we follow others?" The civilian wear he chose in place of the Western lounge suit was the Sun Yatsen jacket with trousers.[21] Although this ensemble was to become known in the West as the Mao suit, it was in fact the distinctively Chinese dress of the political elite on both sides of Chinese politics. A photograph of Mao Zedong and Chiang Kaishek taken in Chongqing during the negotiations following the end of the anti-Japanese war suggests a case of "separated at birth" which was not too far from the fact in political terms (Fig. 7.7). Their suits were virtually identical: well cut, of good material, and faithful to the style established by Sun Yatsen.

In *Song of Youth*, a popular novel and then film of the 1950s, author Yang Mo (1914–1996) not surprisingly confirmed the conclusion to which Mao had come. The story features all three of the garments mentioned by Yang Xianyi: the Western suit, the *changpao*, and the Sun Yatsen suit. The Western suit is worn by the heroine's spoilt, decadent brother, whose backward class attitudes are manifest in the combination of his "well-pressed foreign suit" with "his glossy hair, and his pompous, shallow appearance." The *changpao* is worn by her reactionary husband, a disciple of the liberal philosopher Hu Shi. His thin, rather stooped frame gives him the look of an old-fashioned scholar and is plainly antithetical to the na-

---

19 *BYHB* 14 May 1929.

20 Wang Xing, *Bainian fushi chaoliu yu shibian*, 34.

21 Li Zhisui, *The Private Life of Chairman Mao* (London: Chatto and Windus, 1994), 121.

Fig. 7.7 Chiang Kaishek and Mao Zedong at Guiyuan, the site of peace negotiations between the Communists and the Nationalists after the end of the anti-Japanese war. Their suits are virtually identical except that Jiang's looks better cut and he sports a fountain pen in the left pocket, which was very *comme il faut* among Nationalist cadres.

tionalist body required by the times. In striking contrast to both the above, Jiang Hua, the upstanding young Communist to whom Daojing's destiny is finally linked, appears before her first "in an old felt hat and a grey cotton Sun Yatsen suit, [looking] like a college student of simple tastes, or a clerk in some government office."[22]

Mao's rhetorical question also expressed the sentiments proclaimed by a number of his contemporaries, and probably held by many other men who never put their sartorial choices into words. Wu Jingxiong (John C.H. Wu, 1899–1986), a Harvard Law graduate, was "so Chinese that he refused to wear Western dress." His friend Shao Xunmei, who in the 1920s helped found the Yunshang Fashion Store, shared Wu's sentiments as far as men's clothing was concerned.[23] Emily Hahn (1905–1997), Shao's American lover, recalled that "the first and only time of our acquaintance" that he wore European clothes was when he donned a suit to avoid detection by the Japanese police.[24] Judging by Lu Xun's comment, such attitudes were widespread in intellectual circles. At Beijing's Qinghua University around this time, blue cotton gowns

22 Adapted from the translation. The phrase "grey suit buttoned up to the neck" is used here by the translator to render "ta chuanzhe yishen huibu Zhongshan zhuang"—i.e. "he was wearing a Sun Yatsen suit of grey cotton." Yang Mo, *Song of Youth*, trans. Nan Ying (Peking: Foreign Languages Press, 1978), 245, 253.

23 Emily Hahn, *China to Me* [1944] (Boston: Beacon Press, 1988), 17. On Shao, see Leo Ou-fan Lee, *Shanghai Modern*, 241–54.

24 Hahn, *China to Me*, 98.

were the predominant form of dress, which was a matter of pride in the student community.[25]

It is obvious, however, that these Chinese nationalists all dressed like the greater number of their contemporaries, or at least like their town-dwelling, middle-class contemporaries. The *changpao* might be worn for political reasons, or might simply be what the wearer was used to. Yang Xianyi's reflections on how he might "feel" or "look" in particular forms of dress make it clear that individual decisions about wearing a gown were informed by a strong consensus about what the gown did *not* signify. His choice was interestingly expressed in negative terms: he had three different sorts of clothing at his disposal, but two would assign to him particular performative identities which he was not prepared to assume. He was "reduced" to wearing a gown. Was this for want of a sort of clothing that might allow him to dress up as "himself"? Although he does not elaborate on how the gown made him "look" or "feel," the strategy of negation employed here suggests that in the *changpao*, a habit comfortable, conventional, and unremarkable, he was sartorially invisible.

Of the two "suits" that Yang Xianyi chose not to wear, the Western version was clearly rejected on nationalist grounds. Apparently, this ensemble had lost the international or cosmopolitan attributes that made it acceptable in the opening years of the Republic. The most developed critique of the suit in the Republican era was put in an essay by Lin Yutang, a member of a Shanghai literary circle to which Shao Xunmei also belonged. The essay was first published in English for an American audience and like many of Lin's writings was directed at subverting foreign prejudices against Chinese culture through a combination of reasoned argument and humour. With confidential jocularity, he put it to his readers: "Need anyone who in his native garb practically goes about the house and outside in his pyjamas and slippers give reasons why he does not like to be encased in a system of suffocating collars, vests, belts, braces and garters?" To this example of plain common sense he added arguments about hygiene, aesthetics, climate and democracy, drawing on major tropes of discourse about modern life. In the end, however, his point was that: "the Chinese dress is worn by all Chinese gentlemen. Furthermore, all the scholars, thinkers, bankers and people who made good in China either have never worn foreign dress, or have quickly come back to their native dress the minute they have 'arrived'..." By contrast, those who wore foreign dress were college students, clerks, and the politically ambitious, along with "the nouveaux riches, the nincompoops, the feeble-minded ..."[26] In other words, the Chinese man in a suit was either very young, very vulgar, or stupid.

25 Wen-hsin Yeh, *The Alienated Academy: Culture and Politics in Republican China, 1919-1937* (Cambridge, Mass.: Harvard East Asia Center, 1990), 226.

26 Lin Yutang, "The Inhumanity of Western Dress," 260.

Lin Yutang's strong opinions about the suit were a product of the 1930s. This decade was marked, as we have seen, by a reactionary atavism, a return to the past for cultural inspiration. Governments, both central and provincial, fostered this atavism, and in the uncertain climate of the 1930s world, even people who were critical of the government felt the pull of the past. The iconoclasm of the May Fourth era was replaced by restorationism. Lu Xun commented on this change of ethos in "The Decline of the Suit," written in 1933. The suit had become very popular after the 1911 Revolution, he observed, but afterwards Chinese people had reacted against it, "reviving the old system" of clothing. He was struck by the irony of Manchu clothing (i.e. the *changpao*) filling the vacuum of China's need for an appropriate style of dress.[27]

The decline was by no means absolute. Lin Yutang and Lu Xun were both intellectuals, and writers by profession. Their observations and attitudes were necessarily related to the social circles in which they moved or to which they had access. As noted above, the suit had become well established in some circles, and it was not an inherently anti-patriotic form of dress. On the contrary, how to wear one had long been equated with success or failure in modernising the Chinese self-cum-nation. Chen Bixie, who studied in France and Germany in the 1920s, showed as much in a popular novel serialised in the 1930s, in which the question of what Chinese men wore was placed in a cosmopolitan context.

The novel traces the largely unedifying careers of a number of Chinese students in Paris, the characters apparently based at least in part on real life people.[28] A number of episodes in the novel concern the issue of national prestige but the most developed treatment of this theme concerns the suit-wearing Zhao Qiusheng, the only son of uneducated but wealthy and indulgent parents. The reader first meets him when he is on his way to France, travelling first class. He occasions disgust in the dining room by the way he slurps his soup, and when the ship is passing through the tropics, he causes scandal in the smoking room by taking off the greater portion of his clothing in order to play cards in comfort.

On arrival in France, Zhao is met by Ying Zigu, who has been in France for some years and is very much a man of the world. Ying is both disgusted and dismayed by the sight of his compatriot:

He was wearing a not-so-new morning suit, of which the trouser legs were completely round, with no sign of the proper crease. On his feet were brown leather shoes, covered with a thick layer of filth, and worn with purple socks that had apparently become separated from their suspenders and were bunched up around his ankles. His shirt was greying and the cuffs even more distressingly dirty, while his tie resembled nothing so much as an

---

27 Lu Xun, "Yangzhuang de moluo" (The decline of the suit), quoted in Wang Xing, *Bainian fushi chaoliu yu shibian*, 36.

28 Chen must have been in either France or Germany when Zhang Youyi arrived on the continent after her separation from Xu Zhimo, for hers is among the sagas recounted in the novel through fictionalised characters.

earthworm. On beholding this grimy spectacle, Zigu wondered to himself: "Why did this precious fellow have to end up in France, making Chinese lose face …?"[29]

For Ying Zigu, clearly, Chinese who could wear the suit appropriately—pressed, clean, with matching colours—gave China "face" in the eyes of the world. The antithesis of Zhao in this novel is one (suit-wearing) Professor Liu Wanguang, a strapping fellow who speaks perfect English and has apparently studied boxing as well. In a fist-fight with an Englishman who has insulted Zhao, and China in general, Liu makes short work of his opponent, reducing the foreign passengers on board the ship to fawning admiration.

It is notable that Chen's negative comments on Zhao's suit refer mainly to its state of cleanliness. In combining personal hygiene with poor table manners in the person of this anti-hero, Chen drew on a rich literary tradition in the treatment of hygiene in relationship to cultural progress in China. Western commentators, from John Barrow to Arthur Smith, along with the "Father of the Nation" Sun Yatsen, had linked the issues of clothing and hygiene to criticise and even ridicule the Chinese person as inhabitant of a particular cultured bodily and vestimentary space. In late Qing novels, the Chinese man in a suit had been deployed in ways similar to Chen's use of Zhao, for an identical point. Underneath their civilised clothes, as Paola Zamperini has commented, these be-suited men remained as dirty and lice-ridden as ever.[30] Although the man in a gown could also be ridiculed in this way, the benchmark for civilised behaviour was undoubtedly raised when he donned a suit. The resulting tensions meant that the foundations for the suit in Chinese society were to remain shaky until after the *changpao* and the Sun Yatsen suit had both been marginalised, something that did not happen till the last quarter of the twentieth century.

Gender, dress, and nation

In their commentaries on the suit, Lin Yutang and Chen Bixie both demonstrate a greater preoccupation with a national (China-West) problem than with gender (man-woman) issues. Lin Yutang did have something to say on the subject of women's dress, which he thought about very differently from men's. "Western women," he averred, "long ago achieved simplicity and common sense in their dress;" consequently, "foreign dress for young women of good figures between twenty and forty and for all children" was not only acceptable but to be encouraged.[31] The issue of underclothing, which he raised frankly in the case of men's wear, was lost on him in the case of women. He had no idea of the discomforts

---

29 Chen Bixie, *Haiwai binfenlu* (Carryings on abroad) (Shenyang: Chunfeng wenyi chubanshe, 1997), 20.

30 Zamperini, "On Their Dress They Wore a Body," 316.

31 Lin Yutang, "The Inhumanity of Western Dress," 261.

endured by women wearing 1930s Western clothing: bras, step-ins, silk stockings, slips or full petticoats, and heels, in combination with dresses that were as likely as not to be tight at the waist and difficult to manage in the wind, or when sitting down or bending over. That he could happily envisage a Chinese woman wearing Western clothes also means that he did not see women as the bearers of the national flag. What women wore was a matter of sexual or social rather than cultural interest.

The problem of dress, however, was Janus-faced: looking outward, Chinese commentators saw it in terms of China versus the West, but looking inward, they saw it in terms of men versus women. The two were closely related, as an article by Li Yuyi in 1928 showed:

The fabrics used by men are frequently of the flowing sort, such as silk, which do not lend themselves to the display of the strong beauty of the male. In recent times, those wearing stiff fabrics ... are less and less to be seen. It is even rarer to see anyone displaying the strong beauty of the male that shows the spirit of our great country.

To the problem of the fabrics Li added the problem of colour, which he described as "the ugliest aspect of Chinese people's clothing at the present time." Men's clothing featured as many and varied colours as did women's, all mixed and mis-matched in the most barbaric way. This had deleterious effects on the nation:

Where styles are not differentiated, then sex differences between men and women often cannot be recognised. Under these circumstances, the citizenry's (*guomin*) sense of purpose declines, and there is no elevation of the spirit. Riotous colours show nothing of the refinement of a great country, and can be regarded as a matter of the greatest shame.

Practical advice was offered to remedy this problem. On the one hand, care should be taken with colour coordination. On the other, there were colours suitable for men's clothing: black, dark green, dark purple, deep grey, royal blue and gold.[32]

Li gave expression in this article to a general anxiety about male femininity, and gender confusion more broadly, a subject on which Ye Qianyu commented in a series of cartoons published around the same time (Fig. 7.8). Yu Dafu (1896–1945), among the most famous writers of this period, echoed these concerns in an autobiographical memoir. Among Yu's classmates at school in Hangzhou there were many "whose clothes and accessories were lovely, whose gestures, delicate, and whose speech, quiet and gentle ... There were a few students who didn't think it humiliating being regarded as a woman. They put on fragrance, makeup, and face powder and affected behaviors that showed off their wealth."[33] The effeteness of these "sons of the country gentry," as Janet Ng

32 Li Yuyi, "Meizhuang, xinzhuang yu qizhuang yifu" (Beautiful dress, new dress, weird and wonderful dress), *Funü zazhi* 14, 9 (1 January 1928): 25.

33 Janet Ng, *The Experience of Modernity: Chinese Autobiography of the Early Twentieth Century* (Ann Arbor: The University of Michigan Press, 2003), 85.

Fig. 7.8 He looks like her and she looks like him: three of a series of cartoons about androgynous dress trends by Ye Qianyu in 1928, the year the Nationalist Party established a new government in Nanjing.

shows, was offset in Yu's eyes by the tough masculinity of the village woodcutter with his "dark skin, sinuous muscular body, and rich, masculine voice."[34] This dichotomy was to become a standard literary trope in the patriotic fiction of the early PRC, in which the sturdy bodies of (male) peasants and workers—successors to the *haohan* or "good fellow" types of classical literature[35]—provide a steady counterpoint to the pampered bodies of a decadent and ineffectual old elite.

The problem of male femininity was exacerbated by its opposite, female masculinity. Yu Dafu's woodcutter was not too unlike Liu Na'ou's character, mentioned in the preceding chapter: the revolutionary Xiaoying, with "her masculinised body—her healthy dark skin, strong and flexible arms and legs, and short hair."[36] This vision of athletic prowess is apparent in newspapers of the 1930s, where sporting events involving women were often reported. The sports oval, however, was a performance space. Like the theatre, it allowed and sanctioned costume. For short-haired girls to wear "men's" clothing as ordinary daily dress was another matter. Whether in high fashion, sensible working clothes, the plain dress of the intelligentsia, or the provocative clothing of the transvestite, the "woman-as-man" (*nü zuo nan*) excited a high degree of media interest (Fig. 7.9).

---

34 Ibid., 86.

35 See Louie, *Theorising Chinese Masculinity*, 79-81.

36 Liu Jianmei, "Shanghai Variations on 'Revolution Plus Love,'" 65.

Fig. 7.9 Miss Tao Mo'an in a Western suit, one of numerous pictures of women in men's clothing in the 1930s press.

"Cross-dressing" is a rather inadequate term to describe this phenomenon. To speak of cross-dressing is to suggest a pre-existing stable gender order with well-established vestimentary signs, as in boy/girl, trousers/skirts, short hair/long hair. In fact, gender roles and dress codes were in a state of massive upheaval during the twentieth century. In the late years of the Qing dynasty, girl students were already breaching the limits of acceptable styles for women, and girl soldiers were simply wearing uniforms. This was not entirely due to generational or political rebelliousness. Parents, as discussed in Chapter Four, could well feel that when girls were entering a boys' domain, such as a school, they should wear boys' clothes.

Were such clothes primarily male clothes, or primarily student clothes, soldier clothes, and so on? This question is given salience by a long history of commentary on women in China wearing men's clothes and adopting male personae, and on girls being brought up as boys. In the classic novel *Dream of Red Mansions*, Lin Daiyu is puzzled as to the identity of "Peppercorn Feng" until she recalls that this must be Cousin Lian's wife, "who had been brought up from earliest childhood just like a boy, and had acquired in the schoolroom the somewhat boyish-sounding name of Wang Xi-feng."[37] Feng, it should be noted, is a not very nice character, but the "woman-as-man" figure in literature was not necessarily a negative one.

A number of sympathetic cross-dressing, gender-switching tales were produced by women playwrights in late imperial China. The logic underpinning this literary device was that in a man's clothes, a human being could achieve a social personhood; in a woman's clothes, a girl had to make do with "making herself up with rouge and powder, serving her husband with towel and comb, and begging others for pity."[38]

Although this logic was compelling, the fact that theatres and brothels were the most common contexts for cross-dressing meant that for a girl to dress in a boy's clothes was also associated with moral turpitude. Prostitutes and actors belonged

---

37 Cao Xuexin, *The Story of the Stone*, Vol. 1, trans. David Hawkes (London: Penguin, 1973), 91-2.

38 Wilf Idema and Beata Grant, *The Red Brush: Writing Women of Imperial China* (Cambridge, Mass.: Harvard University Asia Center, 2004), 676-7.

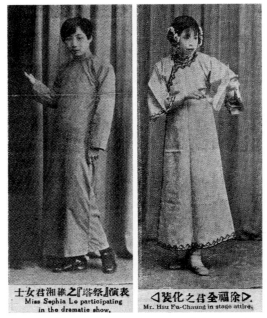

士女君湘蒸之『塔祭』演表
Miss Sophia Lo participating
in the dramatic show.

◁装化之君全福余▷.
Mr. Hsu Fu-Chaung in stage attire.

Fig. 7.10 The actress in a *changpao* and the actor in a *qipao*. In actuality, the *changpao* is not too different from the plain garment worn by many women as "qipao."

to the "mean" classes,[39] inhabiting a social space where girls from "good families" (*liangjia*) feared to tread. On the other hand, when these girls began in numbers to cut their hair, wear boys' clothing to school, and don military uniform, it was clear that the times were changing. This phenomenon was highly visible around the time of the 1911 Revolution and again during the Nationalist Revolution of the 1920s. The "good families" actually provided the conditions for their daughters to aspire to be like their brothers by sending them to school. Girls moved quickly from going to school to demonstrating on the streets and becoming soldiers. Donning a *changpao* was probably the least of a number of transgressive acts they performed.

There were a number of social or occupational roles in which male dress on women was unremarkable. Invisible cross-dressing on the part of the intelligentsia was possible because of the relative ease with which a woman might wear a man's robe, especially in winter. Photographs of women soldiers quite often appeared in the popular press, suggesting a sustained fascination with the sight of women in uniform but also providing visual evidence of the normalisation of soldiering as a female profession. (Nationalist as well as Communist forces included women in arms.) Male dress may also have seemed appropriate on women in certain other professions. When Dr Zheng Suyin, chief obstetrician at the Guangji Hospital, posed for the *Ladies' Magazine* in 1930, she wore a suit coat, shirt and tie with a tailored skirt, hair cut in a short bob.[40]

Another context for cross-dressing was supplied by the performing arts. Theatre audiences in early twentieth-century China were exposed both to men

39 Catherine Vance Yeh, "A Public Affair or a Nasty Game? The Chinese Tabloid Newspaper and the Rise of the Opera Singer as Star," *European Journal of East Asian Studies* 2, 1 (2003): 15.

40 *Funü zazhi* 16, 3 (March 1930): front feature.

playing women's roles and to women performing as men, sometimes on the same stage (Fig. 7.10). Cross-gender performance, an established feature of Chinese theatre, could easily have fallen victim to one of the many campaigns against uncivilised or backward cultural practices. It was saved from such a fate partly by Mei Lanfang (1894–1961) (Fig. 7.11), nationally the most famous player of young female (*dan*) roles in Beijing Opera.[41] The most photographed figure of his time in China, Mei was not only celebrated at home but also acclaimed internationally after tours abroad.[42] The enormous public appeal enjoyed by the stars of Beijing Opera hints at the reservoir of cultural attitudes in China that might have made cross-dressing both controversial and appealing. The *dan* performers were frankly admired as "men of the female gender" (*nüxing zhi nan*).[43] Conversely, the charm of a

Fig. 7.11 Postcard portrait of the wildly popular Mei Lanfang, right, playing Lin Daiyu in "Daiyu Buries the Flowers," a Kun (southern-style) opera based on an episode from the eighteenth-century classic, *Dream of Red Mansions*.

cross-dressed woman—where she was charming—must have resided in her boyishness. Her clothing drew attention to the fact of sexuality even more obviously than the normalised femininity of the *qipao*.

Provocative and flamboyant cross-dressing was common among actresses. Stars photographed for the popular press during the Nanjing Decade included Meng Xiaodong (1907–1977), "famous for her male impersonations," shown in trilby and man's robe;[44] actress Wang Qingkui, dressed in jacket, robe, Chinese-style winter hat, and wearing spectacles;[45] and actress sisters Yang Juqiu and Yang Jufen, both wearing Western men's clothes: suit and tie, handkerchief in

---

41 See Isabelle Duchesne, "The Chinese Opera Star: Roles and Identity," in John Hay, ed., *Boundaries in China* (London: Reaktion Books, 1994), 217-42.

42 See Mark Cosdon, "'Introducing Occidentals to an Exotic Art': Mei Lanfang in New York," *Asian Theatre Journal* 12, 1 (Spring 1995): 175-89.

43 Yeh, "A Public Love Affair or a Nasty Game?" 29.

44 *BYHB* 6 April 1927.

45 *BYHB* 16 March 1927.

Fig. 7.12 "Hollywood heroines—their insurrection in men's suits! The leading fashion of 1933." Marlene Dietrich (first and second from left) visited China for the filming of Joseph von Sternberg's 1932 feature film, *Shanghai Express*. She was one of the most photographed Hollywood stars in the Chinese press.

left breast pocket.[46] Correspondingly, stars such as Marlene Dietrich and Katherine Hepburn were featured in the Chinese press as examples of women in the West wearing men's clothing (Fig. 7.12). Judith Butler's articulation of gender as "performative" is well illustrated by these actresses, so accustomed to performing roles on stage or screen that they could easily do so, perhaps instinctively did so, in their daily lives.[47]

Numerous other photos in the popular press show otherwise unknown young women in men's clothes: two girls in the Asian Tramping Society, looking like a couple of young men out on a hunting expedition (Fig. 7.13); two girls on an outing in the school holidays, one in a *qipao* and the other in Western male leisure suit—golfing cap, jacket, and knickerbockers;[48] two girls sitting in a park, wearing suit coats by way of winter jackets, providing provocative comments on their own otherwise female dress.[49] The photos were often sent to the paper or magazine by amateur photographers, or perhaps by the woman or women photographed. They were inserted into pages otherwise filled with news on any number of topics, including the latest conflict with Japan or the recent visit to Shanghai of a prominent political leader. Photographed side by side, sometimes hand in hand, these young women summoned up images of "two beauties" depicted in old woodblock prints while simultaneously suggesting same-sex sexual preference. Cross-dressing was indeed scandalously publicised in 1930 by a murder trial involv-

46 *BYHB* 13 June 1928.

47 See Judith Butler, *Gender Trouble: Feminism and the Subversion of Identity* (New York: Routledge, 1990).

48 *BYHB* 5 September 1928.

49 *SDHB* 5, 11 (1 April 1934).

Fig. 7.13 Two girls from the Asian Tramping Society, dressed for outdoor activities.

Fig. 7.14 A soldier in the Nationalist Army: an example of the masculinisation of Chinese women?

ing a triangular love affair. The victim of the crime was romantically involved with both a woman and a man, and was killed by the latter when she refused to marry him. She was known for her sartorial predilections: she commonly dressed in men's clothing.[50]

It is clear from the number of such photos that the press, and no doubt the reading public, took a keen interest in signs of male dress on female bodies. Such clothing, in conjunction with associated activities such as sport and profession, was read as a sign of mannishness. "Masculinised women!" proclaimed the caption to a photo montage in the *Women's Pictorial* (Fig. 7.14). A woman gymnast, a woman martial arts expert and a woman soldier were featured.[51] A cartoon in the *Beiyang Pictorial*, "Dressed in her brother's clothes," remarked on the direct, unqualified exchange of gender roles faciliated by the adoption of a suit: the binary oppositions of girl and boy, sister and brother, *qipao* and suit were simultaneously invoked (Fig. 7.15). Had the cartoonist seen an example of such cross-dressing, or seen representations of it in the press? If so, it can be concluded that the sight invited reflection, and the cartoon may be read as a serious comment on gender-cum-sexual confusion in the generally confusing times.

---

50 Liu Xinhuang, *Xu Zhimo aiqing zhuan* (Xu Zhimo's loves: a life) (Daizhong: Zhenxing chubanshe, 1986), 129-30.

51 "Nanxinghuale de nüxingmen" (Masculinised women), *Furen huabao* 26 (Februrary 1935): front features.

Analytical commentaries on such clothing are rather rare. One commentator glossed a photo with the observation that: "These years are the era of women wearing men's clothes. The long gown (*changshan*) has become the *qipao*; further, the riding jacket has become the overcoat!"[52] More commonly, captions identified the person together with the photographer, but supplied few other details. In narrative treatments of sexual preference, gender roles and vestimentary practices, however, writers of the twenties and thirties clearly found the unstable arrangements of their time a compelling metaphor for the nation's crisis. Ling Shuhua's well-known story about two girl students who fall in love offers an excellent illustration: one girl is from the north, and the other from the south, and they are fatally divided when the Nationalist Revolution plunges the country into war.[53]

作 溶 漢 蔣 [裳 衣 的 哥 哥 上 穿]
' Her brother's dress.'' By H. C. Tsiang.

Fig. 7.15 "Dressed in her brother's clothes." Cartoon by Jiang Hancheng, 1927.

The best-known treatment of cross-dressing in the Nationalist period is the film "Girl in Disguise" (*Huashen guniang*) in which a girl dresses up as a young man to visit her grandfather in Shanghai who thinks he has a grandson rather than a granddaughter. In this guise, the "grandson" attracts the affections of another girl, but "himself" falls in love with (another) young man. The film was an instant success. Actress Yuan Meiyun (b. 1917), although a veteran of the screen by the time she was selected to play the key role, shot from relative obscurity to stardom (Fig. 7.16). Three sequels were made in Shanghai, while in Guangzhou the film's popularity prompted a flurry of unremarkable boy-dressed-as-girl movies.[54]

---

52 *SDHB* 5, 11 (1 April 1934).

53 For an English translation, see "Once Upon a Time," Amy D. Dooling and Kristina M. Torgeson trans, in Amy D. Dooling and Krisitina M. Torgeson, eds, *Writing Women in Modern China: An Anthology of Women's Literature from the Early Twentieth Century* (New York: Columbia University Press, 1998), 185-95. For a thoughtful discussion of Ling's fiction, though without reference to this particular story, see Shu-mei Shih, *The Lure of the Modern*, 215-28.

54 Lu Gongsun, *Zhongguo dianying shihua* (Tales from the history of Chinese cinema) (Hong Kong: Nantian shuye gongsi, 1961),Vol. 2, 86-8. For brief accounts of the film in English, see Shuqin Cui, *Women Through the Lens* (Honolulu: University of Hawai'i Press, 2003), 12; Jay Leyda, *Dianying—Electric Shadows: An Account of Films and the Film Audience in China* (Cambridge: Massachusetts Institute of Technology, 1972), 109. A more extended discussion can be found in Chris Berry and Mary Farquhar, *China on Screen: Cinema and Nation* (New

Fig. 7.16 Yuan Meiyun in the 1936 feature film, "Girl in Disguise," (*Huashen guniang*).

"Girl in Disguise" attracted strong criticism from left-wing critics, the more so because Yihua Studio was viewed as selling off its birthright: it had begun life in 1933—the "year of leftist films"[55]—as a small studio under the left-wing director Tian Han (1898–1968), dedicated to the production of realist films with a strong social message. "Girl in Disguise" was a frivolous film, antipathetic to this original mission. Its popularity in 1936 is readily explained by factors separate from issues of cross-dressing and gender-blurring: a comedy with strong sexual references but conservative values, set in seductively comfortable bourgeois households in Singapore and Shanghai, offered an escape from the grim realities that the 1933 realist films had served up in liberal portions. The film ends happily. The topsy-turvy world is set to rights through the disclosure and stabilisation of the main character's original identity, which is seen as pre-existing, authentic, and always there if only those around could see through the confusing, counter-indicating costume.

A similar conclusion was reached in the homoerotic novel *Precious Mirror of Boy Actresses*, composed in equally troubled times in the previous century. In the course of discussing this novel, Keith McMahon draws attention to what he defines as "a cardinal rule" of Chinese fiction: "a normative ending should not be seen as canceling out the wayward body of the story."[56] In other words, the fact that convention is observed in the conclusion of "Girl In Disguise" does not cancel out its content. For the original film and its three sequels all to be great box-office successes suggests a fascination on the part of the audience with a narrative that crossed national boundaries (from Singapore to China) simultaneously with gender boundaries (girl to boy), and that pointed to the troubling if titillating outcomes of such transgressions (homosexual liaisons). The reception of the film, as Gongsun Lu writes, shows that it was in tune with the times.[57]

York: Columbia University Press, 2006), 83-6. Note that Leyda translates the film's title as "Miss Change-Body," while Berry and Farquhar render it as "Tomboy."

55 Yingjin Zhang, *Chinese National Cinema* (London: Routledge, 2004), 68.

56 Keith McMahon, "Sublime Love and the Ethics of Equality in a Homoerotic Novel of the Nineteenth Century: Precious Mirror of Boy Actresses," *Nan Nü* 4, 1 (April 1 2002): 102.

57 Gongsun Lu, *Zhongguo dianying shihua*, Vol. 2, 88.

Considered in light of narrative treatments, media interest in cross-dressing in the 1930s invites a reading as an expression of bemusement over the state of the nation, and the same might be said of individual cross-dressing practices.[58] Every popular publication in the 1930s paid attention to women's dress, but the page that promoted the new spring fashion was likely also to feature news of the latest negotiation with a warlord, the latest Japanese atrocity, or the latest initiative (or lack thereof) by the Nationalist government. Thus in June 1932, while Miss Tan Suxin posed with two friends in a park, Marshal Zhang Xueliang inspected troops in Beijing, Master Zhao Shouyan posed cutely in ancient robe, headdress and fan, and a Cantonese schoolgirl modelled bermuda socks embroidered with the words "resist Japan."[59] In this context, the phenomenon of women donning men's clothes appears crammed with narrative significance, even if that was only one of a number of vestimentary choices being made by people in China at the time.

The drift towards trousers

In 1939, as the anti-Japanese war entered its third year, movie-goers in China were presented with another "girl in disguise" movie, one that returned them to familiar territory. Zhang Shankun's *Mulan Joins the Army* was the third screen version of the Hua Mulan legend, two others having been released in close succession in 1928. There were few years in the first half of the twentieth century when the story of Mulan, read as a tale of resistance to invaders, would not have seemed relevant. In 1939, when Japanese forces occupied much of eastern China, it seemed especially so.[60] As East Asia descended into full-scale war, women moved en masse into trousers, the better to contribute to the war effort. Oei Hui-Lan's stepdaughter was married in Chongqing, the wartime capital of Nationalist China. She wore "baggy padded trousers and a matching jacket,"—an outfit "very different," commented Hui-lan, "from the clothes I would have chosen for her."[61] In the Communist base at Yanan, the women soldiers were hardly to be distinguished from the men (Fig. 7.17). On both sides, millions of men were putting aside their gowns for cadre suits or military uniforms.

---

58 See David Der-wei Wang, "Impersonating China," *Chinese Literature: Essays, Articles, Reviews* 25 (December 2003): 133-63. Wang's focus, however, is on men dressed as women, not the reverse.

59 *BYHB* 18 June 1932.

60 Chang-tai Hung, "Female Symbols of Resistance in Chinese Wartime Spoken Drama," *Modern China* 15, 2 (April 1989): 172-4. On Zhang Shankun, see Poshek Fu, "The Ambiguity of Entertainment: Chinese Cinema in Japanese-Occupied Shanghai, 1941 to 1945," *Cinema Journal* 37, 1 (Fall 1997): 66-84.

61 Koo, *No Feast Lasts Forever*, 222.

In retrospect, it can be seen that the *changpao* was doomed by the chronic violence of the first half of the twentieth century. Already in the last decade of the Qing it was threatened by the rise of militarism, but it could then be hoped that China would be a society divided in orderly fashion between civilian and military functions. Despite the adoption of Western suits as formal wear by the first Republican government, daily wear by that government's prescriptions could be the gown and jacket equally as well as the common suit, and its status was reasserted when it was declared formal wear under the Nationalist Government.[62] In practice, the gown remained in wide use until the communist victory in 1949, although its symbolic meanings intensified during the Nanjing Decade.

Fig. 7.17 Wearing trousers the Yanan way: Kang Keqing and He Zizhen at Yanan in 1937. He Zizhen was Mao Zedong's third wife; Kang Keqing was married to Marshal Zhu De.

During the thirties and forties, however, China was engaged in confrontation with Japan as well as in an internal battle between Nationalists and Communists. Its experience can fruitfully be contrasted with India's in the same period, when Indian nationalists were locked in a struggle with their colonial overlords, the British. In vestimentary terms, the Indian struggle was expressed through *swadeshi* and symbolised by Mahatma Gandhi in his homespun loin cloth. The Indian struggle was featured in the Chinese press and no doubt made an impression. One photo published showed a donkey wearing Western hats and draped with Western clothes, while around him stand young nationalists in white caps and Indian shirts. A placard on the donkey's back reads: "We can not see the advantage of *swadeshi* goods because we are donkeys."[63] Passive resistance, while inevitably accompanied by violence, was the order of the day.

---

62 Chang Renchun, *Lao Beijing de chuandai* (Dressing in old Beijing) (Beijing: Yanshan chubanshe, 1999), 28.

63 *BYHB* 5 May 1932.

In China, the anti-Communist campaign (1929–1933), the anti-Japanese war (1937–1945) and the Civil War (1946–1949) meant that the gown-wearing class was exposed extensively to military dress, whether through personal experience or through the press. China was a nation at war through most of the first half of the twentieth century. Millions of people died in the process. The *changpao* could offer no side a promise of victory. The trousers worn by soldiers of various armies, by the peasantry that supplied the manpower, and by the cadres that managed them, were the clothes of the times. In the end, both women and men adopted them.

8
THE NEW LOOK IN THE NEW CHINA

In the 1950s, Zhang Ailing's friend and fellow-writer Su Qing (1917–1982) surprised an old acquaintance by appearing before him dressed in "people's dress of the women's style" (*nüshi de renminzhuang*). His assumption appears to have been that if there was a *qipao* left to wear in Shanghai, a woman such as Su Qing would have been wearing it. But Su Qing was in sympathy with the times. As Wang Anyi later commented, "in a country and a city turned upside down, women were all in plain colours, for you must know that in the 1950s this was the style of 'fashion' for women."[1] Whether this style of clothing can be spoken of as fashion in any usual sense depends, however, on the spirit in which it was worn.

People in China changed clothes for various reasons in the early 1950s. On the one hand, a sense of excitement and energy, pride in the reunification, and hope for the future meant a profound and widespread empathy for the spirit of the revolution. This manifested itself in a strong sense of identification as "the people," which in vestimentary terms meant wearing "the people's dress." On the other hand, there were people who were afraid or uncertain about what "liberation" would bring. In Shanghai, Noel Barber observed the sudden abandonment of *qipao* for pants and shirt by the city's street girls.[2] Such women sought in "the people's dress" an anonymity that might shield them from unwelcome inquiries as to who they were and what they did.

The transition to a new regime in late 1949 was especially significant for women, who were required to rethink themselves in a theoretical context provided by Mao's critique of the patriarchy. Women's liberation ceased to be a right and became a duty, and the circumstances for identity formation and life-style choices became rather constraining. Lin Huiyin, whose husband Liang Sicheng was renowned as an historian of architecture, was delighted to be appointed to

---

1 Wang Anyi, "Xunzhao Su Qing" (In search of Su Qing), in Su Qing, *Jiehun shinian* (Ten years of marriage) (Taibei: Shibao wenhua, 2001), 5. The "women's style" indicates that Su Qing was wearing a Lenin suit.

2 Noel Barber, *The Fall of Shanghai: The Communist Takeover in 1949* (London: Macmillan, 1979), 2.

Fig. 8.1 Men as workers, women as peasants: a standard gender-cum-occupation binary in Liang Yulong's revolutionary poster, "Great Leap Forward in Technology and Culture" (*Jishu wenhua dayuejin*). It can be seen that the worker-peasant combination was also a male-female one. The worker wears the clothing of the international proletariat; the peasant wears Chinese folk dress.

a full academic post at Qinghua University in 1950. That "freed her," her son wrote, "from being Mrs Liang Sicheng."[3] But Kang Keqing (1911–1992), who had served in the army for twenty years, was made to hang up her uniform in 1949 (see Fig. 7.16). The soldier who had frankly stated that she "was not much interested in women's problems," was put to work in the Children's Welfare Department of the Women's Federation.[4] In a way, she was condemned to being just the wife of her husband, Marshal Zhu De (1886–1976).

Although there were no formal regulations governing what such women should wear in the New China, a complex dress code was developed through the propaganda organs of the ruling party. Posters showing workers, peasants and soldiers—some the work of former calendar poster artists—were one

3 Liang Congjie, "Shuhu renjian siyuetian: huiyi wode muqin Lin Huiyin" (Sudden April days in this human world: remembering my mother Lin Huiyin), in Liang Congjie, ed., *Lin Huiyin wenji* (Collected writings by Lin Huiyin) (Taipei: Tianxia yuanjian chuban gufen youxian gongsi, 2000), xxxv.

4 Lily Xiao Hong Lee and Sue Wiles, *Women of the Long March* (St Leonards: Allen and Unwin, 1999), 220-1.

Fig. 8.2 Images of working women were used on the front covers of the official women's magazine. Their occupational categories were signified by their clothing. Here, a national model in agricultural labour, Ou Zhizhen (left), is dressed in a Chinese-style top in polka-dot fabric, typical of the bright, folkish clothing used to portray peasants in poster art; Zhao Mengtao, party member and model worker at provincial and national levels, wears a white cap and apron over her checked jacket to attend her loom. (This is a commemorative photo: she died in 1963.) Zhang Baomei, employed in technological upgrading of measuring and cutting tools in a factory in Chengdu, wears the cap and jacket of an engineer.

important medium for conveying this code (Fig. 8.1).[5] The press, which was full of photos of China's leaders and of model members of the "people," was another. Novels, plays and films constituted a third. Stories such as *Song of Youth*, discussed in the previous chapter, were constructed around characters dressed in particular styles: the reactionary in his gown, the capitalist in his Western suit, the revolutionary in his Sun Yatsen suit. In all these media, men—dressed in whatever clothes—were represented much more commonly than women. Projections of the new gender and class order were thus skewed by the weight of the politically progressive male.

This order had a surprisingly scientific character, consistent with the revolutionary, Marxist respect for technology. "In Mao's China," notes Tina Mai Chen, "the farther a worker moved along a continuum of manual to mental labor and outdoor to indoor work space, the greater the coverage of the body by white garments."[6] The scientist or doctor was fully clad in white, the peasant very rarely. The working man, sometimes depicted wearing a white shirt beneath his overalls, occupied the middle of the "working white" spectrum. He was granted pride of place in the standard worker-peasant-soldier configuration of numerous visual representations of the social order. The dominance of the male was steadily confirmed in party propaganda. If more than one revolutionary class

---

5 Laing, *Selling Happiness*, 223-34.

6 Tina Mai Chen, "Proletarian White and Working Bodies in Mao's China," *positions: east asia cultures critique* 11, 2 (Fall 2003): 378.

Fig. 8.3 The Lenin suit as depicted in a peace poster, 1955: turned-down collar, double breasted and a double row of buttons. The Russian woman is depicted in a blouse, which was consistent with Chinese perceptions of Russian national dress. The caption reads: "Strive for peace and friendship; oppose the use of nuclear weapons."

and more than one gender was depicted, men were cast as workers and soldiers, women as peasants (Fig. 8.1).

The woman as cadre, worker or soldier was of course often depicted in posters, but rarely in the company of men; and the peasant woman—celebrated through the creation of model workers (Fig. 8.2)—was actually at the bottom of the social heap. In Heilongjiang in the late sixties, Rae Yang was shocked to find that the local men referred to their wives as "stinking dependents," although "after a while even we [educated youth] began calling them "stinking dependents" behind their backs."[7] The charming depictions of peasant girls in film, graphic arts, and photography were belied by the reality. Poorly dressed, quick to age, treated with contempt, subject to gross domestic violence, peasant women inspired not even the reddest of revolutionaries to wear their side-fastened, cotton print, distinctively Chinese tops.

Social status in the early years of the PRC was most recognisable in the form of a male cadre (i.e., party functionary) dressed in a Sun Yatsen suit. Women responded to this vestimentary sign by donning the Lenin suit. Double-breasted with a turn-down collar, modelled on the Russian army uniform (Fig. 8.3), the Lenin suit became popular among women revolutionaries first of all in liberated

---

7 Rae Yang, *Spider Eaters* (Berkeley: University of California Press, 1997), 178-9.

Fig. 8.4 Song Qingling (centre), wearing a Lenin suit, greets Deng Fangzhi, mother of fallen soldier Huang Jiguang, on the thirty-fourth anniversary of the People's Liberation Army, 1 August 1961. She is accompanied by Deng Yingchao, the wife of Zhou Enlai, who is wearing an ordinary cadre suit, with just a single row of buttons. Deng Fangzhi's side-fastening collarless jacket was probably typical of rural women's dress at that time.

areas of the north-east, in the late forties. "Aunty" Zheng from Harbin, born around 1940, recalls as a child seeing newspaper photographs of labour heroines such as China's first woman tractor driver, Liang Jun, and first woman truck driver, Tian Guiying: "They all wore Lenin suits, and looked very smart. I really envied them, and wanted to grow up quickly so that I could wear one, too."[8]

The Lenin suit was status dress for civilian women in the 1950s. On her return to civilian life, Kang Keqing adopted "a simple grey cotton Lenin jacket and trousers," which was to be her dress for her remaining years. She jokingly tried on the high-heeled shoes sent to her by Song Qingling to celebrate a return to civilian life, but they did not really go with a Lenin suit.[9] Jung Chang's mother was also forced out of the army after Liberation, and wore a Lenin suit in place of her uniform. She improved on it by wearing a pink printed blouse underneath, with its collar turned out.[10] Song Qingling continued to don a *qipao*, especially when she was representing China to foreigners; but even she was now commonly to be seen in a Lenin suit (Fig. 8.4).

With women in Lenin suits and men in Sun Yatsen suits, even a well dressed assembly presented a monotonous sartorial spectacle. Those who could not afford such clothes wore simple versions thereof. The colours were blue, green or grey, and the cut of clothes varied little between generation and gender. Propaganda materials ranging from campaign posters to news reports show young girls in skirts and blouses, frocks in bright prints modelled on Russian styles, or even *qipao*s; and family photos occasionally show the same. These were good clothes for special occasions, such as family or national celebrations, or even simply for

---

8 "Fuzhuang: yiqu bufan de Lieningzhuang" (Clothing: the Lenin suit—once gone, never to return), *Guoji xianqu baodao*, 20 March 2006, news.xinhuanet.com/herald/2006-03/20/content_4322357.htm. Accessed 1 October 2006.

9 Lee and Wiles, *Women of the Long March*, 225.

10 Jung Chang, *Wild Swans: Three Daughters of China* (New York: Simon and Schuster, 1991), 227.

photo shoots. The everyday vestimentary scene was another matter. "Look along a street," complained the poet Ai Qing (1910–1996), "and all you can see is a great sheet of blue and black."[11]

The political and economic context for this uninspiring scene was complex. With the end of the Korean War in 1953, China enjoyed a respite from almost continuous warfare over a period of sixteen years, and the time was ripe for economic growth. But cotton harvests in 1953 and 1954 were poor and textile production, unlike the population, failed to expand.[12] Under these circumstances, cotton rationing was proposed as an interim solution for cloth shortages.[13] This had the effect of limiting the variety of cloth available to those who could afford to buy more than the minimum required for daily dress, and consequently constricting the possibilities for the re-emergence of a varied clothing culture. On the other hand, the recycling of old clothes was simultaneously promoted.[14] In 1954, old clothes were of course the clothes that were being worn before the founding of the PRC five years earlier, including the *changpao* and the *qipao*, but the *People's Daily* appeared to endorse the acceptability of such garments when it urged the importance of a diversity of clothing in the People's Republic. The current phenomenon of "men and women, old and young, without distinction, all wearing uniforms" (Fig. 8.5) was identified in the paper as a distinct cultural problem.[15]

An obvious question to be asked about this phenomenon is, what did people in China actually want to wear? An opportunity for them to demonstrate their preferences arose in the mid-1950s, when the Ministry of Culture authorised a campaign to reform the reigning drab fashions. Launched early in 1955, the campaign culminated in nationwide fashion shows the following year, before the Hundred Flowers Movement took over and key figures in the campaign had to turn their attention to other matters. It featured a lively discussion on clothing and aggressive promotion of a different dress aesthetic. For a year or two, the way was open, in theory, for people to wear just what they liked, and also to voice their opinions about what should be worn in the New China.

Fashioning Chinese socialism

In April 1955, a forum organised by a leading current affairs magazine, the *New Observer* (*Xin guancha*), brought together leading arts administrators to discuss

---

11 *XGCBYK* 16 April 1955: 24.

12 Alexander Eckstein, *Communist China's Economic Growth and Foreign Trade: Implications for U.S. Policy* (New York: McGraw-Hill for the Council on Foreign Relations, 1966), 50, 60; *Far Eastern Economic Review* (23 February 1956): 237.

13 *RMRB* 14 September 1954.

14 *RMRB* 17 September 1954.

15 Ibid.

possible future directions for Chinese dress.[16] The forum was chaired by journalist and fiction writer Ge Yang (b. 1916), then editor of the *New Observer*.[17] Her deputy editor and exact contemporary, the artist Yu Feng, was a participant, and was appointed director of the campaign.[18] The standing of the forum is evident in the prominence of the participants: Jiang Feng (1910–1982), head of the Central Academy of Fine Arts in Beijing, Zhang Ding (b.

Fig. 8.5 Cartoon commenting on lack of differentiation in clothing between male and female, young and old. Note that the adult women's suits are different: they are in fact not cadre suits but Lenin suits.

1917), a painter in the traditional style and a professor in the academy, the pianist Zhou Guangren (b. 1928), and the poet Ai Qing who with Jiang had played a central part in the formation of CAFA in 1950, and who held a series of important posts in arts organisations in the 1950s.[19]

The forum marked the proximate launch of the dress reform campaign, but in the preceding months the press had carried a number of articles on associated matters, including cotton rationing, the class nature of clothes, and what Chinese women should wear. On this last issue, a short piece in the *Guangming Daily* established a benchmark with its headline: "Women Should Wear Skirts." The writer offered four points in defence of this stance: making skirts or dresses was more economical than making trousers; skirts were more convenient for walking than trousers; skirts were customary wear among Chinese (a moot point, to say the least); and skirts were attractive.[20] These points can be summed up as frugality, practicality, national culture and aesthetics, and they were the four principles to which propagandists for dress reform consistently returned in the course of the campaign. China's poet laureate Guo Moruo (1892–1978) celebrated them in a poem written to celebrate the opening of the Beijing Clothing Exhibition the following year:

---

16 *XGCBYK* 6 April 1955: 23-5.

17 Huaxia funü mingren cidian bianji weiyuanhuai (Editorial committee for the dictionary of famous Chinese women), *Huaxia funü mingren cidian* (Dictionary of famous Chinese women) (Beijing: Huaxia chubanshe, 1988), 113.

18 Ibid.

19 *BDRC*, Vol. I, 317-9; Michael Sullivan, *Art and Artists of Twentieth-Century China* (Berkeley: University of California Press, 1996), 130-1, 321, 322, 324.

20 *GMRB* 6 March 1955.

Economic, appropriate, beautiful, generous,
Loveliness on the body, loveliness in the mind.
Dress is a symbol of culture,
Dress is an ideological phenomenon.
Socialism brings an everlasting spring.
We should have clothes appropriate to the season.[21]

Setting aside the word "socialism," it is clear that this set of principles was consistent with the tenor of the New Life Movement. Much as was the case in the graphic arts, points at issue in the dress debates of the 1950s were set by debates of the Republican era.[22] It is hard to see how this could have been otherwise. Like Guo Moruo, the participants in the *New Observer* forum had all reached maturity under the Nationalist Government, and they necessarily carried their personal histories into the new era. Their family photos would in all cases have shown the procession of styles through which women, in particular, advanced along the path set by China's modernity.[23] Although the fifties are usually regarded as part of a new period of Chinese history, the decade was close to the forties, and people brought to it the problems identified in earlier times. Their contributions to the clothing reform campaign were informed by their historical experience.

Foremost among these continuities was the issue of national self-respect. Yu Feng later recalled national pride as the driving force behind the campaign,[24] a point suggested also by contemporary reports from Hong Kong. "To impress visitors from Hong Kong," reported the *Far Eastern Economic Review* the following year, "authorities in Canton and Shanghai recently 'encouraged' people there to wear colourful dresses instead of grey and blue tunics."[25] In China, newspapers happily reported the responses of foreign friends to Chinese clothing, especially to the *qipao*, and pointed out the obvious influence of Chinese style on the Paris autumn fashions of 1955, in the wake of the visit of an arts troupe to Europe that year.[26]

The importance simply of how China looked to the rest of the world emerged at several junctures during the *New Observer* forum. Ai Qing commenced his address by pointing out that the anti-Japanese war, during which the cadre-style uniform had become a universal form of dress in the base areas, was now some

---

21 *DGB* 1 April 1956.

22 Julia Andrews, *Painters and Politics in the People's Republic of China, 1949-1979* (Berkeley: University of California Press, 1994), 11.

23 See photos in Li Hui, *Ren zai xuanguo: Huang Miaozi yu Yu Feng* (People in a whirlpool: Huang Miaozi and Yu Feng) (Jinan: Shandong huabao chubanshe, 1998).

24 Interview with Yu Feng, Brisbane, 14 February 1999.

25 *Far Eastern Economic Review* 3 May 1956: 560.

26 *Shanghai xinwenbao* 8 March 1956.

years past, and the special conditions under which this form of clothing had become established no longer applied. His aesthetic sensibilities were adversely affected by the sight of his compatriots en masse in the streets of New China. What they wore "[did] not harmonise at all with the examples of architecture along either side of the street, and the joyful tenor of life [under socialism]." In essence, he wanted clothing in socialist China to proclaim the beauties of social-ism to the world.[27]

The painful sense of being observed and found wanting is evident from com-ments made by other conference participants. Zhou Guangren noted that foreign visitors to the Forbidden City commonly remarked afterwards: "your clothing used to be so beautiful. Why does everyone dress so plainly now?" She remarked also on how much the *qipao* was admired by "foreign friends." Zhang Ding was similarly sensitive to the eye of the foreign beholder, complaining that "when we cultural workers go abroad, we all wear the cadre uniform." He viewed this as quite "unnecessary," when the Western suit had already become an international form of dress. An almost palpable sense of humiliation exudes from his brief comment on this issue: he, the Chinese artist abroad, dressed up like a cadre!

Two other important aspects of the campaign emerge from the record of the forum. One is the significance of the example set by the Soviet Union, to which reference was frequently made at other points during the campaign. Stalin was cited in the course of debates over clothing, and so was Chekhov.[28] Where China was heading, as one commentator declared, "was in the direction of the Soviet Union."[29] Jiang Qing (1914–1991) was shocked at Russian women's preoccu-pation with clothes and money,[30] but other Chinese looked with envy on the relatively lively sartorial scene in Russia. The variety of dress evident in photo-graphs and films brought home the fact that not all socialists dressed alike. "In the Soviet Union," pointed out Ai Qing, "if there are six or seven girls walking along together, they will all be wearing different styles of dress." Their situation was quite different from that of children in China, who "dress up like little old people," all looking like "miniature versions of their fathers."[31]

In terms of vestimentary culture Russians and Chinese were actually mov-ing in different time zones. 1950s China was comparable not to post-Stalinist Russia but to a much younger socialist state. Just as the cadre suit enjoyed mass popularity in 1950s China, so the khaki "Jungsturm" uniform for men and women had become *de rigueur* in young Russian circles in the late 1920s, to the disapproval of the authorities. A campaign was mounted to beautify

---

27 *XGCBYK* 16 April 1955: 24.

28 *Zhongguo qingnian banyuekan* 1 March 1955; 1 January 1955.

29 *Zhongguo qingnian banyuekan* 1 March 1955.

30 Roxane Witke, *Comrade Jiang Qing* (London: Weidenfeld and Nicholson, 1977), 258.

31 *XGCBYK* 6 April 1955.

Fig. 8.6 Commemorative photo of 1952: the girls are wearing *bulaji* and the boys checked shirts to match. The girls seem inexperienced at wearing dresses, arranging their legs just as if they were wearing trousers.

Russian clothing through the production of a "true 'Soviet' fashion of our very own," not only hygienic and practical but also aesthetically pleasing. Fashion shows and exhibitions were to be organised to popularise the new styles.[32] In China, dress designers of the 1950s were thus struggling with issues that had been faced by their Russian counterparts in the 1920s: what sort of clothing was appropriate, what was pleasing, what was desirable, for the happy citizenry of a socialist country?

Nonetheless, Chinese answers to these questions were in part shaped by post-war Soviet attitudes. Sentiments uttered in the Soviet press such as "the Soviet person has become more beautiful, both in mind and soul; his clothes must also be beautiful"[33] were frequently echoed in the Chinese media in the 1950s; and Russian women's magazines, with their plethora of fashion sketches and patterns, helped legitimate the tentative revival of fashion as a topic in the Chinese press.[34] A major new item in the Chinese wardrobe in the early fifties was the

---

32 Lidya Zaletova, Fabio Ciofi degli Atti, Franco Panzini et al., *Costume Revolution: Textiles, Clothing and Costume of the Soviet Union in the Twenties*, trans. Elizabeth Dafinone (London: Trefoil Publications, 1987).

33 Lynne Attwood, *Creating the New Soviet Woman: Women's Magazines as Engineers of Female Identity, 1922-53* (Houndmills: Macmillan Press Ltd., 1999), 164. Punctuation adapted.

34 On fashion in post-war Soviet magazines, see ibid., 163-5.

bulaji or frock, the Chinese transliteration of the Russian term "platje."[35] Often made of printed cloth, belted in at the waist, and featuring a shirt-collar, this simple, distinctively European garment was among the gender-distinctive forms of dress on the streets of Chinese cities in the early fifties (Fig. 8.6). It was inspired by the clothing worn in China by Russian women in the early fifties, and by styles publicised in Russian magazines and films.[36]

The other aspect of the campaign apparent from the forum is that it was largely concerned with women's dress, and to a lesser extent with children's. Zhang Ding was the only conference participant to dwell closely on men's dress, which he raised in connection with both peasants and townspeople. The major issue for everyone, including Zhang Ding, was the lack of gender differentiation in dress. This was not too far removed from the question of national self-respect. Zhou Guangren was perturbed that his foreign friends thought there were no women appearing in public places, because the cadre suit made everyone look male. The nexus between gender differentiation in dress and national culture became plain in the designs developed for women's clothing.

National culture in Yu Feng's fashion theory

The core group of designers consisted entirely of women. They included well-known artists such as Qiu Ti (1892–1958) and Xiao Shufang (b. 1911); Chang Shana (b. 1931), who was the daughter of the artist Chang Hongshu and like him a student of the Dunhuang frescoes; Gu Qun (b. 1928), oil painter and teacher at CAFA; Chen Ruoju (b. 1928), instructor at the Central Academy of Industrial Fine Arts; printing and dyeing expert Wu Shusheng (b. 1925); and Xia Yayi (b. 1921), costume designer for stage performances of popular or folk dance.[37] Their efforts were coordinated by campaign director, Yu Feng, who had responsibility for establishing a theoretical framework for new designs as well as for design production. A survey of her writings reveals the range of historical, cultural and aesthetic issues raised in the course of the campaign.

At a time when debates in the art world over socialist realism versus Chinese-style painting were raging, Yu Feng did not adopt a highly ideological position on painting. She was herself an oil painter, but had great admiration for the

---

35 For this information I thank Professor Konstantin Tertitski, Institute of Asian and African Studies, Moscow State University.

36 Zhang Liangqiong, Zhang Yuxia, Zhou Kaiyan, and Chen Ping, "Cong Zhongguo xiandai wenyuan zhiyezhuang de xingcheng he fazhan kan yinru waili yangzhi de yiban lujing yu moshi" (A route and model for foreign styles considered from the perspective of the form and development of professional clothing for arts personnel in modern China), *Zhejiang gongcheng xueyuan xuebao* 18, 1 (March 2001): 56-7.

37 See Huaxia funü mingren cidian bianji weiyuanhui, *Huaxia funü mingren cidian*; *Meishu* April 1956: 30-3.

work of the aged doyen of Chinese-style painting, Qi Baishi (1864–1957). She had a romantic engagement with folk or rural culture and an intense respect for the national art heritage. While she was keen to see diversity in dress and to that extent was forward looking, her theoretical statements and practical designs showed constant reference to folk culture and to legacies of the past.

The weight Yu Feng placed on maintenance of local culture and handicraft traditions was evident at the *New Observer* forum, where she drew on her travel experiences of the previous year.[38] Echoing comments on the rich texture of rural life made in her essay of that year, she declared her fondness for the colour and variety of local material cultures. In Fujian, she had seen women "all wearing tops of deep or pale pink with loose black trousers. They looked wonderful. When they went off to work each day, each wore fresh flowers in her hair, and each day the flowers were different."[39] Sketches of women in rural dress were contributed by both her and Zhang Ding for the published account of the forum.

In an essay published in *Fine Arts*, Yu Feng elaborated on the theme of folk dress by drawing attention to the attractiveness of clothing culture among the minority peoples. Rural China and minority China probably occupied the same space in her mind, and served similar functions as ways of talking about the antiquity and cultural origins of the nation. She demonstrated the proximity of the two tropes to each other by moving seamlessly from the richness of arts and crafts among the minority peoples to the subject of (Han) rural life:

In the vast rural and the minority areas, we must encourage conservation and dissemination of the regional and ethnic characteristics of the original clothing of the people. The infinite knowledge and talent of the labouring women of the vast rural areas has always been evident in [their hand-crafted garments, such as] head scarves in every pattern and style, their skirts, the uppers of their embroidered shoes. If today we hear that some village and minority girls no longer know how to embroider, this can only be a loss.[40]

The decorative designs she supplied for this article are similar to examples of embroidery from Haimen in Zhejiang, advertised in a 1957 issue of *China's Women* as examples of Chinese handiwork that could be used to beautify clothing (Fig. 8.7). Her attachment to the "old home village," also in Zhejiang, suggests that her own ancestral town may have laid the foundations for her interest in minority culture arts and crafts. Her major essays on her native place date from 1956 and 1979, but her obituary essay for her father in 1939 shows that this attachment was of long standing.[41]

---

38 Yu Feng, "Ziran, shenghuo, chuangzuo" (Nature, life, creation) [1954], in Yu Feng, *Wode guxiang* (My old home place) (Tianjin: Baihua wenyi chubanshe, 1984), 196-206.

39 *XGCBYK* 6 April 1955: 24.

40 Yu Feng, "Fayang fuzhuang de minzu fengge" (Developing the national style in clothing). *Meishu* April 1955: 13.

41 Yu Feng, "Fuqin—faguan, shiren, huajia" (My father: judge, poet, artist) [1939], in Yu

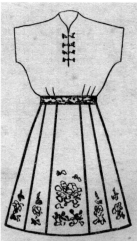

Fig. 8.7 Yu Feng's embroidery design for a Chinese folk-influenced skirt and blouse (right), and embroidery and lace designs inspired by handicraft workers in Haimen, Zhejiang province.

Read alongside her expressions of frank admiration for rural and minority crafts, Yu Feng's statements on urban forms of dress from recent history seem cautious and require reading between the lines. One feature of recent Chinese fashion on which she remarked was the mandarin collar, which had dramatically characterised the revolutionary fashions of 1911 and after subsiding somewhat in the 1920s had re-emerged with flair in the 1930s. Zhang Ailing commented of the mandarin collar that in the 1930s it was "uglier than ever," creating the impression of "an upright, remote little head, the head of a goddess, perched on top of a voluptuous, free-flowing figure."[42] But there is no doubting that it had become the signifier of Chinese style. Yu Feng plainly admired the collar, but her admiration was tempered by utilitarian concerns. "The Chinese-style collar is excellent," she stated, "because we are not accustomed to baring shoulders and revealing the bosom, and our physique is also not well suited to it. But the collar should not be too high or it will impede freedom of movement."[43]

Caution is also obvious in her response to the question of the *qipao*. The strongest statement on the *qipao* at the *New Observer* conference was made by party veteran Yang Zhihua, the widow of Qu Qiubai (1898–1935). Yang's contribution to the conference was a brief letter, which was read out to the meeting and sub-

Feng, *Wode guxiang*, 127-31; "Wode guxiang" (My old home place) [1956], in Yu Feng, *Wode guxiang*, 11-27; "'Wode guxiang' bu ji" (Further to 'My old home place') [1979], in Yu Feng, *Wode guxiang*, 37-48.

42 Eileen Chang, "Chinese Life and Fashions," 72.

43 *XGCBYK* 6 April 1955: 24.

Fig. 8.8 Two designs by Yu Feng. On the left, the embroidered shirring at the waist is attributed to dressmaking practices in rural areas of Jiangnan. The right shows the modified *qipao* with A-line skirt.

sequently published in the report of proceedings. In it she declared her opposition to the *qipao* on class, utilitarian and aesthetic grounds.[44] Yu Feng's statement on the *qipao* at the conference was correspondingly careful. In brief, she said she was not opposed to it. In a later article she wrote of the "poor impression" that young women had of the *qipao*, an unbecomingly tight-fitting garment which was moreover "not practical for nowadays." And young designers were unlikely "even to have seen patterns for it."[45]

Nonetheless, the *qipao* appealed to Yu Feng. As against other garments on offer, it had several advantages. First, it was distinctly Chinese, and unlike the dress of rural women was historically associated with modern, urban, progressive women. It was quite common for the *qipao* to be used as a national emblem, either actually, as when Chinese women went abroad, or figuratively, as in propaganda photographs and posters. Second, women knew how to make it. Home-made garments were the norm in China till the last quarter of the twentieth century, and the *qipao* was relatively simple to make. Third, as Yu Feng noted, many women still had *qipao*s tucked away in cupboards, a wasted resource in a time of cloth shortages.[46] Her affirmation of this obviously Chinese style is evident in her response to the *bulaji*, which dominated new styles shown at the Beijing clothing exhibition in 1956 and available in retail stores there and elsewhere, particularly in Shanghai. "I think that wearing western-style frocks is

44 Ibid., 25.

45 Yu Feng, "Fayang fuzhuang de minzu fengge," 13.

46 Ibid.

fine," she wrote, "but the phenomenon of people not liking or actually ceasing to wear Chinese clothes deserves our attention."[47] The designs she produced during the campaign showed a debt both to folk culture and to the *qipao* (Fig. 8.8).

Yu Feng's attachment to historical and regional national forms was not out of place in 1950s China: Mao Zedong had similar sympathies, and Chinese-style (*guohua*) painting enjoyed strong support among both artists and art lovers. But neither were such tendencies particular to the era. Yu Feng's statements on Chinese dress resonate with the sartorial history of Zhang Ailing, whose commentary on two photographs taken in 1944 anticipate Yu Feng's statements on the importance of retaining local skills in material culture. These photographs show Zhang in a bright floral top, the material for which

Fig. 8.9 Design for a peasant outfit circulated in the clothing reform campaign in 1956. The outfit was modelled live for exhibitions and newspaper pictures.

she had purchased in Canton. "Down in the countryside," she wrote, "it is only children who wear this [fabric]. I brought some back to Shanghai to be made up, thinking to perpetuate the arts of the common people."[48] Learning from the masses and painting from life, fundamental principles in art practice in the 1950s, were compatible with a deep nationalist impulse for locating culture in the past and in the people. In this respect, Yu Feng's statements on the future direction of Chinese clothing culture were not at all Maoist. Rather, they were continuous with earlier twentieth-century concerns about national culture generally.

Chinese fashions and world time

An instinct for the modern to some extent countered nationalist aesthetics in the outlook of the dress reformers. Appealing as folk dress may have been to nationalist sensibilities, Yu Feng did not urge women to follow Zhang Ailing's example and actually wear it. Fashion features and exhibitions in 1956 dictated different fashions for urban and rural women. Just such an outfit as Yu Feng

---

47 Ibid.

48 Zhang Ailing, *Duizhao ji*, 59.

Fig. 8.10 Yu Feng (right), director of the clothing reform campaign, photographed arm in arm with New Zealand visitor Ngaere Te Punga during an excursion to the Summer Palace, Beijing, May 1956.

幾種服裝樣子

Fig. 8.11 Designs by Yu Feng's colleague, Xiao Shufang: a *bulaji* (left) and two different skirts and tops. The mandarin collar on the blouse modelled top right marks the garment as Chinese in style, but the garments have a highly contemporary look.

had described as eye-catching in Fujian was put on display at a fashion exhibition in Tianjin, with a caption indicating that it was suitable for rural women.[49] "New Shanghai Fashion" publicised in *Wenhuibao* in March 1956 showed a fetching rural woman in wide-sleeved flowered print top and neat apron worn with trousers, a design that was circulated in graphic illustrations on leaflets or posters (Fig. 8.9). The recommended style for a woman cadre, by contrast, was a neat shirt-collar frock in plain fabric, belted in at the waist—the professional woman's version of the *bulaji*.[50] While motifs from folk embroidery on a blouse might sign modern dress as Chinese, folk dress could not be used as the basis for how to cut garments worn by urban women. For that, Yu Feng had to look for other sources of inspiration.

The irresistible pull of world time for fashion designers even in the unlikely context of Maoist China is obvious from the designs produced under Yu Feng's direction. In the West, from the 1930s onwards, a disciplined, tailored look

49 *DGB* 1 April 1956.

50 *Wenhuibao* 16 March 1956.

connected with the masculinisation of mainstream clothing competed with retro styles that attempted to recapture the nineteenth-century full skirt and tight bodice formulation. Dior's "New Look" of the late forties is the most famous example of the latter, and retained some influence through the 1950s. In China, fashion exhibitions held in 1956 occasionally featured full-blown "New Look" skirts, with their many yards of material, a style depicted also in newspapers and magazines.[51] This style was deemed suitable for evening wear. Of greater interest are the day-wear designs. The hip-length waisted top, both tapered and full skirts, the loose short overcoat and the bloused bodice were all garments that resonated with contemporary Western fashions. Strolling in the grounds of the Summer Palace in spring 1956, Yu Feng wore an ensemble that made her look quite at home with the members of the New Zealand cultural delegation whom she was accompanying (Fig. 8.10).

Skirts and frocks clearly dominated the thinking of arts circles when it came to imagining how Chinese women of the new era might look. The former had Chinese antecedents, skirts being a standard overgarment for Chinese women of any means right up to the early twentieth century. It is doubtful, however, that these early models were what advocates of the skirt had in mind. The skirt designs produced in the 1950s were clearly in sympathy with Western fashion (Fig. 8.11). The same could be said of the frock, or *bulaji*, which obviously owed much to identification with "uncle Soviet Union," but also tapped into modern world fashions.

The clearest evidence that Chinese artists involved in the dress reform campaign were attuned to shifts in international fashion lies in the modified *qipao*. Modification took a couple of different forms. One was the simple addition of inverted pleats to cover the characteristic side slits in the garment, solving the problem of leg exposure. The other was the adaptation of the *qipao* to a frock design, a fuller skirt reproducing the feminine lines of post-war fashions in the West (Fig. 8.12). Antecedents to the *qipao* frock can be seen in early post-war designs such as produced by Chen Ling for a 1946 fashion folio (Fig. 8.13). With similar designs in the fifties, Yu Feng and her associates affirmed the internationalisation of Chinese dress. Women in China had of course often worn Western clothes in preceding decades, but in doing so they had been moving between different sartorial worlds. Chinese clothes and Western clothes, even if sometimes mixed and matched with each other, were terminologically and psychologically distinct. The *qipao* frock integrated the two styles, while at the same time abandoning a defining feature of the long-line, now classic *qipao* of the 1930s. Its multi-layered historical references, and thus its cultural particularity, became ever fainter.

---

51 *DGB* 1 April 1956; 22 March 1956.

Fig. 8.12 *Qipao*-influenced designs by, from left to right, Yu Feng, Xiao Shufang and Qiu Ti, published in China's leading fine arts journal.

Inherent in the new clothing imaginary was a new apprehension of the Chinese female body. Historically, the clearest systematic distinction between European and Chinese women's dress was a difference in line. Prior to the twentieth century, with the partial exception of the empire line, European women's dress tended to emphasise bust and hips through waisted styles. Chinese dress was the reverse: loose, commodious, and concealing, especially during the nineteenth century when the cut of clothes became very wide. Even the *qipao*, which dominated urban women's dress in the 1930s, was essentially a straight garment. Only with the addition of darts to shape the garment, beginning in the post-war period, was the potential of the long-line *qipao* to show off feminine curves fully developed. The *qipao* frock and the *bulaji*, together with the skirt and blouse ensemble, likewise showed the Chinese woman as presenting bust, waist and hips.

Although the reign of these new fashions was brief, they served to show that the only alternative to jackets and trousers for men and women in blue, green or grey was a highly conventional modern wardrobe, which would duplicate in China the visual differentiation between men and women evident in the hallmark modern societies of the West. In the process of drawing clothes, Yu Feng and her colleagues were also drawing idealised women. These were on the whole unlike the women commonly portrayed in revolutionary art of the Maoist period but they provide a hint of something haunting the imagination of people in

218

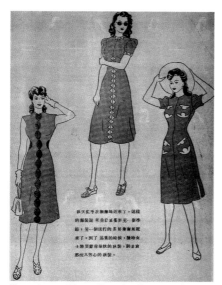

Fig. 8.13 Chen Ling's designs for the "modern lady," 1946.

China as they hurried their society along into the future. The entire campaign appears to have been fuelled by an anxiety that women in socialist China did not look quite right. A certain, internationally recognisable type of gender differentiation was necessary to stamp the New China as new.

There were of course ironies in revolutionary women artists devoting their energies to producing such differentiation. To the extent that they identified with their task, something not easy to assess, they effectively demonstrated the narrow confines within which middle-class women could construct themselves after Liberation. The exaggerated styles of high couture in the West, so necessary to establishing the seasonal look apparent in modified versions of the original creation, are absent from the designs which appeared in publications across the country in 1956. The artists who produced them probably had to trim their own drawings, either in their minds or on paper, in order to fulfill their brief: the design of a modest, practical and at the same time visually appealing wardrobe for the women of the nation. Yu Feng's instinct for the collar, for example, was modified by her concerns for utilitarian dress styles. In this, she was in accordance with her associates in the dress reform project. They had to think small rather than big, and their clothing designs were on the whole conservative. The most striking point of comparison between dress design sketches in Chinese and Western publications in this period is the careful, modest, realist line of the former relative to the latter.

The scope and limitations of the dress reform campaign

The high point of the dress reform campaign occurred in spring 1956, when fashion exhibitions were held around the country. Xiamen, on the southern coast, led the way on 10 March, with Nanjing, Fuzhou, Guangzhou and Tianjin following in short order. On the evening of 24 March, an invited party of six hundred workers, students and cadres gathered at Beijing's New Overseas Chinese Hotel for the national capital's first socialist fashion parade. Among the models were third and fourth year Middle School students, who made an impression on the audience

219

on account of their freshness and vitality.[52] The following week a public clothes exhibition was opened in the Workers' Cultural Palace, attracting 83,000 visitors in the first couple of days. Similar exhibitions were held around the same time in a number of other large cities—Tianjin, Shanghai, Changsha, Chengdu, Chongqing, Shenyang. Travelling exhibitions were organised so that lesser centres would not miss out. A show conducted in Urumqi, Xinjiang, featured "more than 1,000 costumes of Han, Uighur, Kazakh and Russian styles."[53]

The spring of 1956 was a lively period for the Chinese rag trade. Retail outlets were attached to many of the exhibitions, and significant quantities of floral print cloth and made-up dresses were reportedly sold. The exposure given to new fashions at this time placed clothing on the social agenda. The aim of socialism, declared one columnist, was "the improvement of the material life and culture of the people," including the beautification of dress in accordance with the principles of attractiveness, economy and usefulness.[54] *Qipao* and *bulaji*, along with skirts and blouses—including blouses in a *qipao* style—were pictured in press reports of the exhibitions. Men's Western suits were occasionally featured, and newspapers ran advertisements for new shoe styles and new hairstyles to round out the imaginary of a modern Chinese clothing culture (Fig. 8.14).

Yet for women as well as for men, the impact of the dress reform campaign on clothing culture in China was limited. Politics militated against its success. The Hundred Flowers Movement, though not developing into a mass campaign until 1957, was already distracting attention from clothes in 1956. According to Yu Feng, there was less and less time to devote to dress reform as she and her colleagues became caught up in a relentless round of meetings dedicated to political affairs. The press continued to feature articles on dress reform through 1956, but by the first half of 1957 the movement was in its twilight. The spring fashion shows of 1956 had no successors. Patterns for the new styles continued to be published, but newspapers and periodicals in 1957 in general retreated from open propaganda for the diversification of dress styles.

Economic conditions were also unfavourable to radical changes in dress practices. Even in the middle of the campaign, the theme of frugality continued to be sounded: advertisements

Fig. 8.14 Different hairstyles advertised in the summer of 1956: the permed bob was dominant.

---

52 *RMRB* 26 March 1956.

53 *Far Eastern Economic Review* 3 May 1956: 560.

54 *DGB* 9 March 1956.

for new styles were accompanied by calls to "Economise In The Use Of Cloth." Arguments for dress diversity as economically advantageous for the family and the country were consistently advanced in the course of the dress reform movement, but in practice, only the simplest combination of clothes could begin to rival the economy of jacket and trousers. While the simple, straight *qipao* offered clear advantages over the cadre uniform in terms of saving material, revised *qipao* designs added fullness to the skirt at the expense of conserving cloth.

The sudden license to "dress up nicely" (*daban piaoliang*) moreover encouraged a large wardrobe. This point was brought up in a letter to the *China Youth Daily*, allegedly sent by the irate husband of a profligate woman who wanted to buy ever more clothes to keep up with the changing fashions. The newspaper had some stern advice to offer, especially to young women: "Wearing attractive styles of dress is a good thing. But we must also remind those with a taste for fashion: the beauty of frugality and simplicity should not be thrust to the back of your minds. You can also dress up nicely using slightly cheaper materials."[55]

From the point of view of the practicalities of daily life in 1950s China, the campaign itself was poorly thought through. Skirts and dresses were suitable only for wearing in warm weather. Anywhere north of the Yangzi and for much of the country to the south, trousers were necessary in the winter, especially in the absence of woollen stockings. In September 1956, the *Harbin Daily* advertised an autumn wardrobe which for women consisted of box-pleat skirt or *qipao* under jacket.[56] Even if made of heavy cloth, as the text advised, such garments could be worn with comfort only for a month or two in Manchuria. When the *Liaoning Youth Daily* offered its readers a choice of clothing designs six weeks later, the alternatives offered for women were Chinese-style jackets and pants, options appropriate to the cold weather already upon them.[57]

A third, and finally the most significant factor inhibiting a change in clothing culture, was the receptiveness of the populace. In Russia, limited resources and political propaganda did not prevent people from "dressing up nicely." In China, as it proved, the dress reform campaign could not easily effect a change in people's attitudes to what they wore. The move to revive the *qipao* was especially unsuccessful. According to Yu Feng, women were much more likely to don a skirt and blouse than to venture forth in a *qipao*,[58] while from the photographic record, it would seem that ten years after the founding of the PRC, a Chinese girl getting dressed up to celebrate National Day was more likely to be wearing skirt and top than *qipao*. As practical wear, the *qipao* was rejected by the authorities. New police uniforms introduced in 1956 consisted in summer of "white or

---

55 *Zhongguo qingnianbao* 28 June 1956.

56 *Ha'erbin ribao* 1 September 1956.

57 *Liaoning ribao* 17 October 1956.

58 Yu Feng interview.

Fig. 8.15 "We two are of one mind." Cartoon by Chen Jinyan depicting a woman in *qipao* keeping musical accompaniment to a man playing a "right-wing tune". The reference is to Li Jiansheng (b. 1908), a member of the China Democratic League and wife of one of its most prominent representatives, Zhang Bojun. Both were prominent in various official capacities in the early years of the PRC before falling victim to the anti-rightist movement of 1957.

dark green jackets with navy blue trousers for the men and skirts for the women."[59] As leisure wear, the *qipao* continued to be tainted by associations with right-wing politics and cultural decadence (Fig. 8.15).

The cadre suit retained favour among women. In 1956, as the dress reform campaign entered its second year, press reports showed that little had been done to marginalise these forms of dress. One commentator, although anxious to promote dress diversity, also defended the Sun Yatsen suit and the Lenin suit as each beautiful in its own spartan way, and appropriate dress for those who wished to wear them.[60] Another frankly protested against pressures being placed on girl students to abandon their cadre uniforms.[61] Yu Feng early identified ideological prejudices and social conformity as obstacles to the diversification and beautification of clothing (Fig. 8.16):

I think that the most important reason lies not in economic reasons, customary practices of daily life or people being too busy at work, but rather in ideological prejudices. For example, one might think others would conclude that you like dressing up and say that you are following a bourgeois life-style; or that a revolutionary cadre should support a simple style; or that you are dressing up because you are seeking a marriage partner; or that your style is not proper … Therefore, nobody wants to wear beautiful clothes and expose herself to criticism.[62]

This sort of social pressure extended right down to small children. Lu Xiaorong, at school in Chongqing in the 1950s, was elated to be among the little girls chosen to greet a Soviet visitor to the school, but she was dismissed from the group when she turned up for rehearsal dressed for the occasion in a new red woollen cardigan embroidered with flowers. Her astute mother instructed her to take the cardigan back to school and give it to one of the girls who had not found something suitable to wear. The sacrifice paid off: at the end of term, Xiaorong was elected an exemplary stu-

59 *Far Eastern Economic Review* 7 June 1956: 715.

60 *Zhongguo qingnianbao* 16 March 1956.

61 *Zhongguo qingnian banyuekan* 15 June 1956.

62 Yu Feng, "Fayang fuzhuang de minzu fengge," 12-13.

百相观望　　　　江有生作

——还没有人穿……

——有人带头了……

——快回去……

——快回去……

Fig. 8.16 In his cartoon "Beholding each other," Jiang Yousheng echoed Yu Feng's comments on conformity as a factor inhibiting fashion diversity.

dent by her classmates, and the following term she was made class leader.[63]

As Yu Feng also wrote, a clothing culture could not be supplied by professional artists. It was the work of the masses. Insight into actual fashion trends in 1950s China was supplied by the artist Ding Zheng, who pointed to the status of the cadre suit (usually the Sun Yatsen suit for men, Lenin suit for women) as the main impediment to change in clothing culture. He introduced this subject with an anecdote:

In 1950, on the eve of the first of May, Labour Day, I was at a bath house in Beijing when three working men in soiled, oil-stained jackets and trousers came in, just opposite where I was sitting. Each of them was carrying a little bag. What emerged from each bag after they had washed was, in a word, a cadre suit, at that time not yet in widespread use. They donned them in all solemnity, inspecting each other to see whether the garments were too big or too small, too long or too short; but having tentatively tried them on, they proceeded to take them off again, carefully folding them away into their bags and putting their old clothes back on. Except one rather young fellow among them, grinning happily, said to his companions: "I can't wait. I'm going to wear mine today," eliciting the response: "What's the hurry? Think what day it is tomorrow."

In the eyes of these workers, as the writer pointed out, the cadre suit was festive wear, good clothes for a special occasion. But a second example he offers shows it had other meanings as well:

The owner of a department store only yesterday was wearing a silk coat, but today when he takes up his position at the door of the shop to watch the passers-by, he turns out to have changed into a blue cadre suit. A business associate who knew him well came by and made a sly joke: "Congratulations! The boss of the shop has become a cadre!"

---

63 Lu Xiaorong, "Yijian maoyi" (A woollen cardigan), in *Shui yao ren* (Eaten up by water) (Shanghai: Shanghai shiji chuban jituan and Shanghai jiaoyu chubanshe, 2004), 4-5.

Fig. 8.17 "Who's the bride?" asked cartoonist Lu Tian, in a critical comment about the cadre suit as wedding dress. For a rural wedding, traditional-looking clothes were regarded as more suitable than cadre suits (left).

But he responded seriously: "I mightn't be a cadre, but I can certainly be reckoned Chinese!"

Finally, this writer recognised the appeal of the cadre suit to young women (Fig. 8.17):

In the countryside, young women getting ready for their weddings these days don't worry about whether or not they have a dowry but whether or not their parents will let them make a new cadre suit. In fact, the red flowers worn at the breast by bride and groom at a wedding are now often attached to the front of a cadre suit. Young women living in cities have altered their *qipao*s to make short jackets, and over the jackets they wear cadre suits. The reasons do not go beyond this: they have linked together cadre suits and progressive thinking, cadre suits and simplicity in lifestyle, cadre suits and frugality ... Although this is all erroneous, there is no denying that in it we find encompassed the desire of women for progress and for equality with men in life and work, as well as a view of simplicity and frugality as the core elements of Chinese aesthetics.[64]

In brief, the cadre suit appealed to the status-conscious, to patriots, and to women. This encompassed quite a large number

誰 是 新 娘? 魯 田 作

---

64 Ding Zheng, "Tan fuzhuang de bianhua he fuzhuang gaijin wenti" (On the problems of changes and advances in clothing), *Meishu* April 1956: 8.

Fig. 8.18 Skirts and blouses, or an occasional frock, were the order of the day for the commemorative games of the tenth anniversary of the People's Republic. Top, women athletes on parade. Above, cover girls for the tenth anniversary issue of *China's Women*.

of people. It is plain that some people in China merely endured the fashion, wearing it for reasons of fear or unwelcome peer pressure, but it is probable that very many felt good wearing it. Why would they not? Their leaders wore it. It was the dress of the New China, a new era, which they were helping to create. Wearing it, they felt both attuned to their times and linked to the historical, heroic period of Yanan. What is more, when they felt like a change, they did not revert to the *qipao* or *changpao* of the past but rather to cosmopolitan styles. When women athletes donned frocks or skirts and blouses at the games held to mark the tenth anniversary of the founding of the People's Republic of China, it was clear that the hegemony of the *qipao* had been broken (Fig. 8.18).

As it proved, the campaign itself was out of temper with the times. In 1958 the government announced the beginning of a "great leap forward" that in the space of five years was meant to take China into the ranks of the industrialised nations of the world. Not long afterwards, the country was struck by famine. Propaganda campaigns urging frugality in the use of cloth increased in intensity (Fig. 8.19). In "ways and means" columns, women were advised how to cut cloth with minimal wastage, and how to turn an old garment into a new one. Long before the allotted five years had lapsed, people in China

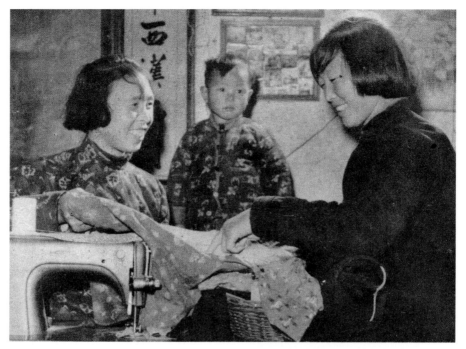

Fig. 8.19 Happy peasants with a shiny sewing machine and clothes of figured cloth, photographed in 1962 for an article on the importance of conserving cloth.

were reduced to making their clothes from "patriotic wool" (*aiguo ni*), or in other words, from scraps.[65]

---

65 Sang Ye, "From Rags to Revolution: Beyond the Seams of Social Change," in Claire Roberts, ed., *Evolution and Revolution: Chinese Dress 1700s–1900s* (Sydney: Powerhouse Museum, 1997), 47-8.

9
DRESSED TO KILL IN THE CULTURAL REVOLUTION

In 1963, Wang Guangmei (1921–2006), wife of President Liu Shaoqi (1898–1969), accompanied her husband on a tour to Southeast Asia. A journalist interviewing her in later years recalled the feature documentary *Chairman Liu Shaoqi Visits Indonesia*, filmed in colour, that had been shown in Chinese cinemas in wake of the tour. Only eight or nine at the time, she retained in adulthood a vivid memory of Wang Guangmei in her "Chinese-style *qipao*, so lovely in appearance, with such an air of elegance and distinction—that affected me powerfully. You could say it was the first glimmerings of sexual awareness in me."[1]

Four years later, in one of the most famous incidents of the Cultural Revolution, Wang was confronted with this fragment of her sartorial past by the self-styled Jinggangshan Corps of Beijing's prestigious Qinghua University. At a mass struggle session, she was charged with being "a member of the reactionary bourgeoisie and the number one pickpocket on the Qinghua campus." Most of the students interrogating her had no doubt seen the film featuring her wearing a *qipao*. They shamelessly recorded the struggle session:

Interrogator: We want you to put on the dress that you wore in Indonesia.

Wang Guangmei: That was summer ... Chairman Mao has said that we must pay attention to climate and change clothing according to it.

Interrogator [amidst laughter]: What Chairman Mao has said refers to the political climate. According to your standpoint, even though you are wearing a fur coat, you will also freeze to death.[2]

---

1 Sun Ji, Fan Jia'an, and Gu Jing, "Wang Guangmei xishuo wangshi" (Wang Guangmei discusses the past in detail), *Huaxia nügong* (Women's work in China) 1, 2002, www.gmw. cn/03pindao/renwu/2004-07/03/content_52318.htm. Accessed 12 November 2005.

2 "The Trial of Liu Shao-ch'i's Wife, 10 April 1967," in Harold Hinton, ed., *The People's Republic of China 1949-1979: A Documentary Survey, Vol. 3: The Cultural Revolution Part 1* (Wilmington: Scholarly Resources Inc., 1980), 1699-700. Romanisation adapted.

Fig. 9.1 Wang Guangmei, wife of President Liu Shaoqi, wearing clothes she was forced to put on during her interrogation by Red Guards.

She was humiliated by being forced to put on a *qipao* too small for her, a necklace of ping-pong balls, and high-heeled shoes. Photos of the event have survived (Fig. 9.1).

The politics of clothing during the Cultural Revolution are a familiar aspect of the social history of the "ten years of turmoil" (1966–1976). In her widely read memoir *Life and Death in Shanghai*, Nien Cheng commented on the problem of what to wear in these years. Nien for many years held a senior position in Shell International's Shanghai office and was able to keep herself and her daughter in an unusual degree of comfort up until the Cultural Revolution. After the initial outbreak of Red Guard activity in Shanghai she made her first venture outside very cautiously, wearing her servant's floppy trousers with exercise shoes and a countrywoman's hat. Dressed thus, she was preserved from experiencing what she saw befall a young girl who was wearing pants with a narrow cut and fashionable shoes. In the middle of the street, the girl was seized by Red Guards, and her shoes and trousers were forcibly removed before the eyes of a jeering crowd.[3]

From the highest echelon of Chinese society to the lowest, at least in urban contexts, women were vulnerable to such attacks during the Cultural Revolution. In some respects, the pattern had been prefigured during earlier decades—in the violence inflicted on girls with bobbed hair in the 1920s, for instance, and in the regulations governing women's dress in the 1930s. In the early years of the PRC, too, women could hardly dress with impunity. Even during the dress reform campaign, it would appear, gossip followed the woman who paid too much attention to her looks; social pressure could make life difficult for her at work and in the neighbourhood; and during a political campaign, when every unit needed a target for struggle, she was an obvious candidate. But actual physical attacks on women on the grounds of what they wore were not a notable feature of those earlier years.

Although there were clear cultural continuities between the fifties and late sixties in China, the early years of the Cultural Revolution are characterised by

---

3 Nien Cheng, *Life and Death in Shanghai* (London: Grafton Books, 1987), 85.

a spirit of violent struggle that exceeded the temper of the mass movements of the fifties by a wide margin. Well-brought up young girls and boys, imagining themselves as warriors in a battle between good and evil, charged in to do battle with the enemies of the revolution. They abused, beat, and tortured their teachers, classmates, neighbours, sometimes even their parents; drove them to suicide, or murdered them; and wrote about it afterwards in tones of perplexity as to how it all happened. "There were over one hundred million of us," wrote An Wenjiang. "Who turned innocent youth into monsters?"[4]

Violence in the Cultural Revolution not infrequently took the form of rape, revelations of which belied the carefully cultivated impression of a society too high-minded to be distracted by sex. Opportunistic rape of young girls by their superiors was apparently quite common, and so too aggravated rape of politically suspect or marginal elements by the shock troops of the revolution. These gender-specific acts of sexual violence in a social context marked by ongoing conflict and the destabilisation of male power reinforces an impression of China being engaged in something like a war in the years of the Cultural Revolution.[5] Fittingly, military uniform was the favoured dress of the era.

Dressing in the spirit of Mao Zedong Thought

Looking back over the past vestimentary era as if from a great distance, Yang Yueqian wrote:

I recall how people dressed up in the ten years of turmoil during the Cultural Revolution, when everyone was under extreme ideological control. The whole country from top to bottom presented a spectacle of blue, green and grey. Styles and varieties for the main part were all attempted imitations of army, navy and airforce uniforms. Most of the designs on any figured cloth showing a bit of colour were over-obvious symbols of "sailing the seas depends upon the helmsman." Red railway lights, red flags on boat prows, and sunflowers were the most fashionable decorative devices.[6]

---

4 An Wenjiang, "Shanghai Rebel," in Zhang Lijia and Calum MacLeod, eds, *China Remembers* (Hong Kong: Oxford University Press, 1999), 119.

5 See Ruth Seifert, "War and Rape: A Preliminary Analysis," in Alexandra Stiglmayer, ed., *The War against Women in Bosnia-Herzegovina* (Lincoln and London: University of Nebraska Press, 1994), 54-72. Seifert offers this analysis specifically as applicable in Western cultures, and against the background of mass rapes in Bosnia-Herzogovina. See further Neil J. Diamant, *Revolutionising the Family: Politics, Love, and Divorce in Urban and Rural China, 1949-1968* (Berkeley: University of California Press, 2000), 303-4. Diamant explains political rape as "a way of reasserting male power against an imagined, folk-religion-inspired threat to young men" (the threat posed by the evil spirit that occupied the womb), but this seems rather too specific an interpretation. That the perpetrators sought to "prove themselves as 'real men' by humiliating class enemies in sexual ways" (ibid., 303) seems more to the point.

6 Yang Yueqian, *Shizhuang liuxing de aomi* (The mysteries of fashion) (Beijing: Zhongguo shehui kexue chubanshe, 1992), 34.

"Sailing the seas depends on the helmsman" was the first line in one of the most popular songs of the Cultural Revolution. The last line was "Mao Zedong Thought is the sun that never sets." Mao Zedong Thought, the never-setting sun, was the guiding principle of Chinese communism. During the Cultural Revolution it acquired an authority that in world history has been rivalled only by religious texts central to great fundamentalist movements. Artworks of this period depict Mao surrounded by joyful acolytes, their ecstatic faces turned as one towards his glorious visage. Memoirs and diaries show young people undergoing great spiritual struggles in their attempts to live truly revolutionary lives, characterised by service to the people, dedication to the Communist Party, and undying love for the Great Leader. The songs they sang were hymns of devotion to the Saviour of the Chinese People. The clothes they wore declared their contempt for the bourgeoisie, capitalism, American imperialism, and Soviet hegemonism, and their commitment to furthering and deepening the revolution under the banner of Mao Zedong Thought.

Naturally, not everyone was a devout Maoist, and even devout Maoists could not live by Mao Zedong Thought alone. Vanity, envy, sexual attraction, fear, peer pressure, and social ambition all entered into choices made about what to wear, as did poverty and opportunity. Nonetheless, revolution was the guiding principle in the culture of daily life during these years, and few could avoid taking it seriously. The vanguard revolutionaries, Mao's Red Guards, set the tone for style among young people. They saw themselves as surrounded by invisible enemies whom it was their duty to expose and destroy. They equipped themselves in battle dress for the task.

For girls, military dress and a military persona meant identification with a Maoist revolutionary tradition going back to before the founding of the Communist Party. In 1919 Mao had written specifically on the issue of what women should wear. He put it to the reader that "if a woman's head and a man's head are actually the same, and there is no real difference between a woman's waist and a man's," there was no obvious reason why women should wear their hair in buns and dress in skirts. He objected also to makeup, "which is the brand of a criminal," to bracelets, rings, and earrings, as well as bound feet. "Schools and families are prisons [for

Fig. 9.2 "Love martial dress, not dressing up." Woodblock print by Zhao Xinfang. This young woman's clothes very obviously pre-date the Cultural Revolution.

women]," he proclaimed. His solution to their predicament was simple: "raise a women's revolutionary army."[7]

The clothes he was describing are clearly the skirt worn with jacket-blouse, before the era of bobbed hair, and before the widespread abandonment of jewellry. More than forty years later, in a very different clothing regime, he reaffirmed his approbation of women in uniform with a poem written after inspecting female militia:

Five-foot rifles, flashing bravely,
On the training ground, at break of day,
How remarkable the spirit of Chinese women:
They love martial dress, not dressing up.[8]

To these solid Maoist foundations, some girls could add a family history in which their mothers as well as their fathers had donned uniform. Mu Aiping's mother had joined anti-Japanese resistance forces in 1937, when she was fourteen years old. Recruited into a training detachment, she was instructed to change into a dark grey army uniform: "her short hair was hidden beneath an army cap, her calves were wrapped in cotton puttees, her tunic fastened by a leather belt."[9] Thousands of children must have heard their mothers tell stories like this, and felt just as Mu Aiping did in 1966. "When I first heard Chairman Mao's call to fight capitalist roaders," she recalled, "I was excited. Always proud of my family background, I pictured myself under a huge red flag, defending Chairman Mao's revolutionary headquarters shoulder to shoulder with my parents, and felt absolutely glorious."[10]

The Cultural Revolution and military fashions

The Cultural Revolution was born of a power struggle in the top echelons of the Communist Party. As a distinct historical time with its own cultural characteristics, the period of this so-called revolution is well illustrated by the contrast between 1965 and 1966 mass gatherings. In 1965, the grounds of the Workers' Cultural Palace in Beijing were filled with women in skirts and dresses dancing with each other in a vast, orchestrated celebration of Labour Day (Fig. 9.3).

---

7 Stuart R. Schram, ed., *Mao's Road to Power: Revolutionary Writings 1912–1949: Volume 1: The Pre-Marxist Period, 1912–1920* (Armonk, NY: M.E. Sharpe, 1992), 353.

8 First published in Mao Zedong, *Mao Zhuxi shici* (Poems by Chairman Mao) (Beijing: Renmin wenxue chubanshe, 1963). See *Mao Zhuxi shici,* www.szxy.org/news/003y/312/maozedong110/mzd.htm. Accessed 28 December 2006.

9 Aiping Mu, *Vermilion Gate: A Family Story of Communist China* (London: Little, Brown and Company, 2000), 80.

10 Ibid., 313. A "capitalist roader" was someone who advocated capitalism for China, or at least was accused of doing so by Mao. The term was directed in the first instance at President Liu Shaoqi.

Fig. 9.3 Workers celebrating 1 May in the grounds of the Workers' Cultural Palace, 1965. Two women in jackets in the right foreground show what women were wearing if they were not involved in the performance.

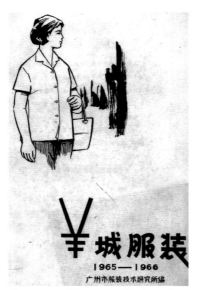

Fig. 9.4 "Canton Clothing," a clothing design booklet produced by the Guangzhou Clothing Technology Research Office, set the sartorial tone for 1965–1966. Whether big changes were anticipated for the years thereafter is not clear.

The dancing women of 1965 were by no means dressed in everyday clothes; clothing designs published in Guangzhou in the same year showed more modest expectations of how women would dress over the coming year (Fig. 9.4).[11] Nor are they evidence of a radically different gender order to that embraced during the Cultural Revolution. To the contrary, as a 1965 "Iron Girl" poster demonstrates, "iron women" of model work units and communes such as Daqing and Dazhai were already being held up for nationwide emulation (Fig. 9.5). But this was the last year for some time that women would be licensed to "dress up nicely." In 1966, a series of mass gatherings in Tiananmen Square yielded some of the most famous images of the Cultural Revolution: serried ranks of students in jackets and trousers and caps in a sea of red flags, all waving little red books and pictured with mouths wide open, because they were roaring in unison "long, long life to Chairman Mao."

11 See Fig. 10.3 for illustrations from the booklet shown in Fig. 9.4.

Fig. 9.5 The iron women from the oil fields of Daqing, China's model industrial site. A year before the Cultural Revolution, *China's Women* used this seventies-looking poster by You Longgu ("Dragon girl" You) to mark its May Day issue. A similar cover was used to mark National Day 1964, for an issue carrying photographs of outstanding welder Gui Ying (above right) and the Women's Day Oil Well Group (below), all of Daqing.

The Cultural Revolution took the form of a mass movement in which everyone in the country was eventually forced to participate, whether as a revolutionary or as a counter-revolutionary. Activists frequently found themselves performing both roles at different stages. The turmoil commenced as a struggle directed against the mayoralty in Beijing, was fanned by a confrontation between two factions at Beijing University, and then spread like wildfire through the press and the educational institutions of the capital and then of the country, after Mao Zedong's endorsement of the radical student faction on 1 June, 1966.[12] In the schools, very young activists began organising themselves into a quasi-military formation that would become a by-word for the Cultural Revolution: the Red Guards.

Rae (Rui) Yang was among the earliest of the Red Guards. Sixteen years old, she was presented with a new bicycle by her father so that she could ride around the campuses of Beijing schools and keep in touch with developments in the revolution. She and her friends heard about the exciting new organisation at Qinghua University Middle School in late June, and decided they wanted to be part of it. They tore off their red "Young Pioneer" scarves (now symbols of the "revisionist

---

12 For a good narrative outline of the Cultural Revolution, see Yan Jiaqi and Gao Gao, *Turbulent Decade: A History of the Cultural Revolution*, D.W.Y. Kwok, trans. (Honolulu: University of Hawai'i Press, 1996).

Fig. 9.6 Song Binbin fastens a Red Guard armband on the Chairman's sleeve, 18 August 1966.

educational line"), turned them into red armbands, and rode along the street with a new look of determination in their eyes:

People noticed our new costume: faded army uniforms that had been worn by our parents, red armbands, wide canvas army belts, army caps, the peaks pulled down low by girls in the style of the boys ... Our eyes were clear and bright. Our cheeks rosy and radiant. Red armbands fluttered in the wind.[13]

These few lines sum up the general look that was to be favoured over the next few years, and the spirit in which it was worn.

Further impetus for the popularisation of military dress was provided by Mao himself when, on 18 August 1966, he appeared before the massed Red Guards at Tiananmen Square dressed in military uniform. The psychological impact of this gesture was the greater because he had rarely been seen in military uniform since the end of the Civil War. Like De Gaulle in the midst of the Algerian crisis, he was using the uniform to assert his standing as leader of the nation; but while De Gaulle had been attempting to resolve a crisis, Mao was intent on deepening one. As commander-in-chief, he effectively signalled by his dress that China was indeed at war.

Such was the message that Song Yaowu took to newspaper readers two days later. Song, a student teacher at Beijing Normal University, had been among the students who were received by Mao in person at the rally, and had the honour of fastening a Red Guard armband on his sleeve (Fig. 9.6). In an article in *Guang-ming Daily*, she reported:

Mao is tall and imposing, his face infused with a rosy light. He was in green military dress, and wearing a green soldier's cap, the bright red of his collar insignia reddening the cockles of one's heart. On seeing the Chairman look so strong, I felt an inexpressible happiness in my heart and wanted to shout: "Everlasting life to Chairman Mao!" When Chairman Mao asked my name, I answered: "Song Binbin." He asked whether it was the "binbin" in the saying *"wenzhi binbin"* (to be refined in accomplishments as well as by nature). I told him it was. He said to me in a confidential tone: "Be militant" (*yao wu ma*).

Reflecting on this conversation made the young revolutionary recall Mao's famous dictum: "A revolution is not a dinner party, or writing an essay, or painting

---

13 Yang, *Spider Eaters*, 122.

a picture, or doing embroidery; it cannot be so refined, so leisurely and gentle, so temperate, kind, courteous, restrained and magnanimous. A revolution is an insurrection, an act of violence by which one class overthrows another." She promptly changed her name from Binbin to "Yaowu"—"I must be militant." Her lengthy article concluded with a clarion call: "China's future belongs to us. The future of the world belongs to us. We must indeed disseminate a 'fighting' spirit, press forward in the great winds and billowing waves of Chairman Mao's class struggle, and implement cultural revolution to the end!"[14]

This militarist spirit was infective. Mao had promulgated it in his May Seventh directive, in which he projected a vision of a totally integrated society in which the people were acquainted with military affairs while the People's Liberation Army engaged in agricultural production and education. Although the PLA came into conflict with radical groups during the violent phase of this "revolution," it emerged with its image enhanced in the eyes of the masses, and the balance between the revolutionary classes shifted decisively in favour of the soldier. Of the key revolutionary classes, the peasant was termed *laodaye* (old grandad), the worker was *bobo* (older uncle) and the People's Liberation Army soldier *shushu* (younger uncle). Of these, Uncle PLA was the most loveable.[15] Soldiers were *liaobuqi* (wonderful, fantastic, unbelievable) during the Cultural Revolution—figures of great charisma and social standing. Girls fell in love with them all over the country, and girls and boys both queued up to join the army.

Those who were not actually soldiers wanted to look like soldiers. Few owned real uniforms but home-made facsimiles that looked more or less authentic abounded. Great care was taken with the choice of cloth, for while the colour scheme was restricted, getting just the right shade of blue or green was critical to the overall effect. Close attention was paid to other sartorial details: the overcoat was ideally a skirt coat, nipped in at the waist; and the trousers had to be full and long, the same width at thigh and calf.[16] Dressed in this way, a young woman could deport herself with considerable self-assurance.

Hao Zhihong, a pupil at Number Fourteen Middle School in Harbin, joined the school's Red Guard Battle Brigade in 1967. Her mother made her an army uniform of green cotton, which she wore with a Mao badge and an armband, strolling down the main street of the city with an air of self-consequence "as though I were a soldier in the People's Liberation Army" (Fig. 9.7). A photographer happened to be lying in wait, and addressed her as she passed his shop:

---

14 *Guangming ribao* 20 August 1966.

15 Xiao Wuliao, *Jiqing shishang: qishi niandai Zhongguoren de yishu yu shenghuo* (Passionate times: Chinese art and life in the seventies) (Jinan: Shandong huabao chubanshe, 2002), 53.

16 Yu Qing, "Hong zhuang su guo" ('Red' clothing, white gaiters), in Shandong huabao chubanshe "Lao zhaopian" bianjibu (Shandong pictorial publishing, "Old photos" editorial section), ed., *Lao zhaopian*, no. 1, 90.

In accordance with the demands of the political situation, the photo shop is planning to produce photos of a group of Red Guards of different ages and occupations to decorate the shop window. We've been outside the door for a whole morning trying to make a choice. I think that comparatively speaking you have a good air and appearance, so I'm asking you to serve as a representative Red Guard!

How could she refuse? A few days later she found herself displayed in glorious colour in the shop window. "At that time there was no colour photography," she recalled, "so the photography shop brought in an experienced artisan to add colour to the photo of every Red Guard."[17]

Fig. 9.7 Hao Zhihong as a young Red Guard in her home-made army uniform. Her armband had "Red Guard" emblazoned under the words "Mao Zedong Thought." The book in her hand is undoubtedly a collection of Mao's writings or sayings.

Army uniforms at this time were very simple. In 1955, rank insignia had been introduced and officers' uniforms were differentiated from the rank-and-file, but in 1965 this reform was reversed and the old Yanan style prevailed once again. This meant that home-made versions, produced by mothers around the country, were easier to sew than would otherwise have been the case. Nothing, however, could compete with the glamour of a real uniform, as numerous memoirs of this time attest:

That was the era when "stinking beauty" was not allowed. *Qipao*s, western suits, tight pants—in the space of a night turned into the "four olds," and were swept into the dustbin of history by the "iron broom" of the proletariat. The only thing worth wearing, the one form of glamour, which took off like a storm, was the yellow army uniform.[18]

The writer of these lines was ten years old when the country was swept with "military uniform" fever. She and her older brother both grew sick with longing for a real soldier's uniform but it was out of their reach and they had to make do with home-made versions until he grew up and joined the army. He sent her an authentic uniform to wear while she was at university in the early seventies,

17 Hao Zhihong, "'36 nian qian de 'cai zhao'" (A 'colour photo' from 36 years ago), *Haerbin ribao* 11 September 2003.

18 Zang Xiao, "Huang junzhuang qingjie" (A passion for a yellow military uniform), *Hefei wanbao* 11 September 2003, www.jhcb.com.cn/epublish/gb/paper6/20030715/class000600004/hwz344499.htm. Accessed 10 November 2003.

wearing which earned her the nickname of "Old Eighth Route" from her admiring fellow-students.[19]

Like jeans and T-shirts in the West at that time, army uniform was very much a young person's fashion, but unlike jeans a uniform was almost impossible to obtain. The best source, as the story of "Old Eighth Route" demonstrates, was the army itself. The army issued its personnel with new uniforms twice a year. Soldiers were supposed to hand in their old ones in exchange, or else pay for them, which they could ill afford. But being in a position to hand out old uniforms was a source of extraordinary social power. "I really valued my uniforms," recalled one soldier. "Although they were old from wear, I didn't want to hand them over to Army Supplies for cleaning cars with, when I was able to repay a few close friends. After my [period of] duty, I gave each of them an old army uniform."[20]

In this curious market, connections were everything. Fourteen-year-old Mu Aiping joined the Red Guards in August 1966, and as the daughter of a major-general in the People's Liberation Army was given the task of obtaining khaki combat gear. Such was the prestige of the Red Guards that she was able to secure a loan of twenty outfits. "At that time," she recalled, "it was not unusual for the Red Guards to be issued with military equipment, including vehicles with drivers, by members with military connections, who gained credit for their contribution to the Cultural Revolution."[21] Her father was enraged (she had acted without his knowledge) and finally forced a return of all the uniforms.

Other fathers sacrificed their uniforms to their children. In Xuzhou, northern Jiangsu province:

... real army uniforms were few. What most people wore were home-made uniforms of cloth that was dyed green. At that time, the dyeing shops in the county capital could only dye things a few colours—blue, black, red—so the workers in the Xuzhou Textile Dyeing Factory had a monopoly on the business. I was ten at that time, and pestered my mother for a uniform. All she could do was buy some wrapping cloth (a coarse cloth used for wrapping items for the post, which didn't need cotton coupons), and dye some for me and my brothers.

The dye used by the writer's mother was supposedly "grass green" but in fact turned the cloth a sort of ochre colour (*tuhuangse*), which not only looked nothing like the green uniform of the PLA but rather resembled the army uniforms of the Nationalist forces—as represented on stage, at least. By happy chance, this family had a "complete Soviet-style officer's uniform" tucked away in a trunk

---

19 Ibid. The Eighth Route Army was the largest Communist military force during the Anti-Japanese war (i.e. World War II).

20 Wen Song, "Junzhuang lianqing" (Loving sentiments about army uniforms), *Xiamen ribao* 3 August 2003.

21 Mu Aiping, *Vermilion Gate*, 330.

Fig. 9.8 Wearing army uniform with attitude. *The Red Detachment of Women* was first performed in 1964, but became one of the most famous model works of the Cultural Revolution.

—with "shining gold epaulettes, a bright red collar, a high topped [army] cap, a great-wide military belt, leather soldier's boots." The brothers in the family quarrelled bitterly over who should have the right to wear the uniform, and ended up rotating it among themselves, a month at a time, till finally it was threadbare here and there, and bleached almost white with washing, although still retaining enormous prestige because the style showed that the wearer had a revolutionary background.[22]

The style was set by the events of 1966, and became entrenched through the practice and ideology of revolutionary struggle. It was effectively promoted, too, by the model artistic works that were approved for performance during this period, which mostly featured themes of revolution and war. The first eight model works were approved in 1967, and of them, Xiaomei Chen has pointed out, "seven were direct representations of the revolutionary war experience." A second tranche of ten works was introduced from 1970 onward, and in thematic terms was not much different.[23] In the films, operas, and ballets among these works, beautiful heroines were often to be seen in graceful, stylised folk dress,

---

22 "Junzhuang de gushi" [Story of a military uniform], xjzpz.51.net/xcjs/26.htm. Accessed 10 November 2003.

23 Xiaomei Chen, *Acting the Right Part: Political Theater and Popular Drama in Contemporary China* (Honolulu: University of Hawai'i Press, 2002), 75-6.

most commonly *shanku* (top and trousers), sometimes worn with a short apron.[24] The logic of the stories invariably placed such clothing in the semi-feudal, semi-colonial era, precluding the possibility of it being appropriate as dress for young revolutionaries. On escaping or being rescued, however, the heroine might change these clothes for the uniform of the revolutionary army, or alternatively owe her deliverance to someone dressed in such a uniform. In this way, the stage and screen showcased uniforms of the People's Liberation Army. *The Red Detachment of Women*, with its chorus line of skimpily-dressed women soldiers, won young red hearts all over China, and entrenched the iconic status of army uniform among them (Fig. 9.8).

The links between army uniform and revolutionary activism became attenuated over time. Wang Shuo, born in 1957, attended Middle School in Beijing in the early seventies. He was an apolitical young larrikin in a city that had been largely emptied of young people. In the early seventies, his peer group, ne'er-do-wells from whom his parents tried to separate him, provided the sort of urban spectacle that would come to be known as street fashion:

There were ten of them, draped over their bikes, all wearing army jackets and slip-on Chinese shoes. They were grouped in front of the traffic cop station at the cross-roads, each pinching a cigarette to his lips, exhaling mouthfuls of smoke while they talked with a sort of excited arrogance. You couldn't help noticing them—laid-back toughs looking pleased with themselves, like they owned the street.[25]

Wang Shuo's account of the "turbulent years" have been greeted as revisionist, but a similar tale is recounted by Jung Chang in her celebrated autobiography, *Wild Swans*. Like Wang Shuo and his brother, the Chang siblings were left more or less to their own devices after their parents were sent to May Seventh cadre school. Her brother, Xiao-hei, took to the streets, hanging around with a gang of boys. They cultivated their own fashion, recalled Jung Chang, wearing "many layers of shirts under an outer garment," and then turning out all the collars—the more, the better; the more, the smarter. They made statements with their shoes and hats, as well, wearing white sneakers without laces and army caps with stiffened peaks, which they thought looked very "imposing."[26]

Concealed—or sometimes explicitly revealed—in all these stories is the way in which clothing served to define in-groups and out-groups. In an era when clothing seemed to have little variety and when overdue attention to clothing laid people open to a charge of bourgeois or other tendencies, an extraordinary amount of energy was invested in managing the details of clothing. This was a

---

24 See Rosemary Roberts, "Gendering the Revolutionary Body: Theatrical Costume in Cultural Revolution China," *Asian Studies Review* 30, 2 (June 2006): 141-59; and on aprons specifically, 156.

25 Wang Shuo, *Dongwu xiongmeng* (The ferocity of beasts) (Hong Kong: Wenquan, 1994), 14.

26 Jung Chang, *Wild Swans*, 370.

time when everyone was looking at everyone else, and not only looking but scrutinising with the closest attention. By these means, people found social groups within which they sought to maximise their security.

Up to the mountains, down to the villages

Between the summer of 1966 and the winter of 1968, the Red Guards were allowed to run amok. Arming themselves with weapons seized from the PLA, they turned factional allegiances into civil war. In December 1968, with President Liu Shaoqi dying in gaol and Chairman Mao serving not only as chairman but also as the "great leader, great teacher, great marshal, and great helmsman," the campaign phase of the Cultural Revolution drew to a close. Mao called on educated youth to embark on their "re-education" out in the countryside, where they could learn from the poor and lower-middle peasants. More than sixteen million students responded to the call, or were made to respond to it.[27] They packed up their bedding and thermos flasks, and set off "up to the mountains and down to the villages." Some never came back. For parents, it was as though the Pied Piper of Hamlyn had whistled their children away.

For the sons and daughters of townspeople, life in the countryside was an eye-opening experience. Nanchu, sent north from Shanghai up to the Great Northern Wasteland, commented on the local girls in "gaudy garments buttoned down the left side," who smoked coarse tobacco in small-bowled long pipes; on the copper-coloured peasants in their "patched, cotton-padded clothes, which they fastened with straw ropes" and probably never washed; and on her fellow sent-downers: a girl from Beijing in over-sized shirt and wide-legged pants; a Shanghai girl wearing narrow-legged pants; a Tianjin girl dressed in dark blue with a stand-up collar; and most surprising, a girl from Harbin whose pants "were hemmed above the ankles" while "her coat had narrow sleeves and brass buttons." Nanchu wondered whether such clothes showed Russian influence.[28]

Mu Aiping ended up in an isolated corner of Shanxi, where the Beijing sent-downers found themselves scratching for roots to eat during the annual spring famine. They were astonished to find that knitting—from home-made, poor quality wool—was seen as a man's job, while shoes were not bought in a store but hand-made by women.[29] Wu Xiaoping, from Xi'an, ended up in an even more remote mountain village, where old men still wore queues (!) and half the population was riddled with sexually-transmitted diseases. She presented her host family with some green knitting yarn, which was used to make a jumper for

27 Chao Feng, *Wenhua da geming cidian* (Dictionary of the Cultural Revolution) (Hong Kong: Ganglong chubanshe, 1993), 21.

28 Nanchu, *Red Sorrow: A Memoir* (New York: Arcade Publishing, 2001), 73, 80.

29 Aiping Mu, *Vermilion Gate*, 408.

Fig. 9.9 Different representations of sent-down youth. Above left, Jie Zhenhua (centre), photographed with two companions, all serving as militia in the northern wasteland of Heilongjiang. Their grim faces and the general poverty of their appearance provide a striking contrast to happy, well-dressed students photographed in the Hunan countryside for a propaganda piece in *China Reconstructs* four years later. The second photo was taken well after the high-tide of the craze for military uniform. The girls wear jackets over jumpers and shirts; the boy in the foreground wears a handknitted sweater. Tracksuits were worn as outer wear and as underwear in these years.

their future daughter-in-law. More than twenty-two years later she returned to the village for a visit, and found that the garment was still being worn.[30]

In the midst of poverty and homesickness, the educated youth strove to retain a sense of identity as vanguard revolutionaries and comrades-in-arms, while struggling with patently unrevolutionary sexual and romantic feelings for each other, or for the local men and women whom they sometimes ended up marrying, condemning themselves to a life-sentence in the countryside. From this complex of positions emerged the descriptions of clothes that feature in virtually every tale of "up to the mountains and down to the villages." Looking back, the sent-downers recalled how they and their peers dressed as clearly as if they had spent those years dating in America.

Among them was Ma Bo, son of the novelist Yang Mo, who in 1968 set off from Beijing with three friends for the Inner Mongolian steppe. His grim account of the gruelling years spent in hard labour and persecution as a class enemy on Huolin Gol became one of the most widely read memoirs of the post-Mao years, not least because he had participated in the political struggle against his famous mother. Its opening chapters portray a frighteningly powerful and violent young man, whose revolutionary ardour was expressed entirely through the deployment of his physical strength. Out on the steppe the worm turned. He

---

30 Wu Xiaoping, "Down to the Countryside," in Zhang Lijia and Calum MacLeod, eds, *China Remembers* (Hong Kong: Oxford University Press, 1999), 133.

was classified a counter-revolutionary, and from beating up class enemies he was reduced to chopping rocks.

His physical appearance showed the effects of the revolutionary struggle. After months of isolation on the mountainside, his trousers, made of hide, "were black with grime and covered with patches of all colours; black hairs stuck out through the holes." A friend commented with some foresight that they "deserved to be in a museum to show students fashions of the seventies." Like religious aesthetes taking pride in the practices of poverty and denial of the flesh, he and his friends paraded the outward signs of their years in the wilderness: "To us, split skin that oozed pus and clothing held together by patches and electric cords were a form of beauty—the scars of a bitter struggle."[31]

To cultivate this form of beauty was a way for young men to assert their manhood (see Fig. 9.9). In a vestimentary regime that severely underplayed gender differentiation in dress, politically progressive girls did dress like boys, and even in actual boys' clothes;[32] but grime, split skin, and holes in their clothes were not part of their make-up. The object of Ma Bo's unrequited love was a girl who "dressed simply … No one had ever seen her in fancy clothes or leather shoes." In summer she wore a "green army shirt and blue cotton trousers." In winter, her army cap, worn without a scarf, "made her look like one of the men from the rear."[33] She had to be careful about what she wore because she had a bad political background. Other girls from the platoon, setting off for a day out at a denunciation session, were all "dressed in new army overcoats and caps, perky as can be." This uniform they could combine with "scarves and silk stockings," purchased not in some black market but at the local regimental co-op store.[34] Army dress was to be expected. The entire body of sent-down youth at Huolin Gol had been organised into "platoons" under the aegis of the Inner Mongolian Production Corps, and lived in a quasi-military regime.

Much the same set of elements—military organisation, army dress, and valourisation of the battle-hardened body, juxtaposed with disturbing traces of sexualised, feminine articles of clothing—is identified in another famous memoir, *Red Azalea*. The author of this book, Anchee Min, was too young to have participated in the Cultural Revolution proper, but in 1974, when she finished school, the "Criticise Lin Biao, Criticise Confucius" campaign was in progress. This involved a sudden intensification of political activity, increased attention to military training,

---

31 Ma Bo, *Blood Red Sunset: A Memoir of the Chinese Cultural Revolution*, trans. Howard Goldblatt (New York: Viking, 1995) 290, 225-6, 215.

32 Xiaomei Chen, "Growing Up With Posters in the Maoist Era," in Harriet Evans and Stephanie Donald, eds, *Picturing Power in the People's Republic of China: Posters of the Cultural Revolution* (Lanham: Rowman & Littlefield Publishers, Inc., 1999), 113.

33 Ma Bo, *Blood Red Sunset*, 327.

34 Ibid., 202-3.

Fig. 9.10 A sent-downer rallies her troops for a struggle against Lin Biao's "capitalist, militarist line." This photo was probably used for a newspaper report on the "criticise Lin, criticise Confucius" campaign. The military-style uniform shows the resurgence of a militarist ethos during this campaign, eight years after the Red Guards first erupted onto the scene.

and heightened political fervour on the part of the young. Seventeen-year-old Anchee was sent to Red Fire Farm on the Chinese coast and was placed in a production brigade which was a model company for "the entire Red Fire Farm Army." The "commander," Yan Sheng, was a Red Guard who had led twenty comrades in a revolutionary struggle to reclaim land by the East China Sea. She told her newly arrived troops that "although we would not be given formal uniforms, we would be trained as real soldiers."

Yan Sheng epitomised the iron maiden of the 1970s—the quintessential "can do" girl who held up half the sky and yielded to none in her determined avoidance of the bourgeois (Western fashion), revisionist (*bulaji*) and feudal (*qipao*) dress styles of the benighted past (Fig. 9.10).[35] To Anchee Min's memory: "She was tall, well-built and walked with authority. She wore an old People's Liberation Army uniform, washed almost white, and gathered at the waist with a three-inch wide belt. She had two short thick braids … She was barefoot. Her sleeves and trousers were rolled halfway up." A smitten Anchee began to imitate her hero's "way of walking, talking, dressing," cutting off her hair to form short braids, hankering after a wider belt. Eventually the two girls became lovers.[36]

Anchee Min was privy to another example of assertive sexuality in the person of her fellow worker, Little Green, a pretty, fair-skinned eighteen-year-old with long hair. She "tied her braids with colourful strings while the rest of us tied ours with brown rubber bands." She sewed her trousers in to give her the appearance of being more long-legged than she was, and also the side seams of her shirt so that they tapered at the waist. She made and embroidered her own underwear, using cloth fragments. Once, a pair of her underpants was stolen, creating scandal in the company. She was discovered at last having sex in the fields with a

---

35 For an equation of the political terms and dress styles, see *Bainian shishang*, 48. On the "iron girls," see Emily Honig and Gail Hershatter, eds, *Personal Voices: Chinese Women in the 1980s* (Stanford: Stanford University Press, 1988), 23-6.

36 Anchee Min, *Red Azalea* (New York: Berkeley Books, 1999), 48, 56.

lover. Brought to accusing him of rape, she went mad after he was executed—a credible parable of love and death in Mao's China.[37]

Memoirs by educated youth of their "sent-down" years provide an alternative lens through which to view a lifestyle that has often been interpreted as careless of fashion and innocent of sexuality. Ignorance of sex was quite prevalent in the seventies, but the great silence that shrouded this fearsome topic was a loud one. Sent-down girls were particularly vulnerable to exploitation. Surrounded by whispers and rumours, exposed to seduction and rape, they were preyed on, victimised, tried as criminals, their lives and careers liable to ruin by innuendo. A culture of gossip, patterns of sexual manipulation and domestic violence, and a lack of personal privacy rendered personal lives wretched. Their clothing was absorbed into a system of signs that told the viewer how they might be categorised politically, and therefore how they were related to the viewer's own prospects for survival.

The seventies

During the 1970s, revolution was normalised. The turbulence of the Red Guard period gave way to a routinised process of revolutionary life, involving political study, demonstrations of revolutionary faith, vigilance against counter-revolutionary elements, and work. A reduction of surveillance activities by revolutionary activists in the streets meant a revival of some variety in clothing. Women interviewed in Xi'an in the 1990s recalled that "after 1969, when the worst of Cultural Revolution radicalism had passed, brides exchanged their Mao suits for Western-style ones"—which meant flat, turned-down lapels with a deep v-neck rather than the button-up style.[38] Shirts constituted an important domain for modest experiments in style. Cut straight and wide, the standard woman's shirt of the late sixties and seventies was called the "spring and autumn shirt." It was produced in plain colours during the sixties but showed greater variety in the seventies when checked or even floral prints could again be seen in profusion.[39] Shanghai, naturally, was a source of such innovations as were taking place. For visitors to Shanghai "it was a must to buy paper patterns to give to relatives and friends back home."[40]

The sent-down youth began returning home if they could, and when they did so they were confronted all over again by the gap between urban and rural life. In 1973, when Nanchu arrived back in Shanghai on leave from the Great Northern

---

37 Ibid., 59-61.

38 Maris Gillette, "What's in a Dress? Brides in the Hui Quarter of Xi-an," in Deborah Davis, ed., *The Consumer Revolution in Urban China* (Berkeley: University of California Press, 2000), 84.

39 Yang Yuan, exec. ed., *Zhongguo fushi bainian shishang* (Given French title: Costumes chinois: Modes depuis 100 ans) (Huerhot: Yuanfang chubanshe, 2003), 17.

40 Ibid.

Wasteland, her mother made her strip off and delouse; her clothes, such as they were, were crawling with lice that—between farm labour in the day and the need to sleep at night—she hardly noticed any more. And Shanghai fashions, as she discovered, had moved on. Young people "no longer wore the green uniform as we did in the countryside ... the attire had gone out of fashion. Mao suits were in." When a young man came courting her, he was dressed in "a dark gray jacket with a short stand-up collar, padded shoulders, and four open pockets."[41] In Chengdu, too, army uniforms were fading away—perhaps literally. "In their Red Guard days," wrote Jung Chang, "the high officials' children favored old Communist army uniforms" but later they "switched to wearing dark-blue jackets and trousers [of a particular shade] ... After they had made this their distinguishing sign, boys and girls from other backgrounds had to avoid it ..."[42] Sent-downers who had been at the very forefront of youth style in 1968 or 1969 found themselves behind the times when they returned home four or five years later.

In the absence of high political tensions, poverty was the major factor inhibiting diversity and experimentation in dress. In Lianyungang, on the poverty-stricken coast of northern Jiangsu, the clothing environment for a period of twenty years from the beginning of the Great Leap Forward to the beginning of the reform era was summed up in two common sayings. One was a comment on the restricted range of styles: "Three sorts of clothing in country and town, four different colours cover the ground." The three sorts of clothing were the cadre suit, the Sun Yatsen suit and the Lenin suit. The four different colours were grey, green, blue, and white. The other comment referred to the shortage of cloth and of money to buy it: "three years new, three years old, stitch and patch it for three years more."[43]

A nine-year cycle, as designer Zhou Guoping later commented drily, was not favourable to any sort of fashion industry. A native of Shantou in northern Guangdong province, a great distance from Lianyungang, Zhou was familiar with this second saying, probably the most commonly quoted of any in reference to clothing of the Maoist years generally. "All clothing at that time was patched," he recalled. "Not patches for fashion like today, but real patches." As a child he learned to darn. His mother was a skilled needlewoman, and under her instruction he learned to cut up clothing that had passed all possibility of being worn, creating useable spans of fabric from patches sewn together.[44]

In this commodity-poor economy, brands had great prestige. Bicycles and watches made in Shanghai, Red Lantern brand radios and Great Front Gate

41 Nanchu, *Red Sorrow*, 161.

42 Jung Chang, *Wild Swans*, 370.

43 Untitled document, www.sats.gov.cn/tjfx/fxbg/200309240150.htm. Accessed 10 November 2003.

44 Personal communication, 14 July 2004.

Fig. 9.11 Representative categories of Chinese women, pictured for Women's Day, 1 March 1974. Clockwise from top right: workers putting up big-character posters for the "criticise Lin Biao, criticise Confucius" campaign; educated youth down on the farm in Henan province, "following the path of uniting with the workers and peasants;" the women's militia on Hainan Island, "protecting the nation with heightened vigilance;" and cadres from the Tibetan, Korean and Yi minorities studying Mao Zedong's works.

(*Da Qianmen*) cigarettes were fashionable. As for clothing, fashion lay not so much in style—in which there was relatively little variety—as in the materials of which garments were made. Most in demand, most up-to-date, were synthetics—again a Shanghai product.[45] The economy was growing steadily in the early seventies, and exports were up.[46] This did not affect a place like Lianyungang very obviously, but it did mean that Shanghai was producing more. Some of the surplus was available for use in a domestic market that had never quite forgotten the charm of fashion.

Through the early and mid-seventies, workers, soldiers and peasants remained the holy trinity of the revolutionary masses and continued to provide legitimacy to representations of women in the mass media. On Women's Day in 1974, the commemorative photo montage in the *People's Daily* depicted women cadres in colourful costume (they were all from the national minorities); factory workers in their caps and aprons busy carrying out the "anti-Lin, anti-Confucius" campaign; sent-down educated youth in their jackets of figured cloth, happily committed to "following the path of unity with the workers and peasants;" and the women's militia on Hainan Island, training diligently to defend the motherland (Fig. 9.11).

The black-and-white format of the photos may preclude immediate realisation that the young women in these various photos are all dressed up, with not a patched elbow in sight. The clothing is on the whole consistent with that displayed to the outside world in glossy propaganda publications such as *China Pictorial* and *China Reconstructs*, in which girls from many walks of life are shown wearing brightly coloured shirts, jackets and even skirts.[47] Skirts on the street at that time were highly unusual, if ever to be seen, while shirts and jackets, if occasionally made of gaily-coloured checked or figured cloth, never really amounted to a great splash of colour on the street. But there may be more to such photos than a desire on the part of the media simply to project a good image of China. From the events unfolding in 1974, it is clear that the Chairman's wife, at least, was starting to think that Chinese girls should be wearing something more fetching, more female, and more Chinese than army uniforms and cadre suits.

The Jiang Qing dress

One of the most enduring images of the Cultural Revolution is the figure of Jiang Qing in army uniform and cap (Fig. 9.12). Appointed deputy director of the Cultural Revolution in 1966 and Politburo member in 1969, Jiang Qing played a prominent role in crafting the revolution, and was eventually made to wear

---

45 www.sats.gov.cn/tjfx/fxbg/200309240150.htm.

46 See "China '74 Focus," in *Far Eastern Economic Review* 4 October 1974.

47 For an example of skirts, see *China Reconstructs* XXIII, 11 (November 1974): 9.

Fig. 9.12 Jiang Qing in the military-style dress that was popular during the Cultural Revolution. She is shown here with a People's Liberation Army cultural troupe.

much of the blame for it. She was directly responsible for what was shown on stage and screen during these years, and used this domain of activity strategically. From it she mounted a series of campaigns to enhance her own position, and to destroy possible threats to Mao, who was the ultimate source of her power. In late 1973, she helped to launch the campaign to "criticise Lin Biao, criticise Confucius," and in 1974 renewed her attack on Wang Guangmei, and by extension the already dead Liu Shaoqi, through a campaign against the hapless Shaanxi Opera Troupe.[48] Amidst signs of improvement in China's economic performance and international relations, "a second Cultural Revolution" was effectively whipped up, with Premier Zhou Enlai (1898–1976) as the actual target. The furious counter-campaign waged against Jiang Qing and her supporters after the death of Mao can be attributed to this stage of the party's internal power struggle.

One of the shots fired in this campaign came in the form of an article in the 8 February issue of the *Tianjin Daily*. The headline was sensational: "Denounce Jiang Qing's Ambition to Ascend the Throne Wearing the Imperial Robe." This might be read simply as a turn of phrase, but the article itself showed otherwise. According to the denunciation, early in 1974 Jiang issued orders to a Tianjin clothing factory to make her a gown with a "hundred pleats skirt, embroidered with plum blossoms, with an outer garment to match," and "three pairs of 'empress shoes' in the Tang style." This was not intended for general wear. To the contrary, Jiang Qing is said to have ordered: "This dress must be unique ... no one else is to be allowed to make an outfit of similar pattern and design."[49] Factory equipment allegedly had to be altered to create the fabric.

The following year, the same paper elaborated on the story with an article entitled: "The 'Empress's clothes' and the 'Jiang Qing dress.'"[50] The link was made clear here between the embroidered gown she wanted for herself and a simpler version that she wished to establish as a new form of national costume. Jiang Qing, charged the article, wanted dresses for "the people" (her subjects) to

---

48 Xiaomei Chen, *Acting the Right Part*, 217.

49 Yan Jiaqi and Gao Gao, *Turbulent Decade: A History of the Cultural Revolution*, D.W.Y. Kwok, trans. (Honolulu: University of Hawai'i Press, 1996), 445.

50 *Tianjin Ribao* 8 February 1977, quoted in Yan Jiaqi and Gao Gao, *Turbulent Decade*, 555, n. 30.

match her "empress wear." Her empress dress provided the model for an "open-necked dress" (*kaijinling qunyi*), minus the plum flowers.[51] The collective author of the articles was the Party Committee Criticism Group of the Tianjin Textile Products Company, which had a direct interest in the Jiang Qing dress because that factory had been charged with the task of producing it.

A detailed account of the making of the Jiang Qing dress—apparently an eyewitness account—was later published in a Chinese-language magazine in the USA. According to the author, one Xiao Gao, on the afternoon of 19 May 1974, Jiang Qing summoned Yu Huiyong, Hao Liang, and Liu Qingtang, core members of the Culture Bureau, to her residence in Beijing. Of these, Hao Liang (a.k.a. Qian Haoliang) was a seasoned performer of martial roles in Beijing Opera and had extensive knowledge of stage and historical costumes;[52] Yu Huiyong (1926–1977) was a composer, and Liu Qingtang (b. 1932) a performer in the Beijing dance company.[53] Three current Beijing Opera performers—women—were also invited to the meeting.

After chatting for a while about model opera matters, Jiang Qing came to the point of her invitation, declaring:

Chinese men have a fixed style of dress called the Sun Yatsen suit, but Chinese women have no [equivalent]. Men and women are equal. The history of men being great and women insignificant must be brought to an end. I want to design a distinctive dress for Chinese women, one featuring Chinese national characteristics.[54]

In brief, she wanted a "national dress" for Chinese women. This was a slightly different matter from the dress that she wanted for herself, but it seems that the two must have been related from the beginning.

The design for the dress was inspired by the pleated skirt worn by court ladies in Tang dynasty paintings. The low neckline was a matter of concern, but a neckband was proposed as a solution. The most arduous part of the undertaking was completing the embroidery, a task entrusted to two instructors at an embroidery factory who kept their machines going twenty-four hours at a stretch to meet the deadline. In the end, Jiang Qing was dissatisfied: she had wanted the flowers to be

---

51 Tianjinshi fangzhipin gongsi dangwei pipanzu (Tianjin Textile Products Company Party Committee criticism group), "'Nühuang yi' yu 'Jiang Qing fu'" (The 'Empress's clothes' and the 'Jiang Qing dress'), *Tianjin ribao* 19 August 1978.

52 In 1968, Jiang Qing forced Hao Liang to drop his surname, Qian, because it was the word for "money." Xiaomei Chen, *Acting the Right Part*, 73.

53 Jiang Qing had recruited these supporters in the course of working with the No. 1 Beijing Opera Troupe and other performance groups to produce revolutionary works. Yan Jiaqi and Gao Gao, *Turbulent Decade*, 400.

54 Xiao Gao, "Jiang Qing fu chulong de taiqian muhou" (Before and after staging the marketing of the Jiang Qing dress), *Meizhou wenhui zhoukan* (Literary Weekly from America), no. 99, www.sinotimes.com/big5/99/jqf.htm. Accessed 10 July 2004.

Fig. 9.13 Imelda Marcos standing where Jiang Qing wanted to be, at Mao's side, in Wuhan, September 1974. On the left is Ferdinand Marcos Jr.

embroidered by hand, not by machine. Two more dresses with hand-embroidered flowers were duly produced—she liked the black one with small plum blossoms, not the camel-coloured one with large blossoms—and there were embroidered shoes to match. Jiang Qing had misshapen feet due to footbinding in childhood, reports Xiao Gao, so she was particular about both the comfort and the beauty of her footwear. Cloth shoes with embroidered tops met her needs.[55]

A possible catalyst for Jiang Qing's dress design interests was the pending visit of Imelda Marcos, due to take place in September. Imelda, unlike most women dignitaries who visited China, was Asian, and the contrast between the former Manila beauty queen and the former Shanghai actress, separated by fifteen years in age, would be great. Li Zhisui, Mao Zedong's personal physician, mentioned the Jiang Qing dress experiment in this context:

In honour of her own meeting with Imelda Marcos, Jiang Qing's tailors had made several costumes fashioned after those of the empress [Wu]. When she saw the elaborate imperial gowns, even Jiang Qing realised how inappropriate they were. She never wore them. What role Mao had in dissuading her, I never knew. But Wang Huirong and Nancy Tang [Mao's aides] told Mao about her gowns, and from Mao's silence I knew he disapproved.[56]

---

55 See also Yan Jiaqi and Gao Gao, *Turbulent Decade*, 425.

56 Li Zhisui, *The Private Life of Chairman Mao*, 586.

Fig. 9.14 Chinese athletes at the opening of the VIIth Asian Games, held in Tehran, 1–16 September 1974.

Imelda not only dressed like a beauty queen; she wore a *terno*, women's national dress in the Philippines (Fig. 9.13).[57] This resonated with Jiang's own desire for a national dress for Chinese women.

According to Xiao Gao, it was after the visit from Imelda Marcos that the mass production of Jiang Qing dresses took place, but evidence of earlier production appears in the photographic record of the 1974 Asian Games, held in Tehran in early September. This was the first "Asiad" in which the People's Republic had participated, since China had previously been represented by the rival regime in Taiwan. At the opening ceremony, nearly two hundred Chinese athletes made an appearance, around a third of them women (see Fig. 9.14). Jiang Qing was in charge of designing the official Chinese uniforms for the games[58] and she decided that the women athletes should wear skirts rather than trousers. Although

---

57 On Imelda Marcos and Philippines national dress, see Mina Roces, "Gender, Nation and the Politics of Dress in Twentieth Century Philippines." Paper presented at the 15th Biennial Conference of the Asian Studies Association of Australia, Canberra, 2 July 2004.

58 Jiang Qing's involvement with the uniforms for the 1974 Asian Games was recalled by a senior functionary with long experience in designing uniforms for China's large-scale sports events, as reported in an article from *Nanfang tiyu* (Southern Sport), "Aoyun jianer lifu ye yao chu huayang: yanse dapei gengdadan gengfu bianhua" (Fresh styles of uniform for Olympic athletes: bolder and richer changes matched with colour), www.sina.com.cn/cn/other/2004-07-10/29245.html. Accessed 11 August 2004.

the individual figures are small in the photo, the design features of the dresses are clear: the skirt is pleated, the sleeves come nearly to the elbow, and the v-shaped neckline is delineated by a wide, white band. This was either the Jiang Qing dress or a prototype of it. It was clearly meant to be some sort of national dress, to match the *tangzhuang* (Chinese-style suits) worn by the men and the *hanbok* of the Korean women, marching along behind them.

The Jiang Qing dress was formally launched on 14 October, when the Tianjin Municipal Committee put the garment on display. Some ambivalence was expressed about it in the formal proceedings. "Whether or not to promote it widely, whether or not to wear it, is a matter of attitude," pronounced the Committee. As for how to promote it: "It has been decided that women cadres in organs belonging directly to the municipality and heads of the Municipal Women's Association should take the lead in wearing it." Further, "it had been decided that the main body of troops (the women textile workers) should fling themselves into battle, [between them] immediately donning one thousand of the dresses."[59]

While Jiang Qing was able to exert influence in Tianjin Municipality, a major effort would be required to ensure the garment's popularisation. She supposedly tried to force the dress onto Mao's aide, Deputy Minister of Foreign Affairs Wang Hairong, and was enraged at Wang's refusal.[60] She had greater leverage over women involved in cultural activities. Women from the ballet and opera companies were selected to model it in public, which they did under sufferance. The same was true of schoolgirls. Chen Chen, born in Beijing in 1959 and now living in Melbourne, was at school in Beijing in the 1970s. She and her classmates were often bussed out to Beijing Airport to welcome visiting dignitaries. In 1975, Jiang Qing dresses were distributed to them to wear on such occasions. Chen Chen hated wearing hers: it was a murky blue in colour, and hung awkwardly. The dresses were made in women's sizes and were too large for the schoolgirls who had to wear them. They had to hold them in with pins at the waist.[61]

This anecdote provides the hint of an explanation as to what happened to all the dresses that failed to sell in the stores. A total of 77,565 garments had been produced in the first two-month production drive. In 1975, an exhibition of the dresses made in fifty-five different varieties of figured cloth was held in Tianjin,

---

59 Tianjinshi fangzhipin gongsi dangwei pipanzu (Tianjin Textile Products Company Party Committee criticism group), "Jiang Qing qun bei zuowei 'xinsheng shiwu' qiangxing tuixiang quanguo" (The forceful promotion throughout the country of the Jiang Qing dress as a 'newly born item'), *Renmin jiyi wushi nian* (Half a century of the people's memories). Zhejiang Normal University Library, lib.zjnu.net.cn/f/remjy/037.htm. Accessed 10 July 2004.

60 Xiao Gao, "Jiang Qing fu chulong de taiqian muhou."

61 Personal communication, Carlton, 13 November 2003.

Fig. 9.15 Left, Beijing Opera star Yang Chunxia in a Jiang Qing dress, meeting the Algerian press. Yang played the part of heroine Ke Xiang in both the stage and film versions of *Azalea Mountain*. Note the close pleating of the skirt. Right, a Chinese and an Algerian performer pose for the camera with an illustrated program of *Azalea Mountain*. The Chinese-style fastening at the neck of the Jiang Qing dress (left) is just visible.

and a further sixty thousand dresses were produced. They were marketed in the major stores at 20 RMB per garment. Failure to sell meant that the cost was successively reduced to a final low of 4 RMB. The loss to the country from failure to recoup the initial investment has been reckoned at 220,000 RMB.[62] Numbers of them must have been distributed for use in schools and for public performances or celebrations, before Jiang Qing quietly dropped the whole embarrassing project.

A few photographic images of the Jiang Qing dress have survived from 1974. In November, the Beijing Opera Company went to Algeria to help celebrate the twentieth anniversary of the beginning of the Algerian revolution with a performance of the revolutionary opera *Azalea Mountain* (*Dujuan shan*).[63] The *People's Daily* and *Guangming Daily* subsequently reported the event with photos of Chinese performers socialising with Algerians. Poor as the quality of newspaper printing was at the time, the Jiang Qing dress is plain to view in both the photos shown here (Fig. 9.15). One provides a good view of the bodice with

---

62 Tianjinshi fangzhipin gongsi dangwei pipanzu, "Jiang Qing qun bei zuowei 'xinsheng shiwu' qiangxing tuixiang quanguo;" Tianjinshi fangzhipin gongsi dangwei pipanzu, "'Nühuang yi' yu 'Jiang Qing fu'."

63 *Renmin ribao* 24 December 1974. *Azalea Mountain* (sometimes translated as *Cuckoo Mountain*) was one of the model operas developed under Jiang Qing's leadership during the Cultural Revolution.

Fig. 9.16 Jiang Qing depicted in a "Jiang Qing dress." The cartoon shows her cronies (the other three members of the Gang of Four) putting up a sign reading "wholesale through the back door" (i.e., selling out the country), over the four characters for "criticise Lin [Biao], criticise Confucius."

its "monk style" neckline and abbreviated sleeves, while the other illustrates the knife pleats of the skirt. That these photos were taken in a foreign country is consistent with reports that Jiang Qing had issued orders that the dress was to be worn by women in Chinese delegations abroad.[64]

In the context of clothing practices in China, the story of the dress compels attention because of Jiang Qing's patent inability to popularise it. Like the reformed *qipao* in the fifties, the Jiang Qing dress was inserted into a vestimentary culture that may have looked boring to the outsider but that was deeply embedded in the complex of aesthetic, political, social and economic realities that both produced and authenticated it. In the years of the Cultural Revolution, young Chinese women in the cities and towns liked wearing army uniforms, which derived their meaning from politics, history, and the very song and dance routines that Jiang Qing had approved as part of the developing revolutionary culture. After the army uniform had had its day, they wore combinations of jacket, shirt, and trousers, sometimes in figured fabrics, or in synthetics, with carefully deployed scarves, in accordance with modest trends set in the large cities. The Jiang Qing dress was culturally meaningless to them. In such a dress, no one could have known what part she was meant to play in what story.

After the death of Mao in September 1976, Jiang Qing was identified as one of an ultra-rightist (later ultra-leftist) and counter-revolutionary "Gang of Four" within the party. Arrested and gaoled, she became the target of attack by the educated youth who under her leadership had first criticised the capitalist roader Liu Shaoqi, and then criticised Lin Biao and Confucius. During the

---

64 Lu Zhongmin, "Guoren bainian fushi: shehui bian
ge de qingyubiao" (Chinese people's dress and adornment in the last hundred years: a barometer of social change), *Renmin ribao: shenghuo shibao* (People's Daily: life times supplement) 24 October 2000; Yan and Gao, *Turbulent Decade*, 445.

campaign against the Gang of Four, cartoonists frequently made allusions to her foray into dress design (Fig. 9.16). The effectiveness of their cartoons was not necessarily dependent on the reader's knowledge of the Jiang Qing dress. In a society where wearing skirts had long been politically dangerous, everyone understood that a woman depicted in a dress was beyond the revolutionary pale. The only exceptions were foreign friends and women from the national minorities. A year after Mao's death, what people wore in China was much the same as in 1974, with women and men in generically similar styles of garment (Fig. 9.17).

In 1980, Jiang Qing was put on trial. In the dock she showed fierce contempt for the proceedings, railing at the court: "I defend Chairman Mao! I am utterly revolutionary!"[65] Such statements were just beginning to be anachronistic. In 1977 Mao's immediate successor, Hua Guofeng, had declared the Cultural Revolution over. In 1978, his longer-term successor, Deng Xiaoping, called for modernisation in the areas of agriculture, industry, defence, and science and technology. In 1979, the first fashion magazine of China's reform era was launched. Women who had loved military dress and not dressing up, who had done whatever their brothers did and held up half the sky, were about to undergo another form of re-education. In fact, while the Gang of Four languished in gaol, the entire society underwent a new sort of cultural revolution.

Fig. 9.17 Family on a Sunday outing in Nanjing, autumn 1977. One year after the death of Mao, dress was still very sober.

---

65 Zuo Lin, "Zhang Sizhi: Wo he Jiang Qing tanbengle" (Zhang Sizhi: the breakdown in my talks with Jiang Qing), *Xin shiji zhoukan* (New Century Weekly), 19 (21 June 2006): 61-5.

10
BREAKING WITH THE PAST

During Mao's lifetime, the subject of what Chinese people wore attracted few in-depth analyses and perhaps it was thought that there was not much to analyse. None the less, clothing was quite prominent in understandings of what constituted the difference between China and the rest. If for politically correct Chinese, clothing at that time differentiated the socialist elect from the rest, for outsiders it was the single most obvious feature about contemporary Chinese culture. Every traveller's tale from this period comments on it, particularly on women's clothing, which struck people as variously simple, practical, unworldly, androgynous, unfeminine or downright ugly.

For everyone, this dress finally came to symbolise China. Nancy and David Milton, Canadian "friends of China," seemed hardly conscious of using a metaphor when they wrote: "as one leaves the custody of the smiling and ingenuous Chinese stewardesses in their baggy cotton uniforms, little red books in pockets, braids down their backs, for their elegantly coiffed and tailored French counterparts, one has already changed worlds."[1] How astonished they would have been to know that a quarter of a century later, the staff of Air China would be wearing uniforms designed by Pierre Cardin.

Reform-era fashions

Fashion was one of many areas in which the opening of a dialogue between China and the rest of the world occurred in the late 1970s. Fox Butterfield, China-watching from Hong Kong in late 1978, wrote that "skirts and dresses [were] reappearing recently on Chinese women for the first time in a decade." The *qipao* was in evidence again, and a Japanese businessman reported having seen women with permed hair, wearing mini-skirts.[2]

---

1 David Milton and Nancy Dall Milton, *The Wind Will Not Subside: Years in Revolutionary China—1964-1969* (New York: Pantheon, 1976), 359.

2 *New York Times* supplementary material, 16 September 1978: 82. *New York Times* was not actually published between August and November 1978 due to a printers' strike. The paper kept all the reports sent in at that time and made them available on microfilm in sequence with the regular issues.

In the same year, the Japanese film *Manhunt*, starring Takakura Ken, was released in China. Interviewed in April 2004, singer Mou Xuanpu recalled the impact:

We were crazy about *Manhunt* then—at that time, I bought a trench coat (*fengyi*) and dark classes to look like [Takakura], and grew my hair ... I remember that trench coat looked great. I saw it for sale in Wangfujing and bought it straight away.[3]

Fashion designer extraordinaire Hanae Mori was invited to China that year, in another sign of strengthening Sino-Japanese relations; and Pierre Cardin also paid his first visit. For Cardin, this was the beginning of a long and ultimately very profitable relationship with China.[4] Again in 1978, Hong Kong shirt manufacturer Yang Yuan-loong came out of retirement to found the Esquel Group, which went on to invest massively in the Chinese cotton industry in Xinjiang, and link it to international fashion production through factories around the world.[5] And in Xinjiang itself, 1978 marked the end of a long period of internal exile for the educated youth who had been sent there during the Cultural Revolution. Four hundred thousand sent-downers began looking for transport to get back home.[6]

In retrospect, it can be seen these were signs of a new era dawning in China's vestimentary history (Fig. 10.1). Wang Anyi, destined to become one of the most famous writers of her generation, arrived back in Shanghai in 1978 after nine years away as a sent-downer.[7] In a short story written after her return, she described the response of the returned educated youth to the new fashion regime in Shanghai, which was slightly but shockingly different to when they had left. At that time, "fashionable Shanghai girls [had] already begun to top their curls with berets set at an angle." The sent-downers hastened to catch up. They were "quick to perm their hair and step into high heels," and looked askance at their rustic looking classmate, the protagonist in the story. "You

---

3 Interview with Mou Xuanpu, "'Zhuibu shengsi lian, jue chang caomao ge': chongwen Ri-ben yinyue" (Undying attachment to *Manhunt*; ceasing to sing the song of the Straw Hat: a retrospect on Japanese music), *Xinlang yule* (New wave entertainment), www.news.xinhuanet.com/audio/2004-04/23/content_1436264.htm. Accessed 28 May 2006. The film referred to is Sato Junya dir., *Kimi yo funme no kawa o watare* (in Chinese, *Zhuibu*), 1976.

4 Wu Alun, "Fashion House Makes it 23 Years in China," *China International Business*, www.cib-online.net/interview.html. Accessed 7 August 2003. The article is an interview with Song Huaigui, 65 years of age, Cardin's long-standing representative in China.

5 Winsome Lane, "Marjorie Yang Speeds up Development of Xinjiang," *Zoom* (Fall/Winter 2002): 36-7.

6 On the return of the sent-downers, in the context of writings by and about them, see Zuoya Cao, *Out of the Crucible: Literary Works About the Rusticated Youth* (Lanham: Lexington Books, 2003), 184-94.

7 Jeffrey Kinkley, "Preface," in Wang Anyi, *Lapse of Time* (Beijing: Panda Books, 1988), n.p.n.

Fig. 10.1 "Two family photos": between August 1976 (a month before Mao's death) and August 1978, Sun Yatsen suits and grim faces give way to global fashions and happy smiles. Cartoon by Xie Peilin.

simply don't care enough about your appearance," they scolded her.[8]

Much more than fashion was signalled by this reversal in attitudes. 1978 marked the beginning of a reform era that would transform the economy and society of China, leaving few areas of life, and few lives, untouched. But what people wore did have a surprisingly important part to play in this transformation. Interviewed by Sang Ye in the 1990s, a Chinese millionaire in Beijing described in detail his road to riches. In 1984, with little but a gaol record to show for his twenty-three years, he embarked on a new life with a license to run a clothing stall. His big break came when he bought into the under-subscribed business in imported seconds, a mix of second-hand and shop-soiled new clothes. "Back then," he recalled, "people were completely fixated with new stuff from overseas, and there wasn't much of it around." With a profit margin of around 500 per cent, he made a small fortune on his first transaction.[9]

This story illustrates perfectly the inherent dynamism of the rag trade in the period of transition to a market economy. Guangzhou showed the effects of this dynamism earlier than Beijing or Shanghai. Much of the above-mentioned clothes-dealer's hard work in setting up his first business lay in trekking to Guangzhou, where he bought his stock, and then back to Beijing, where he sold it. Lying close to Hong Kong and to the reform-era Special Economic Zones,[10] Guangzhou was at that time reliving its historical role as the half-open door through which foreign goods seeped into China. It early profited from the new commercial and industrial possibilities ushered in by the Four Modernisations. In the eighties, Zhencheng Township, in greater Guangzhou, became the "blue jeans capital," of Guangdong, full of factories producing export goods. The surplus was sold to Chinese buyers, no doubt including the future millionaire

---

8 Wang Anyi, "And the Rain Patters On," trans. Michael Day in Wang Anyi, *Lapse of Time*, 27.

9 Sang Ye, *China Candid: The People on the People's Republic*, Geremie R. Barmé with Miriam Lang, eds, (Berkeley: University of California Press, 2006), 16-19.

10 Ezra F. Vogel, *One Step Ahead in China: Guangdong Under Reform* (Cambridge, Mass.: Harvard University Press, 1981), 126.

Fig. 10.2 Bell-bottoms in 1980, worn by actress Shao Huifang in the 1980 film *Spectre*.

from Beijing. The town, writes Ezra Vogel, was "a huge denim market from one end to the other, with hundreds of shops, stalls, and street vendors offering piles of blue jeans."[11]

Some years passed after the beginning of the reform era before a vestimentary transformation of any scale became apparent. Li Xiaobin, born in Beijing in 1957, recorded on camera the tentative experiments with style that his contemporaries were carrying out in the late seventies and early eighties. Already in 1977, perms were being advertised, breaking a long drought in hairdressing. Make-up was being used by young women, who walked arm in arm with their boyfriends now. In the winter of 1979, an enormous advertisement for skin cream, showing a pretty young woman, was hung at Shatan Street junction—Beijing's first commercial street poster of the reform era. In 1980 young men were wearing army greatcoats, fringed scarves, fleecy hats (*yangjianrong maozi*) such as worn by the military, and "froggies" (*hamajing*, as sunglasses were popularly known), even in winter. It was fashionable to leave in place the little label on the lens that showed (truly or not) that one's sunglasses had been imported.[12] Li's photographic record is corroborated by memoirs of the time. "I remember at middle school," writes Qi Xiaochun, "the height of fashion in the winter was a fleecy hat worn with a "slab green" (*banlü*), or army coat, and a mouth mask tucked into a button hole, so as to leave the two strings trailing down your front." This get-up, he comments, was calculated to make the older generations "shake their heads and heave sighs."[13]

Even more provoking were bell-bottomed trousers, which made an appearance around 1980 and sparked debates over whether someone with long hair and big trouser legs could also be a moral person.[14] Close-fitting at the buttocks,

---

11 Ibid., 373.

12 Cha Jianying, ed., *Bashi niandai fangtanlu* (The eighties: interviews) (Beijing: SDX Joint Publishing Company, 2006), 433-53.

13 Qi Xiaochun, "Dui shimao de lijie" (On an understanding of fashion), *Dongfang shibao* (Japan), www.chineseculture.about.com/library/netter/px/unsqixiaochun054.htm. Accessed 18 October 2006.

14 Zhang Jingqiong, *Xi fu dong jian—20 shiji Zhong wai fushi jiaoliu shi* (Western clothing, Eastern influences—a history of fashion flows between China and the outside world in the

with a front zipper for girls and boys alike, cut wide in the lower leg, these were derived from a fashion that had begun to disappear in the West around 1976. It must have made a sharp impression on teenagers at the time. Wang Xiaoshuai (b. 1966) begins his award-winning film *Shanghai Dreams* with a scene of a teacher cutting the bell-bottoms off a pupil's trousers; and in *Platform*, fellow-director Jia Zhangke (b. 1970) depicts a father abusing his son over the same style.[15] Fifty-year-old Cao Guimin, now the owner of two cinemas in Chengdu as well as a vast collection of film memorabilia, recalled in 2005 the deep impression made on him by a photo of Shao Huifang, who wore bell bottoms in the 1980 film *Spectre* (Fig. 10.2).[16] She was playing an actress who was persecuted by the Gang of Four.

In the general populace, changes in colour, fabric and cut were initially more obvious than difference in styles and types of clothing. A comparison of clothing designs in Guangzhou in 1965 and 1981 shows that in the latter year, clothes designers were picking up where they had left off just before the Cultural Revolution. The earlier designs were depicted in black and white on coarse paper, the latter in full, glossy colour; but the clothes themselves are remarkably similar. The short, tailored jackets for women, and casual blouson-style jackets for men being promoted in 1981 were essentially the same as those being designed in 1965 (Fig. 10.3). Nor were even these rather conservative styles in general use. Japanese designer Koshino Junko visited China in 1984, and in the nineties recalled: "ten years ago, the streets of Beijing were grey and blue. They had no relationship to fashion at all."[17] In the same year, the *Beijing Review* reported that most people were still wearing "old-style blue and grey suits."[18] The most obvious new items in street-wear were over-garments such as parkas and reversible coats, useful and fashionable at the same time.[19]

Three years later, much the same complaint could still be made. A contributor to a magazine in 1987 noted "the popularity of jeans, track suits and jackets" but felt that "what is taken up by a few young people can hardly constitute a new tide in Chinese clothing." The writer was especially struck by the failure of older people to experiment with new clothing styles, or alternatively by their failure to stick with new trends. "Among middle-aged and older men, the Sun Yatsen suit has now again overtaken the Western suit," he wrote. "The grim tone they're so fond of goes with their age and outlook." The phrasing suggests that the politi-

---

twentieth century) (Heifei: Anhui meishu chubanshe, 2002), 68.

15 Wang Xiaoshuai, dir., *Qinghong*, 2005; Jia Zhangke, dir., *Zhantai*, 2000.

16 Interview with Cao Guimin, *Beijing qingnianbao*, www.china.com.cn, 22 December 2005. Accessed 28 May 2006.

17 Wang Xu, "Dongjing de yitian" (A day in Tokyo), *Shizhuang* 1 (1996): 16.

18 *Beijing Review* 43 (22 October 1984): 11.

19 Ibid.

Fig. 10.3 Fashion designs in Guangzhou in 1966, just before the Cultural Revolution (top); and in 1981, early in the reform era.

cal tensions engendered by the student demonstrations of December 1986 had sent nervous older people scurrying from their ventures into fashion back to the safe harbour of the cadre suit. In any case, they were evidence, to this observer, that "the reform of China's clothing, far from being a 'new tide,' was headed for conservatism."[20]

From the reiteration of such statements, it can be concluded that change in clothing, like in politics, was proceeding at a pace of two steps forward, one back. Yet institutional signs of a change in clothing culture were strong. In 1981 the Central College of Arts and Crafts in Beijing (since incorporated into Qinghua University) established a special class in clothing design, which it expanded into an undergraduate degree in 1982.[21] One of the first students in the new programme was Li Yanping (b. 1950), formerly a ballet dancer, who in 1984 became the first designer in China to mount an individual fashion show.[22] Another was Chen Hongxia (b. 1957), who spent eight years working in the Guangdong Tractor Factory before successfully applying for entry into the same programme in 1981. In 1988, Chen helped set up a fashion design course in Guangzhou University.[23]

In Guangdong itself, the clothing industry was rapidly changing because of the improved trading environment. Zhou Guoping, born in 1959 in the coastal city of Jieyang, gained his early experience in the graphic arts by copying from propaganda pictures in newspapers and magazines during the Cultural Revolution. After graduating from the Guangzhou College of Arts and Crafts in 1981, he was employed in the design centre of the provincial textile import and export organisation.[24] Liu Yang (b. 1964), enfant terrible of China's re-born fashion industry, enrolled in the Guangzhou Fine Arts Academy in 1983 and made himself obvious there by dyeing his hair yellow, red, or green. Appointed designer at the Guangdong Provincial Silk Import Export Company in 1987, he was soon designing for markets in Europe, the Americas, and elsewhere in Asia.[25] And in the little village of Shaxi, Zhang Zhaoda (Mark Cheung, b. 1963), destined to become one of China's most famous designers, was nurturing his interest in clothing by browsing through magazines sent to him from relatives abroad. Employed in a local garment embroidering factory in Zhongshan, he was talent-spotted by a visitor from Hong

---

20 *Shizhuang* 2 (May 1987): 13.

21 Zhang Jingqiong, *Xi fu dongjian*, 83.

22 Bao Mingxin, Jiang Zhiwei, Cheng Rong, eds, *Zhongguo mingshi shizhuang jianshang cidian* (Dictionary of famous Chinese fashion connoisseurs) (Shanghai: Shanghai Jiaotong Daxue chubanshe, 1993), 126.

23 Ibid., 164.

24 Yuan Hao, "Zhou Guoping: shengming de yishu" (Zhou Guoping: art of a lifetime), *21 shiji rencai zhanlüe* (Given English title: *Talents Herald*), 2 (2003): 23-6.

25 Bao Mingxin et al., eds, *Zhongguo mingshi shizhuang jianshang cidian*, 80-1.

Kong, who provided him with inspiration and guidance. In 1985, with capital investment of 40,000 RMB, he set up his own quality clothing factory back in Shaxi, employing some of the best embroiderers in the area.[26]

To advertise their products, designers needed models. Professional modelling in China was unknown before the 1980s. In the Republican era, models were shop assistants or dance-hall hostesses or society beauties. Pierre Cardin demonstrated the centrality of the model to professional fashion when he brought a group of models to Shanghai for his inaugural China fashion show in 1979. The following year, the Shanghai Garment Company—Cardin's host—established a precedent in China by recruiting twenty reasonably tall young men and women to be trained as models (Fig. 10.4). Other key units in the textile and garments industry followed suit. In 1984, eighteen-year-old Deng Ying, then working in a textile factory, applied for admission to the modelling group recently established by the Beijing

Fig. 10.4 A great leap forward in modelling. Above, China's first modelling class, 1980 (director Xu Wenyuan is first to the left in the front row); below, Chinese models in Paris, 1985. The caption reads: "Chinese fashion invades Paris."

Textile & Fashion Public Service Centre. She became a favourite model of Li Yanping, who used her to showcase fashionable *qipao* designs.[27] *Fashion* magazine recruited its own models, who attracted international attention

---

26 Ibid., 152.

27 *China Reconstructs* XXXVI, 10 (October 1987): 15. On Li Yanping, see Bao Mingxin et al., eds, *Zhongguo mingshi shizhuang jianshang cidian*, 126-9.

时装来自东邻 友谊播于两地

——日本时装表演在沪

摄影:梁大楷

Fig. 10.5 The extravagant line of international fashion design was introduced to the local industry through fashion parades and to Chinese readers more generally through fashion magazines. The caption to this photo feature reads: "Fashion from an eastern neighbour; friendship is disseminated through two lands: a Japanese fashion show in Shanghai."

when Pierre Cardin took them on tour to Paris in 1985 (Fig. 10.5).

Fashion magazines themselves were an important sign of change in the vestimentary realm. The first issue of China's first fashion magazine in many years was published in Beijing in 1979, and a number of others appeared in the eighties (see Table 1). The early fashion magazines were mostly produced by textile and garment manufacturing or trade companies along with higher educational institutions and research groups related to the arts of clothing production. They were strongly pedagogical in character, designed to introduce readers to various aspects of an industry in the process of renovation: textile technology, export standard requirements, fitting, measuring, cutting, ironing, Chinese historical clothing culture, and nation-wide innovations in the production and marketing of textiles and clothing. With four to six issues a year, they typically contained a centre spread of colour illustrations of new styles with attention both to local designs and international fashion. Foreign designs, with their focus on concept, must at first have appeared outlandish to Chinese eyes, but the design gap began to close as the decade wore on, not least because of the exposure to Japanese fashion (Fig. 10.5). The Chinese edition of a Japanese fashion magazine was launched in Beijing in 1985, with fashion photographs and patterns entirely from Japanese contributors.[28] As we shall see, Japanese cultural influence in China had become highly obvious by this time.

Needless to say, the establishment of new degrees, university departments, factories, publications and even modelling troupes signified government support for the creation of a fashion environment. The party leadership of the time in fact took a personal interest in clothing reform. In 1983, General Party Secretary Hu Yaobang called for a general overhaul of Chinese clothing culture. "We must get Chinese people to wear clothes that are a bit neater, cleaner and better look-

---

28 *Shizhuang* 1 (1985): 2.

Table 1: SOME EARLY REFORM-ERA FASHION MAGAZINES, BY YEAR OF
FIRST ISSUE.

YEAR	PUBLICATION	PUBLISHER
1979	*Shizhuang* Fashion	China Silk Import and Export Co., Beijing
1981	*Xiandai fuzhuang* Modern Dress	Beijing Municipal Clothing Research Society and Light Industry Publishing Co.
1982	*Liuxing se* Fashion Colour	China Fashion Colour Society
1984	*Zhongguo fuzhuang* China Garments	China Clothing Design Research Centre
1985	*Denglimei shizhuang* (Chinese edition)	China Fashion Magazine company and Kamakura Bookshop (Japan)
1986	*Shanghai fushi* Shanghai Style	Shanghai Municipal Dress Study Society and Shanghai Science and Technology Publishing Co.
1988	*Shijie shizhuang zhi yuan* Elle	Shanghai Translation Publishing Co. and Daniel Filipacchi Publishing Co.
1990	*Shanghai shizhuang bao* Shanghai Fashion Times	Shanghai Clothing Co.

Source: Various magazines; Bao Mingxin et al. eds, *Zhongguo mingshi shizhuang jian-shang cidian.*

ing," he said.[29] A fashion show was held in Beijing that year, and the wife of
Premier Zhao Ziyang was spotted selecting an open-lapel men's jacket for
her husband's use.[30] Hu and Zhao led the charge into new sartorial domains.
When the members of the Politburo appeared en masse at a press conference
in this same year, they were dressed to a man in Western suits.[31] Some of the
old guard resisted this trend: Deng Xiaoping, for instance, clung resolutely
to his Sun Yatsen suit. But the masses began to follow where the new leaders
led. In 1984, the Beijing Department Store in Wangfujing was selling around
3330 suits daily,[32] and within a decade, the very farmers in the fields were to
be seen in suits. Around the country, millions of men must have been learning
how to knot a tie.

Along with the suits came shirts: whiter, brighter and better cut. Dahua
Shirt factory in Beijing, a major domestic supplier, was making less than a million shirts annually in the sixties. With a new plant, imported equipment and
government investment of over one million American dollars in the eighties,
it was producing six million shirts annually by 1989, for export as well as local

29 *Bainian shishang*, 58.
30 Tie Ying, "First National Fashion Show," 5.
31 *Bainian shishang*, 58.
32 *Beijing Review* 43 (22 October 1984): 11.

consumption.[33] White shirts were not only needed by the reform-era white-collar class; in short-sleeved form, they also continued to reign supreme as summer wear for men, a fashion evident from the 1950s onward. A busy Shanghai street scene in summer looked a sea of white, broken up by islets of women's coloured blouses and dresses (Fig. 10.6), and Shenyang was not too different.[34] But customers were beginning to demand more of their white shirts than they had previously. They liked shirts designed to export specifications, "fitted (instead of square-cut and baggy)."[35]

What women should wear

Fig. 10.6 Shanghai street scene in the 1980s, from an undated photo (detail). The knee-high stockings worn by women are just visible on the woman in black skirt and white blouse on the lower right. The man in a red shirt tucked into his well-fitted pants is in unusually smart, up-to-date clothes. Although a couple of young men are to be seen in T-shirts, the majority of men still wear the conventional white shirt over pants.

As in the 1950s, special attention was paid by the leaders to the need for reform in women's dress. Young women had "the right to dress up," proclaimed Vice-Premier Tian Jiyun in 1984. "The idea of dressing like an old woman ... is outmoded."[36] In the warmer months, the influence of new trends was already obvious on the streets, mainly due to the appearance of skirts and dresses. In 1985 black leather mini-skirts were to be seen, "short till they could be no shorter."[37] Flimsy, even see-through fabrics were used for blouses. Women permed their hair and used make-up with impunity. High heels and strappy sandals were worn with knee-high nylon

33 *China Reconstructs* XXXVIII, 10 (October 1989): 18-19.

34 See Shenyang street scene, 1985, on the front cover of *Beijing Review* 49 (2 December 1985).

35 Tie Ying, "First National Fashion Show," *China Reconstructs* XXXII, 10 (October 1983): 4-5.

36 *Beijing Review* 43 (22 October 1984): 11.

37 *Bainain shishang*, 58.

stockings, in a style unique to China (see Fig. 10.6). Sewing machines became household items, and expanded women's potential for making a variety of clothes, whether for themselves or for family members. Magazines carried instructions for knitters on how to produce patterned instead of plain garments: geometric patterns for men, soft rounded shapes for women, cute animal shapes for children.[38]

In the bric-a-brac assemblage of mid-eighties styles, the *qipao* was hardly to be seen. Early in the reform era, when the jackets and pants of Maoist China were gradually being discarded, it was thought that Chinese women of the post-socialist era would naturally gravitate towards the *qipao* (Fig. 10.7). Surveying the

Fig. 10.7 Was the *qipao* going to make a comeback? The first issue of *Modern Dress* (1981) offered readers a choice between Chinese and Western styles.

Shanghai fashion scene in 1981, one observer noted that the so-called "traditional Sun Yatsen suit had already become [just] formal men's wear, a discreet sort of ceremonial dress," but that for women, "dresses in the *qipao* style, which are the most able to reveal a willowy shape, might be well received."[39] And indeed for a while there was "a brief *qipao* fever" as women turned out their chests and wardrobes for the *qipao*s of yesteryear.[40]

The fever passed and in the course of the 1980s it became clear that the *qipao* was being relegated to the specialist area of designer evening wear. First prize in the Second Chinese Fashion Culture show, held in 1985, went to Liu Ping's ankle-length *qipao*, unconventionally split at the front rather than at the sides and provocatively adorned with a large bow just below the crotch.[41] Two years later, Hu Xiaoping's *qipao*-inspired cocktail dress was selected for the collection of the French Fashion Museum after being displayed at the Fifth

---

38 *Shizhuang* 4 (1985): 38-40.

39 Ming Ji, "Shanghai fuzhuang shichang xunli" (A visit to the Shanghai clothes market), *Xiandai fuzhuang* 1 (1981): 19.

40 Wang Xing, *Bainian fushi chaoliu yu shibian* (One hundred years of fashion trends and global change) (Hong Kong: Shangwu yinshu guan, 1992), 59.

41 *Shizhuang* 3 (1985): 17.

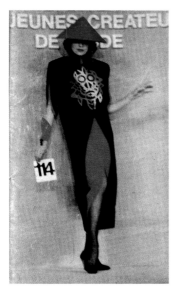

Fig. 10.8 Prize-winning design by Hu Xiaoping, submitted to the International Youth Fashion Competition in Paris, 1987 and featured on the front cover of *Decor* magazine the following year. A student at the Central Arts and Crafts Institute in Beijing, Hu went out to the countryside in search of fashion inspiration. The dress is based loosely on the sheath-like *qipao*. The hem features embroidery designs from Yunnan and Guizhou; a folk paper-cut design adorns the breast; and an elegantly diminished peasant hat tops off the outfit.

International Youth Fashion Competition (Fig. 10.8).[42] As day wear, however, the *qipao* suffered downward mobility. In 1993, the actress-cum-designer Ma Ling (b. 1968) published a collection of her designs in glossy magazine format, with patterns appended. Her evening wear collection featured 1930s-style *qipao*s (Fig. 10.9), but her day wear consisted entirely of conventional skirts, blouses, jackets and frocks in the notionally Western but now actually international style. The patterns did not include any *qipao* designs.[43]

The *qipao*'s sorry standing around this time was noted by a contributor to *Shizhuang*, who noted that before liberation:

the *qipao* was very widespread. After liberation it became a formal dress for state banquets and external activities. When [Deng Xiaoping's] reforms were implemented and the country opened up, things changed enormously. The *qipao* was no longer worn by wives at state functions and was very rarely seen on the streets. It had become just a uniform for hotel staff. Our right and proper national dress had for some reason or other in the end been reduced to this.[44]

To be associated with demeaning employment in the service industry clearly disadvantaged the *qipao*; for it to be worn by entertainers was not much better in the eyes of some women. Interviewed for a fashion broadsheet in May 1995, conductor Zheng Xiaoying recalled seeing a film called "Women of the East" in Moscow, where she was studying at the Tchaikowsky Conservatorium in the sixties. The film featured, among other scenes, one of prostitutes in Hong Kong, wearing *qipao* slit to the thighs. Her reaction to the *qipao* in later years was informed by this association. Performing at an interna-

---

42 See *China Reconstructs* XXXVII, 8(August 1988): 31.

43 Ma Ling, *Ma Ling shizhuang* (Maling fashion) (Beijing: Ma Ling shizhuang fuzhi youxian gongsi, 1993). On Ma Ling, see Bao Mingxin et al., *Zhongguo mingshi shizhuang jianshang cidian*, 3-4.

44 Nie Changshuo, "Nan xing sui gan" (Reflections on the southern tour), *Shizhuang* 2 (1992): 11.

Fig. 10.9 Left, 1930s-inspired *qipao* designs featured in *Maling Fashion* (1993), a one-off publication of fashion designs by a leading young designer of the 1980s, Ma Ling. The cover, right, shows a design based on the May Fourth-style *aoqun*, rather rarely referred to in contemporary fashions. Ma Ling established the PRC's first private fashion enterprise in 1989. She must have retained an affection for this particular design, which is the image used on her business webpage (www.malingfashion.com.cn).

tional musical event in Chongqing, she was deeply embarrassed when one singer performed in a revealing *qipao*. On another occasion in Hong Kong, she refused to appear on the stage in the company of a similarly clad singer.[45]

For younger women, a factor militating against a full-fledged revival of the *qipao* was the strength of new cultural influences entering China as it became reacquainted with the rest of the world. The period of relative isolation had lasted so long that Chinese society had no natural protection against these influences. Continued censorship by the government and even a campaign against "spiritual pollution" could not prevent young people from responding with feverish enthusiasm to the cultural stimulus from outside, especially from the greater East Asian region. In 1980, Nakano Ryoko, the female lead in the influential *Manhunt*, was greeted rapturously in Shanghai when she arrived with a visiting delegation from the Japanese film world (Fig. 10.10). It was not that she was so beautiful, recalls Mou Xuanpu, "but her character really captivated Chinese

---

45 *Zhongguo fushi bao*, 16 (1995).

Fig. 10.10 Japanese film and television had a great impact on Chinese dress in the eighties. Left, the many costumes of Yamaguchi Momoe, who became an icon in China in the early eighties for her role as Sachiko in the television series *A Question of Doubt*. Right, Nakano Ryoko, the female lead in *Manhunt*, received an excited welcome from children in Shanghai Park when she visited China with a Japanese delegation in 1980.

audiences then—on horseback, with her hair flying and her chic clothes, looking by the streetlights for Takakura Ken."[46]

Television ownership permitted increasingly wide and rapid dissemination of new cultural models. In 1978, China had three television sets for every one hundred households. In the six years to 1984 this increased by 533.3 per cent to nearly sixteen in every hundred households, and of course much higher rates again in the cities.[47] The impact was enormous. In 1981, Shanghai television showed an old Japanese series of *Sugata Sanshiro*, the judo saga made famous by Kurasawa's 1943 film of the same name. The hero of the series, Sugata, established a new standard for what a boyfriend should look like, while the spirited Takako sparked a fashion in girls' wear known as the Takako top (*gaozishan*). The following year, girls all over the country became besotted with Japan's super star Yamaguchi Momoe (Fig. 10.10), whose character Sachiko in the television series *A Question of Doubt* inspired a rash of Sachiko look-alikes, wearing Sachiko tops (*xingzishan*) and cutting their hair the Sachiko way (*xingzitou*). The first Hong Kong television

---

46 "Zhuibu shengsi lian, jue chang caomao ge."

47 Hu Teh-wei, Ming Li, and Shangjin Wei, "Household Expenditue Patterns in Tianjin, 1982 and 1984," *The China Quarterly* 120 (December 1989): 789.

series to be shown in China, *Huo Yuanjia*, went to air three years later again, in 1985, and young men on the streets of China were suddenly sporting Beatles-style haircuts in imitation of the heroes. Television also gave exposure to popular singers from Taiwan and Hong Kong. Teresa Teng in an evening gown singing "You ask how deep is my love for you?" replaced Wang Yuzhen in jacket and trousers comparing the compassion of the Communist Party to the depths of Hong Lake.[48]

These new cultural flows not only helped determine the orientation of fashion trends in China; they filled particular styles of clothing with new meanings. He in his trench coat and she in her Sachiko top hinted at the romance of sex, money and power that was endlessly recycled in these foreign films and foreign songs. They were early and unambiguous signs of a post-socialist regime that entailed the overt resexualisation of popular culture in China. In the associated reconfiguration of gender relations, the refeminisation of women was a more demanding task in sartorial terms than the reassertion of a distinctive masculinity, and changes in women's clothing were consequently more dramatic. The difference between a skirt and a pair of trousers was much greater than that between different sorts of trousers, even taking jeans into account. A skirt also meant different shoes, nylon stockings, perhaps a new hairstyle, certainly new ways of walking, sitting, and stooping, probably a different way of looking at the world. In 1979 Cardin shocked his Chinese hosts by demanding the removal of a curtain separating the dressing quarters of the male and female models for his fashion show. "This is work!" he said sternly. "A designer has to see the shape of his models."[49] The cultural gap in attitudes to the body was at that stage enormous. At the Shanghai Garment Company's new modelling school, girls attending their first class in November 1980 were too shy to remove their jackets. They were embarrassed that the woollen jumpers they wore underneath would reveal the shape of their bodies to their male classmates.[50]

In a curious recycling of 1930s strategies, 1980s publishers confronted social shyness about sexuality and nakedness with photos of naked women and scantily dressed sportswomen, adding captions and commentaries about the beauty of

---

48 Teresa Teng (Deng Lijun), who died prematurely in 1995, was the most popular Taiwanese singer of her time, and of her many songs "Ni wen wo ai ni you duo shen ?" (You ask me how deep is my love for you?) is a perennial favourite. Wang Yuzhen sang *Honghu shui* in duet with Fu Ling in the 1961 film, *Honghu chi weidui* (The red militia of Hong Lake). The song remained popular through the 1970s.

49 Xu Wenyuan, *Secai, nülang, wode meng: shizhuang motuoer zhi lu* (Colour, young women, my dream: the fashion model's path) (Guilin: Zhongguo gongren chubanshe, 1991), 27-8. In an earlier publication, I mistakenly attributed this event to a show involving Chinese models. The models involved had accompanied Cardin to China.

50 Ibid.

the human form not dissimilar to those used half a century before.[51] Correspondingly, accounts of the post-Mao fashion renaissance tend to stress the opportunities it offered for women to express their femininity again. "Iron Girl of 'Mao Era' Regaining Feminine Self" proclaimed the *People's Daily* on Women's Day, 2003. The subject of the story was Guo Fenglian, who came to fame as the "iron maiden" in 1963. Guo was the female face of the model commune Dazhai, from which everyone in agriculture was supposed to learn. By "toiling and sweating day after day ... she became the head of Dazhai," reported the paper, "...but at the cost of her femininities [sic]." Now she urges her daughters-in-law to attend beauty salons regularly and keep their hair permed.[52]

The responses of women to reform-era fashions in fact varied greatly. Harriet Evans found that of women to whom she spoke in 1993—"middle-aged, professional"—many were antipathetic to the fashion imagery being produced in the reform era. They had been "brought up to regard gender-neutrality in dress as a signifier of emancipation."[53] This is consistent with the outlook of women of the Cultural Revolution generation described by Lisa Rofel.[54] Women just a little younger might embrace the new fashions with enthusiasm. Yu Li was probably born around 1960. She joined the army and the party in the 1970s, and was one of a PLA team that in 1977 broke the women's small-bore pistol precision and rapid fire world record. But this fast-shooter loved dressing up. When she observed the interest being taken in fashion in the early eighties, she had a flash of inspiration: "be a model!" In 1985, she was in the first troupe of Chinese models to visit Paris (Fig. 10.11).[55]

Generation was just one of a number of variables affecting attitudes to clothing, and it could work in different ways. A number of older women contributed enthusiastically to creating the new fashion era, either through personal example like Guo Fenglian, or in different professional capacities. Li Keyu (b. 1929) had been a costume designer under the old dispensation and became a fashion designer in the new. She went from creating stage costumes for "The Red Detachment of Women" to making designer clothes.[56] Xu Wenyuan (b. 1934) was in her mid-forties when she was placed in charge of the Shanghai Garment

---

51 See Tani Barlow, *The Question of Women in Chinese Feminism* (Durham: Duke University Press, 2004), 289-92, figs 5 and 6.

52 "Iron Girl of 'Mao Era' Regaining Feminine Self," *People's Daily* (English edition), 8 March, 2003.

53 Harriet Evans, *Women and Sexuality in China: Dominant Discourses of Female Sexuality and Gender Since 1949* (Cambridge: Polity Press, 1997), 140.

54 Lisa Rofel, *Other Modernities: Gendered Yearnings in China After Socialism* (Berkeley: University of California Press, 1999).

55 *Shizhuang* 2 (1987): 14-15.

56 Bao Mingxin et al., *Zhongguo mingshi shizhuang jianshang cidian*, 118-19.

Fig. 10.11 Before and after: at the People's Liberation Army fiftieth anniversary commemorative shooting competition in 1977, Dong Xiangyi, Yu Li and Li Yamin (left to right) broke the world record in the women's small-bore pistol (precision and speed) team event. While Dong went on to further feats in this sport, Yu Li became a model. She is photographed here (right) in Paris, 1985.

Company's modelling school. To her fell the tasks of coaxing her students to take off their jackets and reassuring their parents that baring a shoulder was not indecent and would not adversely affect any marriage prospects.[57]

For ordinary women of this generation, moreover, fashion could provide pleasure. It marked a break from the regime of cultural deprivation to which they had been subjected, and satisfyingly reconnected them with a past in which their mothers, if not themselves, had played at being women. After observing a "fashion parade" of older women wearing their own designs, Wang Anyi commented on the realisation, visibly dawning in their faces, that they were women:

They appear to have long forgotten this point. Wearing their sexless clothing they had forgotten their own sex. Carrying out their allotted sexless tasks, they obliterated their own sexuality. They had sexlessly passed their own best years. They seemed, having concluded the best years a woman has, suddenly to have remembered that they were women.[58]

57 See Xu Wenyuan, *Secai, nülang, wode meng.*

58 Wang Anyi, "Ji yici fuzhuang biaoyan" (Remembering a fashion parade), in Wang Anyi,

Herself born in 1954, Wang Anyi appears here to be describing women of her own and her mother's generations (the participants were between forty-two and seventy-four years old). The intensity of her response to this quaint fashion parade must have come somewhere from her own experience or awareness of loss, and perhaps particularly the lost "sent-down" years.

In contrast, Hong Ying, born in 1964, was too young to have been sent down. She was a reform-era teenager. In her autobiography, she records discovering in her teen years that her father was not her biological father; her mother had slept with another man. At a time when the Communist Party was surrendering its self-appointed role as mother of the people ("dearly beloved party, you are our mother"), this true story serves as a narrative appropriate to the times. Growing up in a poverty-stricken and in many respects dysfunctional family, Hong Ying cut loose from her moorings and joined the eighties' equivalent of the beat generation, drifting around China in a haze of alcohol and half-realised aspirations for literary fame. She and her girlfriends "cut each other's hair in outrageous styles not permitted in hairdressers' shops. We dressed simply, like the boys, and in summer often wore skirts without anything underneath, going from one party to the next..."[59] This was not exactly the way her predecessors dressed a decade earlier, but neither was it fashion in the style of Yu Li.

To dress like the boys at some times and to wear skirts without underwear at others was an eloquent expression of the social upheaval of the reform era. "I remember," wrote someone much less rebellious, "that relatives from Hong Kong gave us several pairs of bell-bottoms to take back home, and I only dared to wear them indoors..." To the writer's memory, bell-bottoms were much more likely to be worn by girl hoodlums than by their male peers. "Actually," she reflected, "the popularity of bell-bottoms at that time was not due to aesthetics, but simply to a psychology of rebelliousness in the aftermath of the Cultural Revolution. Especially for girls—daring to wear bell-bottoms meant they had to have courage enough to confront social disapproval."[60]

The clearly stated alternative to bell-bottoms was nice clothing such as described by old-school clothing designer Chen Fumei in 1980. Chen's advice was that young people should dress in neat, appropriate, preferably Chinese-style clothes. The writer offered Zhou Enlai as an excellent model in this regard, always smartly dressed, whatever he was wearing. Girls were to take care, also, to coordinate their clothing, avoiding garish mixes of colour and outlandish combinations such as "a panama hat, a housewife's coat, a soldier's trousers, and student's shoes." They

---

Xunzhao Shanghai (Shanghai: Xuelin chubanshe, 2002), 79.

59 Hong Ying, *Daughter of the River: An Autobiography* (London: Bloomsbury, 1998), 265.

60 "Labaku: bei shiguo fanpan zhouyu de kuzi" (Bell-bottoms: trousers used as an expression of defiance). *Renminwang* (People's web), www.news.tom.com/1002/3291/200597-2452894. html, 7 September 2005. Accessed 18 October 2006.

Fig. 10.12 Girls in dresses, no two alike. With a model worker as its heroine, the 1984 feature film *The Fashionable Red Dress* (*Jieshang liuxing hongqunzi*) made a strong statement in support of pretty clothes for women.

should avoid wearing red, at least if they lived in the city; and attend to their inner beauty as well as their outer.[61] Urged anew to dress up nicely but told as frequently that they had overstepped the mark, girls in this era faced the very problem that Hu Shi had identified in the 1930s when he criticised the dress regulations imposed by Chen Jitang in Guangdong.[62]

As it happened, the boundaries drawn up by Chen Fumei were all transgressed in the film *The Fashionable Red Dress*, released in 1984. Shot on the streets of Shanghai, the film showed working women boldly dressed to go out on the town, model worker Tao Xing'er among them (Fig. 10.12). The moral of the tale was that even a model worker had the right to like pretty things. Another film in the same year, *Girl in Red*, used the time-honoured association of red and revolutionary to portray a girl (in skirt and red blouse) asserting her individuality in the face of pressures to conform. Together these films inspired a proliferation of red skirts, breaking the nexus between red and collectivism, and also between red and peasant that Chen Fumei had not too subtly indicated. After this, Li Xiaobin noted, girls in China finally dared to wear red as fashion, just like girls anywhere else.[63]

---

61 Chen Fumei, "*Zenmeyang cai jiao fuzhuang de mei?*" (What sort of clothing can be called beautiful?), *Zhongguo qingnian* 6 (1980): 20-1.

62 See Chapter Six.

63 Cha Jianying, *Bashi niandai*, 450. The two films are Qi Yingjia, dir., *Jieshang liuxing hong qunzi* (lit. "the red dress is popular on the street"), and Lu Xiaoya, dir., *Hongyi shaonü* (Girl in Red).

Selling clothes ≠ designing fashion

A major driving force behind the sea change in fashion was China's need for economic growth. The export of textiles and garments was fundamental to the implementation of the Four Modernisations, and partly determined the pace and orientation of local fashions. In this domain of economic activity, China was starting from a low base-line. With a long history as an exporter of quality textiles and an enormous labour force, it should have been a dominant force in the international textile and garment trade well before the reform era, but even in the context of the Third World, where it felt reasonably comfortable during the Cold War, it was a poor performer. In 1970, it accounted for less than 5 per cent of clothing exports from developing economies.

The turnaround during the reform era was remarkable. By 1980, in wake of the policy shift in 1978, the share of clothing exports had more than doubled from 4.8 to 10.1 per cent,[64] and the government was beginning to promote ventures overseas in search of new markets. Textile and garment exhibitions were mounted in Sydney in 1980 and 1981, where state entrepreneurs could test the waters in a small, regional market with strong industry protection but a high per capita consumer capacity. Participants took the opportunity to conduct field research. Australians, it was noted, buy around 30 garments per capita per year, of which an average 6.4 were imported. With improved quality, range, punctuality, and price competitiveness "an increase in our exports to Australia is totally possible."[65]

This optimism proved to be totally justified. Australians, who used to make most of their own clothes, were soon making barely any. By the time of the Second China Clothing and Textiles Expo in Sydney, held in 2002, it could be claimed in the promotional material that China had been the world's leading exporter of textiles and clothing for seven years running. The low cost of labour in China made it irresistible to manufacturers. What cost five dollars an hour in the USA and a dollar an hour in Hong Kong in the 1980s only cost sixteen cents in China.[66] China's textile exports as a percentage of world exports peaked early in the reform era, but the labour-intensive garment industry continued to grow, eventually making massive inroads on the apparel retail sector in Europe and North America. All through the Western world, the familiar "made in Hong Kong" label had been replaced by one reading "made in China."

---

64 Yongzheng Yang, "China's Textile and Clothing Exports: Changing International Comparative Advantage and Its Policy Implications," *Asia Pacific School of Economics and Management Working Papers* (Canberra: Asia Pacific Press, 1999), 4.

65 *Shizhuang* 6 (1981): 41.

66 Yao Zaisheng, "Guangdong de shizhuangchang he Shanghai de caifengpu" (Canton's fashion factories and Shanghai's tailor shops), *Xiandai fuzhuang* 6 (1996): 20.

街头时装

Fig. 10.13 Street fashion feature, 1996. At this time, the major fashion organs were not yet full gloss magazines. Much of the local material was still printed on coarse paper, using black and white photography.

Despite this strong performance, observers of the Chinese fashion industry were voicing disappointment about the state of the industry. In 2004, Zhang Wenhe, editor of the Beijing journal *Art and Design*, wrote a gloomy review of Chinese fashion magazines. After its inception in 1979, the fashion magazine in China changed little during the 1980s. The generic magazine was modestly sized and produced on coarse paper, though containing coloured inserts on better quality paper. Textual material well outweighed visual in the contents. Patterns for clothes were a regular feature. In the 1990s, this format gradually disappeared. New magazines appeared—importantly, *Ruili Dress and Beauty* (*Ruili fushi meirong*) in 1995[67]—and some of the old, such as *Fashion*, were reworked. Full-gloss magazines became the norm. Colour spreads, while continuing to show the regional alertness to Japanese and Hong Kong fashions evident in the 1980s, came to be dominated by designs from the big European fashion houses—Versace, Armani, YSL. Street fashion made an appearance in fashion features (Fig. 10.13).[68] Patterns occupied less and less space in popular magazines, before finally disappearing from the major titles. Most of these trends were obvious by the mid-nineties.

After this time, as Zhang Wenhe shows, fashion magazines faced the same problem as the fashion industry more broadly. Foreign titles and Sino-foreign publications were proliferating through copyright purchases, and even as new local magazines emerged, others were closing down. By 2004, just three names, all with foreign connections, dominated the market: *Ruili*, offspring of a Japanese magazine, and now with a whole stable of Chinese magazines to its name; *Fashion*, which had gone into partnership with *Esquire*, *Harper's Bazaar*, and *National Geographic*; and *Elle*, which had been building its Chinese empire since 1988. *Vogue* was just about to make a much-anticipated appearance in Guangzhou.[69] Reflecting on this

67 Zhang Wenhe, "Chinese Magazine Industry: Clothes Horse for Global Fashion Brands," *Rising East* (online version), 4 (May 2006), www.uel.ac.uk/risingeast/archive04/essays/wenhe.htm. Accessed 16 October 2006.

68 *Shizhuang* 3 (1996): 44-7. This issue published the sixth in a series of illustrated articles on street fashion.

69 Zhang Wenhe, "Chinese Magazine Industry: Clothes Horse for Global Fashion Brands."

Fig. 10.14 Designing for the unknown future in 1981. Western-style frocks proved to be more popular than Chinese-style pant suits.

data, Zhang drew a long bow from fashion magazines to the industry as a whole: "We must recognise," he concluded, "that there is currently no fashion industry in our country; even the embryo hasn't been formed, and fashion magazines in China are no more than a clothes horse for the international fashion industry."[70]

Zhang's assessment was consistent with a general pessimism in the Chinese fashion world in the early twenty-first century. Suzhou designer Shi Lin (b. 1942), a front-line participant in the vestimentary revolution of the eighties, was manifestly disappointed at performance in the design sector in the early twenty-first century.[71] China's dominance in the production of clothing, she wrote, was not in dispute, but was directed mainly at providing run-of-the-mill garments for the daily wear of China's millions. Many clothing companies in China did not have a design section at all, but made do with hot items from Shenzhen that they sold inland under their own labels, or picked apart to provide the patterns for their own manufacture. "Without design, there can be no innovation," she wrote, "and without innovative undertakings, there is no future."[72]

---

70 Ibid.

71 On Shi Lin, see Bao Mingxin et al., *Zhongguo mingshi shizhuang jianshang cidian*, 50.

72 Shi Lin, "Zhongguo shejishi haixu nuli" (China's designers still have to work hard), *Zhongguo fangzhi daxue xuebao*, 9 May 2002, www.efu.com.cn/info/technique/2002-5-10/8412.htm. Accessed 3 September 2003.

This critique, intended as a wake-up call to her colleagues when China was on the point of admission to the WTO, did not quite do justice to the efforts and achievements of designers over the preceding quarter of a century. From early in the reform era, designers were labouring to produce a culturally distinctive, internationally recognised and respected brand of fashion. They did not at first know how Chinese fashion was going to develop. The centre-fold of the first issue of *Modern Dress* showed both pretty frilly dresses in the Western style and pyjama suits in a Chinese-influenced style (Fig. 10.14). Both were a far cry from the bell-bottoms that constituted real, live fashion in a sector of the young population, but of the styles, the pretty dresses were a better indicator of future directions in mass clothing for women. On the whole, people in reform-era China wanted to be citizens of the world. Charged with clothing the population not only of China but of many other parts of the world as well, designers' skills were absorbed mostly in producing international styles for the mass market.

In this market, the great challenge was how to capture the upper stratum of wealthier buyers. In 1994, the head of the Luomeng garment manufacturing group went to Paris in full expectation of finding there a market for his very modestly priced suits. When his efforts to attract customers were disappointed, the importance of a recognisable label dawned on him.[73] A "Chinese Famous Brands Fashion" group was established in Beijing that same year, and in company with the Chinese Historical Clothing Research Association launched a Chinese "famous brands" magazine. Eight "famous brands" were featured, including the locally successful Aidekang, founded in 1989 with German investment, and Tianma, known for its shirts. The aim of the magazine was to establish brand recognition for Chinese products.[74] In 1996, the Chinese Famous Brands Development Company was established for the same end.[75]

It proved easier to recognise the phenomenon of the brand name than in practice to create successful labels. In 2001, a national association for the promotion of Chinese brands internationally was founded in accordance with President Jiang Zemin's directive, "establish the national character and create a world brand name." One of its primary tasks is to educate people in China about their own brands, much like "buy British" and "buy Australia" campaigns that have been periodically launched to promote local manufacturing elsewhere.[76] Chinese

---

73 "Chinese Garment Sector Steps into World Market," www.humanrights-china.org/course/Daily2001108142431.htm. Accessed 21 April 2003.

74 *Zhongguo mingpai shizhuang* (Chinese Popular Brand Fashion), 1 (September 1994): 2.

75 Claire Roberts, *Evolution and Revolution: Chinese Dress 1700s-1900s* (Sydney: Powerhouse Museum, 1997), 99.

76 The name of the association is *Zhongguo guoji mingpai fazhan xiehui*, the official English rendering of which is China International Nameplate Development Association. See its website at www.cifbpf.org.

clothing labels have very low recognition among local consumers, so such a campaign is not at all superfluous.[77]

A greater concern in China is that Chinese brand names more generally have little pulling power internationally. In 2005, China had less than a 10 per cent share in world-wide brand name exports, and while most of the top hundred export brands were able to command a 50 per cent or greater share of their respective markets, China's top performer, white goods giant Haier, had only a 10 per cent share of its particular market.[78] Addressing a conference on fashion, the director of Binbin, a very successful clothing chain dealing in its own brand of Western clothes, made it clear that he saw no signs of improvement in the near future. The semiotics of fashion were weighted against China, particular in the domain of off-the-rack styles: "take a Western garment we make in our factories, with the same sort of materials, the same worker, the same machines: stick a top-ranking fashion label like Dior on it, and it sells it for eight to ten thousand; stick Binbin on it, and you'll get two.[79]

In conceptual designs, designers have greater scope for experimentation than when producing set piece garments, but they seem to be constrained by a high degree of cultural self-consciousness when operating in the world context. Designers who at home confidently produce elegant clothing for modern life appear to have difficulty forgetting they are Chinese when facing an international audience, and even greater difficulty in conveying their Chineseness in other than very obvious ways. Lü Yue, one of China's top ten designers in 1997, provided a good illustration of this problem in her "Festival Day" exhibitions in Paris and New York in 1999 and 2000. The parade featured heroin-chic models carrying red paper lanterns, wearing long coats or tunics with loose trousers or very short skirts, all made of red satin, trimmed with fur and embroidered with medallions or chrysanthemums.[80] This was a predictable assembly of elements that must have left the albeit rapturous audience in its comfort zone. Colours and materials alike satisfied established expectations of China, and wayward hairstyles did little to disrupt the impression of an updated *Dream of Red Mansions*.

One impediment to the more creative deployment of historical aesthetics in fashion, and in the arts more broadly in China, is the tight grip maintained by

---

77 In 2004 and 2006 I asked a number of young women to identify a Chinese clothing label they liked, or with which they were familiar, with no quick answer springing to anyone's lips, and sometimes no slow answer, either.

78 Jie Ailan, "Zhongguo pinpai yu shijie pinpai de bijiao" (Comparison of Chinese and International brand names), *Renmin ribao* 5 September 2005.

79 Wei Zhi, "Zhongguo fuzhuang pinpai boyi 20 nian" (Twenty great years of Chinese fashion brands), *Zhongguo fangzhi bao* 27 January 2006.

80 Jiang Ye, ed., *Zhongguo fuzhuang sheji: Lü Yue* (Chinese fashion designer: Lü Yue) (Beijing: Renmin meishu chubanshe, 2004), preface.

the ruling Communist Party on interpretations of history and culture. In the nineties, Marxism-Leninism-Mao Zedong Thought was quietly replaced by patriotism as the guiding principle in Chinese life. This if anything intensified China's preoccupation with success in the international arena while simultaneously encouraging an obsession with the essence of Chinese culture. Lü Yue's "Festival Day" show with its use of red and lanterns, was a case of staging the cultural essence. Zhang Yimou used exactly the same elements for the Chinese performance at the closing ceremony of the Athens Olympics.

Fig. 10.15 Models from the New Silk Route Modelling Company in Qing dynasty costume.

An even more obvious example of national essence on display is the national costume parade, which is a feature of many a Chinese fashion extravaganza (Fig. 10.15). In 2001 the New Silk Route Modelling Company mounted six fashion shows in Berlin which showcased Chinese models, textiles, and culture through a focus on historical costume. Models mounted striking parades of "dignified" Han, "luxurious" Tang, "delicate" Song, "bold" Yuan, "bright" Ming and "elegantly gorgeous" Qing costume. A Xinhua reporter in Berlin showed how such a display could pull the patriotic heart-strings when he thanked the organiser excitedly with the words: "You condensed our Chinese history and culture into a single fashion show. I felt proud to be Chinese."[81] Similar shows had earlier been organised in Paris and New York in 1998 under the rubric "China Millennium." Such a literal appropriation of historical culture suggests that designers have yet to develop an authoritative, or at least a very interesting, view of their own history.

At the same time the politics of international fashion militate against a ready reception of the work of Chinese designers. "China, by definition, is fast fashion," writes Simona Segre Reinach.[82] Since fast fashion is cheap, imitative, and

---

81 "Zhongguo fuzhuang zoujin Bolin" (given English title: China fashion show in Berlin), *Zhongguo zhi yi* 12 (2001): 70-4.

82 Simona Segre Reinach, "China and Italy: Fast Fashion versus *Prêt a Porter*. Towards a New Culture of Fashion," *Fashion Theory: The Journal of Dress, Body and Culture* 9, 1 (1 March 2005): 55.

utterly disposable, it cannot but pose an obstacle to the reception of Chinese designs. After viewing the work of six top Chinese designers in Paris in 2003, Didier Grumbach, president of the French Fashion Federation, had few words of encouragement to offer. "It will take a long time before there are any Chinese labels [worth considering]," he said; "that takes a long, long time to develop."[83] Whether a similar show mounted by Italian designers would have met with a similarly cool reception is impossible to say in the absence of a controlled experiment, but there are undoubtedly ironies in the fact that Chinese kitsch has been successfully marketed by big fashion labels. Speaking at a fashion conference in 1999, Hong Kong designer William Tang expressed bewilderment that his *qipao*-inspired designs on the Paris catwalk in the early nineties failed to make an impression, when with similar designs a couple of years later French designers made fashion headlines around the world.[84]

International relations and vestimentary events

The struggle for recognition by fashion designers has taken place in a complex international situation where China feels truly at ease in the company of few other nations. In the eighties, as discussed above, Japanese culture had a profound impact on popular culture in China. In designer fashion the impact was strengthened by the status of Japanese fashion internationally after 1982, when twelve Japanese designers caused a sensation in Paris.[85] Aspiring designers and models in China seized the opportunity to gain experience in the Japanese industry, and for many—Shi Lin was one, Yu Li another—Japan offered them their first exposure to fashion in foreign lands.[86] The inspiration was comparable to that provided by Japan's victory in the Russo-Japanese war in 1905, and the reasoning was similar. If one Asian country can do it, why not another? A Chinese fashion commentator wrote with wistful optimism in 1987: "In the 1980s, Japanese designers greatly influenced world fashion with designs based on traditional Japanese dress. Perhaps in the 1990s or thereabouts, it will be the turn of Chinese designers."[87]

---

83 "La mode chinoise prend son envol" (Chinese fashion takes off) (5 March 2003), *France3. fr: un site du groupe France Télevisions Interactive*, www.cultureetloisirs.france3.fr/mode/podiumsdailleurs/103017-fr.php. Accessed 3 September 2003.

84 William Tang, keynote address at the ConsumAsian conference on Fashion in Asia, University of Hong Kong, 23-7 March, 1999.

85 See Yuniya Kawamura, *The Japanese Revolution in Paris Fashion: Dress, Culture, Body* (Oxford: Berg, 2004).

86 Bao Mingxin et al., *Zhongguo mingshi shizhuang jianshang cidian*, 50.

87 Wen Tianshen, "New Fashion Trends," *China Reconstructs* XXXVI, 10 (October 1987): 68.

Fig. 10.16 A *qipao* shop in Huizhou, north of Guangzhou. The red skirt and jacket on the left is a Chinese-style wedding dress, of a style that is quite commonly worn instead of the white dress and veil. It is possible that many of the *qipao*s on display here will also be worn at weddings, whether by the guests or by members of the wedding party. A young seamstress is working in the rear of the shop.

The Tiananmen incident in 1989 marked the end of a honeymoon period for reform-era China, and during the 1990s a rise of nationalism around the world affected its interactions with neighbours and trading partners. In 1992, Emperor Akihito visited China in a successful diplomatic move on Japan's part, but relations cooled during Jiang Zemin's return visit in 1995, and were volatile over the next decade. Admiration of Japanese success faded. Interviewed in 2004, designer Han Feng, based in New York, criticised Japanese fashions of the eighties for being "somewhat cold and intellectual," and for being more about the designer than about the people who wore them. Her own aim was "to serve career women, to help them be creative and elegant."[88] This distinction between her own project and that of her famous Japanese peers illustrates perfectly Japan's significance in the construction of Chinese identity and the definition of Chinese goals.

Tensions over the status of Taiwan also intensified in the nineties, when democracy on the island threatened the survival of the "one China" policy. Correspondingly, feelings of patriotism were roused to fever pitch in 1997, when Hong Kong was returned from British to Chinese sovereignty. The *qipao* made a comeback in this year, particularly in Hong Kong itself. A Chinese flavour was anyway infusing international fashion around this time, and Chinese designers hastened to demonstrate their own credentials in this area. In 2000 the *qipao* was given a further fillip by the release of Wong Kar-wai's critically acclaimed film, *In the Mood for Love*. Set in 1960s Hong Kong, the film opens in Shanghai dialect, setting a mood appropriate to the sequence of high-necked *qipao*s paraded gracefully across the screen on the person of Maggie Cheung.[89] *Qipao* shops

88 Daisann McLane, "China's New Fashion Whispers 'Asia'," *International Herald Tribune* 14 September 2004.

89 Wong Kar-wai, dir., *Huayang nianhua* (In the Mood for Love), 2000.

Fig. 10.17 The "New Chinese Jacket" (*xin tangzhuang*), specially designed for the meeting of APEC leaders in Shanghai, 2001. Each garment was presented in a matching silk bag, adorned with the APEC label.

proliferated around the country, and more and more brides began to incorporate the *qipao* into their wedding regalia (Fig. 10.16).[90]

The year of *In the Mood for Love* was followed by the year of APEC in Shanghai, which brought to Chinese shores nineteen regional leaders from the Asia-Pacific rim. It has long been the custom at APEC meetings for the host country to provide an item of regional clothing to the guests, to be donned for a commemorative photo opportunity. In China, a design team was summoned to produce Chinese-style jackets (*tangzhuang*) for the occasion, and on 21 October 2001, television coverage of nineteen regional leaders wearing them was beamed around the world. In consequence, the popularisation of the *qipao* was matched by a fad for *tangzhuang* (Fig. 10.17). Taiwan failed to attend the summit because China would not approve its chief delegate, so had to do without its jacket.

While quarrelling with Japan and Taiwan, China improved its relations with South Korea. Diplomatic relations between the two countries were established in 1992, and laid the base for a mutually advantageous relationship, character-ised by strengthening economic ties. The Asian Economic Crisis in 1997 ap-peared to deal a shattering blow to Korean ambitions in China, but by the turn of the millennium a resurgence of economic activity was evident amid signs of a growing Korean cultural influence in China. Korean restaurants proliferated, and Korean film and pop stars began to attract huge followings. Television audiences became addicted to Korean soap operas such as the historical drama *Jewel in the Palace* (*Dae Jang Geum*), which has attracted enormous audiences in East and Southeast Asia. Cosmetic surgery, pioneered in China by Japa-nese companies, is now virtually a Korean monopoly in Shanghai (Fig. 10.18). Korean fashion boutiques have sprung up everywhere, and massive "Korea City" (*Hanguocheng*) retail complexes have mushroomed in major cities. The children's song "I love Beijing's Tiananmen," could be rewritten, suggested

---

90 A modern, urban Chinese wedding usually involves a number of changes of dress. A bride might begin with a white dress, later change into a *qipao*, and finally don an evening dress.

Fig. 10.19 Korean influence on Chinese high fashion? The line of the hair piece and the gown both suggest that Ma Ke, chief designer for *Liwai* (Exception) was responding to the "Korean current" in 2003.

one journalist, as "I love Beijing's Hanguocheng," so popular is the national capital's Korea City.

In high fashion, Korea has startled Chinese commentators by its extraordinary success in penetrating the elite market. In 2005, leisure wear from the prestigious Korean brand Rapido could command prices between 800 and 2500 RMB, compared to between 500 and 800 for comparable clothing from Adidas. By this year there were sixty Korean labels in the Chinese clothing market, many of them positioned in the top end of the market. More than half had entered the country in just the preceding two years.[91] Japanese and European fashions had by no means been obliterated from the fashion scene: their labels were far too strong for this to be possible. Nonetheless, the Korean influence was strong enough in the early years of the twenty-first century for the "Korean current" (*hanliu*) to be counted a defining characteristic of Chinese fashions in this period. Its impact on local design was clear in the work of Ma Ke (Coco Ma), one of the most interesting designers in contemporary China (Fig. 10.19).[92]

Cultural flows, globalisation, and regional belonging

Despite some resonance between trends in international relations and trends in fashion, it is clear from popular and street fashion that many different variables affect what people in contemporary China choose to wear. Financial resources

91 "Fuzhuang shichang pianchui 'Chaoliufeng' (Korean currents run strong in the clothing market), *Zhongguo fangzhi wang* (China textiles website), www.ramie.comcn/scps05/s006.htm. Accessed 28 May 2006.

92 On Coco Ma, see Douglas Bullis, *Fashion Asia* (London: Thames and Hudson, 2000), 195-9.

are one important factor. The vaunted economic growth in China during the re-form era has produced a great prosperity gap that is broadly evident between city and countryside, and between coast and inland, as well as between people on the top and the bottom rungs of the occupational ladder. In consequence, there is a great distance in more than one respect between the fashion outlets of Nanjing Road and the tailor shops in the old Chongqing, even if the two recognisably belong to the same clothing system (Fig. 10.20).

The mass media, including the internet, constitute another variable, and no doubt the most significant of any. Naturally, the Chinese government makes use of the media for its own purposes, and in this way can help inflect trends affecting fashion among other expressions of contemporary culture. But even given government manipulation and censorship, television and the internet to-gether present consumers in China with a vast smorgasbord of entertainment and information on which they draw for guidance in multiple decisions made about daily life, including where to shop and what to wear. The mix of Chinese, Japanese, Korean, American and European programmes and internet sites avail-able in China is consistent with the mix of subcultures evident on the streets of Chinese cities.

Most obvious among subcultures from a fashion perspective is the "great *ha*" phenomenon, which has both a Japanese and a Korean manifestation. The term *ha* originated in Taiwan and means to like or desire something to the point of being crazy, as in "I really *ha* you" (*wo hen ha ni*). "*Ha ri*," meaning "crazy about Japan," is a neologism invented by a young Taiwanese who, by using the local dialect word "*ha*" instead of a formal Mandarin alternative, wished to identify the particularly Taiwanese character of the phenomenon.[93] As with many fads in Taiwan, both the term and associated cultural practices soon became evident across the strait.

"*Ha*" groupies in China are teenage girls who follow particular bands, watch particular soap operas, and dress up in particular ways. "*Ha* Japan" groupies fa-vour a mix of pastel colours, mini-skirts, and a baroque accumulation of detail. Their "*Ha* Korea" counterparts, who have gained in strength during the Korean culture fever, "wear big pants and tops, so that you can't see any of their feminine

---

93 According to Ming-tsung Lee (Li Mingcong), the term first appeared in Hari Xingzi, *Zaoan Riben* (Good morning, Japan) (Taibei: Jianduan, 1996). The author, otherwise identi-fied only as A Xing, uses "Hari" (*ha ri*) as her pen name. Li Mingcong, "'Qin ri' de qinggan jiegou, yu 'ha ri' de zhuti—yige kua shidai rentong zhengzhi de kaocha" (The structure of feeling in "feeling close to Japan", and the topic of "Japan crazy": a study of cross-generational identity politics), Taiwan Sociology Annual Convention and Conference, 2004. I thank Kuo Mei-fen for this reference. For English-language treatment of the topic, see Ming-tsung Lee, "Absorbing Japan: Transnational Media, Cross-cultural Consumption, and Identity Practice in Contemporary Taiwan," Ph.D. thesis, Department of Social Anthropology, King's College, Cam-bridge, 2005, Ch. 6.

Fig. 10.20 Contrasting sites of fashion in contemporary China. Above left, a dressmaker's shop in the old quarter of Chongqing, with tailors' dummies outside modelling the ready-to-wear garments that have been manufactured on site. Bolts of material are visible within the shop. Clients are measured up in full view of passers-by. Bottom right, "B.Y." (*boya*) fashions, which manufactured off-site and retailed through this little boutique at 220 Urumuchi Road North, one of a number tucked into the wall of an otherwise residential stretch of road.

curves, all you can see is their multi-coloured hair."[94] Girls within the different groups identify strongly with each other, and rely on their carefully cultivated *ha* look for individual and group identity. "I *ha*, therefore I am," quipped one commentator. While the truly eccentric *ha* dress practices are cultivated only by a minority of teenagers operating within particular subcultures, elements of the *ha* look are quite widespread.

Between Japan and Korea as dynamic sources for exogenous cultural inspiration in China, with Taiwan serving as an important mediator, it might seem that the West is a non-player in the Chinese fashion scene. Yet as one Korean in China has written, few of the Korean products entering China are actually Korean in any original sense. Rather, Korea processes and interprets American things for its own consumption, and then exports them to China.[95] Moreover, Europe has its own

---

94 Ann Mah, "Japanese and Korean pop idols set trends for Chinese teens," *International Herald Tribune* 5 March 2005.

95 Li Aoxia, "'Huafeng' he 'Hanliu'" (The Chinese wind and the Korean current), *Shaonian wenyi* (Nanjing) 2 (2006).

groupies in the form of the "young bourgeoisie," or *xiaozimen*, the Chinese latte set. The *xiaozimen* are slightly older and more sophisticated than the *ha* people. They have money, although they do not flash it around. They have a certain "tone": they are educated, and talk about Milan Kundera. They might sing American folk music, but on the whole prefer European to American culture. The flow of their flawless Mandarin is occasionally broken by a smattering of French or Italian. They like foreign movies but not if they are dubbed; they only watch the original versions. They patronise Häagen-Dazs and Starbucks, and *Trends* (*Shishang*) fashion magazine. They roll their eyes. They favour casual dress but avoid obvious designer labels such as Adidas or Nike. A typical *xiaozi* is a girl in jeans trying not to look conspicuous while she works on her laptop in a coffee shop.[96]

A reaction to these various foreign currents in fashion is visible in the *Hanfu* movement, which is directed at reviving and popularising Han dress. This is an ethno-nationalist movement that specifically focuses on Han rather than Chinese culture, although the slippage between the two is considerable and critics have raised concerns about Han chauvinism in the context of the movement.[97] For some of the movement's adherents, Han dress is simply the one-piece wraparound gown of the Han Dynasty (206 BC–220 AD). For others, it is the totality of various sorts of pre-Qing dress, excluding anything definitively identified with the Mongols and other northern peoples. Importantly, the *ruqun*, discussed in Chapter Three of the present book, is featured on Hanfu websites.[98]

Disciples of the movement are mostly students and graduates employed in China's big cities—Beijing, Shanghai, Tianjin, Chongqing, Shenzhen. In September 2003, one enthusiast made headlines in Zhengzhou by walking to work dressed in his Han robe—the first recorded occasion when anyone used the revived costume as ordinary daywear.[99] Most adherents don their apparel simply at festivals, sometimes in connection with the performance of Confucian rituals. The parallels with revivalist rituals in the late twenties, performed by dignitaries wearing antiquated dress, are compelling, and the motivations not dissimilar. "What we are working on," according to a leading proponent, "is not only about bringing back a forgotten fashion. Our driving force is the long lost pride and the eagerness to achieve self-respect while advancing our civilisation."[100]

---

96 Chen Rongli, "Manhua 'xiaozi'" (Leisurely words about "xiaozi"), *Minzu luntan* 6 (2002): n.p.n.

97 See Stephen Wong, "Han follow suit in Cultural Renaissance," *Asia Times* (online edition), www.atimes.com, 26 August 2006. Accessed 12 October 2006.

98 See www.hanfu.org/cn. The main propaganda website, which covers broader issues of Han heritage, is www.hanminzu.com.

99 *Zhongguo xinwen zhoukan*, 12 September 2005.

100 Ibid.

Despite the unambiguous labelling of these different sub-cultures both by the participants and by observers, these various manifestations of influence on fashions in China are evidence not of single, mutually exclusive points of cultural reference in fashion choices (e.g. China, Japan, Korea), but rather of interrelationships that link Chinese youth to other parts of the world, and particularly to other parts of East Asia. The *ha* groupies of Beijing are inspired by their counterparts in the sub-cultures of Shibuya and Harajuku in Tokyo; in Tokyo, in turn, teenagers demonstrate their responsiveness to London and New York by wearing fashions inspired by punk and hip-hop.[101] From the *Hanfu* websites, too, have sprung diasporic offshoots, such as the Toronto Association for the Revival of Chinese *Hanfu*;[102] and the Hanfu movement itself undoubtedly owes much to Korean costume drama for inspiring young Chinese to an interest in their own vestimentary past. Paradoxically, these apparently distinctive, local and localised, culturally specific subcultures show the flows of culture and capital that are commonly associated with globalisation.

At the same time, the strongly regional flavour of the subcultures announces China's embeddedness in that part of the world where it is historically grounded, and where it is surrounded by societies whose historical development in intimately connected with its own. In the English-speaking world, China's position in relationship to the outside is often represented under the rubric "China and the West." Within this paradigm, a reasonable summary of changing fashions in the post-Mao era would be that people in China simply abandoned the so-called "Mao suit" for Western dress. The short history of fashion after 1976 in fact shows that other parts of East Asia, including Hong Kong and Taiwan, have been both highly significant as sources of fashion and also important as brokers of change. Pierre Cardin's name is consistently invoked in accounts of reform-era fashion, but it is open to question whether he would have been invited to design uniforms for Air China if JAL had not already provided the model: tailored, trim and tasteful, in a comfortingly international style that was thoroughly well-suited to the world of modern communications.

---

101 Yuniya Kawamura, "Placing Tokyo on the Fashion Map," in Christopher Breward and David Gilbert, eds, *Fashion's World Cities* (Oxford: Berg, 2006), 63.

102 See www.skycitygallery.com/hanfu/hanfutor.html. Accessed 12 October 2006.

11

CONCLUSION

FASHION, HISTORY, TIME

The words "fashion" and "China" can seem incongruent, particularly when used in an historical context. The vast, solemn, unchanging Chinese empire of the popular imagination is difficult to reconcile with how we think of fashion, and more recent history is indelibly stamped with the image of the Mao suit. Despite a vague consciousness of something called a *cheongsam* associated with the interleaving years, journalists are still commenting with surprise that China has now "discovered" fashion. A phrase such as "fashion in Chinese history" is thus prima facie paradoxical, exposing a range of problems about historical time and cultural practice.

Due to importance accorded to history within Chinese culture, such problems can be detected hovering on the periphery of any discussion of contemporary Chinese fashion. Peter Nolan has identified China's "intense sense of its special place in world history"[1] as a factor favourable to its future success in establishing globally powerful companies. This sense is palpable among fashion designers. "How does Chinese fashion stand in the eyes of foreigners?" asked Ma Ling. She responded to her own rhetorical question with a reference to history:

In discussing this question, we cannot avoid saying that we shut ourselves off for too long. Chinese fashion was not stimulated until our country opened up to the outside. The glorious history of Chinese clothing culture, the richness of traditional handicraft work—especially embroidery and brocade work—all excite vocal interest in the international fashion world. Chinese fashion must compete in ingenuity and beauty on the world stage.[2]

In sympathy with these sentiments, designers consistently return to Chinese history for design inspiration, not only for strategic reasons but also because historical clothing culture remains, for many, the bedrock of their identity as Chinese artists. The "glorious history of Chinese clothing culture" is a legacy that

---

1 Peter Nolan, *China and the Global Economy: National Champions, Industrial Policy and the Big Business Revolution* (Houndmills: Palgrave, 2001), 155.

2 Ma Ling, *Maling shizhuang*, 77.

they have a duty to conserve and enrich. Amidst the froth and bubble of their seasonal fashion shows, a certain cultural seriousness can be observed.

In a recent essay, fashion historian Elizabeth Wilson has commented on the "gulf between classical Chinese culture and the new China," with reference in particular to the urban environment.[3] As she intimates, the destruction of the built heritage in China offers an insight into its loss of vestimentary heritage. The quality of the loss lies not in the absence per se of old forms of clothing from the contemporary sartorial spectacle, but rather in the uncoupling of present and past. Fashion's past in China tends to be located in Europe, or the West more generally, so that shorthand references to past fashion eras—the twenties or the sixties, for example—are references not to Ye Qianyu and Red Guards respectively, but to Chanel and hippies.

It is extremely difficult for Chinese designers to disrupt this paradigm. Feng Ling, born in 1965, turned from painting to clothes design in the late nineties. She combined elements of the Mao suit and army uniforms with the *qipao*, using silks and satins to create a sartorial pastiche of references to the Chinese past. Interviewed in 2005, she described her designs in terms commonly used by Chinese couturiers. "My clothes are very 'China,' yet at the same time very modern," she said, "so they can give others a very persuasive hint about today's China... This clothing is very local, special, and Chinese."[4] But like many adventurous designers in China, Feng Ling faces the problem that her compatriots by and large do not want to wear such clothes: 70 per cent of her customers are foreigners. In other words, Chinese customers find it difficult to recognise local retro as fashion.

Frustratingly, the appeal of Feng Ling's designs to a nice market of foreigners is not matched by a general international recognition for Chinese fashion. Groping towards an effective articulation of the relationship between fashion and history has to date failed to win Chinese designers international acclaim. Their frustrations at this failure are exacerbated by historical memories of humiliation at the hands of foreigners through the Opium War, the Japanese occupation and innumerable other events of the century in between. The conquering heroes of British, American and Japanese industry, whose reign in the Republican era was brought to an end by wars and regime change, have now returned to China in other guises, not least as fashion gurus. In the virtual empire of "la mode," designers from Beijing and Shanghai struggle for product recognition. They walk the streets of their home towns under the shadows of signboards for foreign fashion houses (Fig. 11.1).

---

3 Elizabeth Wilson, " Urbane Fashion," in Christopher Breward and David Gilbert, eds, *Fashion's World Cities* (New York: Berg, 2006), 38.

4 Priscilla Jiao, "Something Old, Something New," *That's China*, (April 2005): 46, www. thatschina.net/20054-p46.htm. Accessed 21 April 2005.

Fig. 11.1 Nanjing Road in summer, 2006, Giordano on the left, Itokin on the right. In the middle distance, on the left and right respectively, are the two great icons of Republican-era consumption, the Wing On and Sincere department stores.

The characterisation of China as the home of Fast Fashion seems likely to intensify the anxieties connected with the bid for international recognition. Fast Fashion, argues Segre Reinach, constitutes a fundamental shift in world fashion culture, marking the next big development after prêt-a-porter, which in turn succeeded haute couture. It relies on perfection of the art of copying, which "China has mastered," she writes, "in an extremely subtle and competent manner."[5] This is far from being the sort of mastery for which China's designers seek acclaim. While prêt-a-porter conferred prestige on Milan, the term "Fast Fashion" will not perform the same service for Shanghai. The contrary seems more probable, with Chinese fashion design belittled rather than enhanced by the only factor that has made its visible in any respect to the rest of the world.

Whether Segre Reinach's analysis will hold good in the longer term remains to be seen. Her mention of copying brings to mind another country that has with wearying frequency been dubbed a nation of copycats: Japan. In Japan, as in China, modern, Western clothing styles have long since replaced older, indigenous forms, and the local fashion industry struggles to compete with the prestige of Western labels. Yet Japan has matched the success of the USA and Italy in adding a new member to the elite cluster of world fashion cities. New York established its credentials in Paris early in the seventies, Milan in the course

---

5 Segre Reinach, "China and Italy," 48.

of the seventies, while Tokyo made a breakthrough in the early eighties that it consolidated in the nineties.[6] One of the factors behind Tokyo's phenomenal feat was the rise of Issey Miyake, a designer of such calibre that in 1988 it could be asked whether he was not "the world's greatest designer."[7]

Size is one of the many differences between Japan and China. China's apparently inexhaustible capacity to supply labour for the mass production of goods may mean, as Chinese commentators gloomily remark, that the PRC is doomed to be the Western world's factory. Certainly it is a much larger "factory" than Japan ever was. On the other hand, India and Southeast Asia are competing with China as producers of textiles and clothing for the world market, and the economic growth of all three regions—East, South and Southeast Asia—must entail changes in their respective industrial profiles of each over time.

A difference more salient to the fostering of design talent may lie in education. Both China and Japan are occasionally mentioned in the international media in the context of school textbook controversies. In Japan this is because an approved textbook might whitewash Japanese wartime aggression. In China it is usually because the government is protesting about Japanese versions of history. The difference is that in Japan historical controversies are possible, while in China they are suppressed. Controversy may well be necessary for Chinese designers to develop a more interesting and diverse range of approaches to their history, enabling them to turn their cultural heritage to good account on the catwalk. Naturally, this cannot be achieved in schools of design alone. The political culture of the country as a whole is implicated.

China and the world: a vestimentary history

How history is written, understood, and internalised is important for fashion's future in China. At present, it is being rewritten from a number of perspectives, many if which have direct bearing on genealogies of dress in China. Most important in this regard is a new alertness in the field to world history in relationship to China. China has often been represented as historically isolationist, especially with respect to the Ming-Qing era.[8] No doubt this view has some validity, especially when China is compared to Europe in the same centuries, roughly from the fifteenth to the nineteenth. Yet the early modern world was one in which China

---

6 Norma Rantisi, "How New York Stole Modern Fashion," in Christopher Breward and David Gilbert, eds, *Fashion's World Cities*, 109; Segre Reinach, "Milan: The City of Prêt-à-Porter in a World of Fast Fashion," in ibid., 124; Kawamura, "Placing Tokyo on the Fashion Map," 60.

7 Georgina Howell, *Sultans of Style, Thirty Years of Fashion and Passion, 1960-1990* (London: Ebury Press, 1990), 48.

8 See recently Julia Lovell, *The Great Wall: China Against the World* (London: Atlantic, 2006).

was engaged with its neighbours and linked to farther flung places through trading networks. Neither its western borders nor its eastern coast was impermeable to cultural influences. Although the use of the term "early modern" in relationship to China is a matter of controversy among historians, there is much to be said for the idea of an early modern world. Such a world was notionally taking shape from around the beginning of the sixteenth century, as far-flung places were brought closer to each other by long-distance communications, trade, and conquest. In this world, China certainly had a significant place.[9]

In this period, as we have seen, China showed the influence of exogenous cultures in new clothing styles or the modification of existing styles. More significantly (since such exogenous influences were longstanding[10]), consumption began to show the effects of increased monetisation, a consequence in part of seaborne trade that linked China through various agents to the New World. Among the consequences were extravagant and "outrageous" clothing evident in the prosperous towns of Ming China. In the pornographic novel *Jin Ping Mei*, written in the late sixteenth century and set in a town on a major trade route, fashion and consumption were linked in a powerful critique of the times and the morals, providing an extraordinary parallel to developments in early modern Europe.[11]

China's susceptibility to creative foreign influences, and particularly to influence from its near neighbours, is a feature of its historical experience that has endured into contemporary times. This may seem so natural a phenomenon as to be hardly worth pointing out, except for the ease with which it is forgotten or overlooked. In the seventeenth century, the country as a whole was taken over by one of these neighbours and became part of the great Qing empire, which lasted until the early twentieth century. The Qing presided over a relatively stable vestimentary regime governed by the dynasty's need for ritual conformity to its standard. Fashion operated within narrow parameters: the motif in an embroi-

---

9 See references given in Chapter Three of this book, and also Lynn Struve, ed., *The Qing Formation in World-Historical Time* (Cambridge, Mass.: Harvard University Asia Center, 2004), passim.

10 See Suzanne E. Cahill, "'Our Women Are Acting Like Foreigners' Wives!' Western Influences on Tang Dynasty Women's Fashion," in Valerie Steele and John Major, *China Chic: East Meets West* (New Haven: Yale Unviersity Press, 1999), 103-17.

11 See Lynn Hunt, ed., *The Invention of Pornography: Obscenity and the Origins of Modernity* (New York: Zone Books, 1993); discussed in Wilson, "Urbane Fashion," 34. *Jin Ping Mei*, circulated in manuscript in the late sixteenth century and then printed in 1610, is a novel of disputed authorship. It is available in English translation as Hsiao-hsiao-sheng, *The Golden Lotus: A Translation from the Original of Chin P'ing Mei*, trans. Clement Egerton, (New York: Paragon Books, 1959); and (still in progress) Xiaoxiaosheng, *The Plum in the Gold Vase, or Chin P'ing Mei*, trans. David Tod Roy, (New Jersey: Princeton University Press, 1993-2006). On the novel's treatment of dress, see Dauncey, "Illusions of Grandeur."

dered work, the colour of the fabric, the width of the sleeve, were all foci for the fashion-conscious gaze.

In the eighteenth century, the commercial manufacture of garments and shoes increased and silk became common for daily wear among the well-to-do, replacing cotton. The theatre became a public instead of a private spectacle, and a source of sartorial creativity.[12] In the early nineteenth century, urban markets increasingly carried exotic goods from the West, and by the later nineteenth century Japan was setting a startling example with various experiments in fashion that China was in some respects to emulate. Too little is yet known about the details of dressing in the Qing for a satisfying cultural history of clothing in this period to have been written, but enough is known about the arts, the economy, and urban life that a view of Qing clothing as lacking in fashion cannot be meaningful. To the contrary, such a view is challenged by historical references to "styles of the times," and "new and strange clothing."

The initial rupture with the old regime in the early twentieth century occurred within the pre-existing domain of apparel. In brief, the radical break with conventional Qing dress did not occur through the adoption of Victorian or Edwardian dresses, but rather through the popularisation in Shanghai of the high-collared, close-fitting jacket worn with narrow-legged trousers, a style worn by students, working women and prostitutes alike (Fig. 11.2).[13] This entailed a metamorphosis of jacket and trousers, central items in the Chinese wardrobe, from loose, wrapper-style garments to close-cut, fitted ones. Even the long gown underwent this transformation. When this occurred, the relationship between clothing and the body was clearly shifting. At the beginning of the century, clothing was hung on the body; people carried their commodious gowns and jackets around gracefully; the fabric was allowed rich play. By the 1911 Revolution, this had already changed; clothing was fitted onto the body, and moved in sympathy with it. By the end of the century, the body—at least at one end of the fashion spectrum—was merely accommodating items of clothing, like ornaments, even if those ornaments had an excessively privileged place in the total aesthetic scheme.

Bodies themselves were changing. The delicate sons and daughters of nineteenth-century gentry families were succeeded by a generation that received physical education in school. In 1917, Mao Zedong published his first article, "A Study of Physical Education," pointing out the relationship between physical fitness and the strength of the nation.[14] In the 1920s, advertisements still showed the classic Chinese beauty of small stature and sloping shoulders with

---

12 Vainker, *Chinese Silk*, 184-91.

13 Luo Suwen, "Lun Qingmo Shanghai dushi nüzhuang de yanbian," 135.

14 Mao Zedong, "Tiyu zhi yanjiu" (A Study of Physical Culture), *Xin qingnian* 4 (1917): 5–12.

goose-egg face and cherry lips. By the 1930s she had been supplanted by a tall, square-shouldered young woman with a bosom, round face, large eyes and full mouth, a type of beauty very familiar from Hollywood. In this decade, the heyday of the *qipao*, China managed to send a team to the Berlin Olympics, and build an enormous sports stadium in Shanghai, before being plunged into war with Japan.[15]

The impact of militarism on Chinese dress in the twentieth century has been noted at several points in this book. While this factor was not without precedent in Chinese vestimentary history, in the twentieth century it was linked to economic, technological and social change of extraordinary dimensions. Ida Pruitt hinted at this link when commenting on the women workers at

Fig. 11.2 Late Qing postcard showing the fitted fashions that prevailed around 1908.

the uniform factories in Tianjin. "Why," she asked, "did the industrial revolution, taking women's work out of their homes, give them always so little and ask for so much, when it first came into any older pattern of life?"[16] Her comment was prompted by the sight of the mass of weary workers leaving the factory gates at dusk, a new phenomenon in the cities of Republican China.

The uniforms being mass produced by factory workers—a new occupational category in China—helped effect a convergence of vestimentary histories, East and West. The Napoleonic wars had conferred a prestige on military uniforms in Europe that was echoed in nineteenth-century fashions. The Great War a century later left a permanent imprint on the way Europeans dressed. Although the relationship between civilian and military dress in the West followed an oscillating pattern, military uniform had an integral place in the national wardrobe of the blueprint modern society.[17] Political leaders in China were not always successful in deciphering the blueprint but they all saw clearly enough one of its external manifestations: the uniform of a successful fighting force. Military uniforms

---

15 See Andrew D. Morris, *Marrow of the Nation: A History of Sport and Physical Culture in Republican China* (Berkeley: University of California Press, 2004), espec. Chapter Six.

16 Pruitt, *Old Madam Yin*, 3.

17 Jennifer Craik, *Uniforms Exposed: From Conformity to Transgression* (Oxford: Berg, 2005), passim, but espec. 34-5, 48-9.

傑子二女藹人孔令公大令公二熙孔儇子大至自家生熙孔委政國
令公士齡宋夫儀子女俊子女君祥 令公左右庭之先祥員府民

Fig. 11.3 A well-dressed family in 1928. The mother of the family, Song Ailing, was sister-in-law to both Sun Yatsen and Chiang Kaishek. Her husband, Kong Xiangxi (H.H. Kung) was a leading figure in the Nationalist Government. They are richly but conservatively dressed, he in gown and riding jacket, she in long vest over wide-sleeved blouse. The girls wear the classic 1920s *qipao*. The elder boy wears a suit, probably appropriate to his schoolboy status. The younger boy has yet to graduate from vest and gown.

accounted for the first great wave of new-style clothing in China, and via the Sun Yatsen suit as well as in their original form continued to be an unusually prominent feature of Chinese dress until late in the century. At the same time, the aesthetics of military dress infected civilian dress more generally, both directly and via European fashions, to yield the trim line of modern Chinese dress.

In retrospect, it can be seen that the last years of Qing rule, indeed the very last five or six years, constituted a crucial period of transition away from a definitively Qing style of dress. The transition was arguably no greater than, even if qualitatively different from, the transition from Ming to Qing dress in the seventeenth century; but it did establish a definitively modern look. It placed the well-articulated body, with its defined limbs and distinct head, at the centre of the vestimentary order. Around this body developed the twentieth-century discourse of fashion that was purveyed through an expanding popular press and supported by competition for custom among local manufacturers and retailers. In the late 1920s, it was still possible to look back and see continuity in dress from the nineteenth century; but even a conservatively dressed family seemed to belong to a different time (Fig. 11.3).

During the May Fourth era, as at the time of the 1911 Revolution, progressive young men imagined themselves as most appropriately clad in Western styles of clothing. This was a sartorial expression of their nationalism. They desired for China a place on the world stage that was consummate with its size and also with its historical role as the Middle Kingdom, the centre of the world. They were impressed by the example of their contemporaries in Japan, and at the same time able to distance themselves from their own cultural heritage by the fact that the last imperial dynasty in China was Manchu, not Han. Changing clothes was a mark in the first instance of their rejection of the Manchus and in the second of their rejection of the past.

Given the readiness with which the suit was adopted at critical junctures of Chinese political history, it must be conceded that the resilience of the man's long gown, a Manchu garment, is a paradox in the history of twentieth-century Chinese dress. Custom, practicality and frugality all helped it survive the years of challenge. Along the way it was re-invested with cultural meaning, so that it ceased to be a Manchu garment and became a Chinese one, at least for men of a certain class. Trousers may have been the dress of the bureaucracy and the military, but the self-respecting man wore a gown when being himself—unless, of course, he was a Communist. In this respect, China between the wars was rather like India, where under the leadership of Gandhi, *swadeshi* and the *dhoti* gained nationalist credentials that helped indigenous dress compete with the powerful suit. In Indonesia, by contrast, Sukarno rejected the indigenous sarong, which he thought had "a demeaning effect" on the wearer, forcing him into the position of servant rather than equal.[18]

After 1949, the Chineseness of the gown was overtaken by its ascribed class character. One of the century's great vestimentary dramas occurred during the twenty-seventh session of the Central People's Government Council in 1953, when Mao Zedong erupted in rage at the philosopher Liang Shuming—"a frail figure," Guy Alitto writes, "clad in an old-fashioned long gown," hailed abroad as a figure of enormous integrity for having refused to forsake the land of his fathers.[19] In a way, Liang won this battle: surviving Mao by twelve years, he emerged from the Cultural Revolution quite unreformed, and put on cap and gown again. But this was among the last of the gowns; in the rapidly globalising clothing climate of the 1980s, it must have been a real curiosity.

Early ideas about changing into Western clothes mostly concerned men's wear. Even though fashionable women did often wear items of Western fash-

---

18 Jean Gelman Taylor, ed., "Official Photography, Costume and the Indonesian Revolution," in jean Gelman Taylor, ed., *Women Creating Indonesia: The First Fifty Years* (Clayton: Monash Asia Institute, 1997), 120-1. I thank Katherine McGregor for this reference.

19 Guy Alitto, *The Last Confucian* (Berkeley and Los Angeles: University of California Press, 1979), 1.

ion and sometimes even donned entire outfits in Western style, it was rare for Western dress to be advocated for women. At the same time, women's dress changed much more markedly than men's during the first half of the twentieth century. In the 1940s it was still possible for a man to wear his father's gown, but if a woman donned the clothes that had been worn at the beginning of the century she would have looked as though she were in fancy dress. The male and female trajectories of vestimentary change were thus quite different, even though they were discursively linked by nationalist commentaries. In this respect, China can be distinguished from a large number of other vestimentary orders in Asia, including India, where women's clothing has remained the more privileged site of cultural heritage. Perhaps it was for this reason that women in China so often adopted men's clothing. They sensed that it was more meaningful culturally.

Liberation was the proximate cause of the decline of the long gown. Its place was taken by the cadre uniform, or Sun Yatsen suit, and gender differentiation in dress was sharply reduced. The great love story that unfolded between the Chairman and the people did not allow too much room for dressing as the "opposite" sex, and the Yanan aesthetic of simplicity and frugality anyway militated against the spirit of display necessary for fashion to thrive. There were trends

in clothing styles, and to a surprising degree the tales of times past testify to young people's preoccupation with clothes during the Maoist years, as well as to their romantic and sexual longings. The overall effect, however, was of a great monastery in which members of a secluded order took pride in the religious habit, right down to the very patches that they sewed on, in imitation of Lei Feng.[20]

Like members of such an order, people in China reacted sharply when the monastery was disestablished. In the post-Mao era, "women wanted to be women" again, or so they were told. It is worth reiterating, however, that women did not want to dress up in *qipao*s, or at least not on a daily basis. Until quite recently, national costume was regarded as something to be worn by backward minority peoples, who are trotted out to provide colour on ceremonial occasions. Han women for the most part have kept pace with the men in sartorial terms. The country's

Fig. 11.4 A fashionable young couple in Beijing, October 2006, dressed more like their peers in other countries than their forbears in China.

---

20 Sheldon Lon, *Sparrows, Bedbugs and Body Shadows: A Memoir* (Honolulu: University of Hawai'i Press, 2005) 114-15.

leaders wear lounge suits and dye their hair black, aspiring to a modern, youthful image that differentiates them sharply from the grey-bearded statesmen of a century ago. Madam Wu Yi, the only woman in the leadership group, might don a *qipao* for evening wear, but otherwise sets an example for fellow women officials by insisting on smart, good quality, contemporary clothing.[21] Like their leaders, the masses have opted for the humdrum, unbeautiful fashions produced by a globalising textile and apparel industry that has somehow made track suits and lounge suits, jeans and T-shirts, skirts and tops, desirable alternatives to the common pants and jacket, *qipao* or *changpao*, of the average Chinese in earlier times (Fig. 11.4).

Fashion and time

The extreme instability of clothing regimes in the twentieth century distinguishes this century from its predecessors. The instability was related to the rapid turnover of political regimes but not explicable by reference to that fact alone, since no previous period of conflict had yielded changes in material culture of quite this order. Technology, trade, ideologies, gender relations, and patterns of daily life in China's great cities had all developed, changed, or diversified to produce a range of possibilities in aesthetics, identities, and material goods that well exceeded in scope anything evident in earlier times. Among the consequences was the capacity of society to support a series of shifts in clothing style in the context of the restless, relentless search for a New China.

Fashion did not lie in these great tidal changes, but in the daily and seasonal choices exercised by consumers in their purchase of fabrics, trimmings, overcoats, underwear, shoes and socks; choices informed by a sharp awareness of the passage of time as measured by the production of these very items, and a valorisation of present relative to the past, again with reference to these items. In making such choices, the citizens of twentieth-century China had been anticipated by their forbears, who in the lively markets of thriving cities of late imperial China had picked and chosen between fabrics, and dressed up in new and strange forms of clothing. In the terminology used to identify these practices—"contemporary styles," "new-time styles"—can be discerned a fashionable impulse that was allowed full play in Shanghai in the 1920s and 1930s. But for reasons discussed elsewhere in this book, twentieth-century fashion can be distinguished from the fashions evident in earlier vestimentary regimes. Most obviously, capitalism, the mechanisation of production, and the popular press had a profound impact on the market for textiles and garments, affecting both its size and its modus operandi.

---

21 Tao Siliang (Deputy Head, China Association of Mayors), "Shuo bu jin de Zhongguo nüshizhang" (The inestimable women mayors of China), preface to *Zhongguo nüshizhang* (China's women mayors) (1995), www.citieschina.org. Accessed 29 October 2005.

It seems probable, too, that fashion entailed a different apprehension of time. In the eighteenth century, Li Dou could write of fabrics becoming outmoded over time, but in the early twentieth century a consciousness of time as measured by fashion sharpened perceptibly. Impressions were replaced by precise calibrations. In 1931, to mark the twentieth anniversary of the Republican Revolution, Shanghai's *Culture and Arts Monthly* published a photo feature on changes in fashion over the preceding last half century. The earliest of the thirty-six photos showed a woman wearing the capacious sleeves fashionable in the late nineteenth century. The most recent photos were of "up-to-date" fashions—*qipao*s of various lengths, and different sorts of overgarment: a waistcoat, a fur wrap, an overcoat, a sleeveless jacket. The chronological progress is itemised: fifty years ago, forty-five years ago, forty years ago, and so on.[22]

An insight into this restructuring of time is provided by the *Beiyang Pictorial* which in 1927, to mark its first anniversary, ran an illustrated feature on "the boys of the Beiyang Pictorial." The "boys" were all grown men by this time and employed in various capacities by the paper. Their adult portraits, sketched by themselves or by a colleague, show modern-looking men with short haircuts, this one in a shirt and tie, that one in gown, a third wearing sunglasses, all entirely imaginable as faces in a newspaper office. Paired with each sketch is a photo of the child that the man once was. Two of the six photos show school pupils in military-style uniform; in the remainder, the boys are wearing gowns. The gowned boys all have heads shaven at the front, giving them a quaint, old-fashioned air.

Wang Xiaoyin, born around 1898, was among the senior members of this group, twelve years old at the fall of the dynasty. He wrote a few verses to accompany his portrait:

No need for mistaken nostalgia for that golden age
Value rather the actual here and now.
Change what you hate,
Love what you have to love,
This is "my world."[23]

Wang's strong affirmation of the present combined with a repudiation of the past was a typical gesture by an intellectual of the May Fourth era. Translated into fashion, such a statement would mean that May Fourth dress styles were bound to be superseded, as *xinhai* fashions had already been. In the longer term, the present itself would be abandoned in favour of the future: Pudong, space, the Olympics, and Fast Fashion. In the world of Chinese couture, however, the past would remain a haunting presence, placing demands on designers that they do not know quite how to satisfy.

---

22 *Wenhua yishu yuekan* 26 (December 1931): frontispiece.
23 *BYHB* 6 July 1927.

LIST OF CHINESE CHARACTERS

A Xing 阿杏
Ai Qing 艾青
Aidekang 愛德康
aiguo ni 愛國呢
An Wenjiang 安文江
Anding [shuyuan] Academy 安定書院
Anhui 安徽
ao 襖
Aoki Masaru 青木正儿
aoku 襖褲
aoqun 襖裙

Ba Jin 巴金
baizhequn 百褶裙
banlü 版绿
Bao Mingxin 包铭新
Bao Tianxiao 包天笑
Beijing huabao 北京畫報
Beijing qingnianbao 北京青年报
Beiping 北平
beixin 背心
Beiyang 北洋
Beiyang huabao 北洋畫報
beizi 背子
bijia 比 甲
Binbin 彬彬
bingtai wei mei 病態為美
bobo 伯伯
boya 博雅
bu he biaozhun 不合標準
bu kai cha 不開叉
Bu Linqing 卜霖慶
bufu 補服
bulaji 布拉吉

Cai E 蔡鍔
Cai Shengbai 蔡聲白
Cai Yuanpei 蔡元培
Cao Fangyun 曹方芸

Cao Guimin 曹贵民
Cao Hanmei 曹涵美
Chang Hongshu 常鴻書
chang majia 長馬甲
Chang Shana 常沙娜
changpao 長袍
changqun 長裙
changru 長襦
Changsha 長沙
changshan 長衫
chaofu 朝服
Chen Bilan 陳碧蘭
Chen Bixie 陈辟邪
Chen Duxiu 陳獨秀
Chen Fumei 陈富美
Chen Hongshou 陳紅綬
Chen Hongxia 陈红霞
Chen Jinbiao 陳錦標
Chen Jinyan 陳今言
Chen Jitang 陳濟棠
Chen Kengran 陳鏗然
Chen Ling 陳玲
Chen Ruoju 陳若菊
Chen Shuying 陳淑英
Chen Yongsheng 陈泳声
Chen Yunshang 陳云裳
Cheng Fangwu 成仿吾
Chenghuang [miao] Temple 城隍廟
chengzi yi 橙子衣
cheongsam (changshan) 長衫
Cheung Maggie (Zhang Manyu) 張曼玉
Chiang Kaishek (Jiang Jieshi) 蔣介石
Chongqing 重慶
Chuansha 川沙
chuisi 垂絲
Chunan nüzi 楚南女子
Chung Wing-kwong (Zhong Rongguang)
    鍾榮光
Chunyang [jin] hat 純陽巾

303

Da jing mao 大经贸
Da Qianmen 大前門
daban piaoliang 打扮漂亮
Dae Jang Geum (Da Chang Jin) 大长今
Dagongbao 大公報
Dah Sun (Da Xin) 大新
Dahua 大华
dajin changyi 大襟長衣
dajin xiaoyi 大襟小衣
dan 旦
Daojing 道静
daopao 道袍
Daqing 大慶
Datong [jie] Street 打銅街
dayi 大衣
Dazhai 大寨
Deng Fangzhi 鄧芳芝
Deng Lijun (Teresa Teng) 鄧麗君
Deng Xiaoping 邓小平
Deng Yingchao 鄧穎超
Ding Huiyin 丁回音
Ding Ling 丁玲
Ding Zheng 丁正
Dong Guiying 董桂英
Dong Xiangyi 董湘毅
Dongxin wachang 東新襪廠
doudu 兜肚
duanru 短襦
duanxiu qipao 短袖旗袍
Dujuan shan 杜鵑山
Dunhuang 敦煌

Fang Yexian 方液仙
Feifei huabao 菲菲畫報
Feng Ling 枫翎
Fenghua 奉化
fengyi 风衣
Fu Chongju 傅崇矩
fu Han 復漢
Fu Ling 傅凌
Fudan 復旦
funü 婦女
Funü huabao 婦女畫報
Funü xinshenghuo yuekan 婦女新生活月刊
Funü zazhi 婦女雜誌
Furen huabao 婦人畫報
fuyao 服妖

gailiang 改良
ganbu zhifu 幹部制服
gaozishan 高子衫

Ge Yang 戈揚
Gong Xiufang 龔秀芳
Gu Mengyou 顧夢游
Gu Qiyuan 顧起元
Gu Qun 顧群
guang 光
Guangdong 廣東
Guangji [yiyuan] Hospital 廣濟醫院
Guangming ribao 光明日报
Guangxu 光緒
Guo Fenglian 郭凤莲
Guo Jianying 郭建英
Guo Moruo 郭沫若
Guofu 國父
guohua 國畫
Guoji xianqu daobao 国际先驱导报
guomin 國民
Guomindang 國民黨
Guowen huabao 國聞畫報
Guowen zhoubao 國聞周報

ha 哈
ha Ri 哈日
Haier 海尔
Haimen 海門
Hainan [dao] Island 海南 島
haipai 海派
hamajing 蛤蟆镜
Han (Chinese) 漢
Han Feng 韩枫
Han Fuqu 韩复榘
Hanae Mori 森英惠
Hanfu 汉服
Hang Zhiying 杭稚英
Hanlin 漢林
hanliu 韩流
hanshan 汗衫
Hao Liang 浩亮
Hao Zhihong 郝志宏
haohan 好漢
haoren yundong 好人運動
haoyi 號衣
He Yingqin 何應欽
He Zizhen 贺子珍
Hefei wanbao 合肥晚报
hei jiansi ku 黑縑絲綺
Hong [hu] Lake 洪湖
Hong Ying 虹影
Hongkou (Hongkew) 虹口
Hongxiang [xifu gongsi] Fashion Store
　　鴻翔西服公司

304

Hu Die (Butterfly Wu) 胡蝶
Hu Shi 胡適
Hu Xiaoping 胡小平
Hu Yaguang 胡亞光
Hu Yaobang 胡耀邦
Hua Guofeng 华国锋
Hua Mulan 花木蘭
huabao 畫報
Huaihai [lu] Road 淮海路
huang caobu gua 黃草布褂
Huang Jiayin 黃嘉音
Huang Jiguang 黃繼光
Huang Naishuang 黃耐霜
Huangpu 黃浦
Huashen guniang 化身姑娘
hudielü 蝴蝶履
Huizhou 惠州
humao 胡帽
Hunan 湖南
Huo Tao 霍韜
Huo Yuanjia 霍元甲
Huolin Gol 霍林郭勒
Huzhou 湖州

Itō Hirobumi 伊藤博文

Ji Jingyi 季静宜
Jia Zhangke 贾樟柯
Jiajing 嘉靖
Jiang Feng 江豐
Jiang Hancheng 蔣漢澄
Jiang Hua 江華
Jiang Peiying 江培英
Jiang Qing 江青
Jiang Yousheng 江有生
Jiang Zemin 江泽民
Jiangnan 江南
Jiangsu 江蘇
Jiangxi 江西
jiankang 健康
Jiao Bingzhen 焦秉貞
Jie Zhenhua 解振华
Jieshang liuxing hongqunzi
    街上流行紅裙子
jietou shizhuang 街头时装
Jieyang 揭阳
Jilian huikan 機聯會刊
Jin 晉
Jin Ping Mei 金瓶梅
Jin Tianhe 金天翮
Jinbu wachang 進步襪廠

Jing'an [si lu] Temple Road 静安寺路
Jinggangshan 井冈山
Jinglun zhenzhichang 景綸針織廠
jingpai 京派
Jingxing zhenzhichang 景星針織廠
jinlian 金蓮
Jinling 金陵
jinü 妓女
Jinyan 金琰
Jishu wenhua dayuejin 技術文化大躍進
Jiuyi [dianji wachang] Hosiery Factory
    久益電機襪廠
juanlian 圈帘
junguomin zhuyi 軍國民主義
junjigua 軍機褂
junjipo 軍機坡
junshihua 軍事化

kaijinling qunyi 开襟领裙衣
kang 炕
Kang Keqing 康克清
Kang Youwei 康有爲
Kangxi 康熙
Ke Xiang 柯 湘
Kong Shangren 孔尚任
Kong Xiangxi 孔祥熙
Koo, Wellington (Gu Weijun) 顧惟鈞
Koshino Junko 小條順子
ku 褲
Kuaile jiating 快樂家庭
kurumaya 車屋
kuzhe 袴褶
Kwok (Guo) 郭
Kwok Chin (Guo Quan) 郭泉

Lao Jiu He 老九和
laodaye 老大爺
Lei Feng 雷锋
leizi 勒子
Li Cefei 李册菲
Li Dou 李斗
Li Gan 李淦
Li Hongzhang 李鴻章
Li Jiansheng 李健生
Li Keyu 李克瑜
Li Mingcong 李明璁
Li Xianglan (Ri Koran) 李香蘭
Li Xiaobin 李晓斌
Li Yamin 李亚民
Li Yanping 李艳萍
Li Yuyi 李寓一

305

Li Zhisui 李志绥
Li Zongren 李宗仁
lianbeishan 連被衫
Liang Jun 梁君
Liang Qichao 梁啟超
Liang Saizhen 梁賽珍
Liang Shuming 梁漱溟
Liang Sicheng 梁思成
Liang Sishun 梁思順
Liang Yulong 梁玉龙
liangjia 良家
Liangjiang 兩江
Liangyou 良友
Lianyungang 連雲港
liaobuqi 了不起
Liaoning ribao 遼寧日報
Likang 利康
Lin Biao 林彪
Lin Cunhou 劉存厚
Lin Daiyu 林黛玉
Lin Huiyin 林徽因
Lin Sumen 林蘇門
Lin Xiantang 林献堂
Lin Yutang 林語堂
Ling Shuhua 凌叔華
lingbao caifeng 拎包裁縫
Linglong 玲瓏
Linxia 臨夏
Liu Chaocang 劉旭滄
Liu Na'ou 劉吶歐
Liu Ping 刘平
Liu Qingtang 刘庆棠
Liu Shaoqi 劉少奇
Liu Wanguang 柳萬光
Liu Yang 刘洋
Liu Pan, Madam (Liu Pan shi)
　　劉潘氏
Liwai 例外
Lu Lihua 陆礼华
Lu Mei 陸眉
Lu, Master [shifu] 陆师傅
Lu Shu 陸書
Lu Tian 鲁田
Lu Xiaoman 陸小曼
Lu Xiaorong 卢晓荣
Lu Xun 鲁迅
Lü Yue 吕越
Luo Dunwei 羅敦偉
Luohanta 羅漢褡
luohua 裸化
Luomeng 罗蒙

Ma Bo 马波
Ma Bufang 馬步芳
Ma Ji 馬繼
Ma Ke 马可
Ma Ling 马羚
Ma Wenying 馬文英
magua 馬褂
Mai furen 麥夫人
majia 馬甲
Maling [shizhuang]Fashion 马羚时装
Manhua shenghuo 漫畫生活
Mao Dun 矛盾
Mao Zedong 毛澤東
maweiqun 馬尾裙
mazi 馬子
Mei Lanfang 梅蘭芳
Mei Ya [zhicheuchang] Factory 美亞
Meishu 美術
Meishu shenghuo 美術生活
Meiya [zhichouchang] Silk Weaving Factory
　　美亞織綢廠
Meng Chang 孟昶
Meng Shu gongji tu 孟蜀宮妓圖
Meng Xiaodong 孟小冬
mengzuogua 蟛蚱褂
Minquan huabao 民權畫報
modeng de xiaojie 摩登的小姐
modeng gouer 摩登狗兒
Mou Xuanpu 牟玄甫
Mu Aiping 穆爱平

Nakagawa Tadahide 中川忠英
Nakano Ryoko 中野良子
Nan Zhili 南直隸
Nanfang tiyu 南方体育
Nantong 南通
Nanyang 南洋
nei 內
Ningbo 寧波
nü changshan 女長衫
nü zuo nan 女作男
nügong 女工
nüshi de renminzhuang 女式的人民裝
Nüxing de choudi 女性的仇敵
nüxing zhi nan 女性之男
Nüzi shijie 女子世界
Nüzi yuekan 女子月刊

Oei Hui-lan (Huang Huilan) 黃慧蘭
Oei Tiong-ham (Huang Zhonghan) 黃仲涵
Ou Zhizhen 歐志眞

306

Pan Yuliang 潘玉良
pao 袍
pi'ao 披襖
piaopiao [jin] hat 漂漂巾
pifeng 披風
pijian 披肩
pingsantao 平三套
pipa 琵琶
Pu Qua (Pukua) 蒲呱
pudi tianguan lü 鋪底天官履
Pudong 浦东
Pukou 浦口
Puyi 溥儀

qi 旗
Qi Baishi 齊白石
Qi Xiaochun 祁小春
qi zhuang yi fu 奇裝異服
Qianlong 乾隆
qimajia 旗馬甲
Qin Liangyu 秦良玉
Qingdao 青島
Qinghai 青海
Qinghua 清華
Qingmo Minchu 清末民初
qipao 旗袍
Qishan 旗衫
Qiu Jin 秋瑾
Qiu Ti 邱堤
Qu Qiubai 瞿秋白
qun 裙

Ren Xiong 任熊
Renmin ribao 人民日报
renminzhuang 人民裝
Rong Zongjing 荣宗敬
Rongchangxiang 榮昌祥
ru 襦
Ruan Lingyu 阮玲玉
Ruili fushi meirong 瑞利服饰美容
rujin 儒巾
ruqun 襦裙
ruyi 如意

shan 衫
Shandong Yuxing 山東裕興
Shanghai 上海
Shanghai xinwenbao 上海新聞報
shanku 衫褲
Shantou 汕頭
Shao Huifang 邵慧芳

Shao Xunmei (Zau Sinmay) 邵洵美
Shatan [da jie] Street 沙灘大街
Shaxi [zhen] 沙溪鎮
Shen Congwen 沈從文
Shenbao 申報
Sheng Cheng 盛成
Shengde [zhizaochang] Weaving Factory
　　勝德織造廠
Shenghuo 生活
Shenxin 申新
Shenyang 瀋陽
Shenzhen 深圳
Shi Lei 石磊
Shi Lin 史林
Shidai huabao 時代畫報
shili yangchang 十里洋場
shimao 時髦
Shinü tu 仕女圖
Shishang 时尚
Shishi huabao 時事畫報
shishizhuang 時式裝
shiyang 時樣
shiyang qun 時樣裙
Shizhuang 时装
shou 壽
shuitianyi 水田衣
Shunde 順德
shushu 叔叔
Song Ailing 宋靄齡
Song Binbin 宋彬彬
Song Huaigui 宋怀桂
Song Meiling 宋美齡
Song Qingling 宋慶齡
Song Yaowu 宋要武
Songjiang 松江
Su Qing 蘇青
Su shi 蘇式
Sugata Sanshiro 姿三四郎
Su-Guang 蘇廣
Su-Hu 蘇湖
Sulun zhenzhichang 蘇綸針織廠
Sun Chuanfang 孫傳芳
Sun Fuyuan 孫伏園
Sun Kamyuen (Jinyuan) 孫金琬
Sun Ke (Fo) 孫科
Sun Min 孙敏
Sun Sun 新新
Sun Xiaobian 孫小辮
Sun [Zhongshan] Yatsen 孫中山
Suzhou jue 蘇州撅

307

ta chuanzhe yishen huibu Zhongshanzhuang
他穿着一身灰佈中山裝
Taiping [men]Gate 太平門
Takakura Ken 高仓健
Tan Suxin 譚素心
Tan Xuerong 譚雪蓉
Tang 唐
Tang [Wensheng], Nancy 唐闻生
Tang Shaoyi 唐紹儀
Tang Yin 唐寅
Tang, William (Deng Dazhi) 鄧達智
tangzhuang 唐裝
Tao Mo'an 陶默盦
Tao Xinger 陶星儿
Taohua [temple] Village 桃花廟
taoshan 套衫
taotouliao 套頭料
Tian Guiying 田桂英
Tian Han 田漢
Tian Jiyun 田纪云
Tianjin 天津
Tianjin ribao 天津日报
Tianma 天马
Tongzhou 通州
Toung Foh Kee [Tang Fu Ji] 湯福記
tuanshan 團衫
tuhuangse 土黃色

wai 外
waitao 外套
Wang Anyi 王安忆
Wang Caiyun 王才運
Wang Guangmei 王光美
Wang Hairong 王海蓉
Wang Qingkui 王慶奎
Wang Shizhen 王世貞
Wang Shuo 王朔
Wang Xiaoshuai 王小帅
Wang Xiaoyi 王小逸
Wang Xiaoyin 王小隱
Wang Xifeng 王熙鳳
Wang Xizhi 王羲之
Wang Yiwei 王伊蔚
Wang Yuzhen 王玉珍
Wangfujing 王府井
Wanli 萬曆
Wei Bi 魏壁
weishang 圍裳
weisheng 衛生
wen 文

Wenhua yishu yuekan 文化藝術月刊
Wenhuibao 文匯報
wenzhi binbin 文质彬彬
Wenzhou 溫州
West Fan Lane (Fanxi xiang) 樊西巷
Wing On (Yongan) 永安
wo hen ha ni 我很哈你
wodan 窩單
Wong Kar-wai (Wang Jiawei) 王家衛
wu 武
Wu Jen-shu (Wu Renshu) 巫仁恕
Wu Jingxiong 吳經熊
Wu Shusheng 吳淑生
Wu Yi 吳仪
Wu Youru 吳友如
Wuchang 武昌
Wuhan 武漢
wusha 烏紗
wutaixiu 五臺袖
Wuxi 無錫

Xi'an 西安
Xia Yayi 夏亞一
Xiamen ribao 廈門日報
xian (xun) 絢
xiancheng 現成
Xiandai fuzhuang 现代服裝
xianshi 先施
Xiao Gao 肖高
Xiao Shufang 蕭淑芳
xiaomajia 小馬甲
xiaoshan 小衫
Xiaoying 曉瑛
xiaozi 小资
xiaozimen 小子们
Xie Bingying 謝冰瑩
Xie Peilin 謝培林
Xie Zhaozhe 謝肇淛
xiguading 西瓜頂
Ximen Qing 西門慶
Xin guancha 新觀察
Xin nüxing 新女性
xin tangzhuang 新唐裝
xin yang 新樣
xingzishan 幸子衫
xingzitou 幸子头
xinhai 辛亥
xinqi 新奇
xinshi 新式
xinshishi 新時式

Xinzhu 新竹
xiquepao 喜雀袍
Xu Dunqiu 許敦伕
Xu Guangqi 徐光啟
Xu Qinfang 徐琴芳
Xu Wenyuan 徐文淵
Xu Xilin 徐錫麟
Xu Zhimo 徐志摩
Xu Ziquan 徐子權
Xueyi 血疑
Xujiawei 徐家衛
Xunwu 尋烏
Xuzhou 徐州

Yamaguchi Momoe 山口百惠
Yan Xishan 閻錫山
Yanan 延安
Yancheng 鹽城
Yang (family) 楊
Yang Chunxia 杨春霞
Yang Hu 楊虎
Yang Jufen 楊菊芬
Yang Juqiu 楊菊秋
Yang Mo 杨沫
yang qian 洋錢
Yang shi 揚式
Yang Xianyi 楊憲益
Yang Xiuqiong 楊秀瓊
Yang Yuan-loong 楊元龍
Yang Yueqian 杨越千
Yang Zhihua 楊之華
Yang, Rae (Rui) 杨瑞
yangbu 洋布
yangjianrong maozi 羊剪絨帽子
Yangzhou 揚州
yangzhuang 洋裝
Yangzi (Changjiang) 揚子 (長江)
yanwei 燕尾
yao wu ma 要武嗎
Yaogong quishan tu 瑶宫秋扇图
yaoqun 腰裙
Ye Qianyu 葉淺予
yesa 曳撒
yi 一
Yi Jing 怡經
Yi Junzuo 易君左
Yihua (gongsi) Studio 藝華公司
yikouzhong 一口鍾
yin 隱
Yin (sisters) 殷
Ying Zigu 應子固

yizi 一字
Yongjia 永嘉
Yongzheng 雍正
You Guangzhao 尤光照
You Longgu 游龙姑
Yu Dafu 郁達伕
Yu Feng 郁風
Yu Fengzhi 于鳳至
Yu Huai 余懷
Yu Huiyong 于会泳
Yu Li 于莉
Yuan Meiyun 袁美雲
Yuan Shikai 袁世凱
Yuan You 袁猷
yuanbaoling 元寶領
Yunshang [shizhuang gongsi] Company
    雲裳時裝公司
Yunying 韞穎

Zeng Jifen 曾纪芬
Zeng Jing 曾鯨
Zhang Ailing 張愛玲
Zhang Baomei 张宝梅
Zhang Binglin 張炳麟
Zhang Bojun 張伯鈞
Zhang Deyi 張德彝
Zhang Ding 張仃
Zhang E 張鄂
Zhang Guangyu 張光宇
Zhang Qi 張七
Zhang Qianying 張蒨英
Zhang Shankun 張善琨
Zhang Wenhe 张文贺
Zhang Xueliang 張學良
Zhang Xun 張勳
Zhang Yimou 张艺谋
Zhang Youyi 張幼儀
Zhang Zhaoda 张肇达
Zhang Zhengyu 張正宇
Zhao Chunlan 趙春蘭
Zhao Dan 赵丹
Zhao Jiasheng 趙稼生
Zhao Mengfu 趙孟頫
Zhao Mengtao 趙夢桃
Zhao Qiusheng 趙秋生
Zhao Shouyan 趙守嚴
Zhao Xinfang 赵信芳
Zhao Yi 趙翼
Zhao Ziyang 赵紫阳
Zhejiang chao 浙江朝
Zhenfeng [mianzhi chang] Cotton Knit

309

Factory 振豐棉織廠
Zheng [ayi], Aunty 郑阿姨
Zheng Mingbiao 鄭明標
Zheng Suyin 鄭素因
Zheng Xiaoying 郑小瑛
Zhengzhou 鄭州
Zhenjiang 鎮江
zhi zhong yishan, bu zhong ren
　　只重衣衫不重人
zhisun 隻孫
Zhong Yanrong 鍾燕榮
Zhongguo funü 中國婦女
Zhongguo fuzhuang 中国服装
Zhongguo guoji mingpai fazhan xiehui
　　中国国际名牌发展协会
Zhongguo huabao 中国画报
Zhongguo mingpai shizhuang 中国名牌
　　时装
Zhongguo qingnian banyuekan
　　中國青年半月刊

Zhongguo qingnianbao 中國青年報
Zhongguo xinwen zhoukan 中国新闻周刊
Zhongguo zhi yi 中国之翼
Zhongshanzhuang 中山裝
Zhou Enlai 周恩来
Zhou Fu 周馥
Zhou Guangren 周廣仁
Zhou Guoping 周国屏
Zhou Muqiao 周慕橋
Zhou Sheng 周生
Zhou Xuehui 周學煇
Zhou Zhongzheng (Chow Chungcheng)
　　周仲錚
Zhu De 朱德
Zhu Runsheng 朱潤生
Zhu Yuanzhang 朱元璋
Zhu Ziqing 朱自清
zhuangshu 裝束
Zhuibu 追捕

TECHNICAL NOTES

Pinyin romanisation is used for all Chinese names, including from Taiwanese written sources, with the following exceptions: Sun Yatsen, Chiang Kaishek, Taipei in the context of an English-language publication, and names of Chinese origin that are well established with other spellings in Hong Kong, Taiwan or foreign language contexts.

Characters for Chinese and Japanese names and terms are supplied in the glossary, with the following exceptions: common place names, including provinces and capital cities, and names sourced in English-language publications, where characters have not also been provided. Traditional and simplified characters have been used in accordance with sources and historical period.

References to Republican-era magazines and newspapers vary in detail according to the information available in the publication. In the transition to new print formats, pagination was occasionally lost, or haphazardly applied.

Revised portions of the following articles by Antonia Finnane appear in this book by kind permission of the respective publishers: "China on the Catwalk: Between Economic Success and Nationalist Anxiety," *China Quarterly* 183 (September 2005): 587–608; "In Search of the Jiang Qing Dress: Some Preliminary Findings," *Fashion Theory* 9, 1 (2005): 1–20; "Yangzhou's 'Modernity': Fashion and Consumption in the Early Nineteenth Century," *positions: east asia cultures critique* 11, 2 (Fall 2003): 395–425; "Yu Feng and the 1950s Dress Reform Campaign: Global Hegemony and Local Agency In the Art of Fashion," in Yu Chien Ming, ed., *Wu sheng zhi sheng(II): jindai Zhongguo funü yu wenhua, 1600–1950* (Given English title: Voices Amid Silence: Women and Modern Chinese Culture (II): 1600–1950) (Taipei: Academia Sinica, 2003), 235–68. "What Should Chinese Women Wear? A National Problem," *Modern China* 22, 2 (April 1996): 99–131.

BIBLIOGRAPHY

ABBREVIATIONS

BDRC   Howard L. Boorman, ed., *Biographical Dictionary of Republican China*
BnF   *Bibliotheque nationale de France*
BYHB   *Beiyang huabao*
DGB   *Dagongbao*
DMB   L. Carrington Goodrich, ed., *Dictionary of Ming Biography*
GMRB   *Guangming ribao*
GWZB   *Guowen zhoubao*
MGRW   Xu Youchun, ed., *Minguo renwu dacidian*
RMRB   *Renmin ribao*
SDHB   *Shidai huabao*
XGCBYK *Xin guancha banyuekan*

NEWSPAPERS AND MAGAZINES
(*original alternative English title)

Section A: Published 1900–1948
Beijing huabao (Beijing pictorial)
Beiyang huabao (Beiyang Pictorial; *Peiyang Pictorial Times)
Dagongbao (*Ta Kung Pao)
Feifei huabao (Feifei pictorial)
Funü huabao (Women's pictorial)
Funü shibao (Women's Times)
Funü xinshenghuo yuekan (Women's New Life monthly)
Funü zazhi (*Ladies Magazine)
Furen huabao (Women's pictorial)
Guowen huabao (National news pictorial)
Guowen zhoubao (National news weekly)
Jilian huikan (Magazine of the federation of industrialists)
Kuaile jiating (Happy family)
Liangyou (*Young Companion)
Linglong (*Linloon)
Manhua shenghuo (Cartoon life)
Mei de zhuangsu (Beautiful dress)
Meishu shenghuo (*Arts and Life)

313

New York Times
Nüzi shijie (Women's world)
Nüzi yuekan (Women's monthly)
Shenbao (*Shun Pao)
Shenghuo (Life)
Shidai huabao (*Modern Miscellany)
Shishi huabao (Times pictorial)
Vogue [Shanghai 1926]
Wenhua yishu yuekan (Culture and arts monthly)
Xin nüxing (New woman)
Zhejiang chao (Tides of Zhejiang)

Section B: Published 1949–2006
Beijing huabao (Beijing pictorial)
Beijing qingnianbao (Beijing youth)
Beijing Review
China Pictorial
China Reconstructs
Da jing mao (Business Weekly)
Guangming ribao (Enlightenment daily)
Guoji xianqu daobao (*International Herald Leader)
Hefei wanbao (Hefei evening paper)
International Herald Tribune
Liaoning ribao (Liaoning daily)
Manchester Guardian
Meishu (Fine Arts)
Nanfang tiyu (Southern sport)
Renmin ribao (*People's Daily)
Shanghai xinwenbao (Shanghai news)
Shizhuang (*Fashion)
The Times
Tianjin ribao (Tianjin daily)
Xiamen ribao (Amoy daily)
Xiandai fuzhuang (Modern dress)
Zhongguo funü (China's women)
Zhongguo fushi bao (Chinese fashion)
Zhongguo fuzhuang (Chinese dress)
Zhongguo huabao (*China Pictorial)
Zhongguo mingpai shizhuang (*Chinese Popular Brand Fashion)
Zhongguo qingnian banyuekan (China youth fortnightly)
Zhongguo qingnianbao (China youth)
Zhongguo xinwen zhoukan (China news weekly)
Zhongguo zhi yi (*Wings)

OTHER WORKS

Aiguo ziyouzhe Jin Yi (Jin Tianhe), *Nüjie zhong* (Warning bell for women), Shanghai: 1903.

Alderfer, Evan B., "The Textile Industry of China," *Annals of the American Academy of Political and Social Science* 152, *China* (November 1930): 184–90.

Alexander, William, *Costumes et vues de la Chine*, Gravés en taille-douce par Simon, d'après les dessins de W. Alexander, Paris: Chez Nepveu, 1815.

——, *The Costume of China Illustrated in Forty-Eight Coloured Engravings*, London: William Miller, 1805.

—— and George Henry Mason, *Views of 18th Century China: Costumes, History, Customs*, London: Studio Editions, 1988.

Alitto, Guy, *The Last Confucian*, Berkeley and Los Angeles: University of California Press, 1979.

All About Shanghai: A Standard Guidebook [1934-5], Hong Kong: Oxford University Press, 1983.

Allman, Jean, "'Let Your Fashion be in Line with our Ghanaian Costume': Nation, Gender, and the Politics of Cloth-ing in Nkrumah's Ghana," in Jean Allman, ed., *Fashioning Africa: Power and the Politics of Dress*, Bloomington: Indiana University Press, 2004, 144-65.

An Wenjiang, "Shanghai Rebel," in Zhang Lijia and Calum MacLeod, eds, *China Remembers*, Hong Kong: Oxford University Press, 1999, 118-26.

Andrews, Julia, *Painters and Politics in the People's Republic of China, 1949–1979*, Berkeley: University of California Press, 1994.

Aoki Masaru, *Pekin fûzoku zufu* (Beijing customs, illustrated), Uchida Michio, ed., Tokyo: Heibonsha, 1964.

——, *Beiping fengsu tu* (Illustrations of Beiping customs), trans. and ed. Zhang Xunqi, Taibei: Changchunshu shufang, 1978.

"Aoyun jianer lifu ye yao chu huayang: yanse tapei gengdadan gengfu bianhua" (Fresh styles of uniform for Olympic athletes: bolder and richer changes matched with color), *Nanfang tiyu* (Southern Sport), 10 July 2004, www.sina.com.cn/cn/other/2004-07-10/29245.html. Accessed 11 August 2004.

Attwood, Lynne, *Creating the New Soviet Woman: Women's Magazines as Engineers of Female Identity, 1922–53*, Houndmills: Macmillan Press Ltd., 1999.

Ayers, William, *Chang Chih-tung and Educational Reform in China*, Cambridge, Mass.: Harvard University Press, 1971.

Bai Yun, *Zhongguo lao qipao—lao zhaopian lao guanggo jianzheng qipao de yanbian* (The traditional *qipao* of China: evidence of its [stylistic] changes in old photographs and old advertisements), Beijing: Guangming ribao chubanshe, 2006.

Bailey, Paul J., "'Unharnessed Fillies': Discourse of the 'Modern' Female Student in Early Twentieth Century China," in Lo Jiu-jung and Lu Miaw-fen, eds, *Wu sheng zhi sheng (III): jindai Zhongguo funü yu wenhua, 1600-1950* (Given English title: Voices amid Silence (III): Women and Culture in Modern China, 1600-1950), Taipei: Academia Sinica, 2003, 327–57.

Bainian shishang: ershi shiji Zhongguo shehui fengqing huajuan (One hundred years of contemporary trends: an illustrated volume on the social ambience in twentieth-century China), *Zhongguo qingnian banyuekan* (special issue) 23, 1999.

Bao Mingxin, "Shanghai Fashion in the 1930s," in Jo-Anne Birnie Danzker, Ken Lum and Shengtian Zheng, eds, *Shanghai Modern, 1919-1945*, Ostfildern-Ruit: Hatje Cantz, 2004, 318-30.

—— and Ma Li, eds, *Zhongguo qipao* (China's *qipao*), Shanghai: Shanghai wenhua chubanshe, 1998.

——, Jiang Zhiwei, and Cheng Rong, eds, *Zhongguo mingshi shizhuang jianshang cidian* (Dictionary of famous Chinese fashion connoisseurs), Shanghai: Shanghai Jiaotong Daxue chubanshe, 1993.

Bao Tianxiao, *Yi shi zhu xing de bainian bianqian* (One hundred years of change in food, clothing, accommodation and travel), Hong Kong: Dahua chubanshe, 1973.

Barber, Noel, *The Fall of Shanghai: The Communist Takeover in 1949*, London: Macmillan, 1979.

Barlow, Tani, *The Question of Women in Chinese Feminism*, Durham: Duke University Press, 2004.

Barnes, Ruth, and Joanne B. Eicher, eds, *Dress and Gender: Making and Meaning in Cultural Contexts*, New York: Berg, 1992.

Barrow, John, *Travels in China*, London: T. Cadell and W. Davies, 1806.

Bashford, James, *China: An Interpretation* [1916], New York: Abingdon Press, 1922.

Beaton, Cecil, *Chinese Album*, London: B.T. Batsford, 1945-6.

Bell, Quentin, *On Human Finery*, London: Allison and Busby, 1947.

Benson, Carlton, "Consumers are Also Soldiers: Subversive Songs from Nanjing Road During the New Life Movement," in Sherman Cochran ed., *Inventing Nanjing Road: Commercial Culture in Shanghai, 1900–1945*, Ithaca: East Asia Program, Cornell University, 1999, 91-132.

Bergère, Marie-Claire, *The Golden Age of the Chinese Bourgeoisie, 1911-1937*, trans. Janet Lloyd, Cambridge: Cambridge University Press, 1989.

Berry, Chris, and Mary Farquhar, *China on Screen: Cinema and Nation*, New York: Columbia University Press, 2006.

Bhabha, Homi K., "Of Mimicry and Man: The Ambivalence of Colonial Discourse," in Homi K. Bhabha, ed., *Location of Culture*, London: Routledge, 1994, 86-90.

Bing Ying, "Dongluan zhong de Minxi" (Western Fujian in turmoil), *Shidai huabao* 5, 2 (16 November 1933).

Bird, Isabella. See under Bishop, Mrs J.F.

Bishop, Mrs J.F. [Isabella L. Bird], *Unbeaten Tracks in Japan*, London: John Murray, 1905.

——, *The Yangtze Valley and Beyond*, London: John Murray, 1899.

Bland, J.O.P., *Recent Events and Present Politics in China*, London: William

Heinemann, 1912.

Boorman, Howard L., ed., *Biographical Dictionary of Republican China*, New York: Columbia University Press, 1967–1979.

Borel, Henri, *The New China*, trans. C. Thieme, London: T. Fisher, 1912.

Borthwick, Sally, *Education and Social Change in China: The Beginnings of the Modern Era*, Stanford: Hoover Institution Press, 1983.

Brandon, Ruth, *Singer and the Sewing Machine: A Capitalist Romance*, London: Barrie and Jenkins, 1977.

Braudel, Fernand, *Capitalism and Material Life, 1400–1800*, trans. Miriam Kochan, New York: Harper Colophon Books, 1967.

Breward, Christopher, and David Gilbert, eds, *Fashion's World Cities*, Oxford: Berg, 2006.

Brook, Timothy, *The Confusions of Pleasure: Commerce and Culture in Ming China*, Berkeley: University of California Press, 1998.

Brouillon, Père Nicholas, *Mémoire sur l'état Actuel de la Mission du Kiang-nan 1842–1855*, Paris: Julien, Lanier et Cie, Editeurs, 1855.

Brown, Kendall H., "Flowers of Taishō: Images of Women in Japanese Society and Art," in Lorna Price and Letitia O'Connor, eds, *Taishō Chic: Japanese Modernity, Nostalgia and Deco*, Honolulu: Honolulu Academy of Arts, 2001, 19-21.

Brownell, Susan, *Training the Body for China: Sports in the Moral Order of the People's Republic*, Chicago: University of Chicago Press, 1995.

Broyelle, Claudia, *Women's Liberation in China*, Michele Cohen and Gary Herman, trans., Atlantic Highlands: Humanities Press, 1977.

Bullis, Douglas, *Fashion Asia*, London: Thames and Hudson, 2000.

Butler, Judith, *Gender Trouble: Feminism and the Subversion of Identity*, New York: Routledge, 1990.

Cahill, Suzanne. E., "'Our Women Are Acting Like Foreigners' Wives!' Western Influences on Tang Dynasty Women's Fashion," in Valerie Steele and John Major, *China Chic: East Meets West*, New Haven: Yale University Press, 1999, 103-17.

Cammann, Schuyler V.R., *China's Dragon Robes*, New York: Ronald Press Co., 1952.

Candlin, Enid Saunders, *The Breach in the Wall: A Memoir of Old China*, New York: Paragon House Publishers, 1987.

Cao Fangyun, "Yifu lüeshuo" (A few words about clothing), *Nüduobao* II, 4 (cumulative number 16) (July 1913): 11-14.

Cao Guimin, interviewed in *Beijing qingnianbao*, 22 December 2005, www.china.com.cn. Accessed 28 May 2006.

Cao Xuexin, *The Story of the Stone*, Vol. 1, trans. David Hawkes, London: Penguin, 1973.

Cao Zuoya, *Out of the Crucible: Literary Works About the Rusticated Youth*, Lanham: Lexington Books, 2003.

Carroll, Peter, "Refashioning Suzhou: Dress, Commodification, and Modernity," *positions: east asia cultures critique* 11, 2 (Fall 2003): 443-78.

Cha Jianying, ed., *Bashi niandai fangtanlu* (The eighties: interviews), Beijing: SDX Joint Publishing Company, 2006, 433-53.

Chan, Wellington K.K., "Selling Goods and Promoting a New Commercial Culture: The Four Premier Department Stores on Nanjing Road, 1917–1937," in Sherman Cochran, ed., *Inventing Nanjing Road: Commercial Culture in Shanghai, 1900–1945*, Ithaca: East Asia Program, Cornell University, 1-36.

Chang, Eileen (Zhang Ailing), "Chinese Life and Fashions," *Lianhe Wenxue* (Unitas) 3, 5 (1987): 66-72.

——, "A Chronicle of Changing Clothes," trans. Andrew F. Jones, *positions: east asia cultures critique* 11, 2 (Fall, 2003): 427–41. See also Zhang Ailing.

Chang, Pang-Mei Natasha, *Bound Feet and Western Dress*, New York: Doubleday, 1966.

Chang Renchun, *Lao Beijing de chuandai* (Dressing in old Beijing), Beijing: Yanshan chubanshe, 1999.

Chao Feng, *Wenhua da geming cidian* (Dictionary of the Cultural Revolution), Hong Kong: Ganglong chubanshe, 1993.

Chen Baoliang, *Mingdai shehui shenghuo shi* (History of social life in the Ming dynasty), Beijing: Zhongguo shehui kexue chubanshe, 2004.

Chen Bilan, *Wode huiyi* (My memoirs), Hong Kong: Shiyue shuwu, 1994.

Chen Bixie, *Haiwai binfenlu* (Carryings on abroad), Shenyang: Chunfeng wenyi chubanshe, 1997.

Chen Fumei, "Zenmeyang cai jiao fuzhuang de mei?" (What sort of clothing can be called beautiful?), *Zhongguo qingnian* 6 (1980): 20-1.

Chen, Jocelyn H-C, "Investigating Garment Fit Requirements for Fashion Brands in Taiwan: A Case Study Based on Oasis and French Connection." Paper presented at Making an Appearance: Fashion, Dress and Consumption, University of Queensland, St Lucia Campus, Brisbane, 10–13 July, 2003.

Chen Juanjuan, "Zhixiu wenwu zhong de shouzi zhuangshi" (The word "longevity" as an adornment on embroidered items), *Gugong bowuyuan kan* (Palace Museum Journal), 2 (2004): 10-19.

Chen Lifu, "Xinshenghuo yundong yu fumu zhi zeren" (The New Life Movement and the Duties of Parents) [1934], in *Geming wenxian, di liushiba ji, Xinshenghuo yundong shiliao* (Documents on the Revolution, Pt. 68, materials on the New Life Movement), Taibei: Zhongyang wenwu gongyingshe, 1975, 171-6.

Chen Rongli, "Manhua 'xiaozi'" (Leisurely words about "xiaozi"), *Minzu luntan* 6 (2002): n.p.n.

Chen Shen et al., *Zhongguo sheyingshi* (History of Chinese photography), Taipei: Sheyingjia chubanshe, 1990.

Chen, Tina Mai, "Proletarian White and Working Bodies in Mao's China," *positions: east asia cultures critique* 11, 2 (Fall 2003): 361-93.

Chen, Xiaomei, *Acting the Right Part: Political Theater and Popular Drama in Contemporary China*, Honolulu: University of Hawai'i Press, 2002.

——, "Growing Up With Posters in the Maoist Era," in Harriet Evans and

Stephanie Donald, eds, *Picturing Power in the People's Republic of China: Posters of the Cultural Revolution*, Lanham: Rowman & Littlefield Publishers, Inc., 1999, 101–22.

Chen Zishan, ed., *Modeng Shanghai: sanshi niandai yangchang baijing* (Shanghai modern: a hundred scenes from the western quarter in the 1930s), Guizhou: Guangxi Shifan Daxue chubanshe, 2001.

China Pictorial Publications & New Silk Road Models Co. Ltd, eds, *Zhongguo xin silu mingmo xiezhen* (China's New Silk Road models in photographs), Beijing: Zhongguo huabao chubanshe, 2001.

"Chinese Garment Sector Steps into World Market," www.humanrights-china.org/course/Daily2001108142431.htm. Accessed 21 April 2003.

Chou, M.T., "Report on Industrial and Social Survey," in Heintzleman to Secretary of State (July 23 1923). File no. 893.40, General Records of the Department of State [USA], RG59 (National Archives).

Chow Chungcheng, *The Lotus-Pool of Memory*, trans. Joyce Emerson, London: Michael Joseph, 1961.

Cipolla, Carlo Maria, *Clocks and Culture, 1300-1700*, London: Collins, 1967.

Clark, Hazel, *The Cheongsam*, Hong Kong: Oxford University Press, 2000.

Clunas, Craig, "The Art of Social Climbing in Sixteenth-Century China," *The Burlington Magazine* 133, 1059 (June 1991): 368-75.

——, *Chinese Export Watercolours*, London: Victoria and Albert Museum, Far Eastern Series, 1984.

——, "Modernity Global and Local: Consumption and the Rise of the West," *American Historical Review* 104 (December 1999): 1497–1511.

Cochran, Sherman, *Big Business in China: Sino-Foreign Rivalry in the Cigarette Industry, 1890–1930*, Cambridge, Mass.: Harvard University Press, 1980.

——, *Chinese Medicine Men: Consumer Culture in China and Southeast Asia*, Cambridge, Mass.: Harvard University Press, 2006.

—— ed., *Inventing Nanjing Road: Commercial Culture in Shanghai, 1900—1945*, Ithaca: East Asia Program, Cornell University, 1999.

——, "Transnational Origins of Advertising in Early Twentieth-Century China," in Sherman Cochran, ed., *Inventing Nanjing Road: Commercial Culture in Shanghai, 1900–1945*, Ithaca: East Asia Program, Cornell University, 1999, 37–58.

—— and Andrew C.K. Hsieh, with Janis Cochran, *One Day in China: May 21, 1936*, New Haven and London: Yale University Press, 1983, 68.

Craik, Jennifer, *The Face of Fashion: Cultural Studies in Fashion*, London: Routledge, 1994.

——, *Uniforms Exposed: From Conformity to Transgression*, Oxford: Berg, 2005.

Cranmer-Byng, J.L., *An Embassy to China: Being the Journal Kept by Lord Macartney During his Embassy to the Emperor Ch'ien-lung, 1793-1794*, London: Longmans, 1962.

Croll, Elisabeth, *Changing Identities of Chinese Women: Rhetoric, Experience, and Self-Perception in Twentieth-century China*, Hong Kong: Hong Kong University

Press; London, Atlantic Highlands: Zed Books, 1995.

Crossley, Pamela, *A Translucent Mirror: History and Identity in Qing Imperial Ideology*, Cambridge, Mass.: Blackwell, 1997.

Crow, Carl, *400 Million Customers: The Experiences—Some Happy, Some Sad of An American in China and What They Taught Him* [1937], Norwalk: Eastbridge, D'Asia Vue Reprint Library, 2003.

Cui, Shuqin, *Women Through the Lens*, Honolulu: University of Hawai'i Press, 2003.

da Cruz, Gaspar, "Treatise in Which the Things of China are Related at Great Length," in C.R. Boxer, ed., *South China in the Sixteenth Century*, Lichtenstein: Nendeln, Kraus Reprint, 1967, 45-239.

Darwent, Charles Ewart, *Shanghai: A Handbook for Travellers and Residents to the Chief Objects of Interest In And Around the Foreign Settlements and Native City*, Shanghai: Kelly and Walsh, 1920.

Dauncey, Sarah, "Illusions of Grandeur: Perceptions of Status and Wealth in Late-Ming Female Clothing and Ornamentation," *East Asian History* 25–26 (December 2003): 43-68.

Davies, Robert Bruce, *Peacefully Working to Conquer the World: Singer Sewing Machines in Foreign Markets, 1864-1920*, New York: Arno Press, 1976.

Davis, John Frances, *The Chinese: A General Description of the Empire of China and its Inhabitants*, New York: Harper and Brothers, 1836.

Deng Ming, ed., and Gao Yan, comp., *Lao yuefenpai nianhua: zuihou yipie* (The New Year prints of old calendar posters: a last look), Shanghai: Shanghai huabao chubanshe, 2003.

Des Forges, Alexander, "'From Source Texts to 'Reality Observed': The Creation of the Author in Nineteenth-Century Vernacular Fiction," *Chinese Literature: Essays, Articles, Reviews* 22 (2000): 67-84.

Diamant, Neil J., *Revolutionizing the Family: Politics, Love, and Divorce in Urban and Rural China, 1949–1968*, Berkeley: University of California Press, 2000.

Dickinson, Goldsworthy Lowes, *Letters From a Chinese Official, Being An Eastern View of Western Civilisation*, London: R.B. Johnson, 1901.

Digby, George, *Down Wind*, New York: E.P. Dutton & Co., Inc., 1939.

Ding Ling, "The Hamlet," in Ding Ling, *Miss Sophie's Diary and Other Stories*, trans. W. F. Jenner, Beijing: Panda Books, 1985, 133-79.

Ding Xiqiang, ed., *Xin Tangzhuang* (The New Chinese Jacket), Shanghai: Shanghai kexue jishu chubanshe, 2002.

Ding Zheng, "Tan fuzhuang de bianhua he fuzhuang gaijin wenti" (On the problems of changes and advances in clothing), *Meishu* April 1956: 7-9.

Dong, Madeleine Yue, *Republican Beijing: The City and Its Histories*, Berkeley: University of California Press, 2003.

Doolittle, Rev. Justus, *Social Life of the Chinese* [1865], Taipei: Ch'eng-wen Publishing Company, 1966.

Dreams of Spring: Erotic Art in China, Amsterdam: The Pepin Press, 1997.

Duchesne, Isabella, "The Chinese Opera Star: Roles and Identity," in John Hay, ed.,

Boundaries in China, London: Reaktion Books, 1994, 217-42.

Dukes, Edwin Joshua, *Everyday Life in China; or Scenes Along River and Road in Fuh-kien*, London: The Religious Tract Society, n.d.

Dyer Ball, J., *The Chinese at Home, or The Man of Tong and His Land*, London: The Religious Tract Society, 1911.

Eberhard, Wolfram, "What is Beautiful in a Chinese Woman?" in Eberhard, *Moral and Social Values of the Chinese: Selected Essays*, Taipei: Ch'eng-wen Publishing Company, 1971, 271-304.

Ebrey, Patricia, "Gender and Sinology: Shifting Western Interpretations of Footbinding, 1300–1890," *Late Imperial China* 20, 2 (December 1999): 1-34.

Eckstein, Alexander, *Communist China's Economic Growth and Foreign Trade: Implications for U.S. Policy*, New York: McGraw-Hill for the Council on Foreign Relations, 1966.

Edwards, Louise, "Women Warriors and Amazons of the Mid Qing Texts *Jinghua yuan* and *Honglou meng*," *Modern Asian Studies* 29, 2 (1995): 225-55.

———, "Policing the Modern Woman in Republican China," *Modern China* 26, 2 (April 2000): 115-47.

Elliot, Mark, *The Manchu Way: The Eight Banners and Ethnic Identity in Late Imperial China*, Stanford: Stanford University Press, 2001.

Elman, Benjamin A., *On Their Own Terms: Science in China, 1550–1900*, Cambridge, Mass.: Harvard University Press, 2005.

Entwhistle, Joanne, *The Fashioned Body: Fashion, Dress, and Modern Social Theory*, Cambridge: Polity Press, 2000.

Epstein, Israel, *Woman in World History: Life and Times of Soong Ching Ling (Mme. Sun Yatsen)*, Beijing: New World Press, 1993.

Erickson, Charlotte J., *British Industrialists: Steel and Hosiery 1850–1950*, Cambridge: University Press, 1959.

Evans, Harriet, *Women and Sexuality in China: Dominant Discourses of Female Sexuality and Gender Since 1949*, Cambridge: Polity Press, 1997.

Fan Hong, *Footbinding, Feminism and Freedom: The Liberation of Women's Bodies in Modern China*, London and Portland, Or.: Frank Cass, 1997.

——— and J. A. Mangan, "A Martyr for Modernity: Qiu Jin, Feminist, Warrior And Revolutionary," *International Journal of the History of Sport* 18 (2001): 27-54.

Fan Jinmin, "Shuoshuo Sushang" (A few words about Suzhou merchants), *Huadong xinwen* (East China news), 1 September 2004, www.people.com.cn/BIG5/paper40/12830/1153970.html. Accessed 9 August 2006.

Fang Chaoying, "Huo T'ao," in *DMB*, Vol. I, 679-83.

Feng Yuemin, "Cong 1875-1925 nian 'Shenbao' guanggao kan Zhongwai 'shangzhan'" (Looking at the Sino-foreign 'commercial war' from advertisements in *Shenbao*, 1875-1925), *Dang'an yu shixue* 2 (2004): 25-9.

Ferro, Marc, *The Great War, 1914–1918*, trans. Nicole Stone, London: Routledge and Kegan Paul, 1973.

Feuerwerker, Albert, "Handicraft and Manufactured Cotton Textiles in China,

1871–1910," *The Journal of Economic History* 30, 2 (June 1970): 338-78.

Finnane, Antonia, *Far from Where? Jewish Journeys from Shanghai to Australia*, Melbourne: Melbourne University Press, 1999.

——, "A Place in the Nation: Yangzhou and the Idle Talk Controversy of 1934," *Journal of Asian Studies* 53, 4 (November 1994): 1150-74.

——, *Speaking of Yangzhou: A Chinese City, 1550–1850*, Cambridge, Mass.: Harvard University Asia Center, 2004.

——, "What Should Chinese Women Wear? A National Problem," *Modern China* 22, 2 (April 1996): 99-131.

——, "Yu Feng and the 1950s Dress Reform Campaign: Global Hegemony and Local Agency In the Art of Fashion," in Yu Chien Ming, ed., *Wu sheng zhi sheng(II): jindai Zhongguo funü yu wenhua, 1600–1950* (Given English title: Voices Amid Silence: Women and Modern Chinese Culture (II): 1600–1950), Taipei: Academia Sinica, 2003, 235-68.

FitzGerald, C.P., *Why China? Recollections of China 1923–1950*, Melbourne: Melbourne University Press, 1985.

Fitzgerald, John, *Awakening China: Politics, Culture, and Class in the Nationalist Revolution*, Stanford: Stanford University Press, 1996.

Fraser, Stewart E., ed., *100 Great Chinese Posters*, New York: Images Graphiques, Inc., 1977.

Fu Chongju, *Chengdu tonglan* (Looking around Chengdu), Chengdu: Bashu shushe, 1987.

Fu Poshek, "The Ambiguity of Entertainment: Chinese Cinema in Japanese-Occupied Shanghai, 1941 to 1945," *Cinema Journal* 37, 1 (Fall 1997): 66-84.

"Fuzhuang shichang pianchui 'Chaoliufeng'" (Korean currents run strong in the clothing market), *Zhongguo fangzhi wang* (China textiles website), www. ramie.comcn/scps05/s006.htm. Accessed 28 May 2006.

"Fuzhuang: yiqu bufan de Lieningzhuang" (Clothing: the Lenin suit—once gone, never to return), *Guoji xianqu baodao*, 20 March 2006, news.xinhuanet.com/ herald/2006-03/20/content_4322357.htm. Accessed 1 October 2006.

Fussell, Paul, *Uniforms: Why We Are What We Wear*, Boston: Houghton Mifflin, 2002.

Gamewell, Mary Ninde, *The Gateway to China: Pictures of Shanghai*, New York and Chicago: Fleming H. Revell Company, 1916.

Garrett, Valery M., *Chinese Clothing: An Illustrated Guide*, Hong Kong: Oxford University Press, 1994.

Gerth, Karl, *China Made: Consumer Culture and the Creation of the Nation*, Cambridge, Mass.: Harvard University Asia Center, 2003.

Gillette, Maris, "What's in a Dress? Brides in the Hui Quarter of Xi-an," in Deborah Davis, ed., *The Consumer Revolution in Urban China*, Berkeley: University of California Press, 2000, 80–106.

Gillin, Donald, *Warlord: Yen Hsi-shan in Shansi Province, 1911–1949*, Princeton: Princeton University Press, 1967.

Godley, Michael, "The End of the Queue: Hair as Symbol in Chinese History," *East*

Asian History 8 (December 1994): 53-72.

Goldsmith, Oliver, *Citizen of the World, or Letters from a Chinese Philosopher Residing in London*, London: G. Cooke, 1762.

Gongsun Lu, *Zhongguo dianying shihua* (Tales from the history of Chinese cinema), Hong Kong: Nantian shuye gongsi, 1961.

Goodman, Bryna, "Improvisations on a Semicolonial Theme, or How to Read a Celebration of Transnational Urban Community," *The Journal of Asian Studies* 59, 4 (November, 2000): 889-926.

Goodrich, L. Carrington, ed., *Dictionary of Ming Biography*, New York: Columbia University Press, 1976.

Greenberg, Michael, *British Trade and the Opening of China 1800–42*, Cambridge: Cambridge University Press, 1951.

Guangdongsheng meishu sheying zhanlan bangongshi (Guangdong provincial office for fine art photography exhibitions), ed., *Dadao "sirenbang" manhua ji* (Collected cartoons on striking down the Gang of Four), Guangzhou: Guangdong renmin chubanshe, 1977.

Guangzhoushi fuzhuang jishu yanjiusuo (Guangzhou garment technology research centre), ed., *Yangcheng fuzhuang* 1965–1966 (Guangzhou garments, 1965–1966), Guangzhou, 1966.

Guangzhoushi shangye fuzhuang yanjiusuo (Guangzhou commercial clothing research centre), ed., *Yangcheng shizhuang* (Guangzhou fashions), Guangzhou: Guangdong keji chubanshe, 1981.

Guo Fuxiang, "Guanyu Qingdai de Suzhong" (On the Suzhou clocks of the Qing dynasty), *Gugong bowuyuan kan* 1 (2004): 65-76.

Guo Jianying, *Modeng Shanghai: sanshi niandai de Yangchang baijing* (Modern Shanghai: one hundred scenes from the 1930s Western quarter), Chen Zishan, ed., Guilin: Guangxi Shifan Daxue chubanshe, 2001.

Guo Weilin, "Mantan nüren de fushi" (Talking about women's dress and adornment), *Furen huabao* 48 (June-July 1937): 4-6.

Hacker, Arthur, *China Illustrated: Western Views of the Middle Kingdom*, North Clarendon: Tuttle, 2004.

Hahn, Emily, *China to Me*, Boston: Beacon Press, 1988.

Hamilton, Robyn, "Historical Contexts for a Life of Qiu Jin," PhD dissertation, Department of History, The University of Melbourne, 2003.

Hanan, Patrick, "*Fengyue Meng* and the Courtesan Novel," *Harvard Journal of Asiatic Studies* 58, 2 (December 1998): 345-72.

Hanshang mengren, *Fengyue meng* (Dreams of wind and moon) [1848], Beijing: Beijing Daxue chubanshe, 1988.

Hao Wen, "Cong shidai shuo dao zhuangshi" (Speaking about dress and adornment), *Shidai huabao* 2, 1 (1 February 1931): 20.

Hao, Yen-p'ing, *The Commercial Revolution in Nineteenth-Century China: the Rise of Sino-Western Mercantile Capitalism*, Berkeley: University of California Press, 1986.

Hao Zhihong, "36 nian qian de 'cai zhao'" (A 'colour photo' from 36 years ago),

Haerbin ribao, 11 September 2003.

Harrison, Henrietta, *The Making of the Republican Citizen: Political Ceremonies and Symbols in China 1911–1929*, Oxford: Oxford University Press, 2000.

Harrist, Robert E., Jr., "Clothes Make the Man: Dress, Modernity, and Masculinity in China, ca. 1912–1937," in Wu Hung and Katherine R. Tsiang, eds, *Body and Face in Chinese Visual Culture*, Cambridge, Mass.: Harvard University Asia Center, 2005, 171-96.

Hay, Jonathan S., *Shitao: Painting and Modernity in Early Qing China*, New York: Cambridge University Press, 2001.

Hinton, Harold, ed., *The People's Republic of China 1949–1979: A Documentary survey, vol. 3: The Cultural Revolution Part 1*, Wilmington: Scholarly Resources Inc., 1980.

Ho, Ping-ti, "The Salt Merchants of Yang-chou: A Study of Commercial Capitalism in Eighteenth-Century China," *Harvard Journal of Asiatic Studies* 17 (1954): 130–64.

Ho, Virgil Kit-yiu, "The Limits of Hatred: Popular Attitudes Towards the West in Republican Canton," *East Asian History* 2 (1991): 87-104.

Hollander, Anne, *Sex and Suits: The Evolution of Modern Dress*, New York: Kodansha International, 1994.

Hong Ying, *Daughter of the River: An Autobiography*, London: Bloomsbury, 1998.

Honig, Emily, "Socialist Sex: The Cultural Revolution Revisited," *Modern China* 29, 2 (April 2003): 143-75.

―― and Gail Hershatter, *Personal Voices: Chinese Women in the 1980's*, Stanford: Stanford University Press, 1988.

Hosie, Lady, *Two Gentlemen of China*, London: Seeley Service & Co. Limited, 1929.

Howell, Georgina, *Sultans of Style, Thirty Years of Fashion and Passion, 1960-1990*, London: Ebury Press, 1990.

Hsiao-hsiao-sheng, *The Golden Lotus: A Translation from the Original of Chin P'ing Mei*, trans. Clement Egerton, New York: Paragon Books, 1959.

Hsiao, Pei-yen, "Body Politics, Modernity, and National Salvation: The Modern Girl and the New Life Movement," *Asian Studies Review* 29 (June 2005): 165-86.

Hsieh Ping-Ying, *Autobiography of a Chinese Girl*, trans. Tsui Chi, London: Pandora Press, 1986.

Hsü, Ginger Cheng-chi, *A Bushel of Pearls: Painting for Sale in Eighteenth-Century Yangchow*, Stanford: Stanford University Press, 2001.

Hu Teh-wei, Ming Li, and Shangjin Wei, "Household Expenditure Patterns in Tianjin, 1982 and 1984," *The China Quarterly* 120 (December 1989): 787-99.

Hua Mei, *Zhongguo fuzhuang shi* (History of Chinese dress), Tianjin: Renmin meishu chubanshe, 1989.

Hua Sheng, "Cong Deguo de weisheng fuzhuang yundong tan dao Zhongguo shimao funü de yanghua" (Comments on the Westernisation of fashionable women in China from the perspective of the healthy dress movement in

Germany), *Linglong* 221 (1936): 167-9.

Huang, Huilan. See Koo, Hui-lan; Koo, Madame Wellington.

Huang Juyan, ed., *Jindai Guangdong jiaoyu yu Lingnan daxue* (Modern Education in Guangdong, and Lingnan University), Hong Kong: Commercial Press, 1995.

Huang, Nicole, *Women, War, and Domesticity: Shanghai Literature and Popular Culture of the 1940s*, Leiden: Brill, 2005.

Huang Renyuan, exec. ed., *Sun Zhongshan yu guomin geming* (Sun Yatsen and the Republican revolution), Hong Kong: Shangwu yinshuguan, 1994.

Huang Shijian and Shao Jin, eds, *Shijiu shiji Zhongguo shijing fengqing: sanbai liushi hang* (Street scenes in nineteenth-century China: the 360 professions), Shanghai: Shanghai guji chubanshe, 1999.

Huaxia funü mingren cidian bianji weiyuanhuai (Editorial committee for the dictionary of famous Chinese women), *Huaxia funü mingren cidian* (Dictionary of famous Chinese women), Beijing: Huaxia chubanshe, 1988.

Hung, Chang-tai, "Female Symbols of Resistance in Chinese Wartime Spoken Drama," *Modern China* 15, 2 (April 1989): 149-77.

Hunt, Lynn, ed., *The Invention of Pornography: Obscenity and the Origins of Modernity*, New York: Zone Books, 1993.

Huters, Theodore, *Bringing the World Home: Appropriating the West in Late Qing and Early Republican China*, Honolulu: University of Hawai'i Press, 2005.

Idema, Wilf, and Beata Grant, *The Red Brush: Writing Women of Imperial China*, Cambridge, Mass.: Harvard University Asia Center, 2004.

Ikeda Shinobu, "The Allure of Women in Chinese Dress," paper presented at a conference on New Gender Constructs in Literature, the Visual and the Performing Arts of Modern China and Japan, University of Heidelberg, 28–31 October 2004.

Ikeda Toshio, "Minsu zaji" (Various notes on popular customs), in Lin Chuanfu, ed., *Minsu Taiwan* (Taiwan popular customs), Taipei: Wuling chuban youxian gongsi, 1994, Vol. 2, 95-108.

Jackson, Beverley, *Shanghai Girls Get All Dressed Up*, Berkeley and Toronto: Ten Speed Press, 2005.

Jami, Catherine, "Western Devices for Measuring Time and Space: Clocks and Euclidian Geometry in Late Ming and Ch'ing China," in Chun-chieh Huang and Erik Zürcher, eds, *Time and Space in Chinese Culture*, Leiden: E. J. Brill, 1995, 169-200.

Jiang Weimin, exec. ed., *Shimao waipo: zhuixun lao Shanghai de shishang shenghuo* (Given English title: Vogue grandma: in searching of the fashionable life of the old Shanghai), Shanghai: Sanlian shudian, 2003.

Jiang Ye, ed., *Zhongguo fuzhuang sheji: Lü Yue* (Chinese fashion designer: Lü Yue), Beijing: Renmin meishu chubanshe, 2004.

Jiangdu xianzhi (Gazetter of Jiangdu county), Wanli edition (1597).

Jiao, Priscilla, "Something Old, Something New," *That's China* (April 2005): 46, www.thatschina.net/20054-p46.htm. Accessed 21 April 2005.

Jiaodong Zhou Sheng, *Yangzhou meng* (Dream of Yangzhou), Taibei: Shijie shuju, 1978.

Jie Ailan, "Zhongguo pinpai yu shijie pinpai de bijiao" (Comparison of Chinese and International brand names), *Renmin ribao*, 5 September 2005.

Jin Lianbo, "'Bulaji' yinfa de caixian" (Guesswork prompted by the "bulaji"), in Lao zhaopian bianjibu (Old photographs editorial section), ed., *Baixing ziji de lishi* (Ordinary people's histories of themselves), Jinan: Shandong huabao chubanshe, 2001.

"Jinzhi funü zhanzu tiaoli" (Regulations for prohibition on footbinding), 10 May 1928. Chongqing Municipal Archives, *Jiaoyu* (Education), Vol. 536, Neiwubu yin, 1937.

Johnson, Linda Cooke, *Shanghai: From Market Town to Treaty Port 1074–1858*, Stanford: Stanford University Press, 1995.

Johnson, Samuel, *Johnson: Prose and Poetry* [1735], London: Rupert Hart-Davis, 1969.

Jung Chang, *Wild Swans: Three Daughters of China*, New York: Simon and Schuster, 1991.

"Junzhuang de gushi" (Story of a military uniform), xjzpz.51.net/xcjs/26.htm. Accessed 10 November 2003.

Kawamura, Yuniya, *The Japanese Revolution in Paris Fashion: Dress, Culture, Body*, Oxford: Berg, 2004.

——, "Placing Tokyo on the Fashion Map," in Christopher Breward and David Gilbert, eds, *Fashion's World Cities,* Oxford: Berg, 2006, 55-68.

Ke Shi, "Guanyu funü de zhuangsu" (On women's dress), *Dongfang zazhi* 31, 19 (1 October, 1934): 205.

Kinkley, Jeffrey, "Preface," in Wang Anyi, *Lapse of Time,* Beijing: Panda Books, 1988, n.p.n.

Ko, Dorothy, "Bondage in Time: Footbinding and Fashion Theory," *Fashion Theory* 1, 1 (1997): 3-28.

——, *Cinderella's Sisters: A Revisionist History of Footbinding*, Berkeley: University of California Press, 2005.

——, *Every Step a Lotus: Shoes for Bound Feet*, Berkeley: University of California Press, 2001.

——, *Teachers of the Inner Chambers: Women and Culture in Seventeenth-Century China*, Stanford: Stanford University Press, 1994.

Koo, Hui-lan [Madame Wellington Koo], *An Autobiography as told to Mary Van Rensselaer Thayer*, New York: Dial Press, 1943.

Koo, Madame Wellington (Oei Hui-lan) with Isabella Taves, *No Feast Lasts Forever*, New York: Quadrangle, 1975.

Kuhn, Philip, *Rebellion and its Enemies in Late Imperial China; Militarization and Social Structure, 1796-1864*, Cambridge, Mass.: Harvard University Press, 1970.

Kwong, Luke S.K., *A Mosaic of a Hundred Days: Personalities, Politics and Ideas of 1898*, Cambridge, Mass.: Council on East Asian Studies, 1984.

"La mode chinoise prend son envol" (Chinese fashion takes off), (5 March, 2003), *France3.fr: un site du groupe France Télevisions Interactive*, www.cultureetloisirs. france3.fr/mode/podiumsdailleurs/103017-fr.php. Accessed 3 September 2003.

"Labaku: bei shiguo fanpan zhouyu de kuzi" (Bell-bottoms: trousers used as an expression of defiance), *Renminwang*, 7 September 2005, www.news.tom. com/1002/3291/200597-2452894.html. Accessed 18 October 2006.

Lach, Donald, *The Preface to Leibniz' Novissima Sinica: Commentary, Translation, Text*, Honolulu: University of Hawaii Press, 1957.

Lai Chi-kong. See Li Zhigang.

Lai, Sufen Sophia, "From Cross-Dressing Daughter to Lady Knight-Errant: the Origin and Evolution of Chinese Women Warriors," in Sherry J. Mou, ed., *Presence and Presentation: Women in the Chinese Literati Tradition*, New York: St. Martin's Press, 1999, 77-107.

Lai Zhizhang, comp., *Taiwan Wufeng Linjia liuzhen ji* (A photographic record of the Lin family of Wufeng, Taiwan), Taibei: Zili baoxi wenhua chubanbu, 1989.

Laing, Ellen Johnston, *Selling Happiness: Calendar Posters and Visual Culture in Early-Twentieth-Century Shanghai*, Honolulu: University of Hawai'i Press, 2004.

——, "Visual Evidence for the Evolution of "Politically Correct" Dress for Women in Early Twentieth Century Shanghai," *Nan Nü* 5, 1 (2003): 68-112.

Landes, David, *Revolution in Time: Clocks and the Making of the Modern World*, Cambridge, Mass.: Harvard University Press, 1983.

Lee, Leo Ou-fan, *Shanghai Modern: The Flowering of a New Urban Culture in China, 1930–1945*, Cambridge, Mass.: Harvard University Press, 1999.

Lee, Lily Xiao Hong, and Sue Wiles, *Women of the Long March*, St Leonards: Allen and Unwin, 1999.

Lee, Ming-tsung, "Absorbing Japan: Transnational Media, Cross-cultural Consumption, and Identity Practice in Contemporary Taiwan," PhD thesis, Department of Social Anthropology, King's College, Cambridge, 2005.

Lee Ming-tsung. See also Li Mingcong.

Legouix, Susan, *Image of China: William Alexander*, London: Jupiter Books, 1980.

Leyda, Jay, *Dianying—Electric Shadows: An account of Films and the Film Audience in China*, Cambridge, Mass.: Massachusetts Institute of Technology, 1972.

Li Aoxia, "'Huafeng' he 'Hanliu'" (The Chinese wind and the Korean current), *Shaonian wenyi* (Nanjing), 2 (2006).

Li Chu-tsing, "T'ang Yin," in *DMB*, Vol. I, 1256-9.

Li Hui *Ren zai xuanguo–Huang Miaozi yu Yu Feng* (People in a whirlpool: Huang Miaozi and Yu Feng), Jinan: Shandong huabao chubanshe, 1998.

Li Jiarui, *Beiping fengsu leizheng* (Inventory of Beiping customs), Shanghai: Shangwu yinshu guan, 1936.

Li Mingcong, "'Qin ri' de qinggan jiegou, yu 'ha ri' de zhuti–yige kua shidai rentong zhengzhi de kaocha" (The structure of feeling in "feeling close to Japan", and the topic of "Japan crazy": a study of cross-generational identity politics). Paper given at Taiwan Sociology Annual Convention and Conference, 2004.

Li Xiaoping, "Fashioning the Body in Post-Mao China," in Anne Brydon and Sandra Niessen, eds, *Consuming Fashion: Adorning the Transnational Body*, Oxford and New York: Berg, 1998, 71-89.

Li Yuyi, "Meizhuang, xinzhuang yu qizhuang yifu" (Beautiful dress, new dress, weird and wonderful dress), *Funü zazhi* 14, 9 (1 January 1928): 24-30.

Li Zhigang (Lai Chi-kong), "Xianxiang yu yingzao guozu: jindai Zhongguo de faxing wenti" (Imagining and Constructing Nationhood: Hairstyles in Modern China), *Si yu yan* 36, 1 (1998): 99-118.

Li Zhisui, *The Private Life of Chairman Mao*, London: Chatto and Windus, 1994.

Liang Congjie, "Shuhu renjian siyuetian: huiyi wode muqin Lin Huiyin" (Sudden April days in this human world: remembering my mother Lin Huiyin), in Liang Congjie, ed., *Lin Huiyin wenji* (Collected writings by Lin Huiyin), Taibei: Tianxia yuanjian chuban gufen youxian gongsi, 2000, xi–xlvii.

Lieu, D.K., *The Growth and Industrialization of Shanghai*, Shanghai: China Institute of Economic and Statistical Research, 1936.

Lin Liyue, "Yishang yu fengjiao—wan Ming de fushi fengshang yu 'fuyao' yilun" (Costumes and customs: late Ming clothing trends and the discourse of "outrageousness"), *Xinshixue* 10, 3 (September 1999): 111-57.

Lin, Li-yueh. See Lin Liyue.

Lin Sumen, *Hanjiang sanbai yin* (Three hundred sonnets from the Han River [Grand Canal]), Yangzhou, 1808.

Lin Yutang, "The Inhumanity of Western Dress," in *The Importance of Living*, London: Heinemann, 1938, 257-62.

Ling Shuhua, "Once Upon a Time," Amy D. Dooling and Kristina M. Torgeson trans, in Amy D. Dooling and Krisitina M. Torgeson, eds, *Writing Women in Modern China: An Anthology of Women's Literature from the Early Twentieth Century*, New York: Columbia University Press, 1998, 185-95.

Lipovetsky, Giles, *The Empire of Fashion: Dressing Modern Democracy*, trans. Catherine Porter, Princeton: Princeton University Press, 1994.

Little, Alicia, *Intimate China: The Chinese as I Have Seen Them*, London: Hutchinson & Co., 1901.

——, *Land of the Blue Gown*, New York: Brentano's, 1902.

Liu Beisi and Xu Qixian, comps, *Gugong zhencang renwu zhaopian huicui* (Given English title: Exquisite Figure Pictures from the Palace Museum), Beijing: Zijincheng chubanshe, 1994.

Liu Fuchang, exec. ed., *Lao Shanghai guanggao* (Advertisements in Old Shanghai), Shanghai: Shanghai huabao chubanshe, 2000.

Liu Jianmei, "Shanghai Variations on 'Revolution Plus Love'," *Modern Chinese Literature and Culture* 4, 1 (Spring 2002): 51-92.

Liu Rendao, ed., *Zhongguo chuanshi renwu minghua quanji* (Collected figure paintings of the Chinese heritage), Beijing: Zhongguo xiju chubanshe, 2001.

Liu Xinhuang, *Xu Zhimo aiqing zhuan* (Xu Zhimo's loves: a life), Daizhong:

Zhenxing chubanshe, 1986.

Lou, Sheldon, *Sparrows, Bedbugs and Body Shadows: A Memoir*, Honolulu: University of Hawai'i Press, 2005.

Louie, Kam, *Theorising Chinese Masculinity: Society and Gender in China*, New York: Cambridge University Press, 2002.

Lovell, Julia, *The Great Wall: China Against the World*, London: Atlantic, 2006.

Lowe, Donald M., *History of Bourgeois Perception*, Chicago: University of Chicago Press, 1982.

Lu, Hanchao, "Arrested Development: Cotton and Cotton Markets in Shanghai, 1350-1843," *Modern China* 18, 4 (October 1992): 491-522.

——, *Beyond the Neon Lights: Everyday Shanghai in the Early Twentieth Century*, Berkeley: University of California Press, 1999.

Lu Xiaorong, "Yijian maoyi" (A woollen cardigan), in Lu Xiaorong, *Shui yao ren* (Eaten up by water), Shanghai: Shanghai shiji chuban jituan and Shanghai jiaoyu chubanshe, 2004, 2-11.

Lu Xun, "Anxious Thoughts on 'Natural Breasts'" [1927], in Yang Xianyi and Gladys Yang, trans., *Lu Xun: Selected Works*, Beijing: Foreign Languages Press, Vol. 2, 353-5.

Lu Zhongmin, "*Guoren bainian fushi: shehui bianqe de qingyubiao*" (Chinese people's dress and adornment in the last hundred years: a barometer of social change), *Renmin ribao: shenghuo shibao* (People's Daily: life times supplement), 24 October 2000.

Luo Dunwei, *Wushi nian huiyi lu* (Memoir of fifty years), Xinzhu: Zhongguo wenhua gongyingshe, 1952, preface.

Luo Jialun, ed., *Guofu nianpu* (Yearly chronology of the Father of the Nation), Taibei: Zhongguo guomindang zhongyang weiyuanhui dangshi weiyuanhui, 1985.

Luo Suwen, "Lun Qingmo Shanghai dushi nüzhuang de yanbian, 1880–1910" (On changes in urban women's clothing in late Qing Shanghai, 1880–1910), in Yu Chien Ming, ed., *Wu sheng zhi sheng(II): jindai Zhongguo funü yu wenhua, 1600–1950* (Given English title: Voices Amid Silence (III): Women and Culture in Modern China, 1600–1950), Taipei: Academia Sinica, 2003, 109-40.

Ma Bo, *Blood Red Sunset: A Memoir of the Chinese Cultural Revolution*, trans. Howard Goldblatt, New York: Viking, 1995.

Ma Ling, *Ma Ling shizhuang* (Ma Ling fashion), Beijing: Ma Ling shizhuang fuzhi youxian gongsi, 1993.

Mackerras, Colin P., *The Rise of Peking Opera: Social Aspects of the Theatre in Manchu China*, Oxford: Clarendon Press, 1972.

Macmillan, Allister, comp. and ed., *Seaports of the Far East: Historical and Descriptive Commercial and Industrial Facts, Figures, & Resources*, London: W.H.& L. Collinridge, 1925.

Mah, Ann "Japanese and Korean pop idols set trends for Chinese teens," *International Herald Tribune* 5 March 2005.

Makepeace, J.A., *A Chinaman's Opinion of Us and of His Own Country*, London: Chatto and Windus, 1927.

Malraux, André, *The Temptation of the West* [1926], trans. Robert Hollander, Chicago: University of Chicago Press, 1992.

Mann, Susan, "Learned Women in the Eighteenth Century," in Christina K. Gilmartin, Gail Hershatter, Lisa Rofel and Tyrene White, eds, *Engendering China: Women, Culture and the State*, Cambridge, Mass.: Harvard University Press, 1994, 27-46.

——, *Precious Records: Women in China's Long Eighteenth Century*, Stanford: Stanford University Press, 1997.

Mao Dun [Shen Yanping], *Midnight*, trans. Hsu Meng-hsiung, Beijing: Foreign Languages Press, 1979.

Mao Zedong, *Mao Zhuxi shici* (Poems by Chairman Mao), Beijing: Renmin wenxue chubanshe, 1963.

——, *Mao Zhuxi shici* (Poems by Chairman Mao), www.szxy.org/news/003y/312/maozedong110/mzd.htm. Accessed 28 December 2006.

——, *Report from Xunwu*, trans. Roger R. Thompson, Stanford: Stanford University Press, 1990.

——, "Tiyu zhi yanjiu" (A Study of Physical Culture), *Xin qingnian* 4 (1917): 5-12.

Marmé, Michael, *Suzhou: Where the Goods of All the Provinces Converge*, Stanford: Stanford University Press, 2005.

Mason, George Henry, *The Costume of China. Illustrated by Sixty Engravings with Explanations in English and French*, London: W. Miller, 1800.

Mayers, Wm. Fred, N.B. Dennys, and Chas. King, *The Treaty Ports of China and Japan*, London: Trübner and Co., 1867.

McCord, Edward, "Militia and Local Militarization in Late Qing and early Republican China: The Case of Hunan," *Modern China* 14, 2 (1 April 1988): 156-87.

McCormick, Frederick, *The Flowery Republic*, London: Murray, 1913.

McIntyre, Tanya, "Images of Women in Popular Prints of the Early Modern Period," in Antonia Finnane and Anne McLaren, eds., *Dress, Sex and Text in Chinese Culture*, Melbourne: Monash Asia Institute, 1998, 58-80.

McLane, Daisann, "China's New Fashion Whispers 'Asia'," *International Herald Tribune* 14 September 2004.

McMahon, Keith, "Sublime Love and the Ethics of Equality in a Homoerotic Novel of the Nineteenth Century: Precious Mirror of Boy Actresses," *Nan Nü* 4, 1 (April 1 2002): 70-109.

Mendoza, Juan Gonzalez de, *The History of the Great and Mighty Kingdom of China* [1588], trans. R. Parkes, ed. Sir George T. Staunton, London: Hakluyt Society, 1853.

Meng Hui, "Pifeng xiaoshi" (A little knowledge about the *pifeng*), in Meng Hui, *Pan Jinlian de faxing* (Pan Jinlian's hairdo), Nanjing: Jiangsu renmin chubanshe, 2005, 81-103.

Meyer-Fong, Tobie, *Building Culture in Early Qing Yangzhou*, Stanford: Stanford University Press, 2003.

Milton, David, and Nancy Dall Milton, *The Wind Will Not Subside: Years in Revolutionary China 1964–1969*, New York: Pantheon, 1976.

Min, Anchee, *Red Azalea*, New York: Berkeley Books, 1999.

Ming Ji, "Shanghai fuzhuang shichang xunli" (A visit to the Shanghai clothes market), *Xiandai fuzhuang* 1 (1981): 19.

Mittler, Barbara, *A Newspaper for China? Power, Identity, and Change in Shanghai's News Media, 1872–1912*, Cambridge, Mass.: Harvard University Asia Center, 2004.

Montesquieu, Charles De Secondat, baron de (1689–1755), *The Persian Letters* [1721], trans. C.J. Betts, Harmondsworth: Penguin Books, 1993.

Morris, Andrew D., *Marrow of the Nation: A History of Sport and Physical Culture in Republican China*, Berkeley: University of California Press, 2004.

Morrison, G.E., *An Australian in China* [1895], Hong Kong: Oxford University Press, 1985.

Morse, Hosea Ballou, *The Chronicles of the East India Company, Trading to China, 1635–1834*, Oxford: Clarendon Press, 1926.

Mu, Aiping, *Vermilion Gate: A Family Story of Communist China*, London: Little, Brown and Company, 2000.

Nagao, Ryūzō, *Shina Minzokushi* (Folk customs of China), Tokyo: Shina minzokushi kankōkai: 1940-1942.

Nakagawa Tadahide, comp., *Shinzoku kibun* (Recorded accounts of Qing customs), Tokyo: Heibonsha, 1966.

Nanchu, *Red Sorrow: A Memoir*, New York: Arcade Publishing, 2001.

"Nanxinghuale de nüxingmen" (Masculinized women), *Funü huabao* 26 (Februrary 1935): front features.

Ng Chun Bong, Cheuk Pak Tong, Wong Ying, and Yvonne Lo, *Chinese Woman and Modernity: Calendar Posters of the 1910s - 1930s*, Hong Kong: Joint Publishing, 1999.

Ng, Janet, *The Experience of Modernity: Chinese Autobiography of the Early Twentieth Century*, Ann Arbor: The University of Michigan Press, 2003.

Nie Changshuo, "Nan xing sui gan" (Reflections on the southern tour), *Shizhuang* 2 (1992): 11-12.

Nie Zeng Jifen, *Testimony of a Confucian Woman: The Autobiography of Mrs Nie Zeng Jifen, 1852-1942*, trans. Thomas L. Kennedy, Athens: University of Georgia Press, 1993.

Nien Cheng, *Life and Death in Shanghai*, London: Grafton Books, 1987.

Nolan, Peter, *China and the Global Economy: National Champions, Industrial Policy and the Big Business Revolution*, Houndmills: Palgrave, 2001.

Pa Chin [Ba Jin], *Family*, trans. Sidney Shapiro, New York: Anchor Books, 1972.

Pagani, Catherine, "Europe in Asia: The Impact of Western Art and Technology in China," in Anna Jackson and Amin Jaffer, eds, *Encounters: The Meeting of Asia and Europe, 1500–1800*, London: V & A Publications, 2004, 298-309.

Pan Guozheng, *Zhuqian sixiangqi: lao zhaopian shuo gushi* (Thinking about Zhuqian: tales from old photos), Xinzhu: Zhushi wenhua chubanshe, 1995.

Pearse, Arno S., *The Cotton Industry of Japan and China: Being the Report of the Journey to Japan and China*, Manchester: International Federation of Master Cotton Spinners' and Manufacturers Associations, 1929.

Pelissier, Roger, *The Awakening of China 1793-1949*, trans. Martin Kiefer, New York: Capricorn Books, 1962.

Peyrefitte, Alain, *L'empire immobile, ou, Le choc des mondes: récit historique*, Paris: Fayard, 1989.

Plauchet, Edmund, *China and the Chinese*, trans. Mrs Arthur Bell, London: Hurst and Blackett, 1899.

Pomeranz, Kenneth, *The Great Divergence: China, Europe, and the Making of the Modern World Economy*, Princeton: Princeton University Press, 2000.

Powell, Ralph L., *The Rise of Chinese Military Power, 1895-1912*, Princeton: Princeton University Press, 1955.

Pruitt, Ida, *Old Madam Yin: A Memoir of Peking Life, 1926–1938*, Stanford: Stanford University Press, 1979.

Purdy, Daniel L., *The Tyranny of Elegance: Consumer Cosmopolotanism in the Era of Goethe*, Baltimore: Johns Hopkins University Press, 1998.

Qi Xiaochun, "Dui shimao de lijie" (On an understanding of fashion), *Dongfang shibao* (Japan), chineseculture.about.com/library/netter/px/unsqixiaochun054.htm. Accessed 18 October 2006.

Qingdai baokan tuhua jicheng (Collected illustrations from Qing dynasty newspapers), Beijing: Quanguo tushuguan wenxian suowei fuzhi zhongxin, 2001.

Qiu Jin (Ch'iu Chin), "An Address to Two Hundred Million Fellow Countrywomen," in Patricia Buckley Ebrey, ed., *Chinese Civilization and Society: A Sourcebook*, New York: Free Press, 1981, 248-9.

——, "Guangfujun junzhi gao" (Draft military organization of the Restoration Army), in *Qiu Jin xianlie wenji* (Collected writings of the martyr Qiu Jin), Taibei: Zhongguo Guomindang zhongyang weiyuanhui dangshi weiyuanhui, 1982, 155-7.

Qiu Jin shi ji, Beijing: Zhonghua shuju, 1958.

Qiu Zhengang, "Guangfuhui you yi nüjie Yin Weijun" (Yin Weijun: another heroine of the Restoration Society), in *Zhejiang xinhai geming huiyilu xuji* (Memoirs of the 1911 Revolution in Zhejiang: continued), Hangzhou: Zhejiang renmin chubanshe, 1984, 64-72.

Racinet, Auguste, *Le costume historique*, Paris: Libraire de Firmin-Didot et Cie, 1888.

Rae Yang, *Spider Eaters*, Berkeley: University of California Press, 1997.

Rankin, Mary Backus, *Early Chinese Revolutionaries: Radical Intellectuals in Shanghai and Chekiang, 1902–1911*, Cambridge, Mass.: Harvard East Asian Series, 1971.

——, "The Emergence of Women at the End of the Ch'ing: the Case of Ch'iu Chin," in Margery Wolf and Roxane Witke, eds, *Women in Chinese Society*,

Stanford: Stanford University Press, 1975, 39-66.

Rantisi, Norma, "How New York Stole Modern Fashion," in Christopher Breward and David Gilbert, eds, *Fashion's World Cities*, New York: Berg, 2006, 109-22.

Rawski, Evelyn S., *The Last Emperors: A Social Hierarchy of Qing Imperial Institutions*, Berkeley: University of California Press, 1998.

Rawson, Jessica, and Jane Portal, "Luxuries for Trade," in Jessica Rawson ed., *The British Museum Book of Chinese Art*, London: British Museum Press, 1992.

Reynolds, Douglas R., *China 1898–1912: The Xinzheng Revolution and Japan*, Council on East Asian Studies, Harvard University, 1993.

Rhoads, Edward J.M., *China's Republican Revolution: The Case of Kwangtung, 1895–1913*, Cambridge, Mass.: Harvard University Press, 1975.

——, *Manchus and Han: Ethnic Relations and Political Power in Late Qing and Early Republican China, 1861–1928*, Seattle: University of Washington Press, 2000.

Ricci, Matteo, *China in the Sixteenth Century: The Journals of Matthew Ricci: 1583–1610* [1615], trans. Louis Gallagher, S.J., New York: Random House, 1953.

Roberts, Claire, ed., *Evolution and Revolution: Chinese Dress 1700s–1900s*, Sydney: Powerhouse Museum, 1997.

Roberts, Mary Louise, *Civilization Without Sexes: Reconstructing Gender in Postwar France, 1917–1927*, Chicago: University of Chicago Press, 1994.

Roberts, Rosemary, "Gendering the Revolutionary Body: Theatrical Costume in Cultural Revolution China," *Asian Studies Review* 30, 2 (June 2006): 141-59.

Roces, Mina, "Gender, Nation and the Politics of Dress in Twentieth Century Philippines." Paper presented at the 15th Biennial Conference of the Asian Studies Association of Australia, Canberra, 2 July 2004.

Roe, A.S., *China as I Saw It: A Woman's Letters from the Celestial Empire*, London: Hutchison & Co., 1910.

Rofel, Lisa, *Other Modernities: Gendered Yearnings in China After Socialism*, Berkeley: University of California Press, 1999.

Rule, Paul, "The Tarnishing of the Image: From Sinophilia to Sinophobia," in Michel Cartier, ed., *La Chine entre amour et haine: Actes du viiiᵉ colloque de sinologie de Chantilly*, Paris: Desclée de Brouwer, 1998, 89-109.

Said, Edward, *Orientalism*, London: Routledge & Kegan Paul, 1978.

Sang Ye, *China Candid: The People on the People's Republic*, Geremie R. Barmé with Miriam Lang, eds, Berkeley: University of California Press, 2006.

——, "From Rags to Revolution: Beyond the Seams of Social Change," in Claire Roberts, ed., *Evolution and Revolution: Chinese Dress 1700s–1900s*, Sydney: Powerhouse Museum, 1997, 40-51.

Schram, Stuart R., ed., *Mao's Road to Power: Revolutionary Writings 1912–1949: Volume 1: The Pre-Marxist Period, 1912-1920*, Armonk, N.Y.: M.E. Sharpe, 1992.

Scott, A.C., *Actors are Madmen: Notebook of a Theatregoer in China*, Madison: The University of Wisconsin Press, 1982.

———, *Chinese Costume in Transition*, Singapore: Donald Moore, 1958.

Segre Reinach, Simona, "China and Italy: Fast Fashion versus *Prêt a Porter*. Towards a New Culture of Fashion," *Fashion Theory: The Journal of Dress, Body and Culture* 9, 1 (1 March 2005): 43-56.

———, "Milan: The City of Prêt-à-Porter in a World of Fast Fashion," in Christopher Breward and David Gilbert, eds, *Fashion's World Cities*, New York: Berg, 2006, 123-34.

Seifert, Ruth, "War and Rape: A Preliminary Analysis," in Alexandra Stiglmayer, ed., *The War against Women in Bosnia-Herzegovina*, Lincoln and London: University of Nebraska Press, 54-72.

Shanghaishi difangzhi bangongshi (Shanghai municipal local gazetteer office), "Zhuanyezhi: Shanghai riyong gongyepin shangyezhi: Diwupian, fuzhuang xie mao shangye: diyijie, yange" (Gazetteer of professions: the Shanghai trade in industrial goods for everyday use: chapter five, the clothes, shoes and hats trade: section 1, historical development), www.shtong.gov.cn/node2/node2245/node66046/node66055/node66156/node66167/userobject1ai61750.html. Accessed 9 August 2006.

"Shanghai funü luohua zhi xinzhuang" (Nakedness in Shanghai women's new fashions), *Beijing huabao* 113 (4 September 1930): n.p.n.

Shanghai xianshi gongsi shizhuang tekan (Shanghai Sincere Company fashion special), Shanghai: 1930.

Shanghaishi Huwanqu dang'anju, Shanghaishi Huwanqu difangzhi bangongshi (Shanghai municipality Huwan district archives and local gazetteer office), eds, *Huaihailu bainian xiezhen* (One hundred years of photographs of Huaihai Road), Shanghai: Shanghai shehui kexueyuan chubanshe, 2001.

Sharman, Lyon, *Sun Yat-sen, His Life and Its Meaning: A Critical Biography*, Stanford: Stanford University Press, 1934.

Shen Congwen, *Zhongguo gudai fushi yanjiu* (Research on Chinese clothing in former times), Hong Kong: Shangwu yinshuguan Xianggang fenguan, 1992.

Sheng Cheng, *Son of China*, trans. Marvin McCord Lowes, London: George Allen and Unwin, 1930.

Sheng Peiyu, *Shengshi jiazu: Shao Xunmei yu wo* (The Sheng clan: Shao Xunmei and I), Beijing: Renmin wenxue chubanshe, 2004.

Shi Lei, "Jindai Shanghai fushi bianqian yu guannian jinbu" (Changes in Shanghai clothing and advances in outlook in modern times), *Dang'an yu shixue* 3 (2003): 36-9.

Shi Lin, "Zhongguo shejishi haixu nuli" (China's designers still have to work hard), *Zhongguo fangzhi daxue xuebao* 9 May 2002, www.efu.com.cn/info/technique/2002-5-10/8412.htm. Accessed 3 September 2003.

Shi Ying, *Minguo shishang* (Republican fashions), Beijing: Tuanjie chubanshe, 2005.

Shih, Shu-mei, *The Lure of the Modern: Writing Modernism in Semicolonial China*, Berkeley: University of California Press, 2001.

Simmel, George, "The Philosophy of Fashion" [1904], *American Journal of Sociology*

62, 6 (1957): 541-58.

Snow, Helen Foster, *Women in Modern China*, The Hague: Mouton & Co., 1967.

Song Qingling jinianji (Commemorative volume on Song Qingling), Hong Kong: Gaibao, 1981.

Staunton, Sir George, *An Authentic Account of An Embassy From the King of Great Britain to the Emperor of China*, London: W. Bulmer and Company, 1797.

Steele, Valerie, and John Major, *China Chic: East Meets West*, New Haven, Yale University Press, 1999.

Stillman, Yedida Kalfon, *Arab Dress From the Dawn of Islam to Modern Times: A Short History*, Leiden: Brill, 2000.

Stoler, Anne, *Carnal Knowledge and Imperial Power: Race and the Intimate in Colonial Rule*, Los Angeles and London: University of California Press, 2002.

Strassberg, Richard, *The World of K'ung Shang-jen: A Man of Letters in Early Ch'ing China*, New York: Columbia University Press, 1983.

Struve, Lynn, ed., *The Qing Formation in World-Historical Time*, Cambridge, Mass.: Harvard University Asia Center, 2004.

Sullivan, Michael, *Art and Artists of Twentieth-Century China*, Berkeley: University of California Press, 1996.

Sun Fuxi, "Shenme shi nüxing mei?" (What is beauty in a woman?), *Xin nüxing* 1, 5 (May 1925): 359-62.

Sun Fuyuan "Xinhai geming shidai de qingnian fushi" (Young people's dress in the period of the 1911 Revolution), in Sun Fuyuan, *Sun Fuyuan sanwen xuanji* (Collected essays of Sun Fuyuan), Tianjin: Baihua wenyi chubanshe, 1991.

Sun Ji, Fan Jia'an, and Gu Jing, "Wang Guangmei xishuo wangshi" (Wang Guangmei discusses the past in detail), *Huaxia nügong* (Women's work in China), no. 1, 2002, www.gmw.cn/03pindao/renwu/2004-07/03/content_52318.htm. Accessed 12 November 2005.

Sun, Lung-kee, "The Politics of Hair and the Issue of the Bob in Modern China," *Fashion Theory* 1, 4 (1997): 353-66.

Sutton, Donald, *Provincial Militarism and the Chinese Republic: The Yunnan Army, 1905–1925*, Ann Arbor: University of Michigan Press, 1980.

Tan Jintu, "Fengrenji zai Zhongguo de zaoqi zhuanbo," (The early spread of the sewing machine in China), in Shandong huabao chubanshe "Lao zhaopian" bianjibu (Shandong pictorial publishing "Old photos" editorial section), ed., *Lao zhaopian* (Old photos), No. 37, Jinan: Shandong huabao chubanshe, 2004, 150-3.

Tang Zhenchang, *Jindai Shanghai fanhua lu* (The flowering of modern Shanghai), Hong Kong: Shangwu yinshuguan, 1993.

Tao, Chia-lin Pao, "The Anti-footbinding Movement in late Ch'ing China: Indigenous Development and Western Influence," *Jindai Zhongguo funüshi yanjiu* 2 (June 1994):141-78.

Tao Siliang, "Shuo bu jin de Zhongguo nüshizhang" (The inestimable women mayors of China), preface to *Zhongguo nüshizhang* (China's women mayors) (1995), www.citieschina.org. Accessed 29 October 2005.

Tao Ye, "Minchu funü de xinzhuang" (New fashions among women in the early Republic), in Shandong huabao chubanshe "Lao zhaopian" bianjibu (Shandong pictorial publishing "Old photos" editorial section), ed., *Lao zhaopian* (Old photos), No. 1, Jining: Shandong huabao chubanshe, 1996, 104-5.

Tarlo, Emma, *Clothing Matters: Dress and Identity in India*, London: Hurst & Company, 1996.

Taylor, Jean Gelman, "Official Photography, Costume and the Indonesian Revolution," in Jean Gelman Taylor, ed., *Women Creating Indonesia: The First Fifty Years*, Clayton: Monash Asia Institute, 1997, 91-126.

Taylor, Mrs Howard, *One of China's Scholars: The Culture and Conversion of a Confucianist*, London: Morgan & Scott, 1904.

Tcheng-Ki-Tong, *Les Chinois Peints par Eux-mêmes*, Paris: Calmann Lévy, 1884.

Thomson, J., *Illustrations of China and Its People*, London: S. Low, Marston, Low, and Searle, 1873-4.

Tianjinshi fangzhipin gongsi dangwei pipanzu (Tianjin Textile Products Company criticism group), "'Nühuang yi' yu 'Jiang Qing fu'" (The 'Empress's clothes' and the 'Jiang Qing dress'), *Tianjin ribao* 19 August 1978.

Tianjinshi fangzhipin gongsi dangwei pipanzu (Tianjin Textile Products Company criticism group),"'Jiang Qing qun' bei zuowei 'xinsheng shiwu' qiangxing tuixiang quanguo" (The forceful promotion throughout the country of the 'Jiang Qing dress' as a 'newly born item'), *Renmin jiyi wushi nian* (Half a century of the people's memories). Zhejiang Normal University Library, lib. zjnu.net.cn/f/remjy/037.htm. Accessed 10 July 2004.

Tie Ying, "First National Fashion Show," *China Reconstructs* XXXII, 10 (October 1983): 4-5.

Tom wenhua (Tom culture), 13 June 2005, cul.news.tom.com/1011/2005613-18050.html. Accessed 17 December 2005.

Tong Te-kong and Li Tsung-jen, *The Memoirs of Li Tsung-ren*, Boulder: Westview Press, 1979.

Tseëlson, Efrat, "Fashion and the Signification of Social Order," *Semiotica* 91 (1992): 1-14.

Vainker, Shelagh, *Chinese Silk: A Cultural History*, London: The British Museum Press, and New Brunswick: Rutgers University Press, 2004.

van de Ven, Hans, "The Military in the Republic," *The China Quarterly* 157 (June 1997): 352-74.

Veblen, Thorstein, *The Theory of the Leisure Class: An Economic Study of Institutions*, New York, B.W. Huebsch, 1912.

Vishnyakova-Akimova, Vera Vladimirovna, *Two Years in Revolutionary China, 1925-1927*, trans. Steven I. Levine, Harvard: Harvard East Asian Monographs, 1971.

Vogel, Ezra F., *One Step Ahead in China: Guangdong Under Reform*, Cambridge, Mass.: Harvard University Press, 1981.

Vollmer, John, *Ruling from the Dragon Throne: Costume of the Qing Dynasty (1644*

–1911), Berkeley: Ten Speed Press, 2002.

Waara, Carrie, "Invention, Industry, Art: The Commercialisation of Culture in Republican Art Magazines," in Sherman Cochran, ed., *Inventing Nanjing Road*, Ithaca: East Asia Program, Cornell University, 1999, 61-90.

Wakeman, Frederic, Jr., "Licensing Leisure: The Chinese Nationalists' Attempts to regulate Shanghai," *The Journal of Asian Studies* 54, 1 (February 1995): 20-1.

Waley-Cohen, Joanna, *The Sextants of Beijing: Global Currents in Chinese History*, New York: Norton, 1999.

Walter, Richard, *Lord Anson's Voyage Around the World, 1740–1744* [1748], London: G.S.L. Clowes, 1928.

Wang Anyi, "And the Rain Patters On," trans. Michael Day, in Wang Anyi, *Lapse of Time*, Beijing: Panda Books, 1988, 27-40.

———, "Ji yici fuzhuang biaoyan" (Remembering a fashion parade), in Wang Anyi, *Xunzhao Shanghai* (In search of Shanghai), Shanghai: Xuelin chubanshe, 2002, 78-80.

———, "Xunzhao Su Qing" (In search of Su Qing), in Su Qing, *Jiehun shinian* (Ten years of marriage), Taibei: Shibao wenhua, 2001, 5-15

Wang, David Der-wei, *Fin-de-Siècle Splendor: Repressed Modernities of Late Qing Fiction, 1849-1911*, Stanford: Stanford University Press, 1997.

———, "Impersonating China," *Chinese Literature: Essays, Articles, Reviews* 25 (December 2003): 133-63.

Wang Ermin, "Duanfa, yifu, gaiyuan: bianfalun zhi xiangwei zhiqu" (Cutting hair, changing dress, altering the calendar: symbolic indicators of reform) in *Zhongguo jindaide weixin yundong—bianfa yu lixian taojihui* (Research Conference on the modern Chinese reform movement—reform and the establishment of the constitution), Taipei: Institute of Modern History, Academia Sinica, 1981, 59-73.

Wang Shucun, *Zhongguo nianhua shi* (A history of Chinese New Year prints), Beijing: Beijing gongyi meishu chubanshe, 2002.

Wang Shuo, *Dongwu xiongmeng* (The ferocity of beasts), Hong Kong: Wenquan, 1994.

Wang Xiaoyi, *Chunshui weibo* (Ripples in spring waters) [1931], Shenyang: Chunfeng wenyi chubanshe, 1997.

Wang Xing, *Bainian fushi chaoliu yu shibian* (One hundred years of fashion trends and global change), Hong Kong: Shangwu yinshuguan, 1992.

Wang Xu, "Dongjing de yitian" (A day in Tokyo), *Shizhuang* 1 (1996):16-19.

Wang Yarong and Wang Xu, "Shen Congwen and His Book on Ancient Costumes," *China Reconstructs* XXIX, 11 (November 1980): 28-33.

Wang Yuru, "Economic Development in China Between the Two World Wars (1920–1936),"in Tim Wright, ed., *The Chinese Economy in the Early Twentieth Century: Recent Chinese Studies*, New York: St Martin's Press, 1992: 58-77.

Wang Zheng, *Women in the Chinese Enlightenment: Oral and Textual Histories*, Berkeley: University of California Press, 1999.

Wei Minghua, *Yangzhou shouma* (Thin horses of Yangzhou), Fuzhou: Fujian renmin chubanshe, 1998.

Wei Zhi, "Zhongguo fuzhuang pinpai boyi 20 nian" (Twenty great years of Chinese fashion brands), *Zhongguo fangzhi bao* 27 January 2006.

Wen Song, "Junzhuang lianqing" (Loving sentiments about army uniforms), *Xiamen ribao*, 3 August 2003. Accessed from *Haifeng wang* (Haifeng website).

Wen Tianshen, "New Fashion Trends," *China Reconstructs* XXXVI, 10 (October 1987): 68.

Widmer, Ellen, "*Honglou meng ying* and Three Novels by Women of the Late Qing" Paper presented at International Symposium on Women, Nation and Society in Modern China (1600–1950), Research Institute of Modern History, Academia Sinica, Taipei, 23-5 August 2001.

Wilson, Elizabeth, *Adorned in Dreams: Fashion and Modernity*, London: Virago, 1985.

——, "Urbane Fashion," in Christopher Breward and David Gilbert, eds, *Fashion's World Cities*, New York: Berg, 2006, 33-9.

Wilson, Verity, *Chinese Dress*, London: Victoria and Albert Museum, 2001.

——, *Chinese Textiles*, London: V&A Publications, 2005.

——, "Dressing for Leadership in China: Wives and Husbands in an Age of Revolutions (1911–1976)," *Gender and History* 14, 3 (November 2002): 608-28.

Witke, Roxane, *Comrade Jiang Qing*, London: Weidenfeld and Nicholson, 1977.

Wong Hwei Lian and Szan Tan, eds, *Powerdressing: Textiles for Rulers and Priests from the Chris Hall Collection*, Ex. Cat., Singapore: Asian Civilisations Museum, 2006.

Wong, Stephen, "Han follow suit in Cultural Renaissance," *Asia Times* (online edition), www.atimes.com, 26 August 2006. Accessed 12 October 2006.

Wu Alun, "Fashion House Makes it 23 Years in China," in *China International Business*, www.cib-online.net/interview.html. Accessed 7 August 2003.

Wu Jen-shu. See Wu Renshu.

Wu Renshu, "Mingdai pingmin fushi de liuxing fengshang yu shidafu de fanying" (Popular styles of clothing among the common people of Ming times, and the reaction of the gentry) *Xinshixue* 10, 3 (September 1999): 55-109.

Wu Wenxing, "Riju shiqi Taiwan de fangzu duanfa yundong" (The movement for unbinding feet and cutting hair in Taiwan during the Japanese occupation), in Li Youning and Zhang Yufa, eds, *Zhongguo funüshi lunwenji* (Collected essays on the history of Chinese women), Taibei: Taiwan shangwu yinshuguan, 1988, 465-510.

Wu Xiaoping, "Down to the Countryside," in Zhang Lijia and Calum MacLeod, eds, *China Remembers*, Hong Kong: Oxford University Press, 1999, 127-35.

Wu, Leonard T.K., "The Crisis in the Chinese Cotton Industry," *Far Eastern Survey* 4, 1 (16 January 1935): 1-4.

Xia Shaohong, *Wan Qing wenren funü guan* (Literati views of women in the late Qing), Beijing: Zuojia chubanshe, 1995.

Xianshi gongsi 25 zhounian jinian ce (Sincere Company 25th anniversary commemorative volume), Shanghai Municipal Archives Q227-84.

Xiao Gao, "Jiang Qing fu chulong de taiqian muhou" (Before and after staging the marketing of the Jiang Qing dress), *Meizhou wenhui zhoukan* (Literary Weekly from America), no. 99, www.sinotimes.com/big5/99/jqf.htm. Accessed 10 July 2004.

Xiao Wuliao, *Jiqing shishang: qishi niandai Zhongguoren de yishu yu shenghuo* (Passionate times: Chinese art and life in the seventies), Jinan: Shandong huabao chubanshe, 2002.

Xiao Zili, *Chen Jitang*, Guangzhou: Guangdong renmin chubanshe, 2001.

Xiaoxiaosheng, *The Plum in the Gold Vase, or Chin P'ing Mei,* trans. David Tod Roy, New Jersey: Princeton University Press, 1993-2006.

Xie Zhaozhe, *Wuzazu* (Five miscellanies), Taibei: Weiwen, 1977.

Xinshenghuo yundong yaoyi (Main principles of the New Life Movement), Wuhan: Hubei Police Bureau Press, 1937. Chongqing Municipal Archives 776/2.

Xu Qingyu, "Xinshenghuo yundong yu wenhua" (The New Life Movement and Culture) [1935], in Pamier shudian bianjibu (Pamier bookshop editorial section), ed., *Wenhua jianshe yu xihua wenti taolunji, xiaji* (Collected articles on the establishment of culture and the problem of Westernisation, part 2), Taibei: Pamier Shudian, 1980.

Xu Wenyuan, *Secai, nülang, wode meng: shizhuang motuoer zhi lu* (Colour, young women, my dream: the fashion model's path), Guilin: Zhongguo gongren chubanshe, 1991.

Xu Xinwu, "The Struggle of the Handicraft Cotton Industry Against Machine Textiles in China," *Modern China* 14, 1 (January 1988): 31-49.

Xu Youchun, ed., *Minguo renwu dacidian* (Greater biographical dictionary of the Republican period), Shijiazhuang: Hebei renmin chubanshe, 1991.

Yan Fu, "Gan sujiechu xiaomajia!" (Hurry up and undo the little vest!"), *Nüzi yuekan* 1, 1 (8 March 1933): 36-7.

Yan Jiaqi and Gao Gao, *Turbulent Decade: A History of the Cultural Revolution*, D.W.Y. Kwok trans., Honolulu: University of Hawai'i Press, 1996.

Yang Kelin, ed., *Wenhua dageming bowuguan* (The Cultural Revolution Museum), Hong Kong: Dongfang chubanshe, 1995.

Yang Xianyi, *White Tiger*, Beijing: self-published, 1999.

Yang Xiaoqing, ed., *Xinshenghuo gangyao* (Principles of New Life), Chongqing: Chongqing gonganju jingcha xunliansuo, 1936. Chongqing Municipal Archives 774/2.

Yang Xingmei, "Nanjing guomin zhengfu jinzhi funü chanzu de nuli yu chengxiao" (The Nanjing government's prohibition of footbinding: efforts and effectiveness), *Lishi yanjiu* 3 (1998): 113-29.

Yang, Yongzheng, "China's Textile and Clothing Exports: Changing International Comparative Advantage and Its Policy Implications," *Asia Pacific School of Economics and Management Working Papers*, Canberra: Asia Pacific Press, 1999.

Yang Yuan, exec. ed., *Zhongguo fushi bainian shishang* (Given French title: Costumes chinois: Modes depuis 100 ans), Huerhot: Yuanfang chubanshe, 2003.

Yang Yueqian, *Shizhuang liuxing de aomi* (The mysteries of fashion), Beijing: Zhongguo shehui kexue chubanshe, 1992.

Yao Zaisheng, "Guangdong de shizhuangchang he Shanghai de caifengpu"(Canton's fashion factories and Shanghai's tailor shops), *Xiandai fuzhuang* 6 (1996): 20-1.

Ye Qianyu, *Xixu cangsang ji liunian* (Telling of the changing landscape, remembering the passage of the years), Beijing: Qunyan chubanshe, 1992.

Yeh, Catherine Vance, "A Public Affair or a Nasty Game? The Chinese Tabloid Newspaper and the Rise of the Opera Singer as Star," *European Journal of East Asian Studies* 2, 1 (2003): 13-51.

Yeh, Wen-hsin, *The Alienated Academy: Culture and Politics in Republican China, 1919–1937*, Cambridge, Mass.: Harvard East Asia Center, 1990.

——, "Shanghai Modernity: Commerce and Culture in a Republican City," *The China Quarterly* 150 (June 1997): 375-94.

Yen Ching-hwang, "Wing On and the Kwok Brothers: A Case Study of Pre-War Overseas Chinese Entrepreneurs," in Kerrie L. MacPherson, ed., *Asian Department Stores*, Richmond: Curzon Press, 1998, 47-65.

Yi Junzuo, *Xianhua Yangzhou* (Chatting at leisure about Yangzhou), Shanghai: Zhonghua shuju, 1934.

Ying Dawei, *Taiwan nüren* (Women of Taiwan), Taibei: Tianye yingxiang chubanshe, 1996.

Yingzi, "Gege niandai de tongzhuang," in Lao Zhaopian bianjibu, ed., *Fengwu liubian jian cangcang* (Witnessing the tides of change), Jinan: Shandong huabao chubanshe, 2001, 99-106.

Yongzheng Yang, "China's Textile and Clothing Exports: Changing International Comparative Advantage and Its Policy Implications," *Asia Pacific School of Economics and Management Working Papers*, Canberra: Asia Pacific Press, 1999.

Yoshida-Krafft, Barbara, "Wang Shih-chen," in *DMB* Vol. II: 1399–1405.

Yoshitake Oka, *Five Political Leaders of Modern Japan: Itō Hirobumi, Ōkuma Shigenobu, Hara Takashi, Inukai Tsuyoshi, and Saionji Kimmochi*, trans. Andrew Fraser and Patricia Murray, Tokyo: University of Tokyo Press, 1986.

Yu Chien Ming (You Jianming), "Jindai Zhongguo nüzi jianmei de lunshu (1920–1940 niandai)" (Modern discourses on the strong beauty of Chinese women, 1920s–1940s), in Yu Chien Ming, ed., *Wu sheng zhi sheng(II): jindai Zhongguo funü yu wenhua, 1600–1950* (Given English title: Voices Amid Silence (II): Women and Culture in Modern China, 1600–1950), Taipei: Academia Sinica, 2003, 141-72.

You Jianming. See Yu Chien Ming.

Yu Feng, "Fayang fuzhuang de minzu fengge" (Developing the national style in clothing), *Meishu* April 1955: 12-13.

——, "Ziran, shenghuo, chuangzuo" (Nature, life, creation) [1954], in Yu Feng, *Wode guxiang* (My old home place), Tianjin: Baihua wenyi chubanshe, 1984,

196-206.

Yu Qing, "Hong zhuang su guo" ('Red' clothing, white gaiters), in Shandong huabao chubanshe "Lao zhaopian" bianjibu (Shandong pictorial publishing "Old photos" editorial section), ed., *Lao zhaopian* (Old photos), no. 1 (Jining: Shandong huabao chubanshe, 1996), 90-2.

Yuan Hao, "Zhou Guoping: shengming de yishu" (Zhou Guoping: art of a lifetime), *21 shiji rencai zhanlüe* (Given English title: *Talents Herald*), 2 (2003): 23-6.

Zaletova, Lidya, Fabio Ciofi degli Atti, Franco Panzini et al., *Costume Revolution: Textiles, Clothing and Costume of the Soviet Union in the Twenties*, trans. Elizabeth Dafinone, London: Trefoil Publications, 1987.

Zamperini, Paola, "Clothes that Matter: Fashioning Modernity in Late Qing Novels," *Fashion Theory* 5, 2 (2001): 195-214.

——, "On Their Dress They Wore a Body: Fashion and Identity in Late Qing Shanghai," *positions: east asia cultures critique* 11, 2 (2003): 301-30.

Zang Xiao, "'Huang junzhuang' qingjie" (A passion for a yellow military uniform), *Hefei wanbao* (Hefei Evening Paper), 11 September 2003, www.jhcb.com.cn/epublish/gb/paper6/20030715/class000600004/hwz344499.htm. Accessed 10 November 2003.

Zarrow, Peter, "Historical Trauma: Anti-Manchuism and Memories of Atrocity in Late Qing China," *History & Memory* 16, 2 (2004): 67-107.

Zhang Ailing, *Duizhao ji: kan laozhaoxiang bu* (Juxtapositions: looking at an old photo album), Hong Kong: Huangguan chubanshe, 1994.

——. See also Chang, Eileen.

Zhang Deyi, *Diary of a Chinese Diplomat* [1872], Beijing: Foreign Languages Press, 1992.

Zhang Jingqiong, *Xi fu dong jian—20 shiji Zhong wai fushi jiaoliu shi* (Western clothing, Eastern influences—a history of fashion flows between China and the outside world in the twentieth century), Heifei: Anhui meishu chubanshe, 2002.

Zhang Liangqiong, Zhang Yuxia, Zhou Kaiyan, and Chen Ping, "Cong Zhongguo xiandai wenyuan zhiyezhuang de xingcheng he fazhan kan yinru waili yangzhi de yiban lujing yu moshi" (A route and model for foreign styles considered from the perspective of the formation and development of professional clothing for arts personnel in modern China), *Zhejiang gongcheng xueyuan xuebao* 18, 1 (March 2001).

Zhang Lilan, "Liuxingjie de beixiju" (Tragedies and comedies in the world of fashion), *Furen huabao* 25 (1935): 9.

Zhang Qianyu, "Shizhuang xinjiang" (New comments on fashion), *Kuaile jiating* 1 (1936): 28-9.

Zhang Wenhe, "Chinese Magazine Industry: Clothes Horse for Global Fashion Brands," *Rising East* (online version) 4 (May 2006), www.uel.ac.uk/risingeast/archive04/essays/wenhe.htm. Accessed 16 October 2006.

Zhang Yingjin, *Chinese National Cinema*, London: Routledge, 2004.

Zhang Zhongli, "The Development of Chinese National Capital in the 1920s," in

Tim Wright, ed., *The Chinese Economy in the Early Twentieth Century: Recent Chinese Studies*, New York: St Martin's Press, 1992, 53-7.

Zhao Jiasheng, "Yifu caifa ji cailiao jisuan fa" (Cutting garments and calculating the amount of material), *Funü zazhi* (1 September 1925): 1450-3.

Zhiqing laozhaopian (Old photos of educated youth), Tianjin: Baihua wenyi chubanshe, 1998.

Zhongguo dier lishi dang'anguan (Second Historical Archives of China), ed., *Minguo junfu tuzhi* (Illustrated account of military uniform in the Republican era), Shanghai: Shanghai shudian chubanshe, 2003.

"Zhongguo fuzhuang zoujin Bolin" (Given English title: China fashion show in Berlin), *Zhongguo zhi yi* 12 (2001): 70-4.

Zhonghua minzu fuzhitu (Chinese national clothing scheme, illustrated), Nanjing: Guohuo weichihui, 1912.

Zhou Shaoquan, "Mingdai fushi tanlun" (An essay on Ming costume), *Shixue yuekan* 6 (1990): 34-40

Zhou Xibao, *Zhongguo gudai fushi shi* (History of ancient Chinese costume), Taibei: Nantian shuju, 1989.

Zhou Xun and Gao Chunming, *Zhongguo gudai fushi fengsu* (Ancient Chinese costume), Taibei: Wenjin chubanshe, 1989.

——, Zhongguo lidai fushi (Chinese costume through history) Shanghai: Xuelin chubanshe, 1994.

——, *Zhongguo yiguan fushi da cidian* (Dictionary of Chinese costume), Shanghai: Shanghai cishu chubanshe, 1996.

Zhu Jiang, *Yangzhou yuanlin pinshang lu* (An appreciation of the gardens of Yangzhou), Shanghai: Shanghai wenwu chubanshe, 1984.

Zhu Runsheng, "Runer de mianhuai—yi fuqin Zhu Ziqing" (Runny's fond recollections: remembering my father Zhu Ziqing), *Yangzhou wenxue* 18 and 19 (1990): 16-18.

Zhu Weisheng, *Coming Out of the Middle Ages: Comparative Reflections on China and the West*, trans. and ed., Ruth Hayhoe, Armonk: M.E. Sharpe, 1990.

"'Zhuibu shengsi lian, jue chang caomao ge': chongwen Riben yinyue" (Undying attachment to *Manhunt*; ceasing to sing the song of the Straw Hat: a retrospect on Japanese music), *Xinlang yule* (New wave entertainment), news.xinhuanet. com/audio/2004-04/23/content_1436264.htm. Accessed 28 May 2006.

Zolbrod, Leon, and L. Carrington Goodrich, "Hsieh Chao-che," *DMB* Vol. I, 546-50.

Zuo Lin, "Zhang Sizhi: Wo he Jiang Qing tanbengle" (Zhang Sizhi: the breakdown in my talks with Jiang Qing), *Xin shiji zhoukan* (New century weekly), 19 (21 June, 2006): 61-5.

Zurndorfer, Harriet, "From Local History to Cultural History: Reflections on Some Recent Publications," *T'oung Pao* LXXXIII (1997): 387-96.

INDEX